PARIS

The present work is based on "Paris monumental", photographed by Max and Albert Hirmer, © 1974, Flammarion, Paris.

PARIS

MICHEL FLEURY

ALAIN ERLANDE-BRANDENBURG

JEAN-PIERRE BABELON

FLAMMARION

From the french by J.-L. Hargreaves

THE GALLO-ROMAN PERIOD AND THE EARLY MIDDLE AGES

THE GALLO-ROMAN PERIOD: THE EMPIRE AT ITS HEIGHT

Although Paris now has only two monuments left from the Gallo-Roman period (les
Thermes de Cluny and les Arènes), Rome left its mark nonetheless. It can still be seen in the 2 and 3
lay-out of certain thoroughfares and, most of all, in the city's development as a whole, under
Roman control as it was for some nine centuries.

On arriving, the conquerors had found a run-down village—the Lutèce (Lutetia) of the
"Parisii" confined to the small Ile de la Cité. This they enlarged, building a beautiful city on
the high ground to the south, giving it a favourable aspect as was their wont. The city thus
lay on the main road from Orléans which crossed the Seine over two bridges, one on either
side of the island, and then continued northwards to the pass of la Chapelle. This thorough-
fare still exists today in the form of the Rue Saint-Jacques and the Rue Saint-Martin. At the
time, it was the main highway, the "cardo" of Lutetia. The new city was cut to a very large
"pattern", to use Paul-Marie Duval's expression, and only filled the bounds set for it very
slowly, stretching down the slope of the hill. On the hilltop itself a vast, closed forum was
built in the second century, at right angles to the Orléans road, replacing an earlier forum. It
was rectangular in shape, surrounded by porticoed shops, with a temple and a basilica in the
middle. Nearby, to the south-west, were some small public baths (thermae) (first century
and early second century). The opulent district stretched westwards over the area which is
now the Luxembourg Gardens. The great public baths to the north (Thermes de Cluny) were 2
built at the bottom of the hill at the end of the second century and the beginning of the third
century. Their imposing ruins can still be seen today. The baths were flanked by some other,
slightly older baths to the east, and to the west by a small theater. These three buildings
marked out the "monumental front" of Lutetia towards the north, on the edge of the marshy
ground bordering the river. The amphitheater (Arènes de Lutèce) was on the outskirts to the 3
east. An aquaduct fifteen kilometres long brought water to the city from springs lying to the
south.

We hardly know anything about the lay-out of the Ile de la Cité at the height of the Empire.
There was probably a temple there, but there is no evidence that the Boatmen's Pillar, parts 1
of which were found in the foundations under the choir of Notre-Dame, was erected on the
island.

The marshy right bank does not seem to have been inhabited at the time and the temple of Mercury on the hill of Montmartre was right outside the city. No regional influence can be discerned in the architecture of Lutetia's monuments at the height of the Empire. In their lay-out, the Thermes de Cluny and the Arènes resemble other monuments of the Roman world. The building method, too, is typical—Roman bonded brickwork, originally rendered in red, and of an admirable regularity at Cluny. Of the sculpture which decorated the building there now only remains the mighty prow-shaped brackets which take the thrust of the arches in the "frigidarium" of the Thermes du Nord. At the Forum and the Arènes, however, excavations have unearthed some sculpted pieces which give some idea of the rich, even heavy, ornamentation of the buildings. The interiors were for the most part painted or decorated with marble panels.

Modelled sculpture flourished quite remarkably at that period. It was truly original, manag-
ing to follow Roman models and yet, at the same time, to preserve a robust vein of native
inspiration. The reliefs on the Boatmen's Pillar show that the Gallic influence coexisted with 1
motifs borrowed from Rome.

The barbarian invasions towards the end of the third century laid waste the beautiful Gallo-Roman city on the left bank, which had been an open city. The Cité was then fortified with a wall, whose foundations were built of blocks from the ruined monuments to the south of the city, or even of engraved stones from the cemeteries. Those buildings still remaining on the island from the height of the Empire were rased to make more space. New monuments were then built in the restricted space protected by the ramparts. Although only unrecognisable bits and pieces now remain of the palace where the Emperor Julien lived before it became the palace of the French kings (now the Palais de Justice), excavations have uncovered the ruins of other buildings of the period which are better preserved.
Next to the northern rampart (the present site of the Flower Market) there was a building with sturdy foundations, the purpose of which remains unclear. To the south-east of this, on the western side of the present parvis of Notre-Dame, there rose a vast edifice whose shortest side was some twenty meters long. Its powerful basement was supported by buttresses—it was doubtless surmounted by a vault. Its construction method of bonded brick is the same as that of the Thermes de Cluny. Despite its extraordinary robustness it is less regular and less carefully built than the latter. The evidence suggests that is was a public building: perhaps a civil basilica built beside the highway which crossed the Cité, on its way from south to north. It has long been thought, though wrongly so, that the city was reduced to the Ile de la Cité at this juncture. In fact parts of the great buildings of the Roman city at its height most certainly survived, and the Forum's vast quadrilateral was even given ramparts in order that it might be used as a secondary refuge. There is no doubt that Lutetia, which had flourished when the Empire was at its height, now resumed its life again on the slopes of the Montagne Sainte-Geneviève, though on a somewhat diminished scale. The discovery of buildings, dating from the period when the Roman Empire was on the wane, which display a workmanship more rustic than that of the preceding period, testifies to this fact.
During this period the Empire's frontiers were shrinking; because of this the city acquired a new importance, one demonstrated by the fact that the military emperors of the fourth century stayed there.

THE EARLY MIDDLE AGES

We hardly know anything of Paris (the name supplanted that of Lutetia at this time) during the somber period of the fifth century. The city emerges again at the beginning of the sixth century as the royal seat of Clovis, remaining for a long time the source of his success. The lands of the former Gallo-Roman city were reconquered—a fact borne out by the existence in the Merovingian period of eleven religious foundations on the left bank. On the right bank there are only traces of five such establishments. A few decorations only—for instance, the capitals and shafts of columns—now remain of the two great funerary basilicas, Sainte-Geneviève and Saint-Vincent (later Saint-Germain-des-Prés) which were destined to receive the bodies of Clovis and his son Childebert I, as well as those of their descendants. However we do still have a description as well as the foundations and some other parts of the Merovingian cathedral built by Childebert in the Cité between 511 and 558. It was immense, the largest in Merovingian Gaul, some 36 meters wide and around 75 meters long. It had a porch with a bell-tower and two large rectangular halls on either side; its nave was ten meters wide, flanked on both sides by double aisles like Saint Peter's and Saint John the Lateran in Rome. In 1847 several of its magnificent columns of ancient marble were found as well as one of the white marble capitals which adorned them (no doubt owing to the fact that ancient monuments were used again in new buildings). They are now in the Cluny Museum. The blossoming of Merovingian art in Paris was not confined to monumental art; it can also be seen in remarkable examples of the goldsmith's craft, from Saint-Germain-des-Prés in particular. This creativity coincided with the Merovingian kingdom's period of prosperity and expansion, and with the growth of Paris on the site of the old Gallo-Roman city.

The monumental Paris of the latter half of the early Middle Ages is completely lost to us. Under the Carolingians the city's role declined in favour of the new imperial residences to the east. The city probably lived off its past, till the catastrophic Norman invasions completed its ruin. Raids by barbarians began in the ninth century: churches were pillaged and burnt when they could not be ransomed. In 885 siege was laid to the city; it was not lifted till 886 after all the suburbs had been destroyed. Nothing was left of the extended southern part of the city, built by the Romans and reconquered by the Merovingians—an artificial graft at the best of times. When Paris was reborn, it was to be near the river, which served as its lifeline, and on the right bank at that, which then became the heart of the city for several centuries.

When we consider the sumptuous and sudden blossoming of architecture in the eleventh and twelfth centuries, the Ile-de-France appears as one of the regions least endowed with remains of Romanesque art. The never-ending waves of destruction, and the fact that Gothic art was born here suffice to explain this lack. Yet a close inspection of those religious monuments still remaining, sometimes reveals elements dating from this period. Such signs as do exist suggest that the Ile-de-France did in fact share in the building fever that gripped Western Europe in this period, though it perhaps lacked the strong regional influence which mark Alsace, Normandy, Provence or Burgundy. The Ile-de-France, a region of crossroads, served by a magnificent river, was torn at the time between a liking for the astonishing architectural triumphs of Normandy and others yet further afield. Those great monuments, which can still be seen in Paris or are known to have existed there, provide precious confirmation of
4 to 9, 15, 12 and 13 this fact. Saint-Germain-des-Prés, Saint-Martin-des-Champs, Saint-Pierre-de-Montmartre
10 and 11 and the former church of Sainte-Geneviève, were powerful, rich abbeys favoured repeatedly by royal goodwill. It is interesting to note that, from the time of their foundation, these abbeys were situated outside the city and they did not merge with it till a very late date. Thus Philippe Auguste's wall, built on the left bank in the early years of the thirteenth century, took in the abbey of Sainte-Geneviève but cut the grounds of Saint-Germain in two, leaving the abbey outside—where a small market-town grew up round it. On the right bank, the new wall built in the middle of the fourteenth century at the behest of Charles V, enclosed the priory of Saint-Martin-des-Champs, already protected by a wall of its own. Subsequently the law of 16 June 1859 included Montmartre in Paris. When they were built, all these churches were surrounded by farm land or vineyards and looked very different from the way they do now, suffocated as they are by other buildings or cut off by sad rivers of asphalt. Originally these monasteries were founded on land abandoned after the Germanic invasions or Norman incursions. They thus had the space to spread out, especially on the left bank, abandoned to a greater extent than the right bank. They soon provided the economic focus around which little urban centers grew up. Some of them, like Saint-Germain-des-Prés, devoted themselves more particularly to spiritual undertakings. It is difficult now for us to imagine the role which this abbey played at the time of its foundation by Childebert in the sixth century. During the Carolingian period it became an intellectual centre and under the monk Ingelard in the eleventh century it tried to carry on the Carolingian tradition. The part it subsequently played in the study of French national history in the renaissance of the seventeenth and eighteenth centuries is well known.

The monks' determination to preserve the heritage of the past provides the key to understanding the prodigious revival of the arts in the eleventh century; a revival which totally transformed the architectural face of Europe. Without wishing (after Vitet and Viollet-le-Duc) to dwell at length on the now acknowledged conflict between the Romanesque art which appeared in the monasteries and the Gothic which developed in the cities, one must nevertheless admit that the most imposing monuments to have survived are the creation of the monasteries. Indeed how could it have been otherwise, when at that time the city was at the infant stage of its artistic development. We are moreover only just beginning to grasp the important part played by the great abbeys of Paris in that immense burst of artistic creativity. The eleventh century saw a new church built at Saint-Germain. The entire western half still remains: the entrance tower and the two bell-towers, nestled between the transept and the choir, were built in the same period by Abbot Morard (990-1014), who must have been planning the complete rebuilding of the church. The work's austere lines and rigour of form reveal the first gropings of artists launching themselves into architecture on the grand scale.

The joints are still thick, but the stone, cut already with great skill, foreshadows the remarkable stylistic successes of the twelfth century. The craftsmen's marks, which can be found scattered over the building's interior, make it clear that the churchmen took on real stone masons for the work. This remarkable first attempt thus represents a complete break with the earlier Romanesque art of the period, when Lombard masons used hammers to break the stone. This popular art, to be seen in many churches of Lombardy, Catalonia, Provence and the Rhineland, was not destined to have a future. The North, which had kept the Carolingian traditions alive, had at that time already launched itself on an enthralling adventure—one eventually to culminate in Gothic architecture.

The nave of Saint-Germain bears witness to the eager experiments of the architects of the eleventh century. As Jean Hubert has demonstrated, it dates from the building works carried out half a century later. The progress achieved in that period is fantastic. On the technical level, the stones are cut with precise arrises and the joints have been reduced to their simplest form. One can also discern a new mastery in the architect's handling of the plan, with a more carefully thought-out relationship between the width of the nave and that of the aisles. The nave also reveals new experimentation. Rejecting the principle of partitioning, the architect has tried to integrate the different volumes by cutting large arcades opening onto the aisles.

The curve of these arcades has been carefully worked out, and they create a new rhythm, reminiscent of antiquity. The desire to break up the monotony of flat walls can be seen in the architect's decision to apply a semi-column to the pillar, on the central nave side—an innovation whose usefulness was then open to question. In this way the bay was created. Yet another innovation was to have a long-term influence: great windows were cut at the top of the walls. It was only the absence of vaulting—the present vaults date from the seventeenth century—which made such architectural daring possible, since the wall had to bear only the weight of a wooden framework. The architects of the late eleventh century and the early twelfth century faced the following problem: to have a well-lit nave covered with a roof or to have a dark, narrow nave which could be vaulted. We now know that quite a few buildings originally planned without vaulting, were then in fact vaulted when they were built. Of course, all this experimenting was not lacking in drama; for instance the vaulting at Cluny collapsed in 1125. The architectural experiments which can be observed at Saint-Germain-des-Prés did not in fact originate there. The great abbeys of the north formed a vast international network at that period, and the links between them burst the narrow confines of region and nation asunder. The progress achieved in any one abbey was then passed on to the others with a speed hard to imagine. Saint-Germain for its part was indebted for many of its features to the experimenting in Normandy. The same however cannot be said of sculpture: both its iconographic and stylistic sources are to be found elsewhere. Before the Revolution
the nave at Saint-Germain still possessed an astonishing collection of capitals, some of which 4 and 5
have been preserved in the Cluny Museum; the others, still in place, were restored or repainted, in a most dreadful fashion in the middle of the nineteenth century. They now defy all analysis. The twelve capitals in the museum, by way of contrast, shed much light on the historical ups and downs of the sculptural renaissance in the eleventh century. They are thought to date from the middle of the eleventh century and as such they can be considered the "incunables" of stone sculpture. On these capitals, the most clumsy workmanship mingles with work of the highest quality, as though three sculptors of quite different training
and temperament had shared the task. One of them, responsible for the Christ in Majesty, 5
was capable of powerful work in vigorous relief. This new feeling for relief was probably due to the artist's trying to imitate metalwork: in the Christ in Majesty for instance the hem of the statue's robe would seem directly inspired by it. Here, a sculptor rediscovered for the first

time the beauty of relief. Yet, as we shall see, the style of these capitals wielded little influence in the Paris of that period. Isolated works such as these, probably by a foreign artist, harked back to the past in many ways.

Whilst Saint-Germain helps us to understand the importance of eleventh century Paris, the
end of that century and the beginning of the next were a very different story. The complete
destruction of Sainte-Geneviève to make way for the Rue Clovis in the beginning of the nine-
teenth century, constitutes one of the cruellest losses ever suffered by Paris. Only a few capi-
tals escaped destruction and they can now be found in the Louvre, the Musée de Cluny and
10 the Ecole des Beaux-Arts respectively. The church's bell-tower—the tour Clovis—for its
part now stands lost amidst the Lycée Henri IV. The choir and the eastern part of the nave
were rebuilt at the end of the eleventh century. The first bays of the nave, with sumptuous
11 columns surmounted by capitals, were not built before 1100. The concept of plastic art
revealed in these capitals is very different from that in the "Maître du Christ de majesté".
The figures and the intertwining foliage are in low relief. Yet the figures are presented in a
manner harking back to antiquity, which foreshadows the zodiac of Saint-Denis of 1140.
But there are even earlier capitals inspired by the style of Sainte-Geneviève. For instance
15 those of the tower of Saint-Martin-des-Champs which were probably repaired at the begin-
ning of the twelfth century. On the capitals of the church's choir, the ornamental foliage
stands out in sharp relief—a clear example of architectural development when compared
with Sainte-Geneviève. During this period, the Ile-de-France was testing its creative powers
in architectural experiments which eventually produced Gothic art. Thus all buildings which
date slightly before the middle of the twelth century may be seen falling on either side of an
ideal boundary separating Romanesque from Gothic art.

GOTHIC ART

TO THE MIDDLE OF THE THIRTEENTH CENTURY

Though Paris does not appear to have been a great artistic center in the early half of the century, the same cannot be said of the latter half. Then it was that Paris established itself as the capital, whilst the Capetian monarchy enlarged its domain considerably, reinforcing its power at the same time. The Ile-de-France played a vital role, moreover, in the discovery of a new style, the eventual successor to Romanesque art. Even if the choir of Saint-Denis, finished for its consecration in 1144, does not possess all the elements of Gothic art, it nevertheless marks such a complete break with the art of earlier periods that it must be considered the first Gothic monument. The intersecting ribs, though important, were but a means to an end; of more significance is the architect's evident desire to create a new volume. The architect of Saint-Denis fulfilled this dream, integrating the side-chapels radiating from the choir with the ambulatory by means of an extra arch. This astonishing achievement, which aroused the admiration of his contemporaries, was the fruit of repeated experimenting, the traces of which can still be seen in several monuments in the Paris region and even in Paris itself. It is not, however, always easy to tell if such buildings are earlier than the choir of Saint-Denis since a lack of documentation makes it impossible to establish exact dates. Thus archeologists do not always agree about the exact dates at which the choirs of Saint-Martin-des-Champs or Saint-Germain-des-Prés were planned. The problem is endlessly discussed in the hope of establishing whether their architects knew the choir of Saint-Denis or whether their work merely foreshadows it somewhat clumsily. Whatever the truth of the matter, none in fact managed to create anything as revolutionary as the choir of Saint-Denis.

In this respect Saint-Martin-des-Champs is without doubt one of the most irritating ex- 15
amples: a fair number of archeologists believe it to be the work of Abbot Hugues I, who died in 1142. This early date would explain the church's many awkward features: its irregular plan, the unsatisfactory arrangement of the vaulting of the aisles, the unharmonious proportions of the central chapel, the use of both groined and ribbed vaulting, as well as the general heaviness of the building form. The capitals, a large number of which have been heavily restored, are purely Romanesque in stylistic inspiration. The radiating chapels, on the other hand, are already merged with the volume of the ambulatory. If the late date is right, the choir of Saint-Martin-des-Champs would then have foreshadowed that of Saint-Denis. The choir of Saint-Germain-des-Prés, for its part, known to have been complete when the altar was consecrated in 1163, seems later than that of Saint-Denis and has little in common with it. The radiating chapels are clearly separated from the ambulatory—a plan which resembles that of Noyon cathedral to which it has been correctly compared. Before the windows were enlarged in the seventeenth century, the great arcades were crowned with a triforium with double arcades on the second storey and little windows on the third. The absence of any influence from Saint-Denis is demonstrated by the use of archaic features, astonishing at such a late date: the most obvious ones are the use of the rounded arch and the decorations of some of the capitals. It seems that in the mid-twelfth century, architects were engaged in parallel experiments, though quite unknown to each other despite the close proximity of the various monuments. In 1163 Paris established its pre-eminence with the reconstruction of
Notre-Dame. The last of the great cathedrals in what is now known as the first period of 16 to 26
Gothic art, Notre-Dame benefited from the experience gained at Sens, Senlis, Noyon and, in particular, Laon, built only a few years before Notre-Dame itself. The architect employed by Maurice de Sully was a man of great ability; his plan was an extremely original one but it was subsequently altered before the building work was finished. The plan, though ample, was yet

of an admirable simplicity: the nave is flanked by double aisles extending beyond the small transepts to surround the apse. The plan is extremely compact and lacks any extraneous elements. Following the custom of the time, the architect included an elevation on four levels: great arcades, galleries, oculi taking the place of triforium, and high windows. One of the building's greatest failings is its general darkness, a feature criticised repeatedly through the centuries. To improve this state of affairs, the windows were enlarged around 1230 to the detriment of the oculi. The ribbed vaulting is sexpartite—in other words an extra arch has been included, spanning the nave to make the vaulting of an oblong bay possible. The search for unity can already be clearly discerned in the lack of alternating piers, for instance. In fact the extra thrust of the vaulting, lighter than the others, was usually taken by a weaker pier. But here the architect has discarded this solution, which anyway created an unfortunate irregularity of rhythm, opting instead for piers of the same diameter in the great nave. Composite columns form a regular rhythm in the magnificent nave. A vestige of alternation can nevertheless be found in the aisles, where the sturdy piers, with twelve little columns attached, are arranged with remarkable skill.

The architect's overriding concern to create a flush elevation can also be seen in the transept crossing. The thrust of the ribs, coming downwards towards the nave, is taken by smooth pilasters, which thus form supports with cut-off corners. Yet other technical innovations reveal the mastercraftsman's skill. In the double ambulatory the triangular vaults without ribs overlap each other and are separated by beams. The vaulting of the galleries, meanwhile, originally rose from the outside wall to clear the bays and let in more light. Notre-Dame in fact dates from the end of a period of experimentation. The aim of all its innovations (oculi, composite columns, uniform supports) was to create profoundly "integrated" archi-
12 tecture. Yet for all that, the massive appearance of the architecture suggests a return to Romanesque ideas: the walls are no longer two-fold, thus banishing the effect of illusion and lightness achieved in other buildings. The exterior confirms this impression: the church appears solidly bedded in this moving riverscape, where the waters divide to enclose the mag-
16 nificent apse.

The facade was not added till considerably later, between 1190 and 1210—a time when great new discoveries had already transformed the development of Gothic architecture. In 1194 the first stone of Chartres cathedral was laid, followed by that of Bourges a year later. A new aesthetics was emerging and Notre-Dame already seemed out of date. However, Chartres and Bourges could not have been built without the vital discovery made during the building of Notre-Dame. In 1185 flying buttresses appeared for the first time in the nave of the Paris cathedral. This meant that the Gothic architect could finally realise his long-standing dream, reducing the building to a skeleton of stone spanning enormous bays.

In the late twelth and early thirteenth century the influence of Notre-Dame de Paris was felt not only in Paris itself and its region but also much further afield. In Paris, Saint-Julien-le-
14 Pauvre, begun in 1170, has sexpartite vaulting—rare in such a little church—and composite columns; the architect has also used alternation. In Saint-Séverin the architect again used composite columns in the first bays of the nave, as well as the principle of the double ambulatory with its special vaulting. Ideas borrowed from Notre-Dame are particularly noticeable in churches close to the capital, whilst further afield at Bourges, the architect again uses the Paris plan but with an entirely new elevation.

The north of France played as important a role in the birth and development of Gothic sculpture as it did in that of architecture. Artists were commissioned to carve statues on the columns that were to decorate the western facade of Saint-Denis (completed for its consecration in 1140) and the Royal Portal of Chartres (1145). As time went on, these projecting statues stood in their own right, as they became ever more detached from the fabric of the

building. This startling innovation, which ushered in a new concept of sculpture in the
round, spread throughout the north. Two important Paris churches bear witness to this fact:
Notre-Dame and Saint-Germain-des-Prés. The sculptures of the Portal of Sainte-Anne were 21
put to use again around 1220 in the west facade of Notre-Dame. The oldest of them date from
around 1150 and the more recent ones from 1165. They come from the former church of
Notre-Dame, which Etienne de Garlande was busy restoring until his death in 1160; the
work was continued thereafter. These sculptures appear to be the work of several artists. One
of them, who was obviously very influenced by the art of Chartres, carved the Virgin of the
tympanum; another, who was evidently more attached to the graphic style of earlier times,
carved the right side of the lintel and the extraordinary head belonging to the statue of David,
formerly on the right-hand splay, and now in the Metropolitan Museum in New York. A
third must have done the left part of the lintel with its long figures in stiff poses. Finally, a
fourth, younger artist is probably responsible for the figures of the tympanum, carved in
stronger relief and with greater suppleness of style. There is also the magnificent fragment of
the column-statue in the Louvre; the subtle treatment of its folds has no equal in stone sculp- 24
ture; only metalwork—the dies for seals for instance—can rival the precision of these undu-
lating folds. This same team of craftsmen must subsequently have crossed the Seine, drawn
by the building work at Saint-Germain-des-Prés, then in full swing. The recumbent figure of
King Childebert, in place by 1163 though nowadays exiled to Saint-Denis, is so close stylisti-
cally to the right-hand lintel of Notre-Dame that it is most probably by the same craftsman.
By way of contrast, it is harder to be sure about the statues of the western portal which were
destroyed during the Revolution. Our entire knowledge of them is based on a bad eighteenth
century engraving. Yet even this reveals the style of the Portal of Sainte-Anne.

In the decade after 1180, the style of Senlis prevailed in Paris. The only evidence of this
remaining now is the two arch moldings and a torso, all of uncertain origin, now in the
Louvre. The early thirteenth century saw a definite reaction against this supple style, though
the astonishing headless statue in the Carnavalet Museum is half-way between the Senlis
style and that of the period around 1200. On the other hand the new concept of plastic art,
inspired by antiquity, can be seen in all its nobility in the extraordinary torso now in the
Cluny-Museum. This, like the statue of Carnavalet, comes from the central portal of Notre-
Dame. The artist has indeed carved a work worthy of antiquity. The sculptures of the tympa- 21
num (except for "Christ showing his Wounds" and "The Angel with Nails", both carved
around 1220) are inspired by the style of Sens which dominated the major building enter-
prises of the time. The long, fluted folds mold the figures, covering the legs of the Virgin and
those of Saint John with magnificent flowing curves. The figures' expressions impart a
serene gravity, suggesting the world beyond. The Portal of the Virgin on the left is composed 21
with extraordinary skill: it is a monumental page, one of the masterpieces of Gothic sculp-
ture. Its authors achieved a marvelous balance between monumental strength and subtlety
of form. After this, sculptors merely reproduced the style. Eventually the decade 1240-1250
saw an abrupt reaction against the style, which had by then exhausted itself.

"RAYONNANT" ART

In the mid-thirteenth century, Paris, until then an artistic center subject to outside influences, suddenly became a creative center in its own right; one which transformed the development of style in architecture and sculpture, as well as in the so-called minor arts: illumination, ivory work and the goldsmith's art. It was a period when Paris was still protected by a sturdy wall on both banks of the river, built by the King Philippe Auguste; to the west there was also the protection afforded by the Louvre, an advanced fortified position in

itself. Thus the capital went through a period of extraordinary developments in all fields: economically, with the powerful guild of the "marchands de l'eau" (river merchants), intellectually, with the University, and also artistically. A kind of rivalry grew up between the King, Louis IX, and the prelates, monks, and great lords; a rivalry which fostered the spread of an "art de cour" or court art. The many busy building sites attracted craftsmen, providing
28 to 32 work for several years. At the Palace the Sainte-Chapelle was being built, at Notre-Dame the transepts were being extended, at Saint-Germain-des-Prés the refectory and the Virgin's
15 chapel were being built, the refectory at Saint-Martin-des-Champs, and, at the Temple, a fore-nave. Work was also being done at many other places which we now only know of from documents. Some of these monuments have disappeared and can now only be studied from drawings and engravings—not always accurate ones at that. Some of these monuments, however, have managed to escape destruction. A specialist in this period, Robert Branner, distinguishes two distinct phases; in the first, from 1240-1250, the "style de cour" or court style was not a single coherent entity but rather a multiple one. Paris, it seemed, was trying to confirm its universality by absorbing as many contemporary trends as possible. The Sainte-Chapelle, the north transept of Notre-Dame and the fore-nave of the Temple belong to this first period. Around 1260 this diversity slowly gave way to a more integrated style; the art de cour blossomed out in all its varied possibilities, and with a mastery of style that carries right on into the fourteenth century with the chapel of Navarre at the collegiate church at Mantes. The second phase is more difficult to discern in Paris as nothing now remains of most of the monuments built then: l'Hôpital des Quinze-Vingts, the Collège de Cluny and all the monasteries are today but evocative names.

The artist's freedom expressed itself in those aspects of architecture which require draughts-

manship—the windows, blind arcades and the different parts of the facade. With time, the approach became increasingly linear, a trend which culminated in the facade of the right transept of Notre-Dame around 1260, and in the chapel of Navarre (14th century), where the delicacy of outline rivals metalwork. At the same time, impassioned experiments were under way to find ways of raising the vaulting of buildings as high as possible and of piercing as many windows as possible in the walls, thus virtually replacing them with stained-glass windows. The discovery of the flying-buttress did away with galleries which were no longer needed for buttressing. Thus was created a new visual unity between the clerestory windows and the triforium, now perforated, whilst the mullions of the high windows extended into the triforium. The nave of Saint-Denis represents one of the important stages in this development: there, Pierre de Montreuil reduced the wall to its simplest expression by a masterly use
30 of pillars, transforming it into a framework for the glass. The upper storey of the Sainte-Chapelle in Paris is another striking example. Here, the supporting structures have been thinned right down. The opacity of stone walls has given way to the translucency of walls of glass enclosing the interior volume. Stained glass is obviously of paramount importance in this development; indeed the whole architectural concept seems to have been designed with the sole aim of achieving the largest surface of glass possible. A close partnership in fact developed between the architect and the stained-glass artists, from which there sprang those immense stained-glass windows, the daring and boldness of whose design still arouses both astonishment and wonder. Another innovation in this line also proved a great success: the
32 enormous rose windows which were let into the whole breadth of the transept facades. Pierre de Montreuil set the example with the transepts of Saint-Denis, then Jean de Chelles followed
19 with the north transept of Notre-Dame, followed in turn by Pierre de Montreuil himself in the south transept. Inspired by the general design of the western facades, these two artists created for the facades of the transept a model which was to last right through the Middle Ages.

As in the case of architecture, recent research has revealed the importance of the capital's
artistic centers in the development of sculpture in the mid-thirteenth century. Paris has been
unusually privileged in that a great number of the works of this period have survived. They
can, moreover, be dated with such precision that one can follow the development of plastic
art through almost a third of the century. As mentioned, this development started with an
abrupt break with the preceding style. In fact the two sculptures "Christ showing his
Wounds" and the "Angel with Nails", inserted in the older tympanum of the central portal 21
of Notre-Dame around 1240, in other words somewhat later than the rest of the work, both
reveal in embryo the future development of sculpture in the second half of the century. The
figure of Christ with its monumental nobility inaugurated the "classical" style, which can be
found generally in Paris, whilst the "Ange aux clous", with his smile and the molded folds of
the drapery, heralds the Mannerist trends which blossomed in Reims. The classical style can
also be seen in the famous statue of Childebert from the pier of the refectory at Saint-Ger- 8
main-des-Prés which, an inscription suggests, dates from before 1244. This statue is so close
stylistically to the "Christ montrant ses plaies" that it could be the work of the same artist.
The four apostles of the Sainte-Chapelle, now in the Cluny Museum, are examples of this 29
style in full bloom. Moreover the statue of Saint John, with its Attic-style head, must be seen
as the highest achievement of this style—one which can never be surpassed. Parisian artists
remained faithful to the classical style till the fourteenth century. At Notre-Dame, two art-
ists seem to have shared the work on the portal of the north transept. The first artist—"Le
Maître de la Vierge" or Master of the Virgin—did the scenes of the miracle of Theophilus.
The figures are tall and slender with well-sculpted heads, and the poses are lively. The
second artist did the lintel, the last two scenes of the legend of Theophilus and the arch mold-
ings. Here the figures are squat, bundled up in thick drapery, the faces lack expression and
the gestures spontaneity. Indeed the sculpture of the north transept is very disappointing
compared with that of the south transept where the genius of the Parisian artists blossomed
forth in full. The arrangement of figures in a frieze has been abandoned in favour of more
elaborate compositions: the groups of figures are arranged and some of them seethe with
movement (Lapidation de saint Etienne—the Stoning of Saint Stephen). The poses of the
figures are also more complex (Lapidation de saint Etienne) and more agitated (Docteurs
disputant avec saint Etienne, Doctors arguing with Saint Stephen). Some mannerist touches
can be seen here and there in the drapery and in the negroid features of a Roman soldier. But
the real mastery of the Parisian artists is best seen in the famous statue of Adam, now in the 26
Cluny Museum, originally from the interior decoration of the south transept of Notre-Dame.
Here for the first time, a sculptor of the Middle Ages dared to compete with the art of antiqui-
ty by sculpting a nude figure in vigorous relief, its different planes flowing gracefully into
each other. The Parisian art of the mid-thirteenth century thus draws to a close with one of
the great masterpieces of Gothic sculpture. Indeed the portals of Notre-Dame seem to have
been the last great undertaking of the thirteenth century. The royal building sites were then
closed down and the craftsmen were drawn away to other, more active centers.

THE EARLY HALF OF THE FOURTEENTH CENTURY

The death of Saint Louis (1270) marked the decline of Paris as an artistic center, both for sculpture and architecture. The great architectural undertakings which had given the city a new face, were now at an end. Nevertheless, right at the end of the century and throughout the fourteenth century, a new phenomenon appeared which was to play a vital role in the development of art: royal or princely patronage—the importance of which Philippe Le Bel understood well. It was linked to a certain social evolution and to a new concept of man in society; one of its side effects was the construction of new monuments: palaces and manor-houses in the civil sphere, and private chapels in the religious sphere.

In 1298, Philippe Le Bel launched important building works in the point of the Cité, an undertaking which transformed the old Kings' Palace into one of the most magnificent resi-
33 to 35 dences of the period, if Jean de Jandun is to be believed. The fire of 1618 completely ravaged the Great Hall with its statues of all the kings of France fastened to its pillars. The fire of 1776 then completed the destruction. Nowadays, there only remains the lower Hall of the men-at-
35 arms, "Salle des gens d'armes"—commonly called the Hall of Saint Louis, its open spiral stair-
33 case which gave access to the Great Hall and the four towers of the palace wall, which have, unfortunately, suffered from over-restoration. Such was the great king's most ambitious architectural undertaking in Paris; the example he set was to be followed thereafter. For example, Mahaut d'Artois (a woman most unfortunate in her daughters whose conduct besmirched their husbands, the king's sons) during her long life employed a whole galaxy of artists, drawn to Paris by the artistic activity there. Jeanne d'Evreux also adopted a policy of princely patronage. Other people of distinction too, religious orders and even ordinary private individuals built colleges, chapels and oratories, none of which now remain. The chapel of the Collège de Navarre, the Chapelle des Grands-Carmes, the Chapelle Saint-Yves, the Chapelle Saint-Julien-des-Ménétriers, the Eglise du Saint-Sépulcre and Saint-Jacques-de-l'Hôpital can only be conjured up nowadays with the help of iconographic documents. Only the refectory of the couvent des Bernardins, now a fire station (24, rue de Poissy, 5e arrondissement), built by the French Pope Benedict XII in 1338, has escaped the general destruction. We are thus prevented from appreciating the artistic development of the first half of the century.

The flourishing of architecture called for appropriate sculpture. Hence the astonishing blossoming of devotional sculpture, specially created for oratories and chapels. Monumental sculpture did not however disappear completely. Indeed, if one compares the few stumps remaining of Philippe Le Bel's palace with the four sculptures of the Priorale Saint-Louis at Poissy, also founded by Philippe Le Bel, one realises what marvellous simplicity the royal sculptors achieved. The feeling for the monumental has been replaced by an artistic sensibility closer to reality. The style spread beyond Paris; its appearance in Normandy was due to
27 Enguerran de Marigny, who sent for the King's sculptors. The statues of Saint-Jacques-de-l'Hôpital, found in the middle of the last century and now in the Cluny Museum, show that the monumental style, also found in the portal of the Saint-Sépulcre continued in use. Nevertheless, these statues display a liking for the anecdotal which a sculptor of the previous century would have found unacceptable, as well as a feeling for volume, which is unlike that of the thirteenth century. Complex drapery arrangements and the cascading folds of clothes were most popular, as clearly seen in the innumerable Virgins with Child or the statues of saints which craftsmen sculpted in alabaster or marble to meet the growing demand of an eager clientèle.

THE PATRONAGE OF CHARLES V

The reign of Charles V (1364-1380) saw an important stylistic revolution, which altered the course of artistic development. The appearance of a new phase of Gothic art is thus generally put in the 1380s. Charles V, whose liking for intellectual endeavour and art of all kinds—architecture, sculpture, the goldsmith's craft and the illuminated decoration of books—aroused the admiration of his contemporaries, knew how to command the service of the greatest artists of the age. Indeed he made them work without respite. The close contacts between artists from very different places, yet united by a common task, inspired new discoveries. Here, Raymond du Temple seems to have been a leading personality; he was close enough to the King for the latter to be godfather to his son, and he probably directed most of the royal building works, or at the very least oversaw their completion. Though an architect himself, he seems also to have supervised the work of sculptors, to whom there are numerous references in the texts of the period; Jean de Saint-Romain, Jean de Launay, Jean de Liège, Jacques de Chartres and Guy de Dammartin sculpted the statues for the famous spiral staircase of the Louvre. Other artists are only mentioned in passing—a certain André Beauneveu, for instance, who proved incapable of working for the same prince for very long on account of his unstable character. Though in the King's service, these sculptors also took on commissions from elsewhere; some of them worked for those close to the court. Today nothing remains of this amazing burst of architectural activity which revolutionized the appearance of Paris at the height of the Hundred Years War. Time and man have conspired to sweep away these great achievements. Chronicles, annals, accounts and inventories help us only to guess at the vastness of the undertaking. Charles V transformed the Louvre of Philippe Auguste into a sumptuous residence which then set the fashion. He raised the walls, added windows, brightened up the roofs with pinnacles and furnished the living apartments in luxurious style. It was under the direction of Raymond du Temple that the amazing spiral staircase was built—the wonder of his contemporaries. The King's health, however, would not permit him to live in the Louvre, so he went to the Marais, where he had the Hôtel Saint-Pol done up, enlarging and decorating it in a less sumptuous and more intimate style. He also had major alterations done to the Palais de la Cité, which had been rebuilt by Philippe Le Bel. Religious buildings were not neglected either. The King founded monasteries, the Couvent des Célestines and the Couvent de Saint-Antoine, extending his bounty to many others besides. The same was true of military architecture. The city had spread considerably on the right bank and this necessitated the building of a new wall; the city built it on the King's orders. To the east, the city was protected by the Bastille Saint-Antoine (Fortress of Saint Anthony), the foundation stone of which was laid on 22 April 1370 by Hugues Aubriot, provost of the merchants. Financial aid from the King made the building of both fortress and wall possible. This formidable fortress, built to a polygonal plan with sides of unequal length, was a novelty by virtue of the high connecting walls, which rose up to the level of the towers. In this plan, the rampart walk took the form of a projecting gallery supported by brackets, which ran right round the fortress, hugging its sinuous contours. Such a plan made flexible defence tactics possible; it was used again in a number of fifteenth century fortresses. Today, only the Château de Vincennes at the gates of Paris can give us some idea of this brilliant period of architectural activity.

The importance of the capital was even more marked in the field of sculpture. Most of it has unfortunately been destroyed: for example, none of the Louvre statues have survived, including three of the royal couple; nor is anything left either of the statues which adorned the east side of the Bastille and also the Hôtel Saint-Pol. The various religious buildings, constructed with the King's help, have also vanished. The only statues to have escaped are the two marvellous ones from the church of the Celestines, now in the Louvre. They bear witness to the great achievements of the team of sculptors assembled by the King. The feeling for plastic art, the different concept of volume and the monumental treatment, represent a complete break with the style of the fourteenth century; they also already herald the stylistic revolution of Sluter, at Champmol.

Charles V seems to have played an important part in these innovations. Owing to his personality, his open-mindedness and special feeling for art, he was able to promote the kind of relationship between artists from very different backgrounds, which engendered a community of style. For the first time—in France at any rate—people realised what an effect patronage could have on the development of the arts. In this respect, Charles V inevitably reminds one of Louis XIV. Patronage was on a level with politics; not only was Paris under self-scrutiny, France, and the whole of Europe too, had their eyes fixed on the capital, avidly following all that happened there. In Paris, the spirit of competition was such that those close to the King, all infected with the feverish desire to build, now turned to the artists of the royal team. Patronage in France then spread wider as Jean de Berry, Philippe le Hardi, Louis d'Orléans, Clément VII, the anti-pope, and Cardinal Jean de Lagrange, all called on the royal craftsmen to build palaces and churches and to sculpt for them. Thus the new style spread throughout the kingdom. The death of the King in 1380 and the minority of his unfortunate son, Charles VI, both contributed to the general dispersal of artists to whom Paris could no longer offer enough work. Thus one of the most brilliant periods of art in the capital came to a close.

THE FIFTEENTH CENTURY

During this period, Paris ceded to others the role of international capital of the arts, and, as royal patronage waned, it was succeeded by princely patronage. Strangely enough, architectural developments were little affected by the various factions which tore the capital apart during the first third of the fifteenth century. Indeed, Charles VII's return to Paris in 1437 did not, as might have been expected, signal a period of renewal; there had in fact been one considerably earlier. Small churches were enlarged or completely rebuilt to very different plans. At Saint-Nicholas-des-Champs, for example, the bell-tower and the seven western bays were built from 1420 onwards, on the orders of Abbot Lebeuf. Then in 1429, the finished choir of Saint-Laurent was consecrated by Bishop Jean du Chastelier. Thereafter, building work was

not resumed before the end of the century. At Saint-Germain-l'Auxerrois, the nave and the
36 transept were built around 1423; the porch, of Burgundian inspiration, was built by Jean
Gaussel from 1435-1439. The feverish desire to build did not grip the capital again till the second half, more particularly the last few years, of the century. The style of the nave at Saint-Médard suggests that it dates from the middle of the fifteenth century. At the church of Saint-Séverin, the church wardens had the five eastern bays of the nave rebuilt in 1450, though the first stone of the new choir was not laid till 1489. In fact Gothic architecture
43 stretched well beyond 1500. The plan of Saint-Gervais-Saint-Protais, for example, was
drawn up right at the end of the XV century. But it then took more than a century to build this church, which remains Gothic in structure. Other churches bear witness to the longevity of the Gothic style: Saint-Merry, for instance; its crypt dates from 1515, the nave, with its
58 and 59 exuberant portal, from 1520 and the choir from 1552. At Saint-Etienne-du-Mont, it is diffi-
45 and 46 cult to pronounce on what is strictly Gothic and what Renaissance, whilst at Saint-Eustache
the style of decoration is entirely Renaissance though the building remains Gothic in plan. In all these buildings, architectural simplicity goes hand in hand with lavish decoration. At Saint-Germain-l'Auxerrois, for instance, the exuberantly decorated porch contrasts
38 strongly with the nave. At Saint-Séverin, the choir with its marvellous twisted pillar provides
a marked contrast with the western bays, and at Saint-Merry the west portal. In Paris, flamboyant architecture developed a special style of its own as the architects strove to build up vast, luminous volumes by developing the bays to the maximum.

40 The end of the century is marked by a renewal of civil architecture: the Hôtel de Sens, unfor-
tunately greatly disfigured by recent restoration, and, more important, the Hôtel of the ab-
41 and 42 bots of Cluny. The plan of the latter and the design of its interior included many important
innovations, which subsequently influenced future developments. Here, for the first time, we find the new style which was to transform French architecture.

Paris was not transformed in a day under the influence of what we now call the "Renaissance." The medieval city possessed a sturdiness all of its own, and its central core, tortuous and teaming with life, only finally yielded to Haussmann's pickaxe. Indeed, though Humanism found fertile ground in Paris, the new forms met with considerable resistance from the Parisian bourgeoisie, attached as they were to the traditional manner of building. The birth of classical architecture on the banks of the Seine is thus closely linked to the personal initiative of successive sovereigns. The extremely slow progress of the new style can only be explained by the capricious, halting relationship which Charles VIII, Louis XII and François I maintained with their capital.

Gothic art, meanwhile, enjoyed great popularity both in domestic and religious architecture.
In this respect, the great residences provide good examples: those of the archbishops of Sens 40 to 42
or the abbots of Cluny, both sumptuous Parisian seats of the high clergy. The great secular
lords for their part had to follow the peregrinations of the court and thus had no time to re-
style their pied-à-terres in the capital. Meanwhile, the churches of Saint-Séverin, Saint- 38
Etienne-du-Mont, Saint-Jacques-de-la-Boucherie, Saint-Gervais and Saint-Merry were ei- 58 and 59, 44, 43
ther built or completed in this century, in a flamboyant style of magnificent subtlety. The King, for his part, liked the new art inspired by Italianism and antiquity. Indeed, the aesthetics of the Renaissance followed his person like the wake of a ship. It was by virtue of the royal visits that the new style first appeared in Paris but then, like the staring crowds themselves, it disappeared in the narrow streets of the city. However it was this new style which gradually familiarised the middle classes with the Orders of antiquity, the images of mythology and allegory, and with the ambitious plans for urban life which the new learning inspired.

The first signs of this new approach can be seen in Louis XII's decision to rebuild the Pont Notre-Dame and the houses on it. This was to be the capital's introduction to town planning—of the authoritarian and theoretical kind. In this plan, a large rectangular gateway lent perspective, whilst the facades of the houses were all built to one design with symetrically placed windows, and use was made of stone bonded with brick. Despite the medieval plan of its gabled houses, the Pont Notre-Dame heralded the dawning of the modern age on the banks of the Seine. At that time too, the Chambre des Comptes (Audit chamber) was being built as well as the outside staircase of the Sainte-Chapelle, both examples of Louis XII style in Paris, which have vanished long since.

These, however, were but trifles. From the time of Etienne Marcel, the King had not felt safe in Paris. During the English occupation he had taken a liking to the Val de Loire. Charles VII, Louis XI, Charles VIII and then Louis XII also regarded it as their favourite place of residence, transforming Ambroise or Blois. To begin with, François I followed their example and created Chambord. But Pavia and Spanish captivity had made him think again; he needed the Parisians' loyalty and their financial support. To keep them contented, the King realised there would have to be a rapprochement between the monarchy and the capital. Thus in 1528 he announced that Paris would be his habitual residence.

At any rate he moved the permanent court to the Ile-de-France (Fontainebleau, Villers-Cotterêts, Saint-Germain-en-Laye, Madrid in the Bois de Boulogne), and took an active interest in the great building works going on in Paris. He was personally responsible for planning the new Louvre, the Hôtel de Ville (for this task he forced the municipal magistrates to take on the Italian Dominique de Cortone, known as the Boccador).

It is to the King that we also owe the first stone embankment, the demolition of fortified
gates, the building of new streets and the immense new church of Saint-Eustache, veritable 45 and 46
cathedral of the right bank, which was not completed until the following century.

Under Henri II the problem was different. The ball had started rolling, and private builders abandoned the Gothic style. A new style had been created, a specifically French adaptation of antiquity by architects such as Pierre Lescot, Philibert de l'Orme and Jean Bullant, all of whom worked on the great Parisian sites. The royal presence, too, was increasingly felt. There was, for example, Henri II's magnificent official entry into the capital in 1549, when
49 to 51, 65 the Fountain of the Innocents was built as was the new Louvre by Pierre Lescot, and the great private mansions like those of the High Constable of Montmorency and those of the Guises, all decorated by the best artists. Paris thus took its place amongst the most famous art cities of Europe.

During the wars of religion, the monarchs stayed ever more frequently in Paris. Henri III was himself really a Parisian, aware of the great city's problems. Despite the difficulties of the times, everyone who held a rank at court—and the Italians were foremost—had a fashionable house built there. Only the new quarters could provide the architects with the space necessary for their work; districts where land had recently been sold in lots, for example the area which today surrounds the Rue des Francs-Bourgeois and the Rue de Sévigné. There we
53, 54 can still find a whole "Marais" district, as it were, dating back to the sixteenth century. It is built in the style of Charles IX or Henri III, a style which wavers between the classicism of Philibert de l'Orme and the overworked mannerist style of the Du Cerceau family.

9 When the reign of the Valois ended, the abbots' palace of Saint-Germain-des-Prés was built for the Cardinal de Bourbon, King Charles X of the League. The palace is made of brick and stone, built with a harmony of colours which his nephew and triumphant competitor, Henri IV, was to retain.

In the early half of the seventeenth century, Paris underwent a spectacular transformation—a source of great wonder at the time. When Henri IV entered the city in 1594, it was exhausted and ruined; the long siege had been a terrible ordeal. Those Parisians who had stayed in the city had been unable to look after their houses, which were consequently utterly neglected. Some of them had been demolished by gunfire or for strategic reasons; rents were at their lowest. The city finally surrendered to the King after his conversion to Roman Catholicism. But, as the price of his victory, the King had to make the Louvre his home and start the mammoth task of rebuilding and restoring the city. In this he had three aims: to gain the Parisians' loyalty and give them confidence, to further his own prestige and, at the same time, to provide a short-term solution to the threat of unemployment.

Well served as he was by the hard-working Sully, Henri IV took a personal interest in town planning. He found moreover that he had inherited from the Valois, from his mother-in-law, Catherine de Medici, and his brother-in-law, Henri III, plans for the capital. He decided to put them to full use, a possibility which his predecessors had doubtless never envisaged. There was, for instance, an urgent need for a connecting road between Saint-Germain and the Louvre district. Henri IV had the Pont-Neuf finished, the first bridge of its kind as it had 47 no houses on it but was provided with pavements. He then finished the task by adding a whole new network of roads. At the tip of the Ile de la Cité, he built embankments and a 48 square of regular plan (the Place Dauphine). The old Palais de Tournelles took up a lot of space in the district of the Marais du Temple, and so the King had a huge square laid out enclosed by high buildings—the Place Royale (Place des Vosges). The prior of the Temple 52 decided to divide up the vast domains lying to the north-east; the king then planned a square of semi-circular shape, surrounded by administrative buildings and bordering on the ramparts—the Place de France. It would have been built but for the King's assassination. To provide a useful link between the Louvre, the habitual Royal residence, and the Palais des Tuileries—a second residence built by Catherine de Medici outside the ramparts—the King built the Galerie du bord de l'eau (the Riverside Gallery), which spans the surrounding wall and the defensive moat.

In this rapid process of transformation, Paris even changed color. Whilst the Louvre arcades were built in stone, in the classic style of the preceding period, the new squares blossomed into a polychromy of brick and stone beneath slate roofs. The new style evoked a familiar good naturedness, very much in harmony with the common sense of Henri IV himself. The houses built for private individuals—the Hôtel Chalon-Luxembourg, for example—display a 55 similar mixture of colors.

Under Louis XIII, the wave of building work encouraged by Henry IV attained such proportions that private initiative became the driving force behind the expansion of the town, despite the monarchy's efforts to restrain too rapid a development. New districts sprang up everywhere; the age of the great property developers had begun, with such men as Louis Le Barbier, Christophe Marie and the architect, Louis Le Vau. They invested their capital in the Pré-aux-Clercs, in the Ile Saint-Louis, in the Marais du Temple, and also to the north of 57 the Louvre, and around the Palais Cardinal (Palais-Royal), buying land by the acre and selling it by the yard. The new streets and embankments were lined with private residences in freestone, built by financiers, members of Parliament and of the Chambre des Comptes (Audit chamber) by ministers and by great lords.

These residences are sober; the sculpted ornamentation, opulent and gay, was put on the pediments of the dormer windows and the other window lintels, except in certain residences which remained faithful to the more elaborate aesthetics of the preceding century, the Hôtel

56 de Sully, for instance. Engravings were done of the most beautiful of these Hôtels as soon as
they were finished. They thus became known to the general public and were soon the object
of admiring comments. Some of the best architects, such as Pierre Le Muet, Jacques Le Mer-
cier, François Mansart and Louis Le Vau, built residences of this type. Le Mercier extended
the old Louvre, whilst the regent Marie de Medici had Salomon de Brosse build the Palais du
60 Luxembourg. The embossed Italian-style ornamentation of the latter was done on the
Queen's express orders.

Meanwhile the resurgence of Catholic spirituality, reflected in the blossoming of both reli-
gious orders and congregations, meant that many convents and churches were being built.
The new churches were built, with variations here and there, according to the new Italian
canon of religious architecture perfected by Vignola in the Gesù of Rome. These included:
62 and 63 Saint-Gervais (facade), Saint-Paul-Saint-Louis, the Visitation, the Val-de-Grâce, the Sor-
61, 84 bonne, the Oratoire, Saint-Sulpice... Next to the Gothic spires, the first domes now rose up
into the Paris skies, changing the cityscape considerably. Paris in fact began to look like
Rome.

Under the regency of Anne of Austria, the innovations achieved by the aforementioned archi-
tects (also by Antoine Le Pautre) meant that in designing private residences, it was now pos-
sible to achieve greater effect and flexibility in the facades, and greater variety and conve-
nience in the living areas. The Hôtel de Beauvais, for example, with its skilfully thought-out
triangular courtyard, provides a good example of the architect's victory over a most unpro-
mising site. It is a masterpiece of the creative spirit, spurred on by difficulties.

In this period, interior design displayed an exuberance never to be seen again. The walls,
doors, coffered ceilings and archings were covered with guilded woodwork, decorated with
rich sculpture, with painted panels, and pictures. Alcoves and mantelpieces were framed
57 with stucco. Today the Hôtels Lambert, Lauzun, Amelot de Bisseuil, the arcades of the
Palais de Mazarin (Bibliothèque Nationale) and Anne of Austria's appartments in the
Louvre, give us a glimpse of the brilliant magic of colours which provided the setting for the
conversations of "Les Précieuses", those XVII century devotees of refinement.

But the monarchy was soon ready to leave Paris once again. The sad memories of the
Fronde, and a desire to live outside the suffocating, nauseous city decided Louis XIV against
living in the Louvre. He took up the itinerant habits of his predecessors, making one particu-
lar château his favourite—and then his home. His growing passion for Versailles, and the
enormous sums he poured into beautifying it, might well have run counter to the interests of
Paris, had not Colbert defended them. He flattered the King into making his capital the most
beautiful in the world, the "dwelling place of his glory" as the psalm puts it.

The French army was victorious everywhere, and so the ramparts of the city were demo-
lished in 1670 and replaced by a wide, shady walk, the "nouveau cours". Triumphal arches
celebrating Louis' victories were then built there: the Porte Saint-Martin and the Porte
71 Saint-Denis. On the left bank, vast utilitarian monuments were put up, majestic as palaces.
64 There was the Collège Mazarin (Palais de l'Institut) built by Le Vau opposite the Louvre, its
central dome rising above a concave facade. But there was also building in the nearby coun-
70 tryside, where an immense barracks for old soldiers (les Invalides) was built, as was a scien-
tific establishment (the Observatoire) and an alms-house (la Salpêtrière). On the right
bank, Le Vau carried on the building work on the Louvre around the Cour Carrée. The King
consulted the Italian Bernini about the main facade opposite Saint-Germain-l'Auxerrois,
67 deciding finally on a French colonnade. This majestic yet incommodious embellishment was
then built in front of an empty palace, which no sovereign ever made his home.

After Colbert's death in 1683, the architect Jules Hardouin-Mansart became the most
69 powerful man in Paris. It was he who built the lovely church of the dome behind the build-

ings of the Invalides. It is one of the most perfect examples of French classicism, inspired by 70
the drawings of François Mansart. He also built the new royal squares, contributing thus to
the rapid growth of Paris towards the west. First, the Place des Victoires with its circular
plan, centering on a statue of Louis XIV on foot, then the Place Vendôme, a much bigger, 72
chamfered square, centering on an equestrian statue of the King. The building of the second
square, planned over and over again, was accompanied by a great calculated surge of specu-
lation over the nearby land bordering on the ramparts.

Encouraged by these enterprises, private builders kept up the pace. The new quarters of the faubourg Saint-Germain and Saint-Honoré, competing on either side of the Seine, blossomed with luxurious mansions. These were veritable palaces, built on much larger sites than previously. Hardouin-Mansart, Bullet, Robert de Cotte, all designed entrance courtyards with service yards as well, surrounded by low outbuildings for the servants. The main buildings, overlooking big gardens, harbour great spaces specially designed for receiving guests—entrance halls, stairways, antichambers and drawing rooms. The living quarters, by way of contrast, were designed with comfort and convenience in mind—lower ceilings, alcoves and concealed passages and staircases for the servants to use.

The architecture is majestic in style, enlivened by the interplay of pediments, forepart and joint-lines beneath the curbroofs, whence dormer windows were gradually to disappear. Meanwhile the polychrome effects of the Mazarin period and the beginning of the great Reign, gradually began to disappear from interior design. At the end of the century, interior decoration consisted of carved woodwork, painted in white and gold, whilst ceilings were white with golden cornices. This period aimed at achieving a well-lit environment; a design which was rich and yet simple, effective in a sober way. Buildings on a more modest scale had facades broken by regular openings and moldings of simple design which gave rhythm to the groups of bays. A good example is the uniform design of certain streets, the Rue de la Ferronerie (even numbers) for example and the Rue du Roule. During this period, ironwork was griven a new prominence. Formerly merely considered a useful accessory, it was now recognised as an actual element of the facade, an indispensable softening note, tempering the harshness of the stone. The balconies of the Place Vendôme were purposely designed by Hardouin-Mansart, and their removal would disturb the delicate harmony of the square.

The death of Louis XIV marked the end for Paris of an era under the tutelage of Versailles, which, like the old king himself, had lasted too long. After a brief sojourn at Vincennes and then at the Tuileries, the young Louis XV might have gone back to live at Versailles in 1722, but the spirit was never the same thereafter—the King was no longer the judge and mover of men or things, and Paris, which had gained its intellectual independence during the Regency—the City opposed to the Court—was to exert its triumphant attraction on the sovereign's courtiers and his most intimate entourage. It was in the salons of the great financiers of the faubourg Saint-Honoré that the philosophers, men of letters, men of science and the artists met and set the style for the Age of Enlightenment—one of a radical change in mentalities.

On the architectural level, the style had changed well before the disappearance of Louis XIV. The decoration of the apartments at the Grand Trianon, and then of certain rooms at Versailles itself, already foreshadows rococo art. The deaths of Le Brun in 1690 and of Hardouin-Mansart in 1708 were important landmarks in this transformation of taste. The latter's demise in particular cleared the field for a varied galaxy of architects, who were to leave
73, 77 their mark on Parisian building under the Regency. While Robert de Cotte, Bullet, Delamair and Lassurance remained faithful to a majestic, soberly decorated classicism, others, such as Germain Boffrand, devised livelier facades with concave or convex effects. Some—Jac-
79 and 80 ques V Gabriel, for example, or Jean Aubert at the Hôtel Biron—isolated the main building completely, while still others cluttered their facades with exuberant, sculpted ornamentation around window frames (masks, garlands, decorative keystones, shells and foliage) and on the voluminous brackets of balconies. In the latter area, the role of draughtsmen and ornamental sculptors was of prime importance; it is they who created the true rococo style, born of the art of Berain and Audran and revitalized by Italian baroque or Flemish influences: Meissonnier, Toro, Oppenord or Pineau. While restraint remained the hallmark of facades, owing to the traditional Parisian aversion for any baroque extravagance, in interior
75, 76 decoration the new inspiration was given freer rein. The straight line was banished; the marble of mantelpieces, the wood of wainscoting, mirror frames, or overdoors, the stucco of cornices, the bronze of lamp brackets, yield to the fantasy of curves and counter-curves, shells, palmtree trunks and garlands of flowers with the same ease as the wrought iron of balconies and staircases. The asymmetric, the exotic or the extraordinary, reign though treated with a great mastery of line and volume.

Thanks partly to the architects of the great hôtels and partly to others less well known, who practised exclusively in Paris, humbler buildings soon began to exhibit signs of the same spirit. We can still see facades dating from this time in all the old districts of Paris—wide or nar-
81 row, decorated with surprising care, like the superb portal of N° 4 Rue Monsieur-le-Prince, or the entrance to the Cour du Dragon (which no longer exists). This attractive, florid style was used by certain Parisian designers right up to 1750—Denis Quirot, for example, or Pierre de Vigny.

It had, however, found its critics well before then, who disapproved of all the rococo "chicories" in the name of reason and nature: Voltaire, Blondel and Caylus in the 1740s. The famous Italian journey of Marigny, Cochin and Soufflot (1750), during which they had the opportunity to admire in situ the art of classical antiquity (Herculanum), hastened the offensive of neo-classical taste against those who still went for an essentially decorative style, an offensive reinforced by the vogue for palladian art in England. Thus the Louis XVI style was to assert itself well before the accession of the king whose name it has been given.

"Architecture," wrote Sébastien Mercier under Louis XVI, "in the last twenty years alone, has reverted to an excellent style, especially where embellishments are concerned. Count

Caylus has revived the Greek taste in us and we have finally renounced our Gothic lines. The interiors of houses are arranged with a charming commodiousness absolutely unknown to all the peoples of the earth."

In mid-century, a single man—Ange-Jacques Gabriel—formed the transition, drawing his inspiration from the art of Versailles before the rococo interlude, a classical art without aridity or superfluities. It was he who was responsible for the last royal square, laid out in honour of Louis XV and endowed since 1830 with the conciliatory name of Place de la Concorde. The 82
two buildings by Gabriel which form its north side, with their high stylobates and their colonnades, are still close to Perrault's Louvre, whereas the idea of this vast parade-ground, open on three of its sides on to the Tuileries gardens, the tree-lined Avenue des Champs-Elysées and on to the Seine, belongs to a new urban universe, that of great vistas and of marriages between buildings and nature. The same character marks the Ecole Militaire, where the neoclassical quest is perhaps more noticeable. Besides, the spirit of the century favoured great projects: squares, vistas, civic buildings, thoroughfares and canalizations had to respond to the needs of the citizen, as they did in Ancient Greece or Rome.

There was another factor which played a role in the transformation of the city during the latter half of the eighteenth century: the spirit of profit and speculation, and it was a prince of the blood, the Duke of Chartres, who set an example by letting out three sides of the garden of the Palais-Royal. Before long they were sprouting arcades, ingeniously designed by Victor 92
Louis to accommodate trading of the most profitable kind.

"The speculators have called in the contractors who, blueprint in one hand and estimate in the other, have fired the capitalists' spirit," wrote Sébastien Mercier. "Gardens have turned into stone and tall buildings catch the eye in places where we used to behold vegetables growing... Sainte-Geneviève and the parish of the Madeleine are surrounded by cranes hoisting enormous blocks of stone into the air. In the plains of Mont Rouge one sees these wheels, 25 to 30 foot in diameter, turning and working out the quarries." New districts like the Chaussée d'Antin and the "grands boulevards" became covered with tall, homogeneously designed buildings offering rented accommodation. In other districts, smaller numbers of great, palatial residences were going up, and more "small houses" with refined decor, gener- 91
ally in outlying suburbs, to please a blasé society that was fleeing the crowds and seeking a heavy simplicity combined with the Anglomania that reigned supreme.

The renovation of the design of facades, based on the principles of antiquity, on a strictly architectonic decoration—with the exception of a few bas-reliefs—and on the opposition of bare walls and surfaces scored with joint lines, was accompanied by a new choice of simplified volumes. The hôtel was readily compressed into a cube, like Palladian villas, one side of which sometimes opened directly on to the street. The basic cube was combined with cylinders or smaller cubes to provide circular drawingrooms, small rooms jutting out into an English garden, in short, a completely new geometry, at which Belanger, Rousseau, Brongniart and Cellerier excelled.

At the same time care was taken to equip the city with public buildings whose ancient classical style would give them a kind of moral guarantee, for more than a century linking the use of the column with respect for the established order. The Palais de Justice, the Mint, the 88
Schools of Medicine and Law, the Mont-de-Piété, the theaters, the hospitals—all of them donned this imposing finery over the next twenty years. Ledoux, advocate of a more austere architecture whose columns, with no base and scarcely any capital, were modelled on those of Paestum, sought new modulations to match the building to its function, or rather, to the ideal, his reluctance to deviate from established systems, combined with his visionary imagination, made his projects—admirable though they seemed on paper—very difficult to realise, as well as very costly. The building of the surrounding wall by the Farmers General,

94 punctuated by veritable temples destined—paradoxically—to serve as offices for the salt tax
collectors, was a terrible financial drain on the Crown and the City, and became the backdrop
for the first scuffles of the Revolution.

As far as religious architecture was concerned, the tradition of so-called Jesuit architecture
continued, at least during the first part of the century. Soufflot, supported by the Marquise
de Pompadour, introduced innovation by building, on the top of the high ground on the left
85 bank, the monumental Sainte-Geneviève's Church, now the Panthéon with its nineteenth
century disfigurements. An admirer of Gothic cathedrals with their lofty elevation and light-
ness, he sought to transpose their qualities into the architectural language of Augustan
Rome without abandoning that prestigious possession of European classicism, the cupola
resting on a tambour with columns. Following these efforts born of an initial eclecticism,
there was a return to sources, towards what was known of Christian origins. Chalgrain at
Saint-Philippe-du-Roule and Brongniart at the church of the Capucins at Antin (Saint-
Louis d'Antin) recreated Palaeo-Christian basilicas, whose gloomy interiors seemed more in
83 keeping with the piety of the age than the wide bays and baroque scenography of Saint-Roch.
The time was drawing near when impressionable souls would take a delight in reading the
"Génie du Christianisme"—the "Spirit of Christianity".

Michelet was quite right when he said that the only great monument in Paris dating from the French Revolution is the Champ-de-Mars. The period was hardly one to favour great building projects, although there were plans to carve new arterial roads through Paris—a scheme which was to be helped by the sale of public properties such as convents or the town-houses of émigrés. The style of the Revolution—spartan Louis XVI under the Convention, becoming more flamboyant under the Directory—was best reflected in the ephemeral decor of those great patriotic festivals which took place in the Champ-de-Mars itself.

Napoleon, on the other hand, took pains to stamp his own imprint on the banks of the Seine. "The Emperor wishes his capital, now the most important capital city in the world, to have an appearance in keeping with its illustrious destiny", he declared to the Corps Législatif in 1807. All his ideas about Paris are embodied in that remark: the universal supremacy he believed he had secured for himself, and to be reflected by his capital—now the center of the world and a place of pilgrimage for foreign delegations. Napoléon was encouraged by the example set by Henri IV and Louis XIV; he was familiar with the great town-planning schemes of the eighteenth century; he wished to rival the eternal monuments of ancient Rome. Moreover, faced with the spectre of unemployment and therefore of revolution, he wanted to pursue the politics of grandeur in reorganising and modernising the city. This meant halls, markets, slaughterhouses, new water supplies, quays, sewers, and the street-numbering of houses. The dominant artistic style was based on the most austere period of classical antiquity: Egyptian fantasies were soon abandoned, to make way for the art of imperial Rome, from Trajan to Septimus Severus. This was the inspiration for the triumphal arches at the Place du Carrousel and the Etoile, for commemorative columns like the one in 97, 98
Place Vendôme, for temples like the Madeleine or the Bourse, and for the huge palaces the 72, 96
Emperor dreamed of building on the banks of the Seine, at Chaillot and at the Champ-de-Mars, for the King of Rome, the University and the Archives. On the other hand, it was the sober urban architecture of Northern Italy which inspired Fontaine's beautiful designs for the arcaded houses on the Rue de Rivoli, with their long covered walkway reminiscent of the arcades of the Palais Royal. Fontaine's arcades lined the new east-west road which had become a necessity once the Place de la Concorde was finished. Besides, the Emperor believed that new streets such as this were indispensable if the monuments to his own glory and to the Ancien Régime were to be displayed to their best advantage: "If Paris is to be made more beautiful, we must tear down more than we build [...] We must create great spaces in this conglomeration of blackened stone, old rubble [...] and human flesh", he is said to have declared in a statement which heralds the work later to be carried out by his nephew Napoléon III.

The changes that took place in Paris during the Restoration and at the beginning of the July Monarchy were due to private enterprise, as had also been the case under Louis XIII, in the wake of Henri IV's personal town-planning policies. Private initiative was helped by a spectacular increase in the population which reached the million mark during that period. Members of the financial world—bankers and stockbrokers—were more responsible for mapping out new development areas than they ever had been under the First Empire. Following the lines of development that Paris had taken under Louis XIV, these new areas stretched out towards the West along the right bank: François Ier, Beaujon, the Madeleine, Europe, Saint-Georges and eventually as far as the Monceau plain. It was classicism's last fling before the pompous eclecticism of the Second Empire. One can still distinguish strains of creativity in the best work carried out between 1816 and 1835; it has a certain charm and originality, and a geniune Attic quality which transcends the stark severity of the Empire style. Instead it draws on the benign charms of Roman and hellenistic architecture and occasionally even borrows from the best traditions of the French Renaissance.

The carvings on the Gaillon fountain, Petiot's statues on the Pont du Carrousel, and some private houses in Saint-Georges (the "New Athens") all bear witness to a style totally free of pastiche; original works of religious architecture include the Chapelle Expiatoire, and the churches of Saint-Vincent-de-Paul and Notre-Dame-de-Lorette—in them the spirit of Ingres' paintings has been translated into architecture.

Continuing the painterly comparison, we find shades of Delacroix in the revived interest in the Gothic style, with the restoration of Notre-Dame and the Sainte-Chapelle being undertaken as a work of national interest; shortly afterwards came the building of Sainte-Clothilde, the first in a long series of architectural pastiches. Louis-Philippe's desire to celebrate "all the glories of France" may be seen in the same light, as can the completion of the Arc de Triomphe at the Etoile with its bas-reliefs of heroic scenes, the tomb of Napoléon, the Molière fountain and Place de la Concorde. But it was only in the last years of his reign that the citizen-king became really interested in town-planning to the point of taking up Napoléon I's development programme. It was too late to build Les Halles: the modest street linking Les Halles to the Marais and named after "papa Rambuteau", prefect of the Seine, had barely been completed when, in February 1848, the régime fell.

Napoléon III, the last sovereign of France, wanted to be a town-planner. His reasons were the same as those of Henri IV; his primary objective was the immediate creation of building sites to placate the restless workers. The improvement of Paris was a field specially reserved for the prince-president, later to become Emperor. He assembled a team of energetic men—Haussmann, Belgrand, Alphand—who were responsible for buildings, waterworks and green spaces respectively. "Paris is the heart of France. We must make every effort to beautify this great city. We must build new streets and make the dark, airless, crowded areas healthier places to live—we must allow health-giving light to shine everywhere within our walls", declared the prince in December 1850. Then work started. A new network of roads was built, cutting through the city center and running from north to south (Boulevard de Sébastopol, Boulevard du Palais and Boulevard Saint-Michel) and from east to west (the extension of the Rue de Rivoli as far as Rue Saint-Antoine, and plans for Boulevard Saint-Germain). These roads were wide to cope with the expected traffic, and had connecting roads linking their main points—in particular the Rue de Turbigo which ran to Place du Château-d'eau (now renamed Place de la République) where barracks were later built to help maintain order. Inevitably, much had to be demolished to realize these plans: the Cité was ruthlessly flattened. The straight line became the order of the day. "A street a league long!" Victor Hugo once exclaimed. "Just think how wonderful that would be!... What a prospect! Let us just hope that such a ridiculous plan never comes to pass".

The buildings being constructed all over Paris showed great diversity. Metal's potential had only recently been recognized and was used on a grand scale in the Bibliothèque Nationale
100 and Bibliothèque Sainte-Geneviève, in railway stations (Gare du Nord) and was soon to be used in churches (Saint-Augustin). Although visible from the outside, the metal was always hidden behind a stone facade so as not to marr Haussmann's noble perspectives. But now it suddenly burst into sight much to the astonishment of the Parisians and even of the architect himself who had employed this new technique only on the insistence of Napoléon III: the building in question was Les Halles, Victor Baltard's central market with its famous iron and cast-iron "umbrellas" which were much maligned by successive generations and recognised as having outstanding functional and aesthetic qualities only when the time came to demolish them. Apart from these famous examples, Haussmann's buildings were in an eclectic style that borrowed elements from every period but ended up looking

bland and derivative. Gothic continued to be the traditional style for religious architecture; but the tall, opulent buildings that housed middle-class families on the new boulevards or in the Monceau area were a mixture of French Renaissance, Louis XIV, Louis XV, or Louis XVI. Both Philibert de l'Orme and François Mansart were guilty of this kind of hotchpotch of styles—as in the final section of the Louvre, a gigantic task which was completed only shortly before the fire started by the Commune. The subsequent disappearance of the Tuileries Palace now makes the building look absurdly like two huge arms trying to embrace empty space; but in spite of its heavy detail there is still something admirable about the competence and scale of the project; it gives the little triumphal arch an air of importance that its builders had never suspected.

There was a smooth transition in style from Second Empire to Third Republic. The appear-
ance of Parisian streets gives no hint of a change in 1870: the same pompous style of build-
ings lines the boulevards and avenues that brought the Haussmann plan to its completion
after it had been interrupted by Sedan. It was even left to the Republic to finish off what was
to have been the theater for the Imperial Court's musical extravaganzas—the Opéra.
Designed by Charles Garnier, the Opéra was a genuine masterpiece and marked the revival of 102
polychrome architecture such as had not been seen since the Place des Vosges. But from then
on, styles were no longer to bear the names of sovereigns or régimes. Instead, their impetus
came from the Great Exhibitions—those commercial events which the industrialised west-
ern world organised with ever-increasing enthusiasm. The exhibitions held during the
Second Empire had already created an international stir in the fields of architecture and the
decorative arts. To the one held in 1878 we owe the pseudo-moorish palace of the first Tro-
cadero (destroyed in 1937), which added a new ingredient to the eclecticism that was still the
order of the day. The exhibition of 1889 gave us a monument remarkable in a different
way—an engineer's act of defiance towards architects, a challenge in metalwork soaring
into the Parisian sky—the Eiffel Tower. As for the 1900 exhibition, it was to herald an "art 104
nouveau".

The last art movement to illustrate Paris's creative role in the history of architecture was "art nouveau". Of course there were many other influential centres, such as Nancy, Vienna and Brussels, but the widespread fame of the 1900 Universal Exhibition, at which the new century seemed to be paying homage to the French capital, and the interest shown by the
107 public authorities in the work of Hector Guimard (his Métro entrances are still evidence of this) carried on the old tradition of great Parisian styles.

In fact, art nouveau soon tailed off into absurd aberrations. The state authorities and, "a fortiori", the city authorities were not powerful enough to conceive and carry out any substantial town-planning operations other than those planned by Haussmann or left unfinished by him. The increase in population, due mainly to mass immigration from the provinces, the anarchic expansion of private construction, the enormous suburban sprawl, and the ageing accomodation in the densely populated central and eastern areas of the city all contributed to the disfigurement of Paris and its environs.

That was the position at the outbreak of the First World War, which put a stop to all building for five years. When peace came, France was unable to reestablish her influence in the field of architecture. The predominating influence was increasingly an international one, with its roots in America with Frank Lloyd Wright and Mies van der Rohe, and in Germany with Walter Gropius and the Bauhaus group. These great creative artists, whose work is perfectly in tune with the modern painting and sculpture of the 1920s (Van Dœsburg, Mondrian, the De Stijl Dutch movement), won many important commissions to build factories, social centers, houses, blocks of flats, and exhibition halls; Paris, by contrast, could boast only one or

109 two isolated examples of pioneer work, such as Mallet-Stevens' cubism and early buildings by Le Corbusier.

Official commissions were, however, going to a Frenchman who was becoming extremely famous in another sphere of architecture—Auguste Perret. Since the middle of the nineteenth century (the first patents came at intervals between 1855 and 1868) reinforced concrete had offered new possibilities to construction engineers. It was found to be a convenient structural material, particularly for public buildings. Perret was quick to recognise its full potential. With Anatole de Baudot, he was one of the first to see it as a dignified material which demanded an aesthetic of its own, suited to the new forms it could create. However, although he rigorously applied this principle to his first designs (the garage in Rue de Ponthieu) the new aesthetic soon became associated in his mind with the durability of classical construction: Perret liked to think of himself as carrying on the tradition of François Mansart and Gabriel. Whether he covered his concrete surfaces with facings, or left them quite bare, he continued to design in facades—facades which still paid homage to the outlines of stone architecture with columns, cornices and bays. With the exception of his "building" in the Rue Raynouard, his work does have the advantage of blending in well with the old Parisian architecture and of following harmoniously on from the capital's four centuries of classical architecture. But the severe perfection of his designs is somewhat lacking in tension and vertical thrust, and it no longer moves us. This is particularly true of his later works. There are a few exceptions, however: the beautiful church at le Raincy really does exploit all the possibilities of concrete and glass and soars up into the sky; and the Champs-Elysées theater is a fine example of a true marriage of the arts with its perfectly integrated decor. Here, Perret has come very close to the eternal spirit of classicism, and at the same time has provided a particular social group with appropriate surroundings for their leisure pursuits. The Republic still had a taste for palaces and colonnades, fountains and terraces, and especially for allegorical statuary—each year a new crop of famous men appeared in public squares and at crossroads. The exhibitions held in the 1930s helped to satisfy the appetite for palaces. The first of them was the colonial Porte Dorée exhibition of 1931, which contributed the Colonial Museum by Laprade and Jaussely. Some 1,200 meters of "Normandy" style bas-reliefs are housed under its babylonian peristyle.

For the Universal Exhibition of 1937 Perret designed the Museum of Public Works whose rotunda is embellished with a colonnade, a reinforced concrete "tholos". The Chaillot hill was also the site for two prestigious cultural centres: the Museums of Modern Art and the Palace of Chaillot. The most one can say for the Museums of Modern Art is that they have aged badly; the Palace of Chaillot is a wonderful symbol of the stiffness and pomposity of 111
pre-war official art. In contrast to the design of these impractical museums, however, the period was turning to functionalist architecture which was used to good effect in certain school complexes, for example, and at the Salle Pleyel. Elsewhere, pastiche and eclecticism were still the order of the day—as in the Institute of Art and Archeology's moorish palace, or the Romano-byzantine basilica of Saint-Pierre-de-Chaillot.

The Second World War brought a new hiatus, this time even longer than the 1914-18 one had been. The housing crisis coincided with a rent-freeze; both helped to accelerate the process of deterioration among old buildings, and encouraged the undisciplined construction of cheap blocks of flats built for economy and totally devoid of elegance. Social facilities were inadequate, and the motorcar was gradually beginning to encroach on public areas. So the first years of this period of "reconstruction" have barely any works of interest to offer. For a long time Paris and the Parisians shied away from high quality modern architecture, which at the time was symbolised by the name Le Corbusier.

Modern architecture arrived on the banks of the Seine through the intervention of an international organisation: the Unesco Palace, a collective work, was built in 1958. But it soon became clear that any large administration which tried to settle within Paris's twenty arrondissements was likely to have a short life there. Concessions to historic surroundings, height restrictions—even when contravened—the cost of land in Paris, and the proliferation of services and car-parks were all serious threats to large new complexes. Unesco feels stifled in its palace and wants to leave; the Radio and Television center, wedged between a residential area and the Seine, will one day suffer the same fate. The best large-scale projects are therefore to be found on the periphery of the city, where new sites proportionate to their size can be created.

The high price of land may cause the death of the city. It has become more and more costly and financially risky to preserve ancient buildings, and people of limited means are moving away in droves as office blocks and luxury appartments go up in the old districts. The process seems irreversible. Finally, the idea of clearing large areas of ground for the benefit of the community has proved to be a childish illusion; now that Les Halles have gone, the way would have been open for a Central Park with real greenery stretching from Saint-Eustache to the Fountain of the Innocents, but will this remain a utopian dream?

The reproductions which follow are arranged in chronological order. This principle is applied to the architectural works as a whole whilst we also reproduce various elements of each dating from different periods.

The reproductions which follow are arranged in chronological order. This principle is applied to the architectural works as a whole whilst we also reproduce various elements of each dating from different periods.

1. The Pilier des Nautes (The Boatmen's Pillar).

Five sculptured, quadrangular blocks of the pillar still remain. They were discovered in 1711, incorporated into the wall foundations under the choir of Notre-Dame. Sculpted in bas-relief on these pieces are the deities of the Roman Pantheon, with either their Celtic or Roman names (Jupiter—to whom the monument was dedicated, no doubt appeared at the top of the pillar—Vulcan, Castor and Pollux, Mars, Mercury, Venus, Fortune and four other goddesses). There are also Gallic deities (Esus, Tarvos Trigaranus, [C]ernunnos, a god with stag's antlers, the initial letter of whose name is uncertain, and Smert[rios], provider of plenty who was likened to Hercules).
There are numerous examples of this type of votive column, a type of monument peculiar to Gaul. The origin and date (between 14 and 37 AD) of the Pilier des Nautes are clearly given in the inscription on one of the five aforementioned blocks: TIB(ERIO). CAESARE. AVG(VSTO) . IOVI . OPTVMO[.]MAXSVMO . [S(ACRVM).]NAVTAE . PARISIACI (.) PVBLICE . POSIERVN[T.] "In the reign of Tiberius Caesar Augustus, to the very good and great Jupiter, the boatmen of Paris consecrate this dedication at their own expense."
On the four sides of the block bearing this inscription, there are six figures with helmets carrying lances and shields. Three of them have beards and three do not, portraying no doubt the oldest and youngest of those who dedicated the column; there are also three draped figures. These scenes probably depict the consecration of the monument by the Paris boatmen in the reign of the Emperor Tiberius. Associating their native gods to the gods of Rome, the boatmen built the pillar in honour of Jupiter, the most powerful god of all. Esus and Tarvos Trigaranus are portrayed on the same stone frieze as Jupiter and Vulcan. There are thus two Gallic gods and two Roman gods at the top of the monument. On each panel there is a tree. In the panel showing Tarvos Trigaranus, the tree appears in the centre, in front of the Bull on whose back and forehead the Three Cranes are perched amidst the boughs. The scene illustrates the Gallic myth of the woodcutter god felling the tree whose leaves hide the bull and the three birds.

2. The Thermes du Nord or Thermae of Cluny.

The Thermes du Nord (Palais des Thermes or Thermes de Cluny) were the most important public baths in Lutetia. The monumental ruins of this enormous building, 100 meters by 65 meters, still stand, as does a vast vaulted hall. The mighty groined vault of the "frigidarium" also remains, supported by enormous stone brackets, shaped like the prows of great ships and decorated with arms. This symbolic decoration bears witness to the part played by the Nautes du Parisis (the Boatmen of Paris) in the building of these baths, a place where they perhaps met regularly. The Nautes du Parisis, an important guild of the Seine boatmen, has also left us a famous inscription. Judging by the extreme care with which the baths were built and the sturdiness of the walls, the baths belong to a period of prosperity. They most probably date from the last quarter of the second century or the first quarter of the third century.

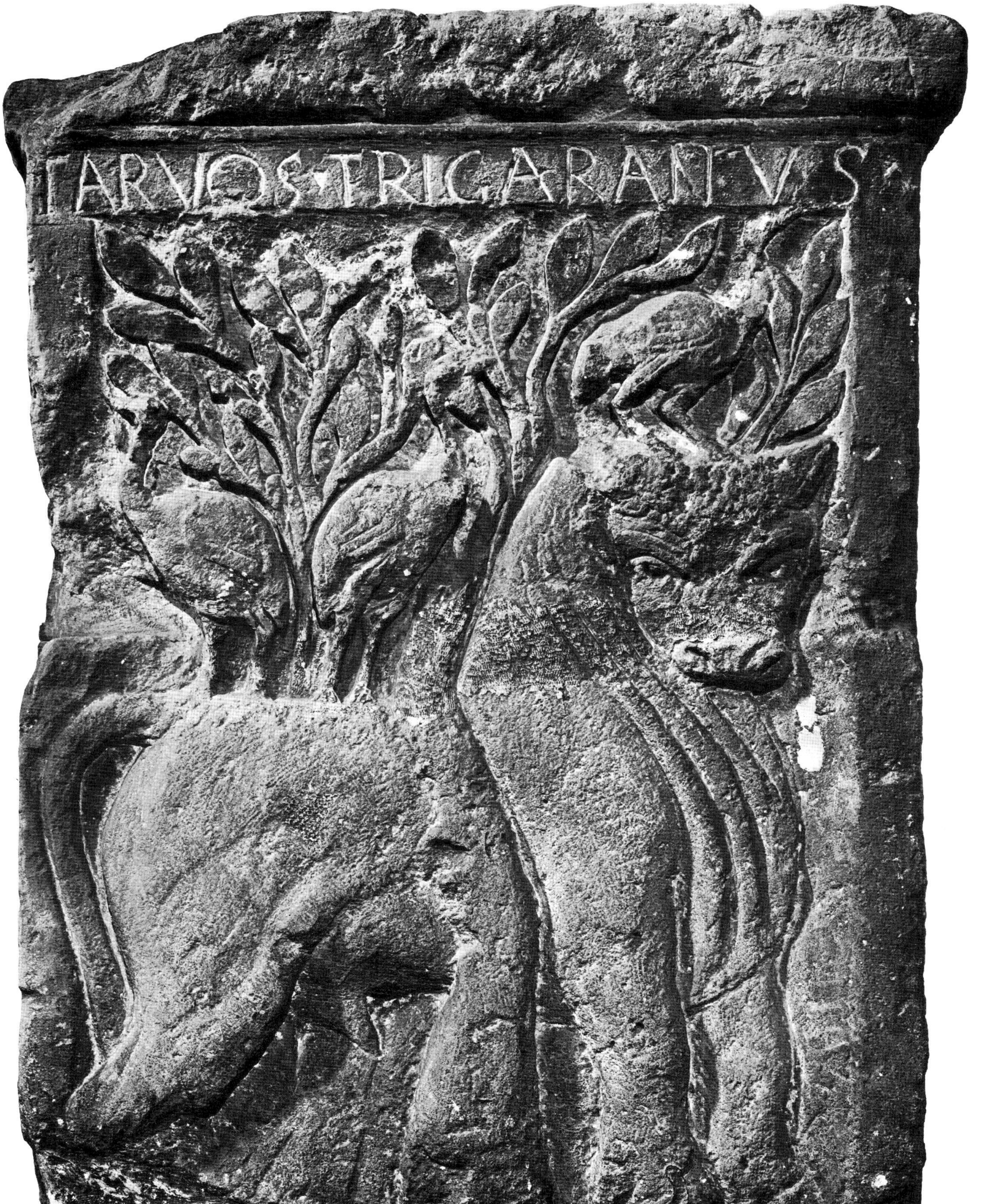

1. The Boatmen's Pillar: Tarvos Trigaranus, the Bull with three Cranes. Cluny Museum.

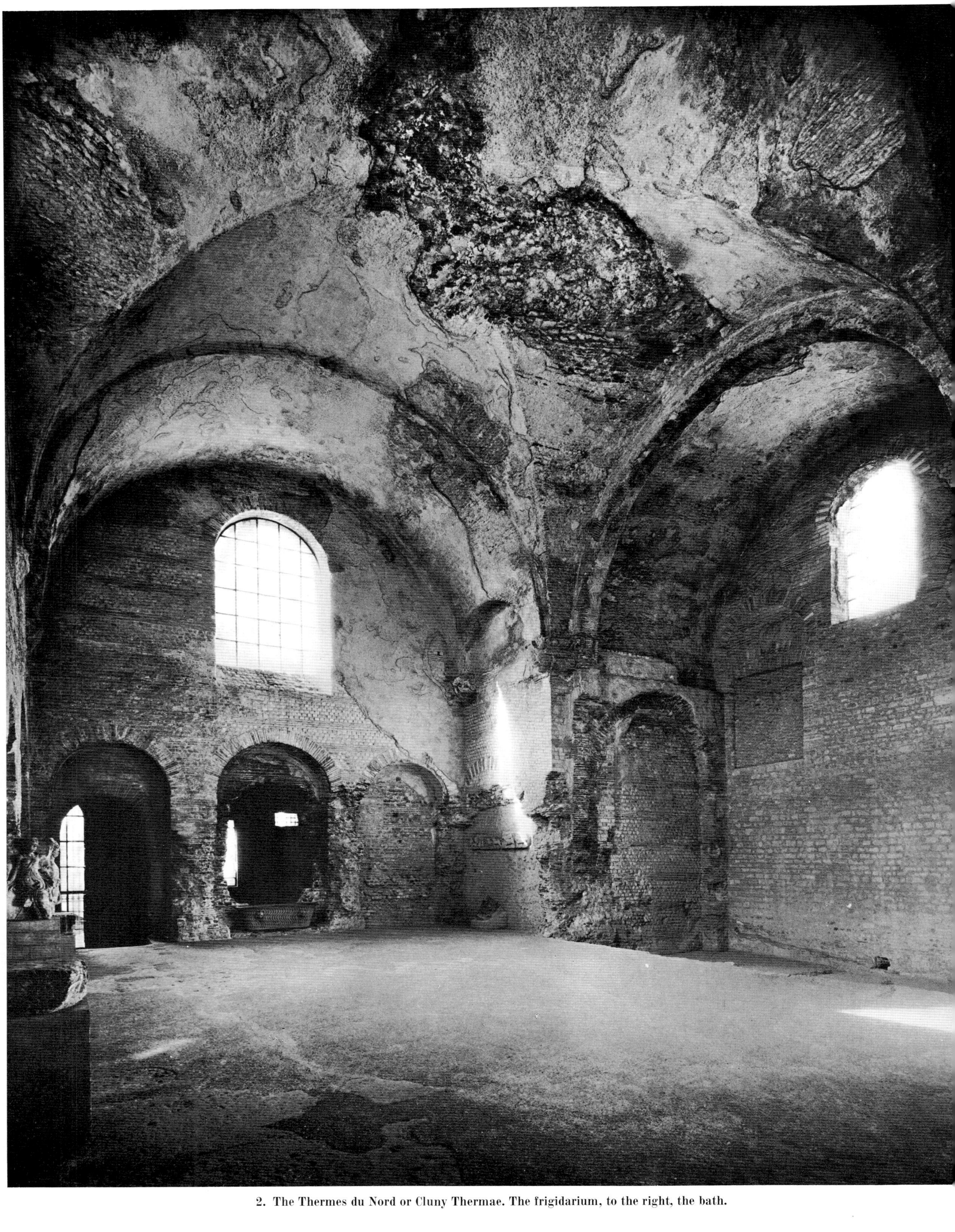

2. The Thermes du Nord or Cluny Thermae. The frigidarium, to the right, the bath.

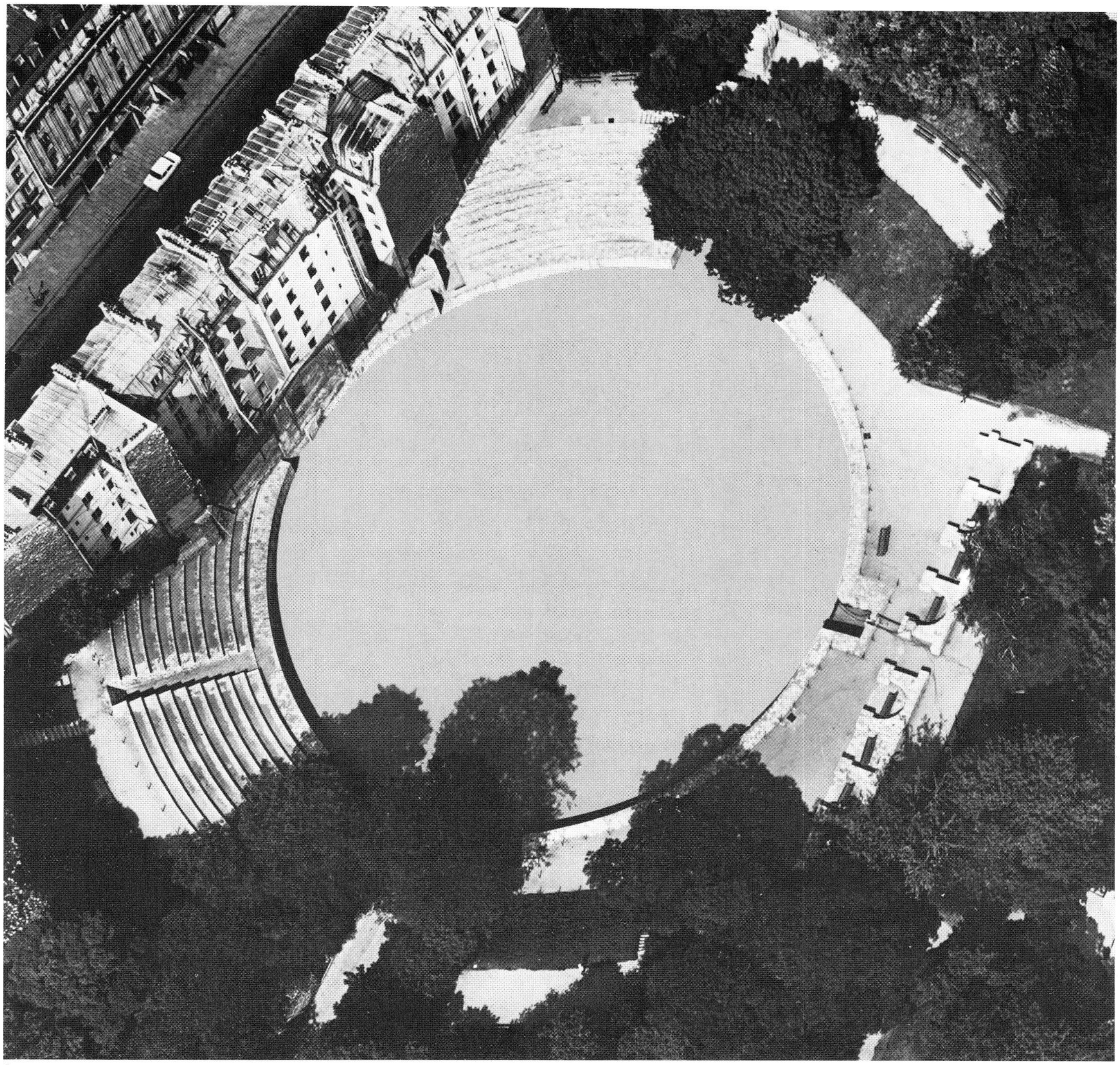

3

3. The Arènes de Lutèce (The Amphitheater of Lutetia).

The "Arènes de Lutèce" are in fact an amphiteater with a stage, a place of entertainment with a double purpose: it was used both for theatrical performances and for circuses (contests involving men or animals, hunts, etc). The arena was built at the end of the first century AD outside the city, to the east. The tiers, some thirty-five of them (only the first ten have been restored) extended round half of the monument only, towards the west. The top-most flights rested on a structure, its facade towards the exterior, with a large opening in the east for the stage. This was very long (41 meters) and had nine recesses, alternately rectangular or semi-circular in shape, which were painted and no doubt held statues. The whole was richly decorated. The arena was in the center, on a lower level—an irregular oval of vast dimensions (52.50 × 46.8 m). There were two wide entrances on the major axis, built on an inclined plane. This vast building could hold more than fifteen thousand spectators.

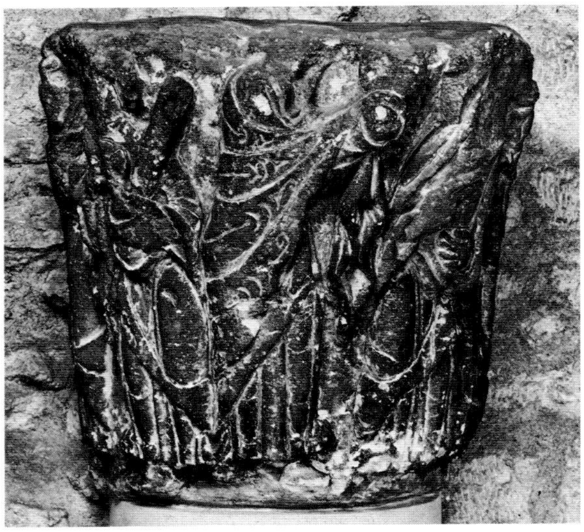

4

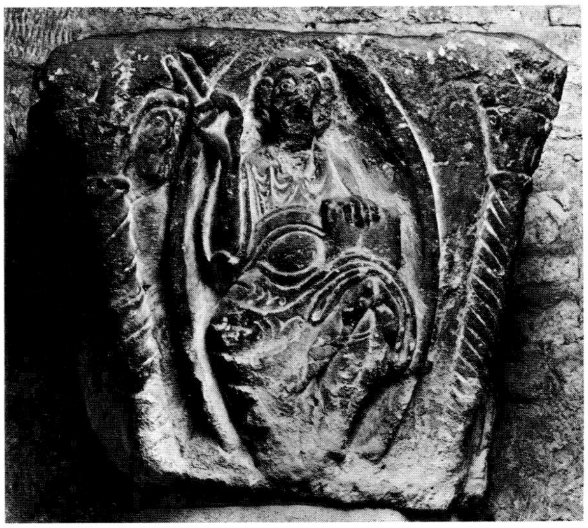

5

4 to 9. The Church of Saint-Germain-des-Prés and the Abbots' Palace.

The basilica of Saint-Vincent-Sainte-Croix, founded in the seventh century by Childebert, rapidly became, under the name of Saint-Germain-des-Prés, one of the most important abbeys in Paris. The abbey remained powerful right through its history and welcomed the leading intellectuals of every period. One of the side-effects of the reform of Saint-Maur, adopted in 1631, was to make it into the center of learning which subsequently laid the foundations of French national history. Of the main buildings only the abbots' palace and the church have survived. The latter is dominated by the impressive, massive stone tower built by Abbot Morard (990-1014). Supported at the western corners by buttresses, the tower has two spiral staircases on the east side. A few sparse openings without splays or decoration enliven these astonishing bare surfaces, which bear witness to the progress made by the masons of the Ile-de-France in the early years of the elventh century.

The nave of Saint-Germain-des-Prés was not built at the same time as the bell-tower. The nave is in fact on a sloping axial line and the different storeys of the bell-tower do not correspond to those of the nave. The remarkable progress that was made between the building of the two different parts means that the nave cannot be earlier than the middle of the eleventh century.

The architect's concern to integrate the bay of the aisle with that of the nave is reflected in the height of the great arcades. But we must wait for the architects of the Gothic period for the success to be complete. A new liking for decoration is also evident: the great arcades are relieved by two ovolos and on the exterior there are string-courses between the windows.

The capitals at Saint-Germain-des-Prés can be considered the incunables of Romanesque sculpture. Although quite a few of them, restored in the nineteenth century, defy analysis, the twelve in the Cluny Museum can be examined in detail. Although they were all sculpted in the same period, most probably under the direction of the same mastercraftsman, there are such differences between them that one can distinguish the work of at least three sculptors, all of different temperament. One of them, the sculptor of the "Christ en gloire" (Christ in Glory) has created a powerful work which expresses the new feeling for relief.

4 and 5. Saint-Germain-des-Prés. Two capitals now in the Cluny Museum.

6. Saint-Germain-des-Prés. The bell-tower and the south side of the church.

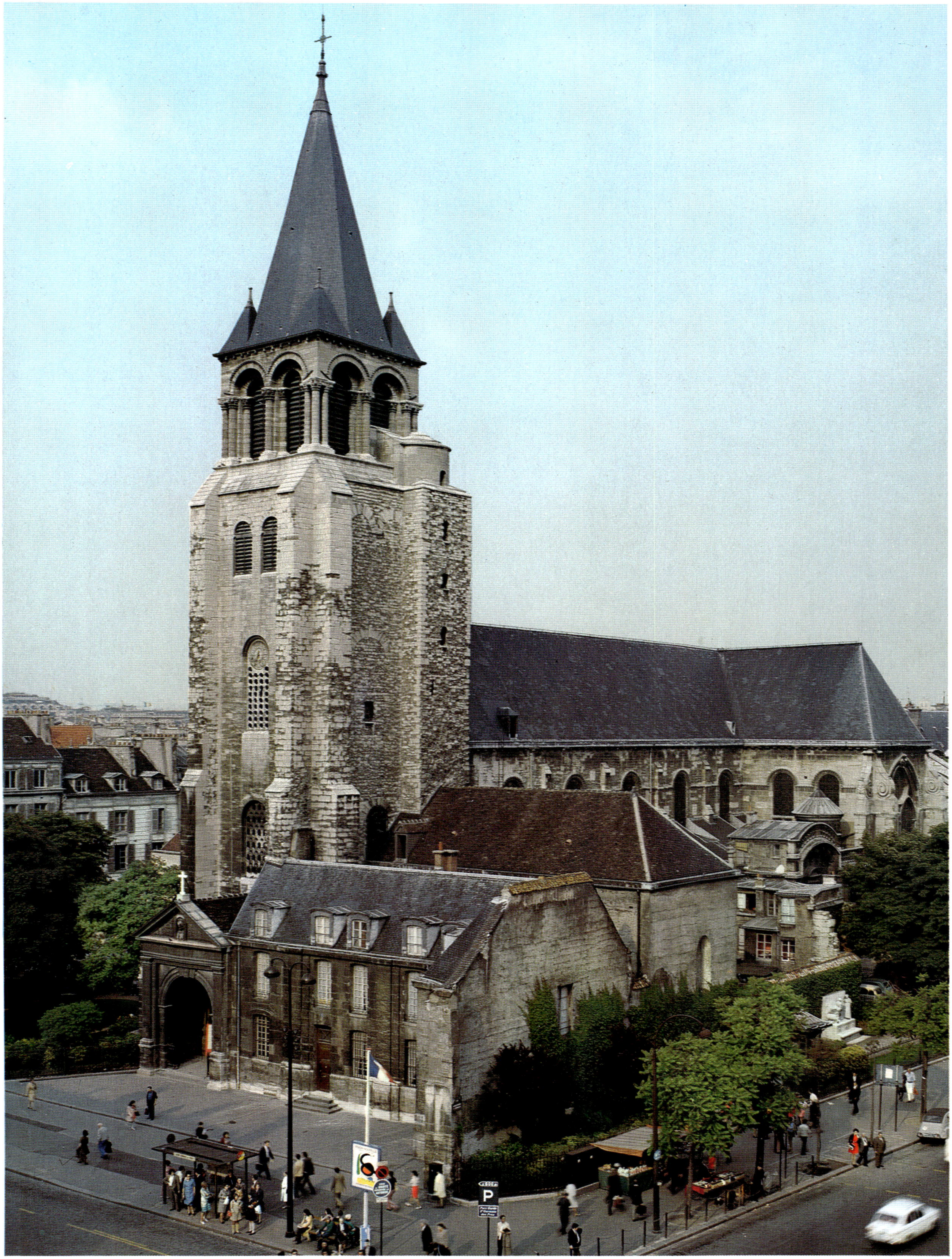

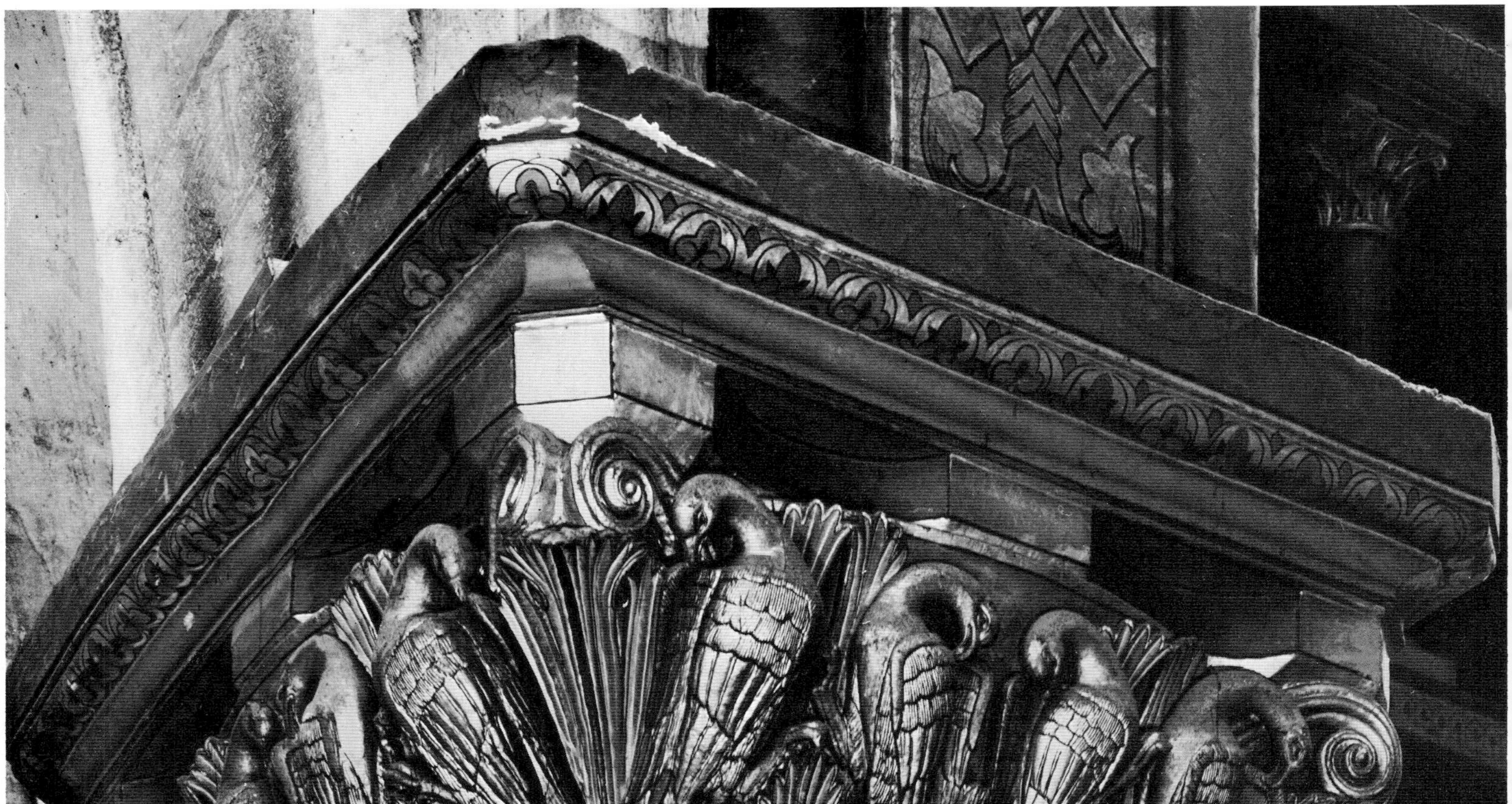

7. Saint-Germain-des-Prés. Capital.

8. The statue of Childebert, from the refectory of Saint-Germain-des-Prés. Louvre Museum.

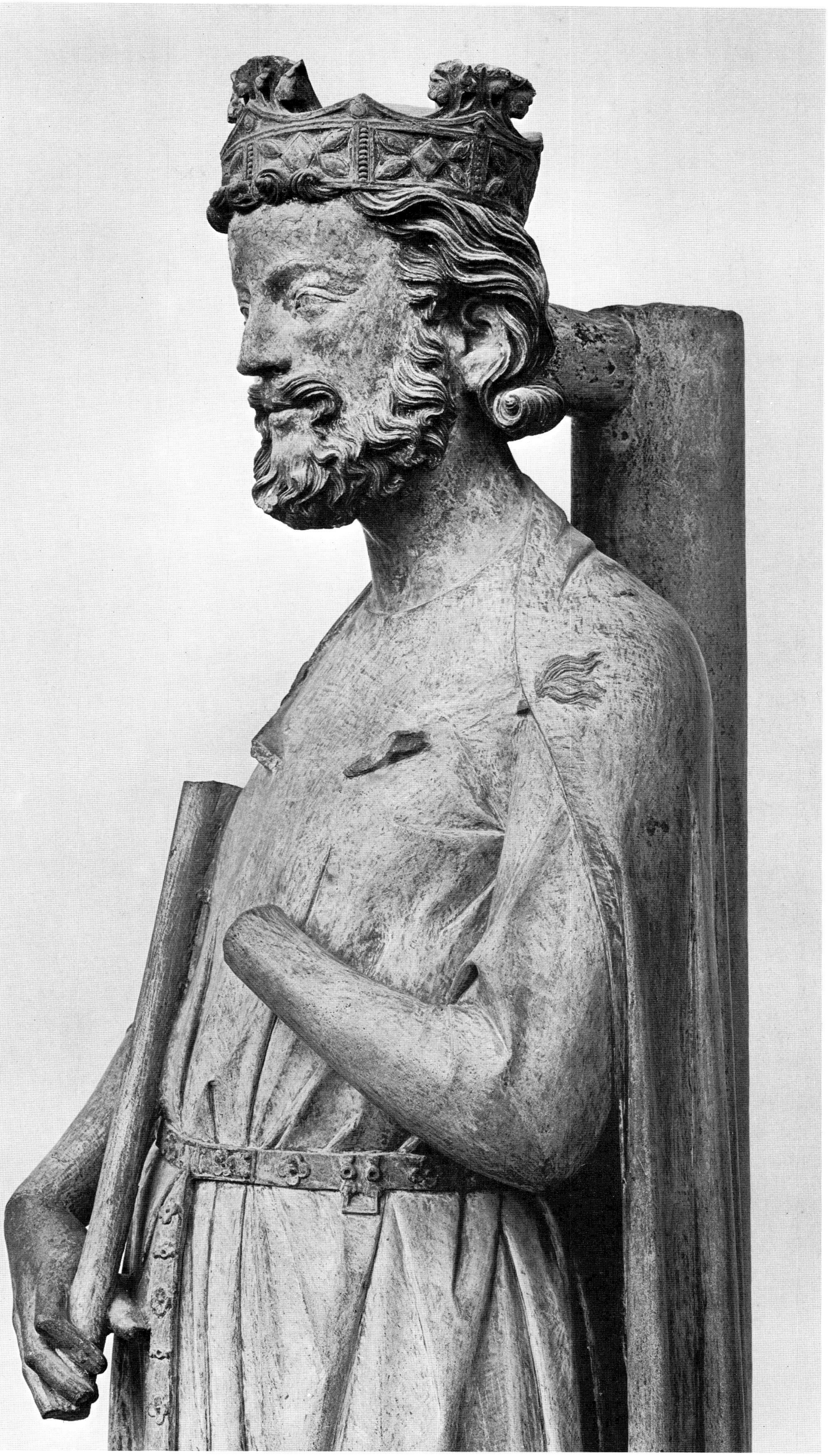

It is generally thought that the choir of Saint-Germain-des-Prés was finished in time for its consecration by Pope Alexander III on 21 April 1163, though it is not known when work on the choir first started. In plan and elevation, it is curiously similar to that of Noyon cathedral: their plans could be superposed with the three bays on the right, the hemicycle with four columns, the simple aisles, the five radiating chapels and the four rectangular chapels. In the elevation, the similarity can only be seen in the first story: at Noyon there is an extra story of galleries but the Paris elevation only has three stories: large arcades, triforium altered in the eighteenth century and clerestory windows. Compared to those of Saint-Denis and Saint-Martin-des-Champs, the choir of Saint-Germain is more archaic-looking: in the south bays, the great arcades are still of semi-circular design and the radiating chapels are treated as separate volumes and have their own vaulting with five branches of ribs. The lesson of Saint-Denis had not been learnt. The general proportions confirm this impression: they are still very heavy with beams whose arrises only are chamfered and arches made up of an arris between two toruses, the full arch predominates as opposed to the Gothic arch, whilst the openings are not as bold as those of Saint-Denis. The sills of the high windows were lowered in the eighteenth century to the detriment of the triforium which took on the present rectangular shape. The arrangement of the exterior volumes gives the same impression: the horizontalism of the Romanesque period predominates rather than the verticalism of the Gothic period. The flying buttresses, which were added at the end of the twelfth century, have established a link (which the architects did not plan) between these two volumes, which were quite distinct originally.
Despite the numerous archaisms, due recognition must be given to the firmness with which the architect designed his plan and drew up his elevation. There are no hesitations in the design of the exterior or in the thrust of the arches. The sculpted capitals are of interest too, particularly since they have not been restored. The capitals on the columns of the choir are among the most beautiful: very finely sculpted, they are still Romanesque in style and reflect that horror of the void which drove the sculptor to decorate the whole vase. The one reproduced (ill. 7) is so close to that of Sainte-Geneviève (ill. 11) that they seem to be by the same artist. Some of the capitals in the radiating chapels, on the other hand, were sculpted by the same atelier whilst others already foreshadow the Gothic capitals.

8. The Statue of Childebert from the Refectory of Saint-Germain-des-Prés.

The refectory of Saint-Germain-des-Prés was built by Pierre de Montreuil under Abbot Simon (1239-1244). It was savagely destroyed during the Revolution and now only the great west bay remains and the statue of Childebert from the pier of the door letting onto the cloister. The statue can be dated with precision and the "Mannerist" treatment of the face recalls the "Christ montrant ses plaies" on the central portal of Notre-Dame.

9. The Abbots' Palace of Saint-Germain-des-Prés.

The final upheavals of the religious wars, the League and the siege of Paris did not favour building projects. The abbots' palace of Saint-Germain-des-Prés is one of the few buildings dating back to those cruel years. It was started in 1586 for the abbot of the day, the cardinal Charles de Bourbon, uncle of Henri IV and the man chosen as king under the name Charles X, by the members of the League. The palace, built by the mason Guillaume Marchant, and finished around 1590, was at the time still surrounded by a green precinct. It looked like a little château constructed in that harmonious blend of brick and stone which then remained fashionable under Henri IV. In front there is an entrance courtyard and at the back a garden surrounding the chevet of the church. The main part of the palace has nine sections with a high pavilion at right angles. With its great slate roof and series of pediments, the overall outline of the building is most lively. The abbots' palace was then altered between 1690 and 1699 for the Cardinal of Furstenberg; a little square, formerly the stable yard, now bears his name.

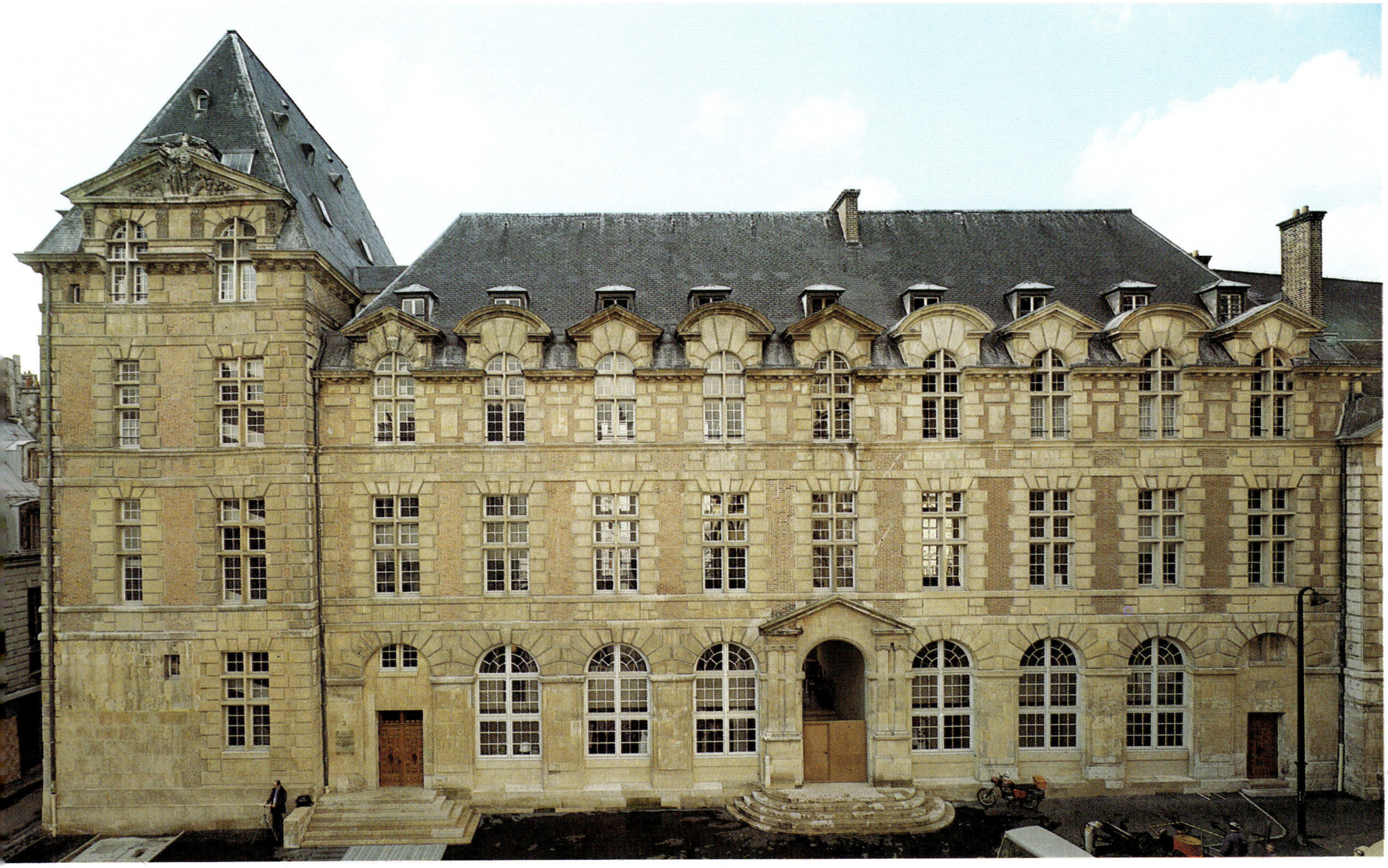

9. The Abbots' Palace of Saint-Germain-des-Prés, the façade on the street, 3 and 5, Rue de l'Abbaye, 6th Arr.

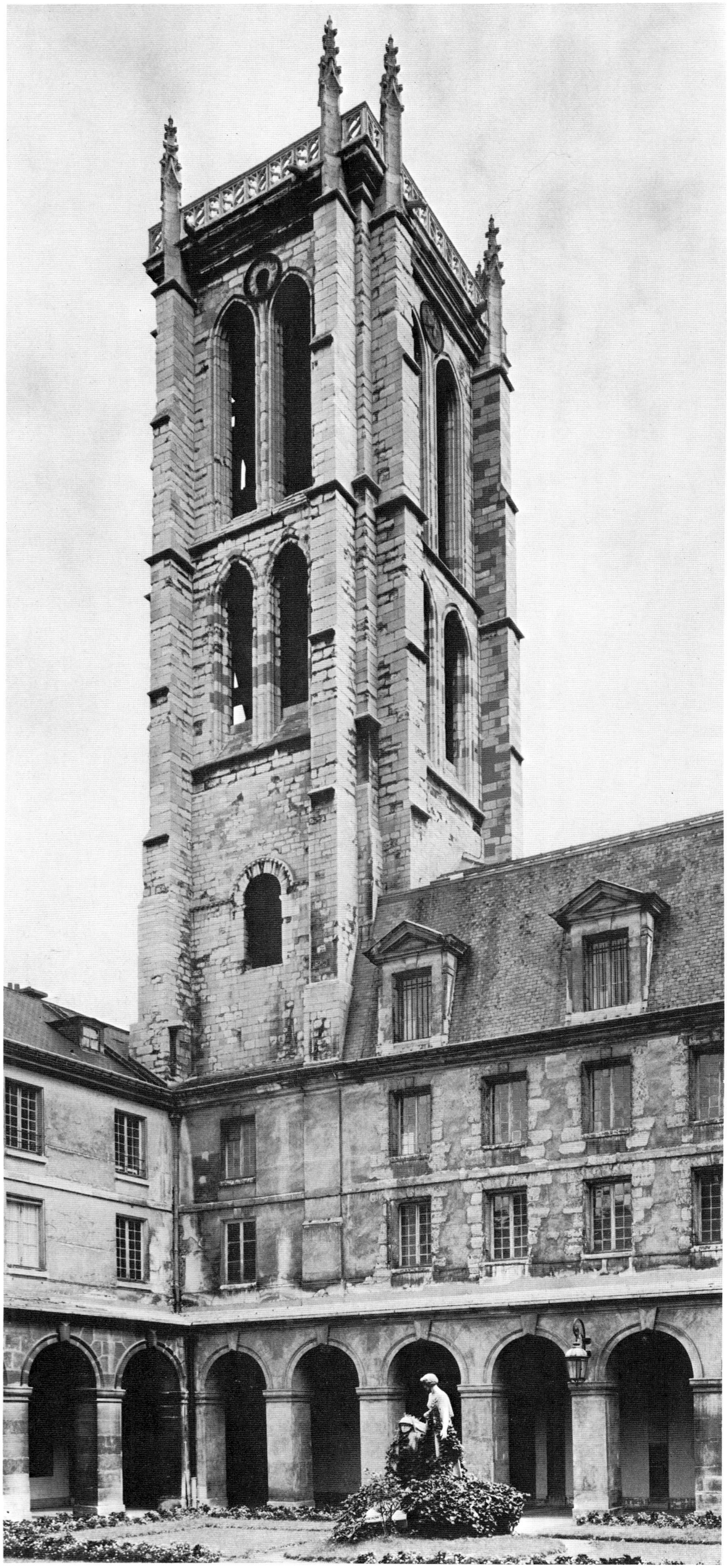

10

10 and 11. The former Abbey of Sainte-Geneviève.

It was King Clovis who, after his conversion, founded Saints-Apôtres which later took the name of Sainte-Geneviève. We know little of the original building and little more of the building which was destroyed when the Rue Clovis was built. At the time, it had a nave with nine bays opening onto the transept and a choir with astonishing chapels. The superb bell-tower, which still stands, was built as an annex on the south side, on a level with the transept. The different phases of building were probably as follows: at the end of the eleventh century the new apse and the elevated western parts of the nave were built. In the reign of Philippe I (1060-1108) the precentor Thibaud built the first story of the tower. Building then continued in the twelfth century with the great round piers of the western part of the nave. One of the capitals, now in the Cluny Museum cannot be earlier than the middle of the twelfth century. The four birds worked in relief on the vase are almost modelled in the round. The refectory on the Rue Clothilde is the only surviving monastic building of Sainte-Geneviève dating back to the Middle Ages. It is not in its original state however as a new story was put in to accommodate the chapel of the Lycée Henri-IV. As a result the present-day visitor feels almost crushed by the ribbed vaults. Also the bases of the pillars are now located in the kitchens. On the exterior, the western facade has buttresses placed at regular intervals to emphasise the vertical design of the building. It is very simple with openings surmounted by quatrefoils. The interior reveals the delicate architecture of the first third of the thirteenth century, with ribbed vaults on an oblong plan, whose thrust is taken by delicately decorated capitals. The ceiling beam rests on magnificent brackets decorated with elegant foliage. The keystones of the arches still bear sculpted heads.

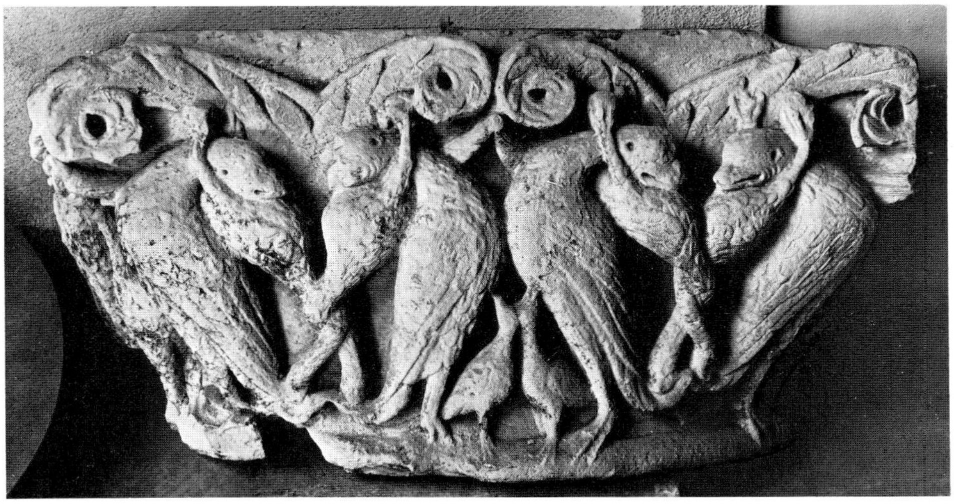

11. Sainte-Geneviève. Capitals decorated with birds. Cluny Museum.

10. Sainte-Geneviève. The church tower,
known as the "Tour Clovis", inside the Lycée Henri-IV.

12 and 13. Saint-Pierre-de-Montmartre.

Louis VII acquired the church of Montmartre to found a convent, after a conversation with Thibaud, prior of Saint-Martin-des-Champs. Work started on the choir; the last bay of the nave, the transept and the choir itself were finished when Eugène III came to celebrate its consecration in 1147. The first three bays which were not entirely ready at the time, were only finished in the second half of the century. The apse was rebuilt in the twelfth century for reasons which remain unknown. Its plan, which resembles that of Saint-Julien-le-Pauvre closely, can be found in several churches, quite a few of which belong to the same period. Despite the heavy restoration work at the beginning of this century, the church remains a good example of the tentative beginnings of Gothic architecture. Many of its features are still Romanesque; some of the capitals belong stylistically to the first half of the twelfth century. The right-hand bay of the choir, which dates from the first stage of building work, reflects the architect's hesitations. The arches and beams and the wall-ribs with their heavy outlines rest clumsily on the supporting columns. The arches of the last bay of the nave are not earlier than the fifteenth century and date from the same building phase. The bay itself has an interesting elevation with three storeys. The function of the openings over the great arcades remains unclear though some people think they may be the remains of a royal gallery. The central apse, later rebuilt, probably had a semi-dome originally. Its present vaulting shows what mastery the architects had attained. The ribs are more delicately outlined and their thrust is taken by fine little columns rising from the ground. The wide bays allow more light into the building and the wall-ribs of the windows rest on very fine little columns whose bases are supported by the abacuses of the central columns. The architectural ambition is just as noticeable on the exterior with the different molding of the windows resting on columns set into the piers. Despite the lack of height, the concept of volume emphasises the break with the world of Romanesque.

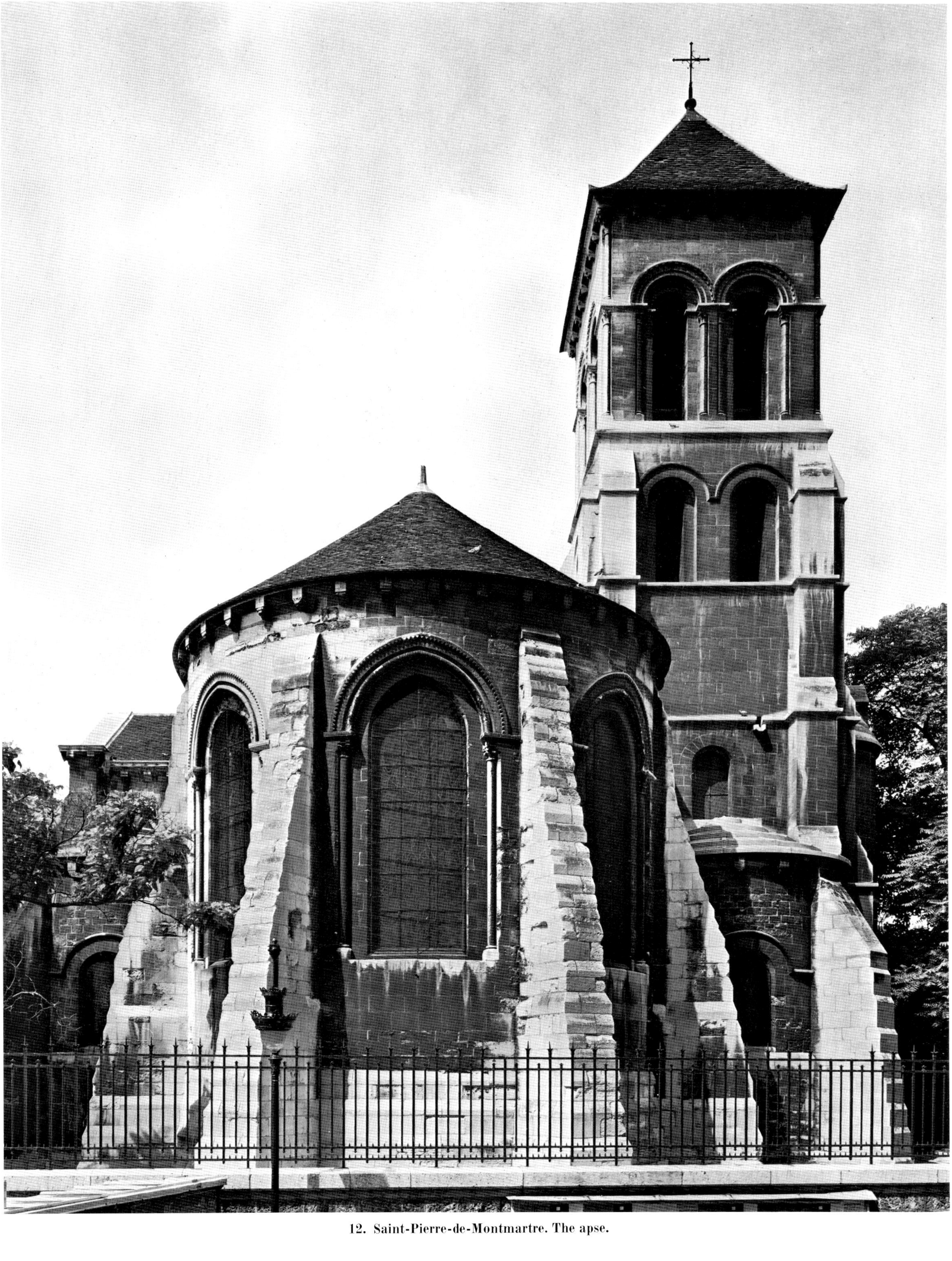

12. Saint-Pierre-de-Montmartre. The apse.

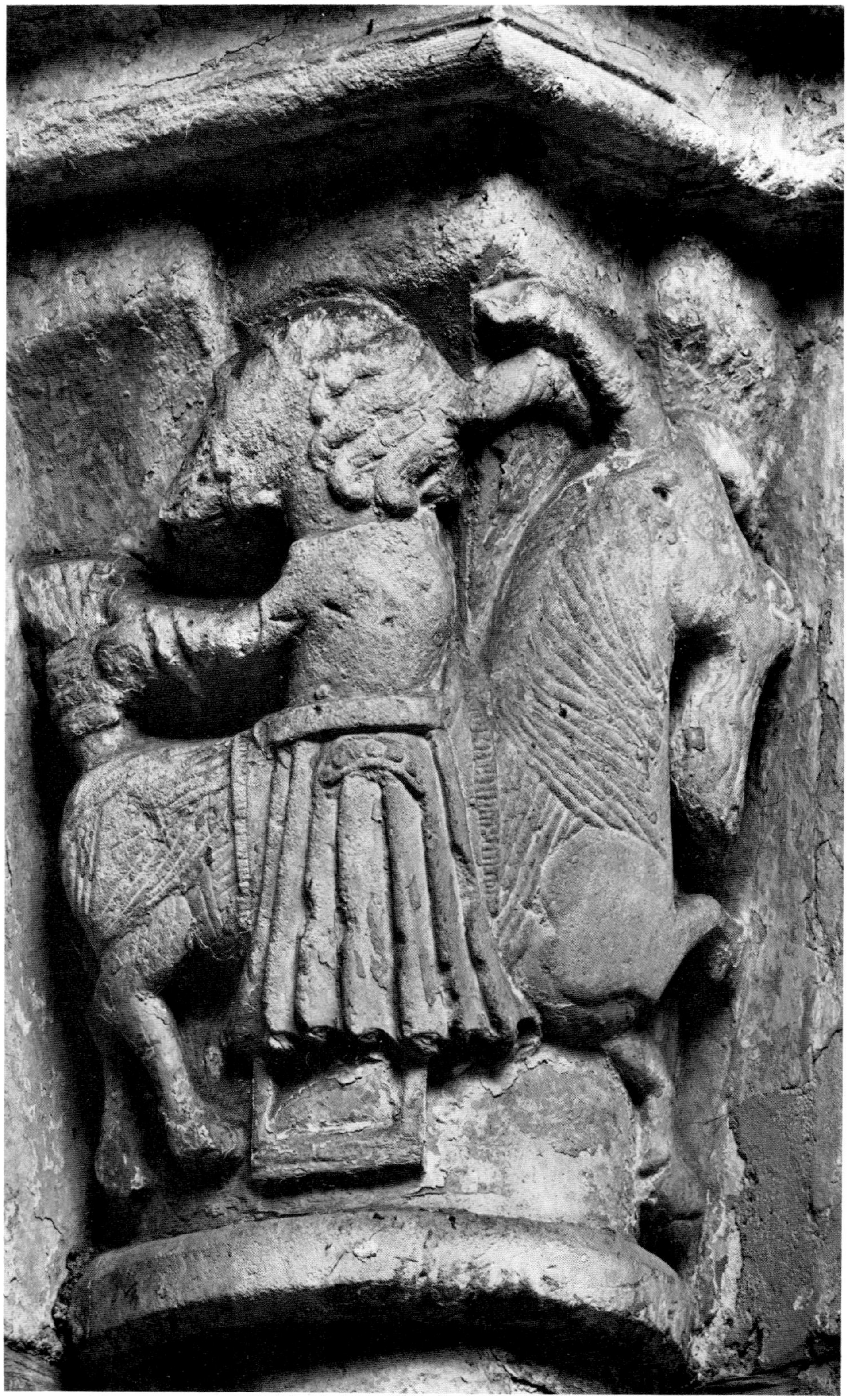

13. Saint-Pierre-de-Montmartre. A capital of the nave. Lust (?).

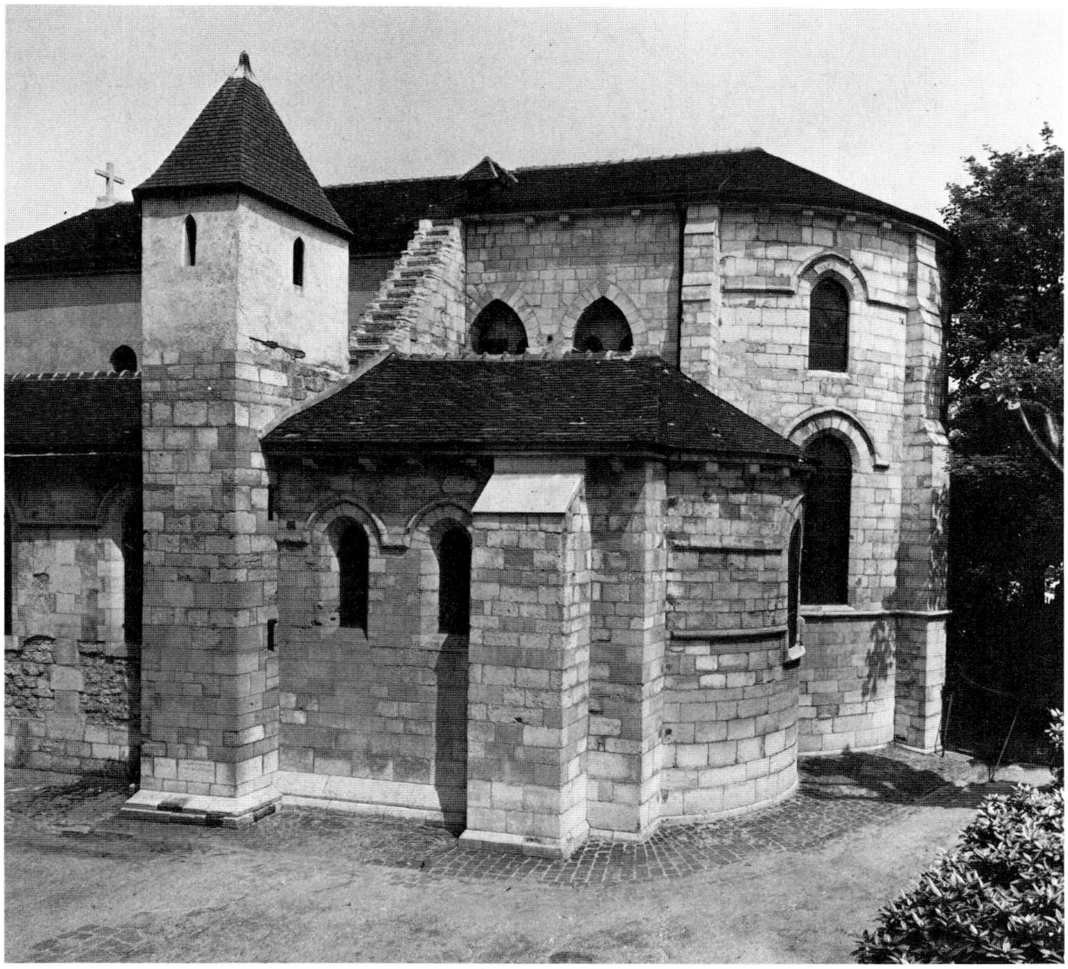

14. Saint-Julien-le-Pauvre. The apse.

14. Saint-Julien-le-Pauvre.

Although there is no documentary evidence indicating when work started on the church of Saint-Julien-le-Pauvre, its architecture suggests that it was around 1170. This little church with its countrified look in fact took nearly a century to build; the nave does not seem to have been finished before the middle of the thirteenth century. Its original appearance has been greatly altered by the destruction of the facade and the first two bays of the nave as well as by repeated restoration. Nevertheless the east side of the church has some interesting features. The church's plan is in fact very similar to that of Saint-Pierre-de-Montmartre, but the elevation resembles those of very large buildings: the bay of the choir and the bay before the absidiole have sexpartite vaulting. The architect has used alternation in the choir bay with a column as the weak pier. Here the influence of Notre-Dame can be clearly distinguished. In this bay the elevation has two storys whilst in the apse it has three, with two stories of superposed windows. This strange arrangement probably results from a change of plan during building.
Equally interesting are the many sculpted capitals, especially those on the columns of the weak pier. Sculpted in a vigorous style, their ornamental foliage moulds the low vases to perfection. On the north side there are the famous siren-birds which Huysmans described so marvellously.

15. Saint-Martin-des-Champs.

The choir of Saint-Martin-des-Champs represents a vital stage in early Gothic architecture as it is now generally thought to be the work of the prior, Hugues I (1130-1147). It has a double ambulatory opening onto very small radiating chapels and a longer trefoiled central chapel. However the lay-out is clumsy: the first bay of the choir is not regular, the central pillars of the apse are set far apart to give a view of the axial chapel, the ambulatory varies in width, whilst the plan and dimensions of each chapel differ slightly. The design of the vaulting is also irregular and has had to be adapted to the clumsily placed supports. The architect has moreover used two different kinds of vaulting: ribbed vaulting in the apse and the central chapel and groined vaulting in the ambulatory. Such clumsiness is probably due not only to the architect's experimenting but also to the fact that he may well have been restricted in his work by existing buildings. The bell-tower which flanks the choir, for instance, is of earlier date, and excavations in 1913 unearthed the remains of an apsidal chapel on the south side. Whatever their significance, the architect's hesitations reveal a new concept of architecture. Shortly before the architect of Saint-Denis set to work (1140-1144), the architect of Saint-Martin had tried to integrate the volume of his radiating chapels and get the air circulating freely through this volume. On the exterior, moreover, he managed to disguise the irregularities of the interior with great subtlety on the exterior. The two levels of the apse are superbly developed beneath the gable of the thirteenth century nave. Yet the concept of volumes in different tiers still belongs to Romanesque art. The capitals, which have not been restored, are also inspired by Romanesque sculpture; they are the work of many artists from different regions.

In the thirteenth century the priory of Saint-Martin-des-Champs underwent major alterations: a new precinct was built, of which a tower still remains (7, Rue Bailly); the nave of the church was rebuilt and a new refectory was started. In spite of nineteenth century restoration work, affecting in particular the decorations of the capitals and the brackets, the refectory is one of the great architectural successes of the period. The great rectangular hall, 42.80 meters long and 11.70 meters wide, is divided by fine columns mounted on high polygonal bases. Great bays surmounted by oculi flood the room with light, displaying the fineness of the architecture to full advantage. The reader's chair, set into the north wall and roofed with ribbed vaulting, is surrounded by a balustrade which rests on a decorated bracket. The same delicacy of decoration can be seen in the hall's main door with its bare tympanum.

15. Saint-Martin-des-Champs. The Refectory, now a library.

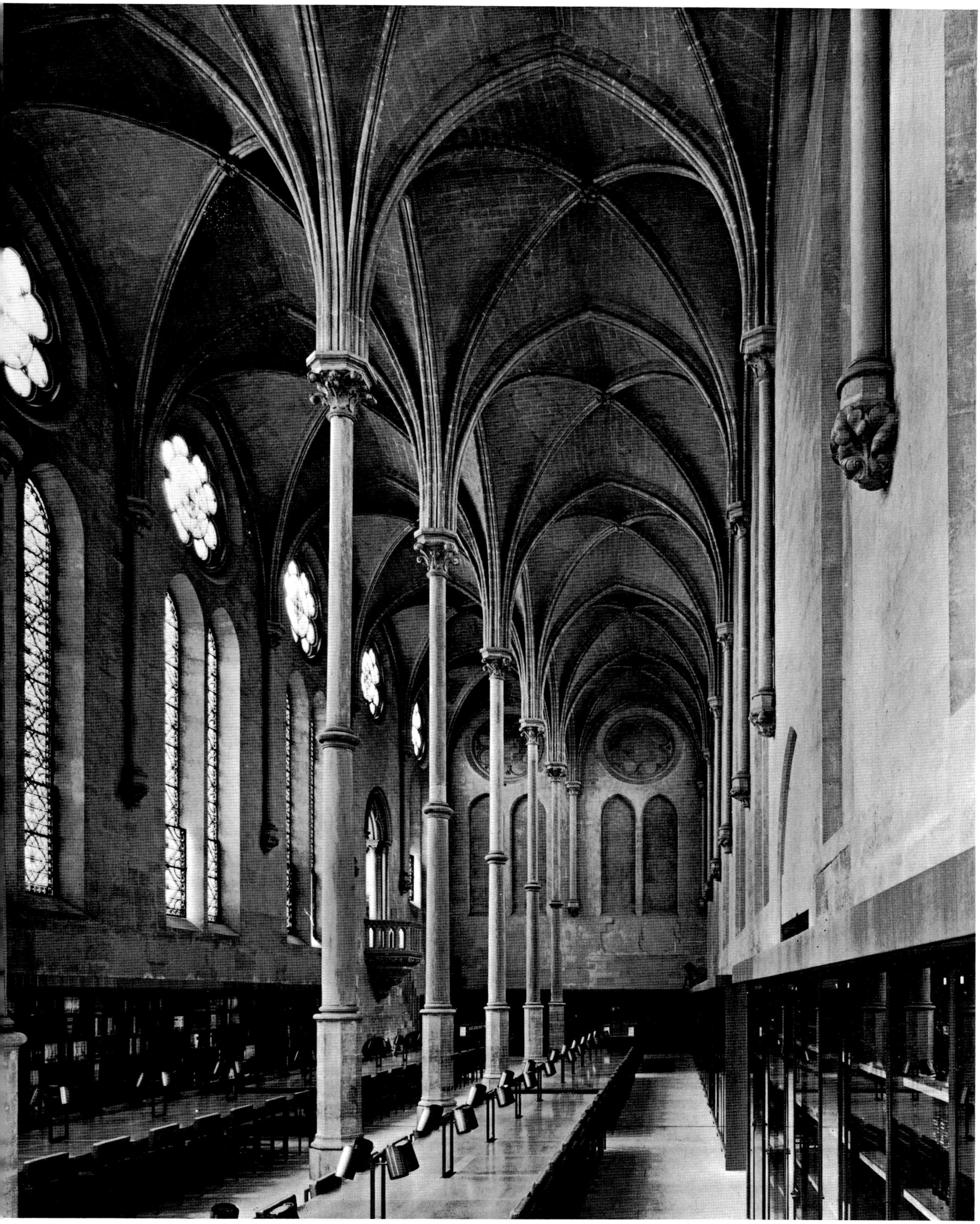

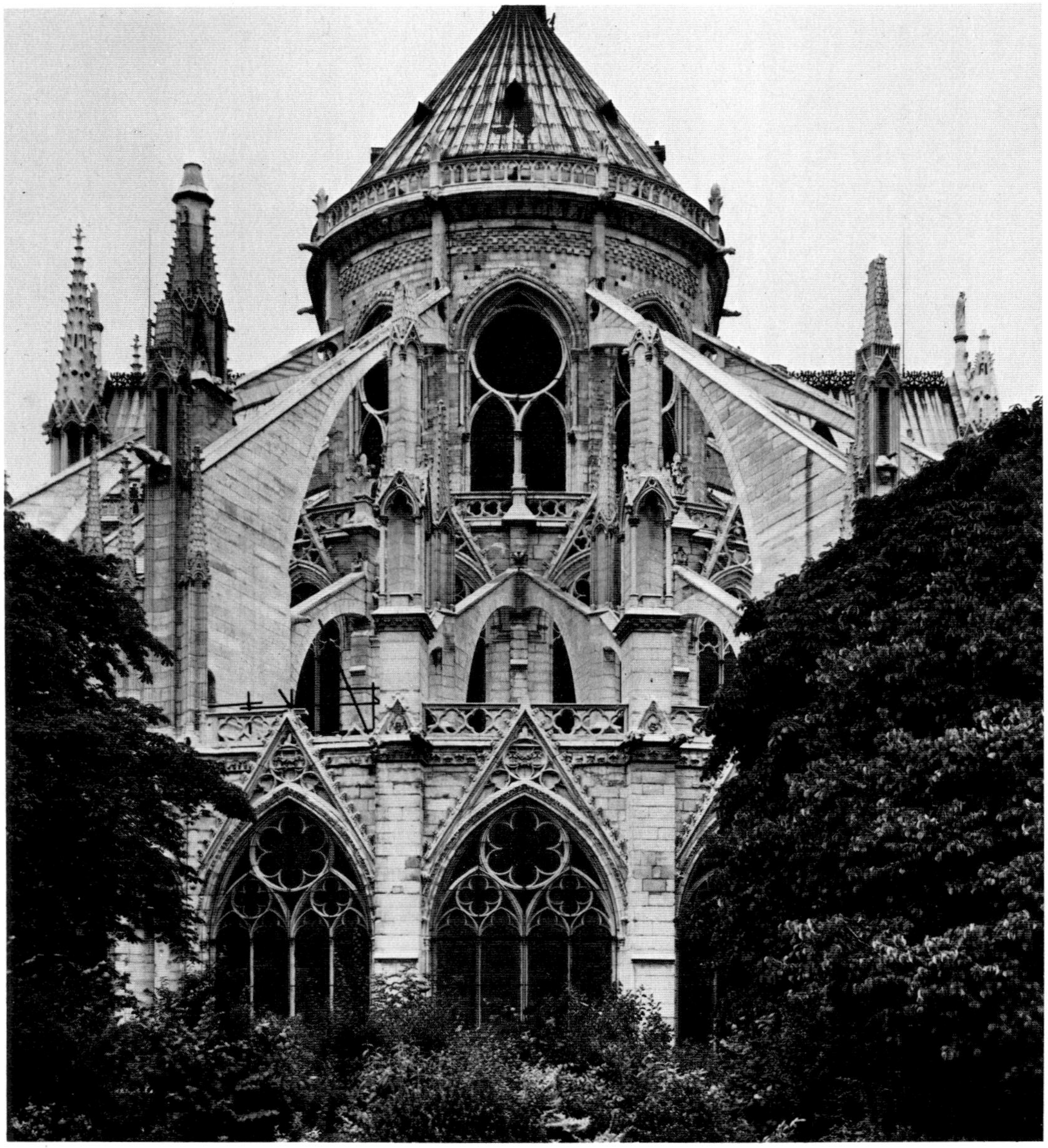

16. Notre-Dame. The apse.

16 to 26. Notre-Dame.

The actual date when building work started at Notre-Dame is not recorded. Robert d'Auxerre notes only that bishop Maurice undertook its reconstruction. It is most probable that at the time of his election (12 October 1160), he had already thought of it, since it was quite obviously necessary. Work in fact started with the choir, which was almost finished in 1177 when Robert de Torigni admired it. In 1182, Henri de Château-Marçay, the Papal Legate, consecrated the high altar. Building work then progressed rapidly on the transept, the roofing of which was finished in 1198. In the meantime Maurice de Sully had died (1196) and Eudes de Sully had succeeded him (1197-1208). At that point the nave was more or less finished and work had already begun on the lead roofing. Eudes de Sully immediately had the western facade done; by 1225 it had already risen to the base of the great pierced arcaded screen. The towers and the arcaded screen were not finished till the second quarter of the thirteenth century. The cathedral planned by Maurice de Sully was finished in 1245.

Its appearance was however soon transformed by alterations. In the second quarter of the thirteenth century, chapels were built between the piers of the nave buttresses with the result that the transepts were then recessed. Jean de Chelles first rebuilt the facade of the north transept with a connecting bay and then, on 12 February 1258, he laid the first stone of the south transept, which was finished by Pierre de Montreuil. Meanwhile the high windows were enlarged and their sills were lowered to meet the extrados of the galleries. The aim was to let more light into the church, which was still very badly lit. The various alterations had another effect: since the original flying buttresses of the nave had been double ones, they now had to be reduced to single ones, a feat of singular boldness. At the end of the thirteenth century and in the early fourteenth century, Pierre de Chelles, who had planned the work, and his successor, Jean Ravy (1318-1344), built the chapels of the choir, the superb flying buttresses of the apse and let windows into the angles of the galleries, removing the original rose windows in the process. The cathedral was then finally complete; later work consisted mainly of decoration or restoration. The plan chosen by Maurice de Sully is one of extreme simplicity: the nave flanked by double aisles extends, uninterrupted at the transepts, into the long choir, surrounded by a double ambulatory without chapels. The nave with double aisles echoes that by Suger at Saint-Denis. The elevation has four storeys, the custom of the period. The third storey with its marvellous rose windows disappeared later when the windows were enlarged. The oblong bays are roofed with sexpartite vaulting whose thrust is taken by sturdy round piers, all of them the same. Alternation between strong and weak piers is only used in the aisles of the nave. Notre-Dame harks back to the past more than it foreshadows the future: the great galleries disappeared later, quadripartite vaulting was used subsequently and the small columns taking the thrust of the ribs were then extended to the floor to emphasize the vertical divisions of the bays.

The traditional character of Notre-Dame's architecture is seen at its best in the apse its superbly rounded masses rising up in layers, forming a pyramid. The effect, more usual in Romanesque architecture, is somewhat diminished by the flying buttresses which are of later date. The addition of chapels radiating from the ambulatory only serves to underline the massive appearance of the apse. The higher flying buttresses, added in the fourteenth century, give a lighter effect to the two upper levels. The western facade echoes the harmonious facades of the Norman churches of the Romanesque period, although the proportions are grander. It has a unity of composition rare in the Gothic period. Each level is clearly marked by horizontal lines which run across the full length of the facade, so that the two towers can only be seen above the pierced arcaded screen. The south and north sides display this same horizontal division interupted only by the two maginificent facades of the transept which were built in the middle of the thirteenth century. However the present single flying buttresses, replacing the original double ones, have lessened the tiered effect which was doubtless more marked originally. The spire above the crossing, added by Viollet-le-Duc, also reflects the desire to give Notre-Dame a lighter, more upsoaring appearance—a quality which the Paris cathedral noticeably lacks.

The sculptures on the portals' tympana and arching have escaped all restoration, with the exception of the two lintels of the central portal. The sculpture of the tympanum of the central portal—with the exception of "Christ showing his Wounds" and the "Angel with Nails",

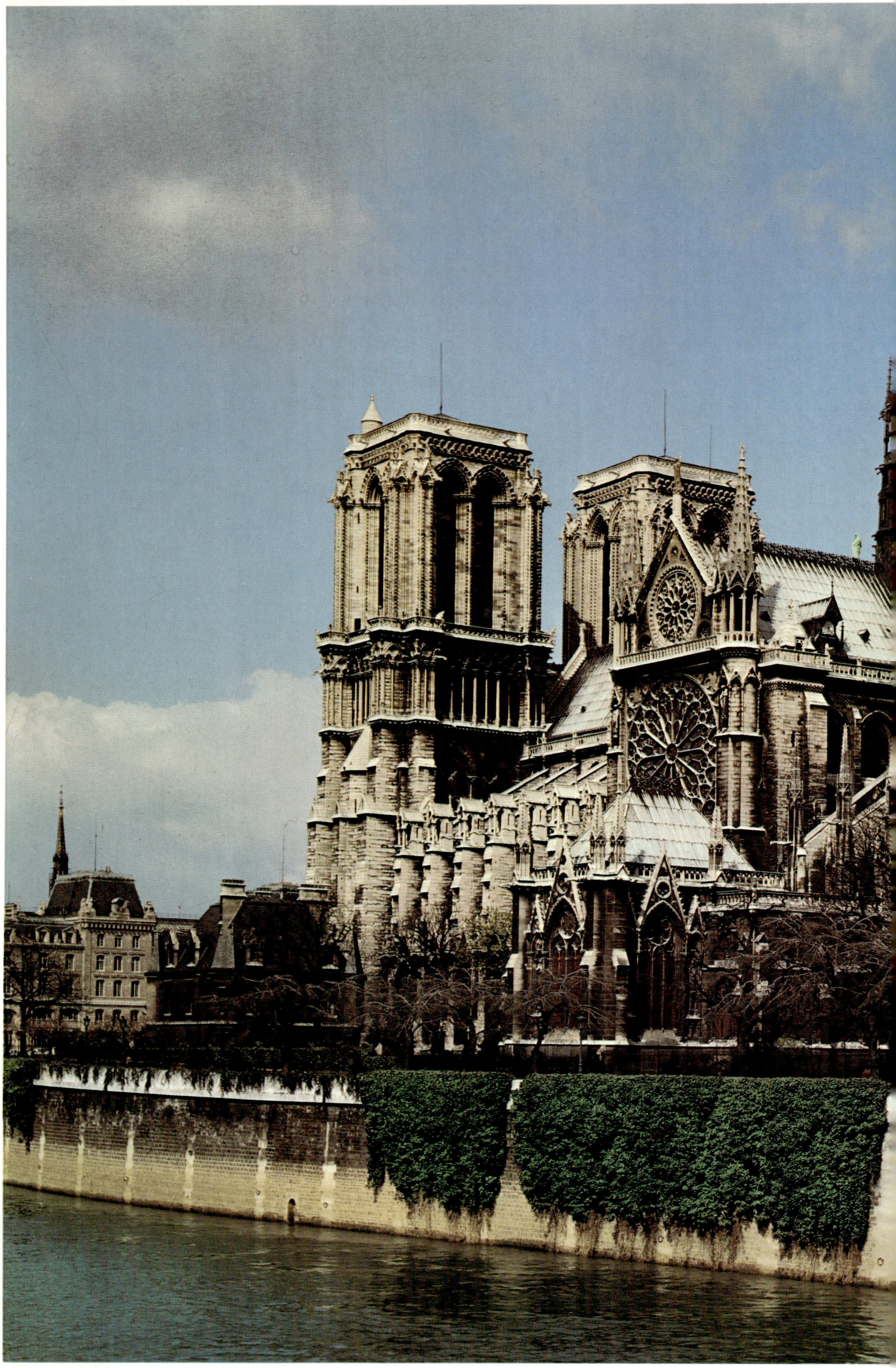

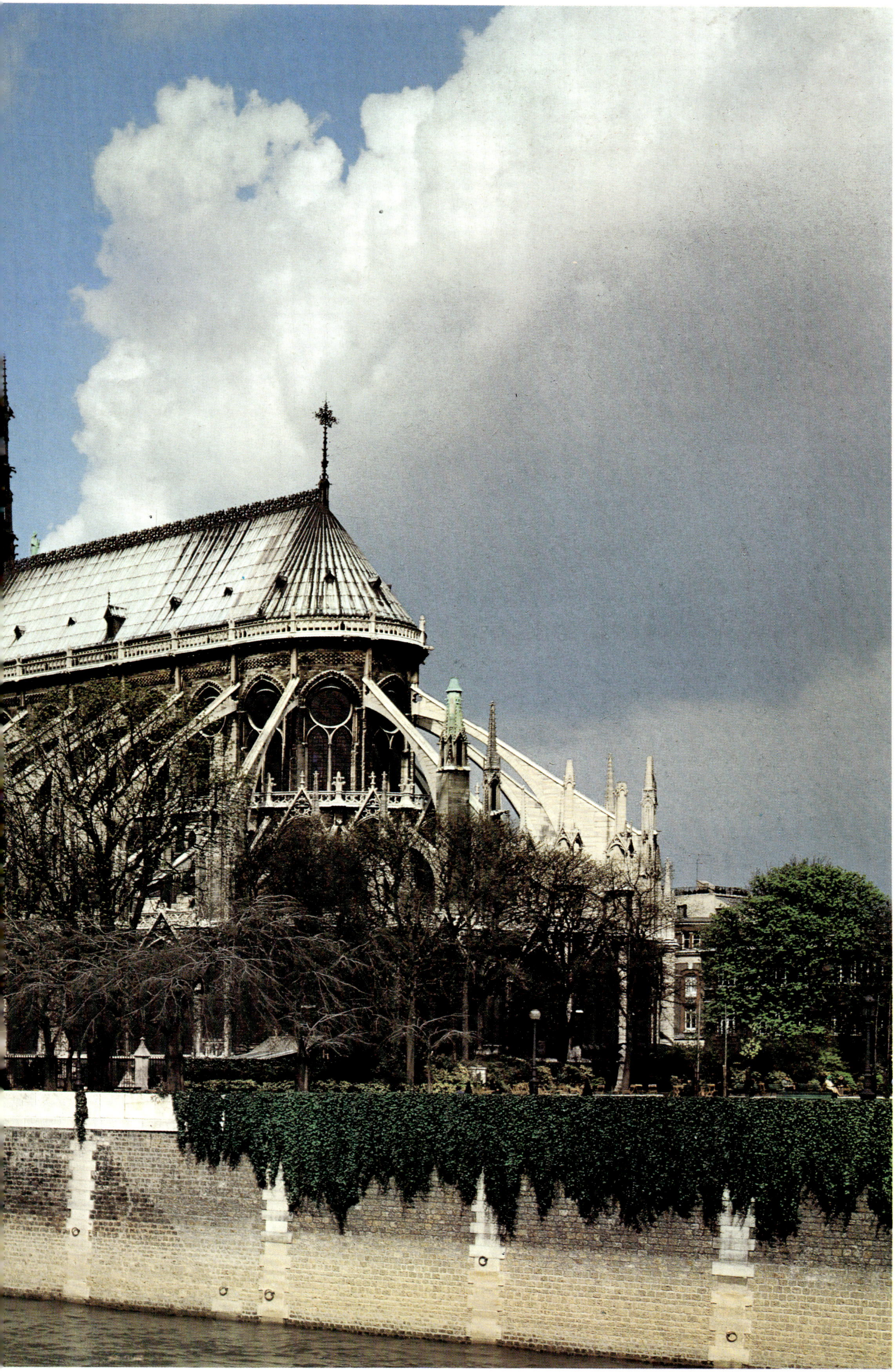

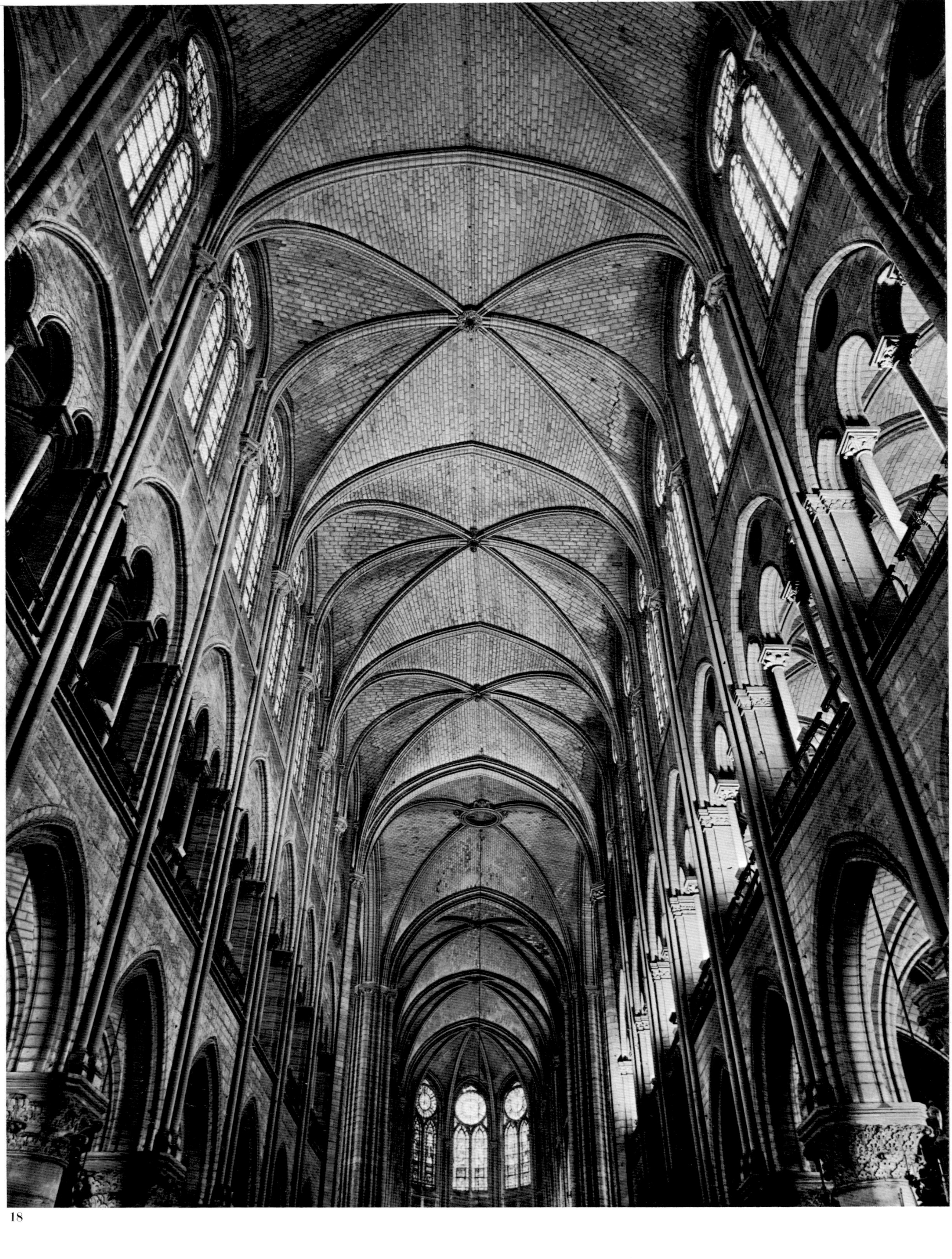

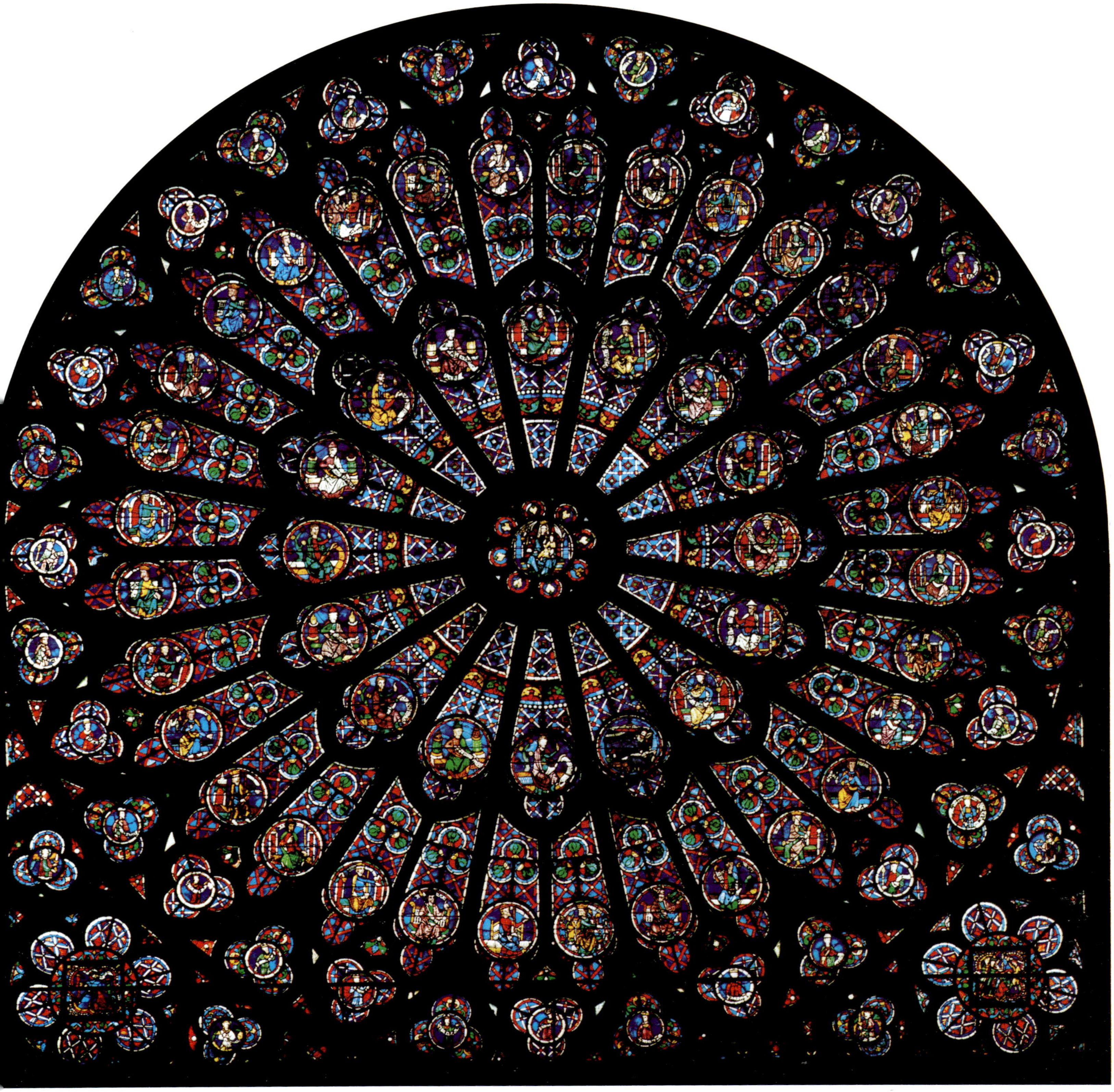

19. Notre-Dame. The rose window of the north transept.

17. Notre-Dame. The apse and the south side.

18. Notre-Dame. The vaulting of the nave.

sculpted around 1220—are inspired by the style of Sens which prevailed in the major building works of the time. The long, fluted folds mould the figures, covering the legs of the Virgin and those of Saint John in magnificent curves. The faces radiate a serene gravity, suggesting the world beyond. Saint Anne's portal on the right bears sculptures of very different periods and in different styles, which were added around 1220. In the tympanum, the Virgin beneath a canopy is flanked by two angels and by Saint-Germain and the king Childebert. The upper lintel displays scenes of Christ's childhood whilst in the lower lintel there are scenes from the life of Saint Anne and the Virgin. In the arch moldings the angels, kings, prophets and old men of the Apocalypse glorify the Virgin. Drawings originally done for Montfaucon enabled sculptors of the nineteenth century to restore the original decoration of the piers. Parts of this survived, including the torso of Saint Peter (Musée du Louvre), the head of David (Metropolitan Museum, New York) and the Saint Marcellus (of the pier) now in the north tower. The column-statues were done in the twelfth century, between 1150 and 1165, as were the tympanum, the upper lintel and nearly all the arch moldings. After the portal's installation, work was then completed on the lower lintel, the eight arch moldings of the first tier, the two incense-bearing angels who filled the space between the archings and the tympanum.

The left portal had a scene of the Crowning of the Virgin inspired by a new iconographic formula: the Dormition and the Assumption have in fact been blended into a single scene in the lintel. In the lower lintel, on either side of the Ark of the Covenant are the patriarchs and kings. The archings are filled with angels, patriarchs, kings and prophets. The door jambs have little bas reliefs of the zodiac and seasonal occupations.
Around 1250 Jean de Chelles rebuilt the north facade of the transept. The portal was dedicated to the Virgin; the lintel bears scenes of Christ's childhood and, above that, the legend of the monk Theophilus is portrayed. In the arch moldings there are angels, virgins and doctors and on the pier, the Virgin and Child. Before the Revolution, the piers bore the Three Kings on the left and the three theological Virtues on the right.
The south portal, started in 1258, is devoted to the legend of Saint Stephen, sculpted on the lintel and the tympanum.

20. Notre-Dame. The west facade.

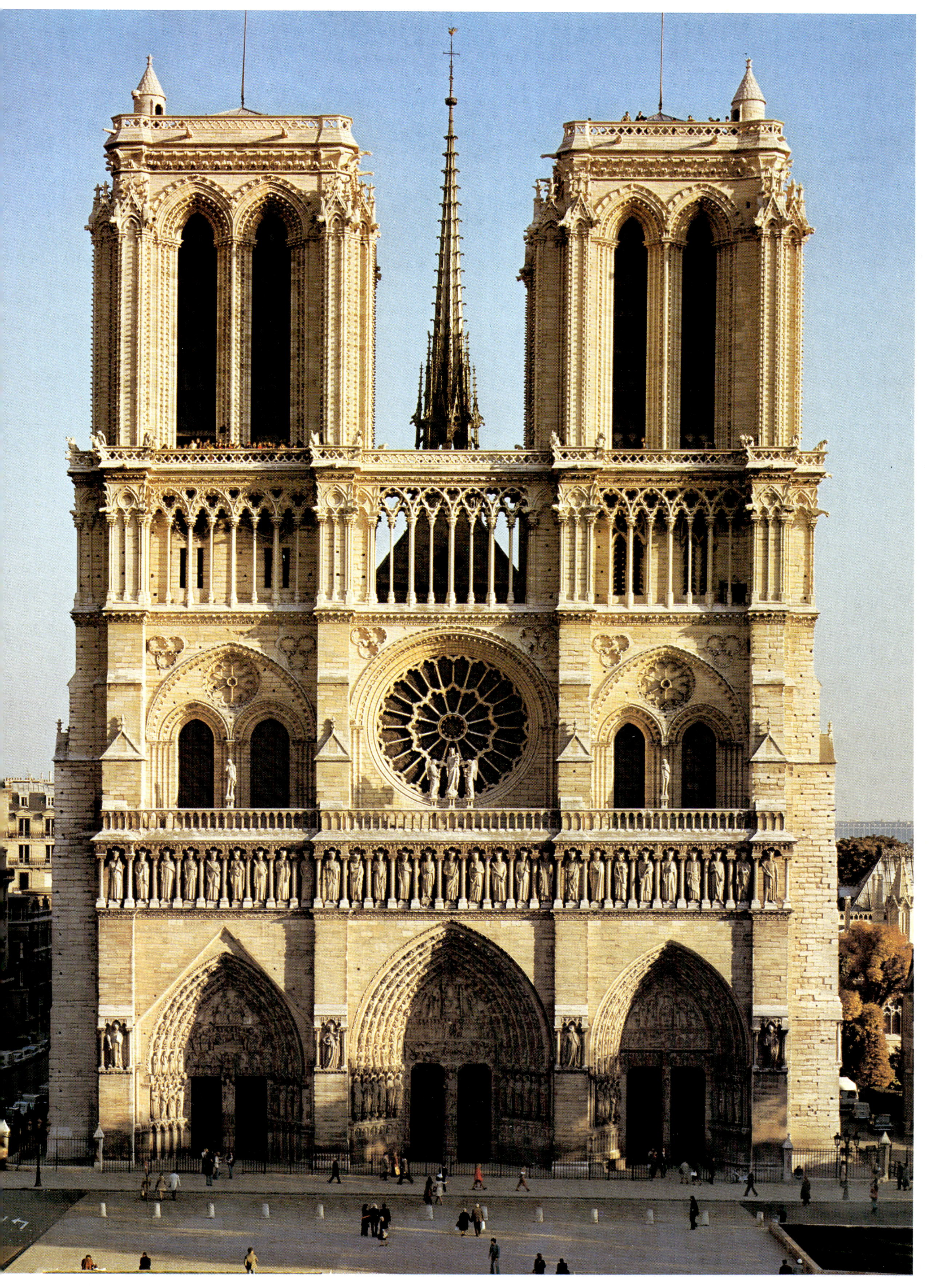

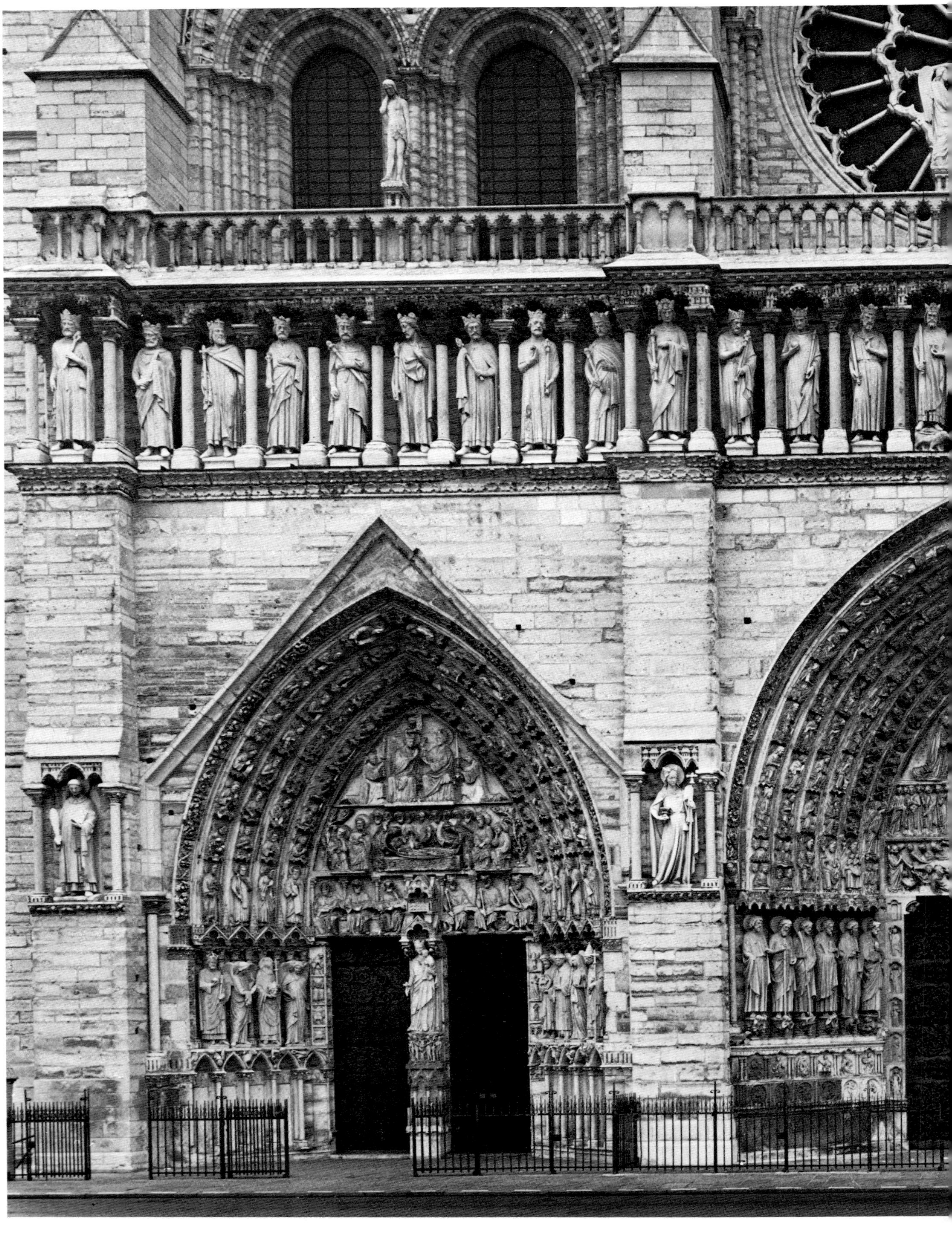

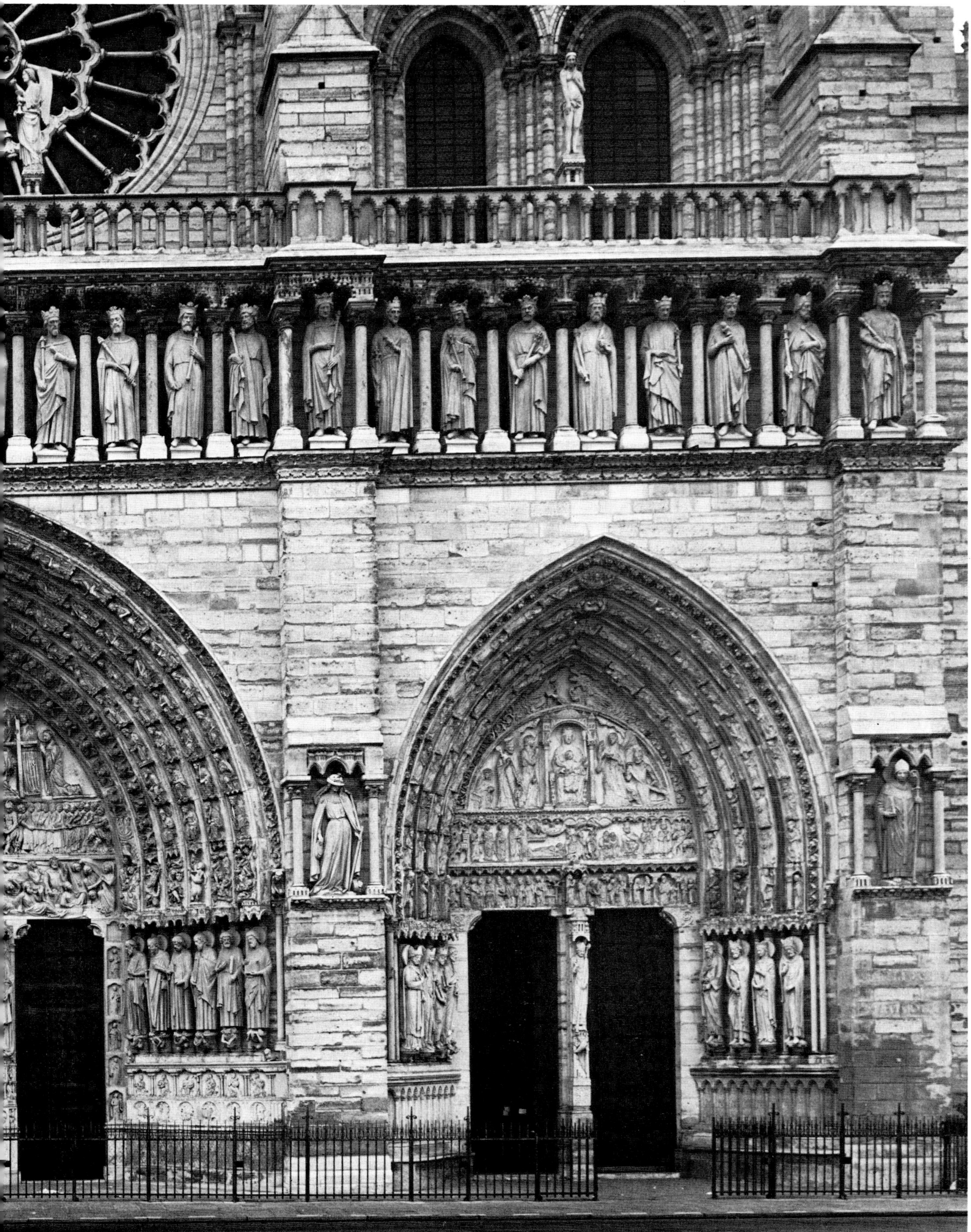

21. Notre-Dame. The three portals: on the left, the portal of the Virgin; in the center, the portal of the Last Judgment; on the right, the portal of Saint Anne.

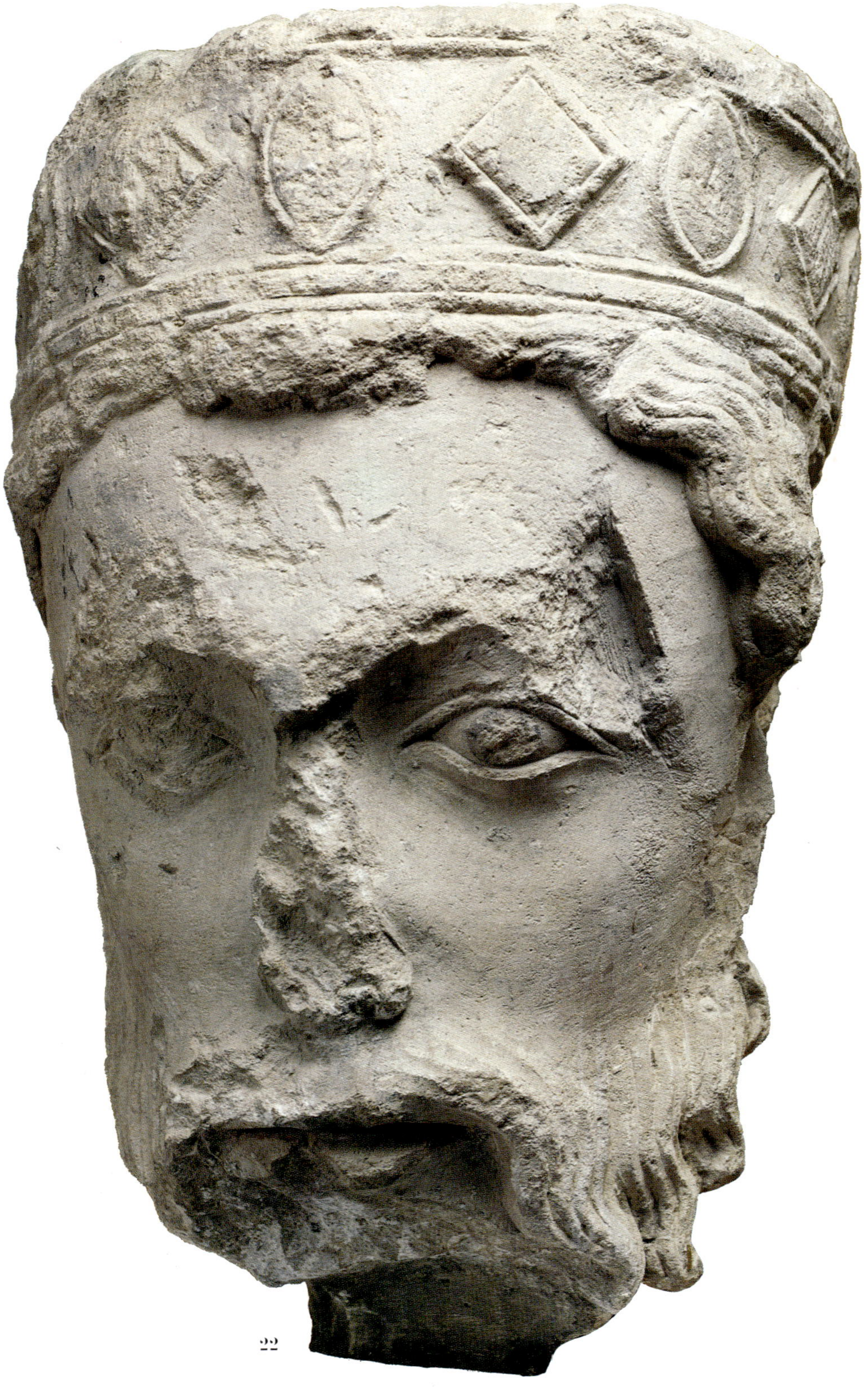

22

22 and 23. The Kings' heads from Notre-Dame.

The arcade of the Kings of Judah, stretching from one tower to the other above the three porches of the facade of Notre-Dame, remained a mystery till 1977. When restoring it, Viollet-le-Duc imagined a style which, it has now been shown, was very far from the original. During the restoration of the Hôtel Moreau, twenty-one heads were found in April 1977 at 22, Rue de la Chaussée d'Antin, where they had been hidden in a hole for safe-keeping, shortly after the Revolution. They shed new light on the sculpture of the early thirteenth century. Despite the fact that they were placed high up on the facade, the artist took the trouble to brighten them up with paint. Broken, crumbling and mutilated though they are, their freshness and beauty is still most moving.

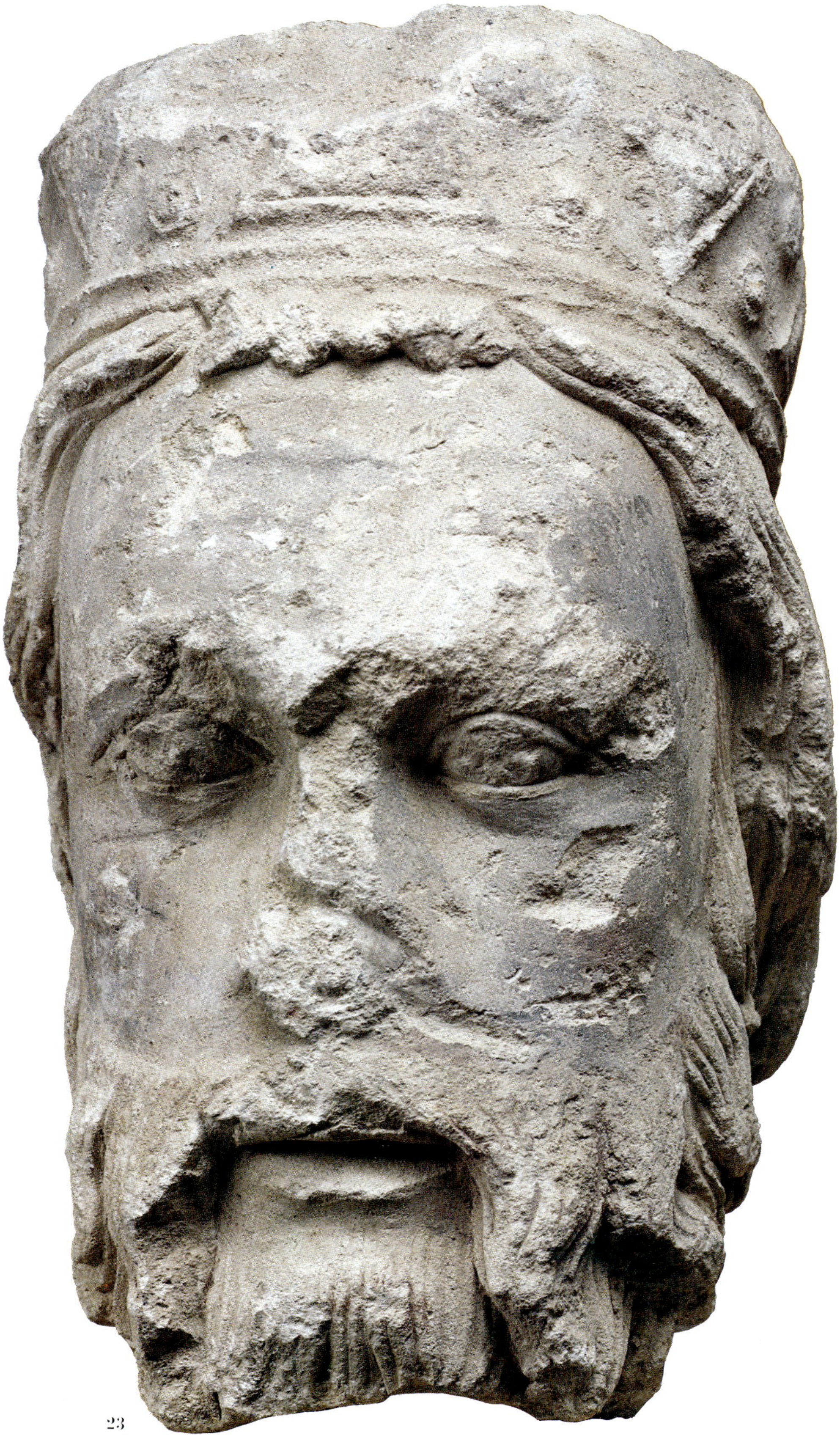

23

22 and 23. Kings' heads from Notre-Dame. Now in the Cluny Museum. They form part of the collection of sculptures found in the foundations of the French Bank of Foreign Trade (Hôtel Moreau).

64

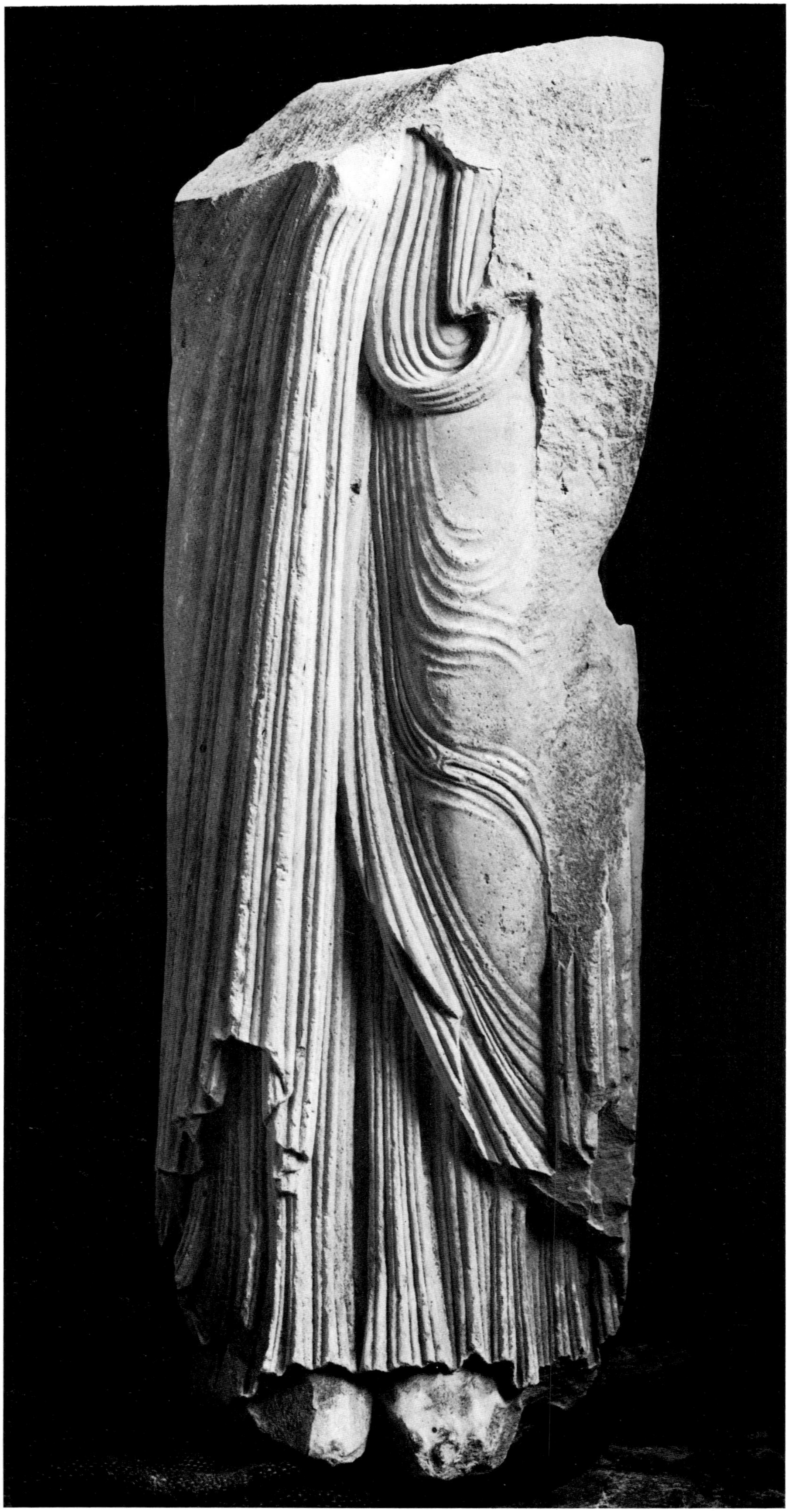

24

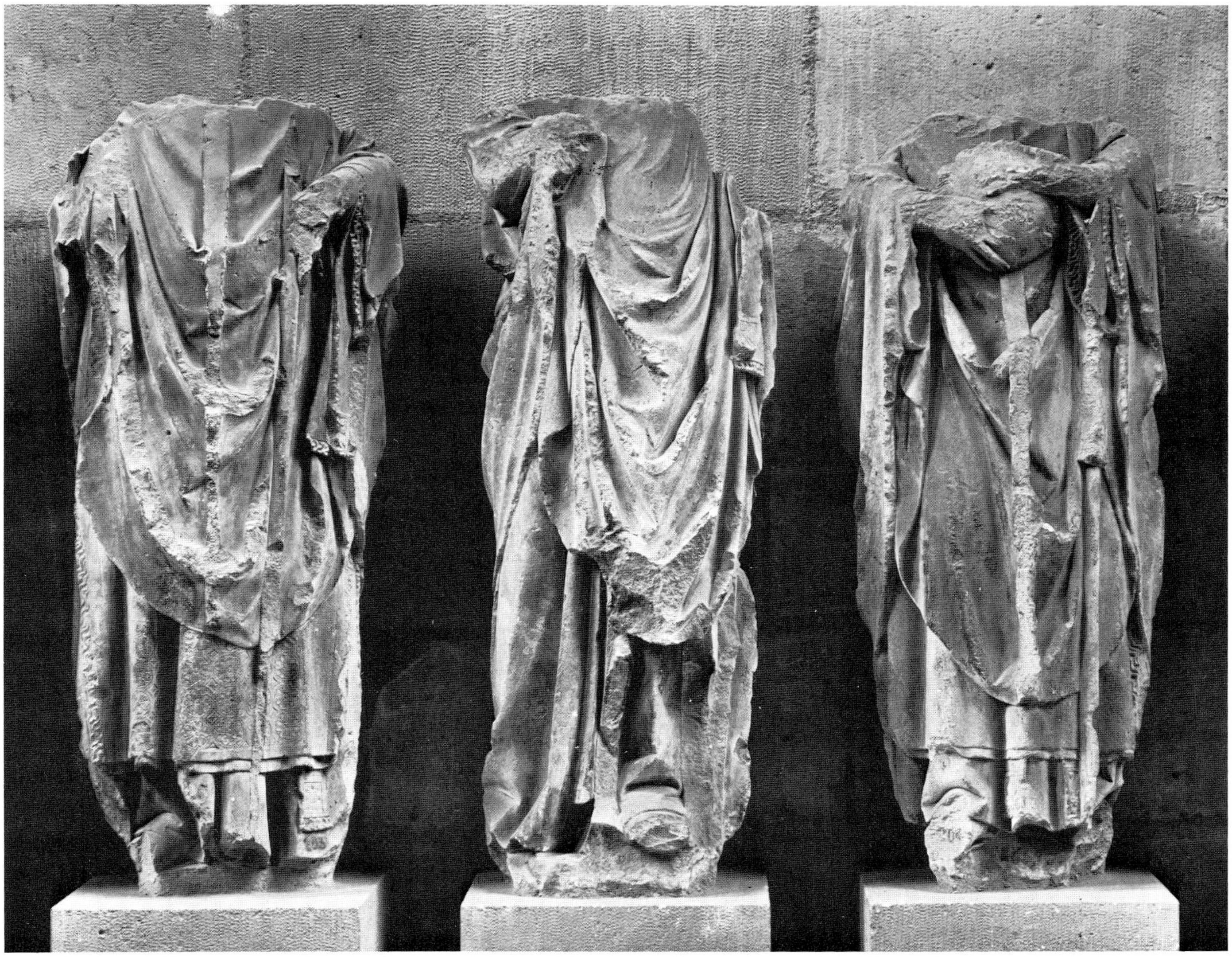

25. Notre-Dame. Three statues from the south transept (north tower).

24. Notre-Dame. Statue of Saint Peter from the portal of Saint Anne. Louvre Museum.

66

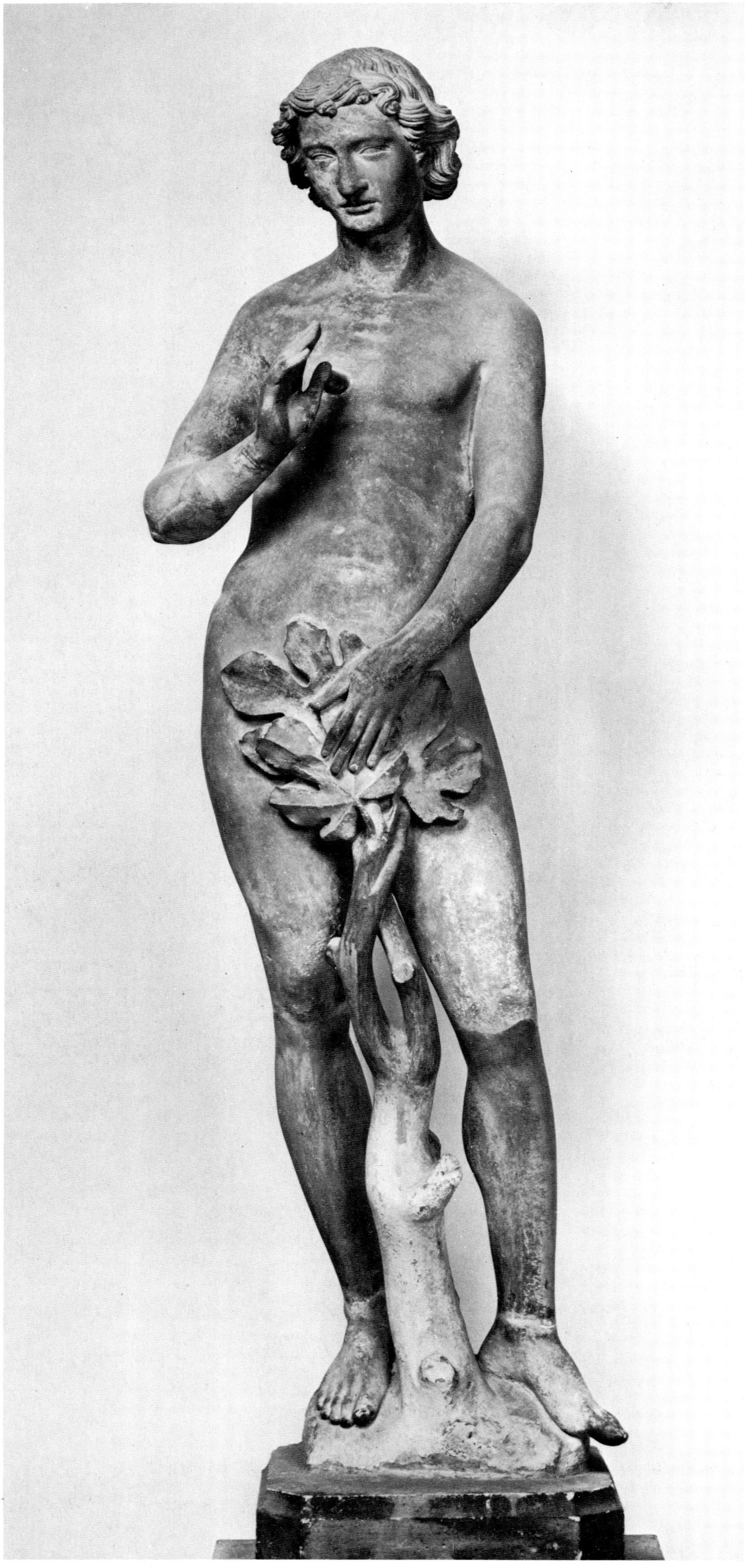

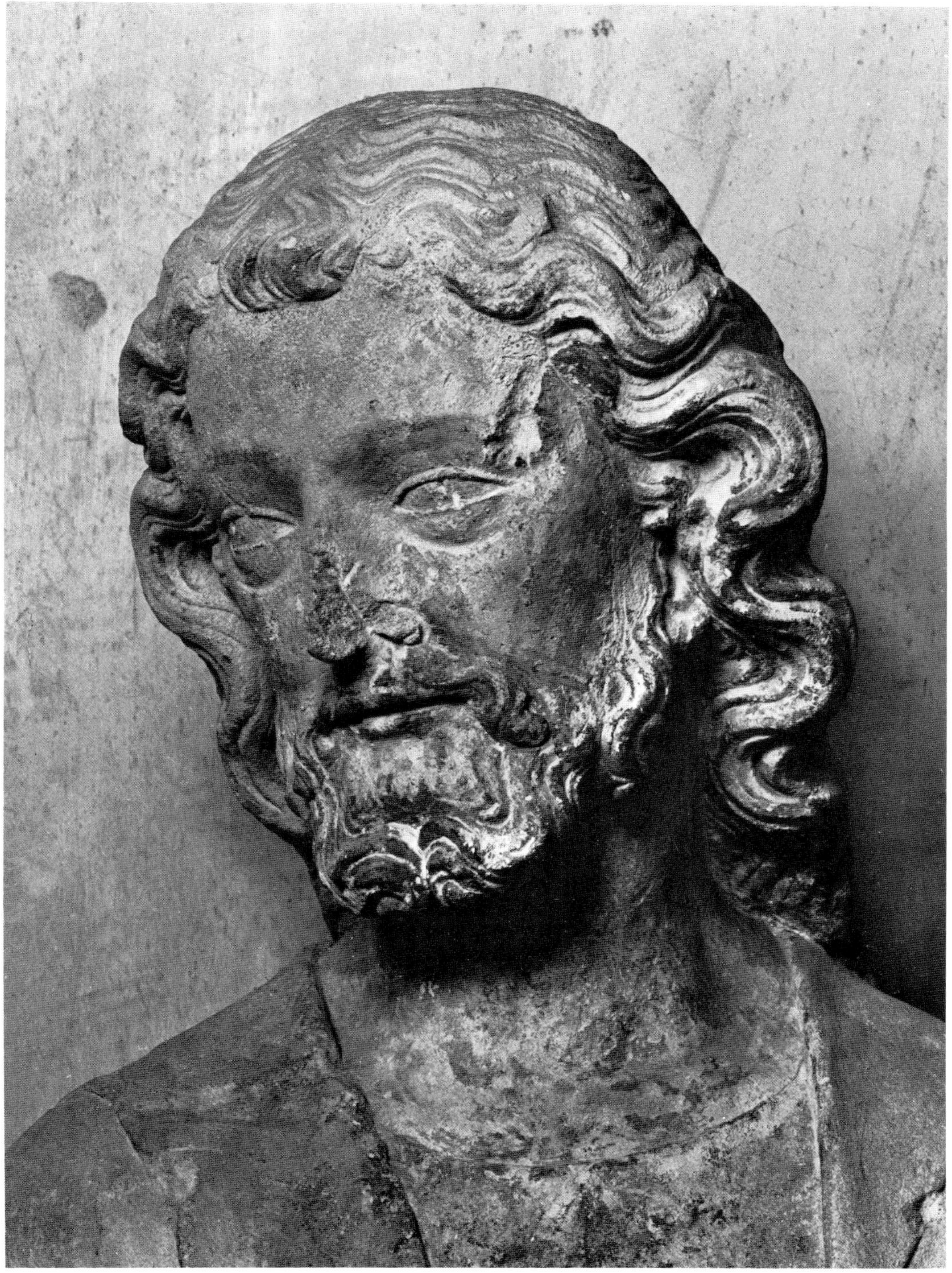

27. An apostle from Saint-Jacques-de-l'Hôpital. Cluny Museum.

27. An apostle from Saint-Jacques-de-l'Hôpital.

The death of Saint Louis (1207) marked the end of the great royal building projects. Private individuals then took over the initiative, building colleges, chapels and even churches. On the present site of numbers 129-133 of the Rue Saint-Denis, a confraternity built a hospital and a vast chapel for pilgrims journeying to or from Saint-Jacques-de-Compostelle. It was the Queen, Jeanne d'Evreux, who laid the first stone on 18 February 1319. Like the Sainte-Chapelle, the chapel's interior was decorated with statues attached to the little columns which took the thrust of the ogival arches. Nothing now remains of the building except these statues, sculpted by Guillaume de Nourriche and Robert de Launnoy from 1320 to 1325. Buried no doubt during the Revolution, they were found in 1846 when a building was being put up on the same site.

26. Notre-Dame. Statue of Adam from the interior of the south transept. Cluny Museum.

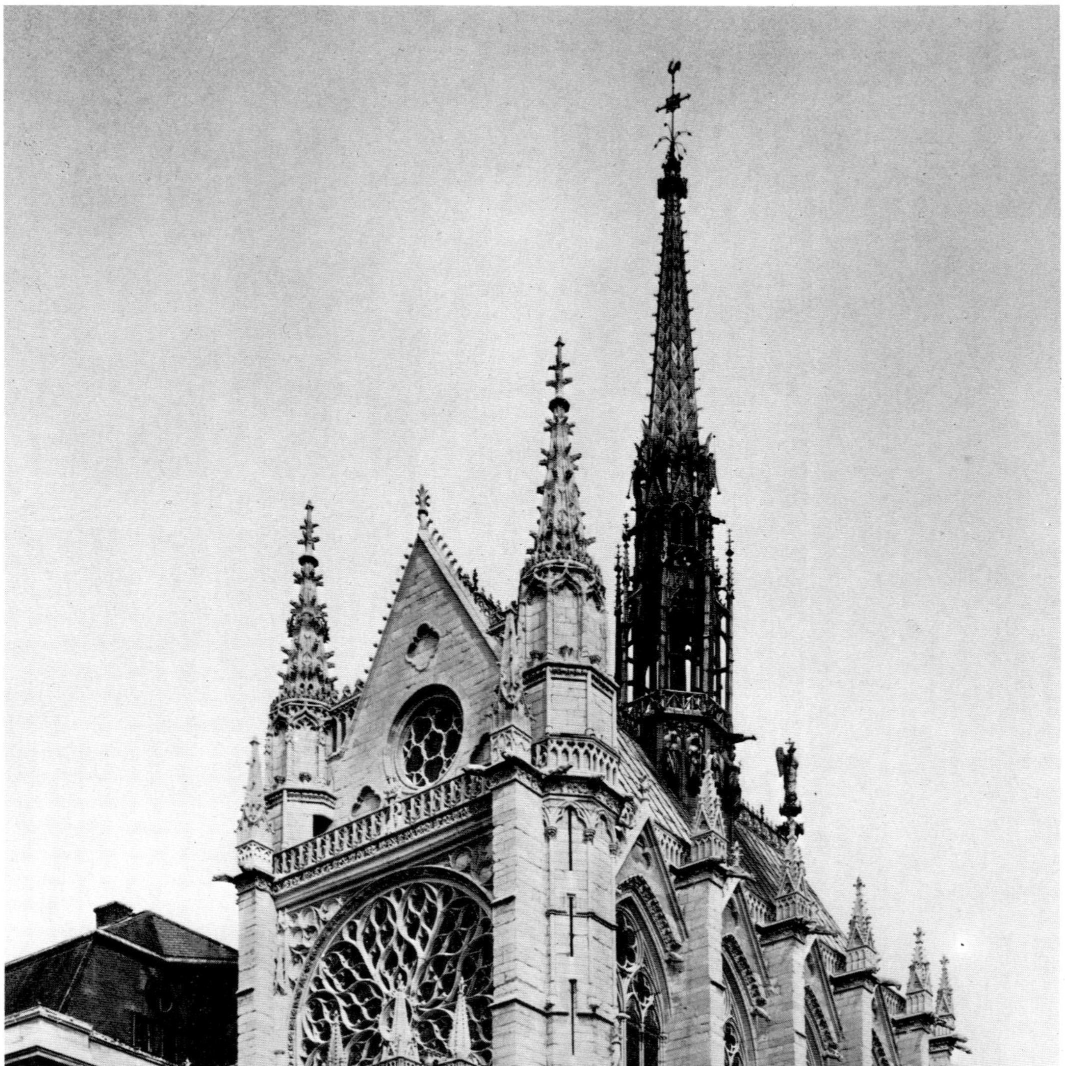

28. The Sainte-Chapelle. The west facade and the south side.

28 to 32. The Sainte-Chapelle.

On acquiring the relics of the Passion, Saint Louis decided to build a two-storey building in his palace to house them. Although the actual date when work started on the Sainte-Chapelle is not known (somewhere between 1239 and 1243), we do know that the building, with its stained-glass windows and sculptures, was ready for its consecration in 1248.
The plan of the upper storey is extremely simple: a hall with four bays of rectangular plan. On the ground floor there are sturdy columns set at a short distance from the walls, providing the first storey with a solid foundation. The same simplicity can be seen in the external elevation: the airy construction with its great windows soars upwards from its massive base. The ascending buttresses form a solid link between the two storeys. They give the building a vigorous rhythm and dynamism to be found again only in the "art de cour" or court art. The buttresses, moreover, enabled the architect to cut great openings into the walls of the first floor. Inside, the effect is striking. The architect has managed with great subtlety to make this glass cage solid and secure. Light streams from all directions, drowning what little wall is left, whilst the columns supporting the vaulting seem to disappear before our eyes. These columns project by about a meter or so from the windows and between them the lancet windows rise to twelve meters. Their graceful, soaring lines make them seem even taller than they are, as do the slender mullions separating them. This glass cage rests on a base without windows decorated with a blind arcade which runs its whole length.
The rigorous style of the architecture constrasts with the magnificence of the decoration. This includes the capitals with their ornamental foliage, showing all the different kinds of trees in the Ile-de-France, the paintings of the quatrefoils, which have been overrestored and spoilt, the angels nestling on the cornerstones and the cordon separating the two levels. There is also the vigorous design of the abaci, the bases and the ogival arches made to catch the light. Twelve statues of the apostles attached to the pillars bear witness to the genius of Saint Louis' sculptors. Quite a few of the statues were remade in the nineteenth century; inspired by the beautiful fragments preserved in the Cluny Museum.
The stained-glass extends over 600 square meters and more than two-thirds of it dates back to the thirteenth century, whilst the remaining third was beautifully redone in the nineteenth century. The work was shared by three Parisian ateliers. The "main" atelier produced work of fine technical quality in a supple style. The second atelier created more varied compositions of greater expressiveness and refinement. The third atelier, meanwhile, and the most interesting, varied the faces and expressions by applying the paint very skilfully.
The western rose window, which bears the monogram of Charles VIII, dates from the second half of the fifteenth century. The Apocalypse shines out with brilliant clarity in a harmony of colors, each in many shades: golden yellow, pale yellow, green-yellow, blue-green, sky blue, slate grey, royal blue, deep violet, blue-violet, crimson-pink, crimson-garnet, vermilion-red and ruby-red. Green and yellow nevertheless predominate in this spectrum of colors. Engraving on double glass is used abundantly in this window made (according to Louis Grodecki) between 1485 and 1498.

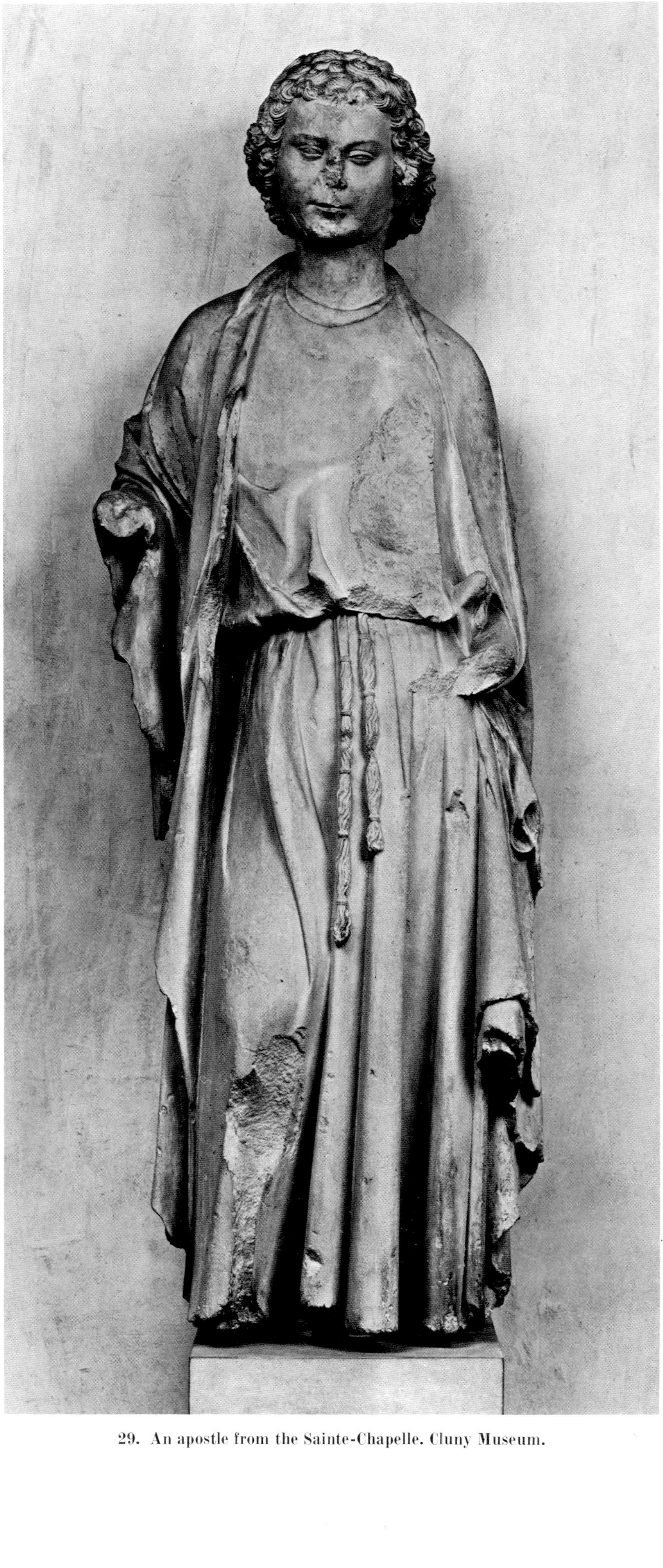

29. An apostle from the Sainte-Chapelle. Cluny Museum.

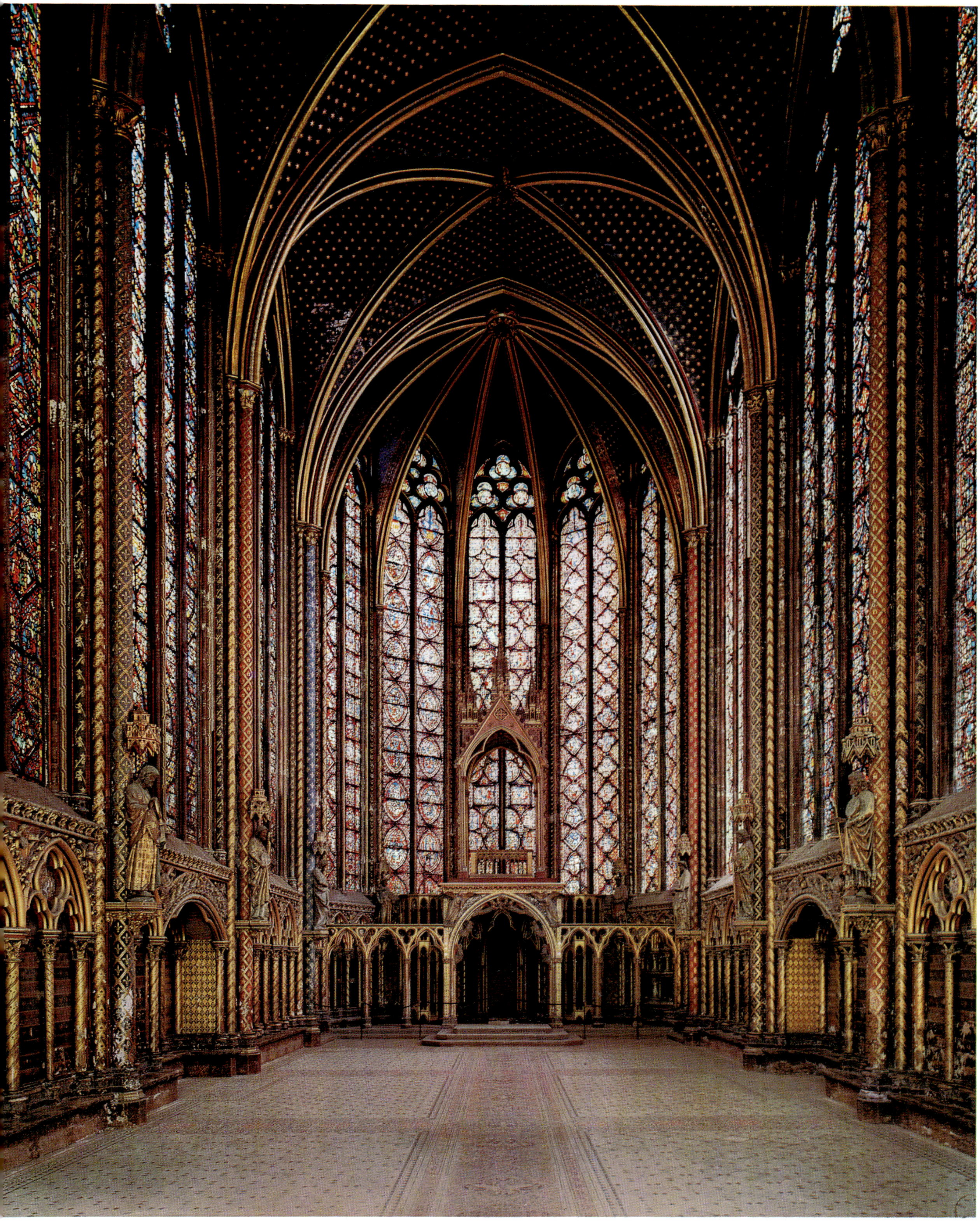

30. The Sainte-Chapelle. The high chapel.

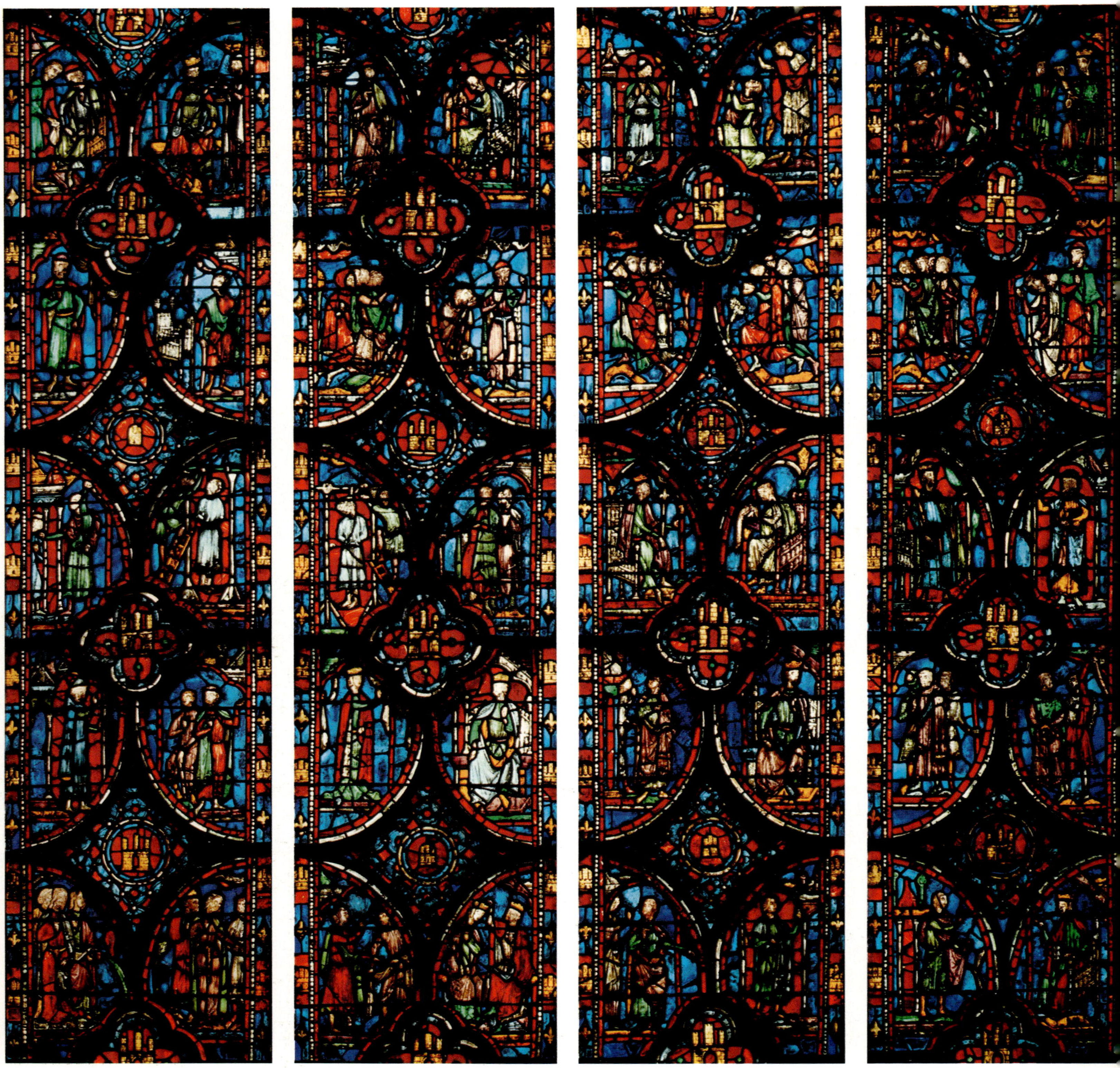

31. The Sainte-Chapelle. Stained-glass windows in the third south bay.

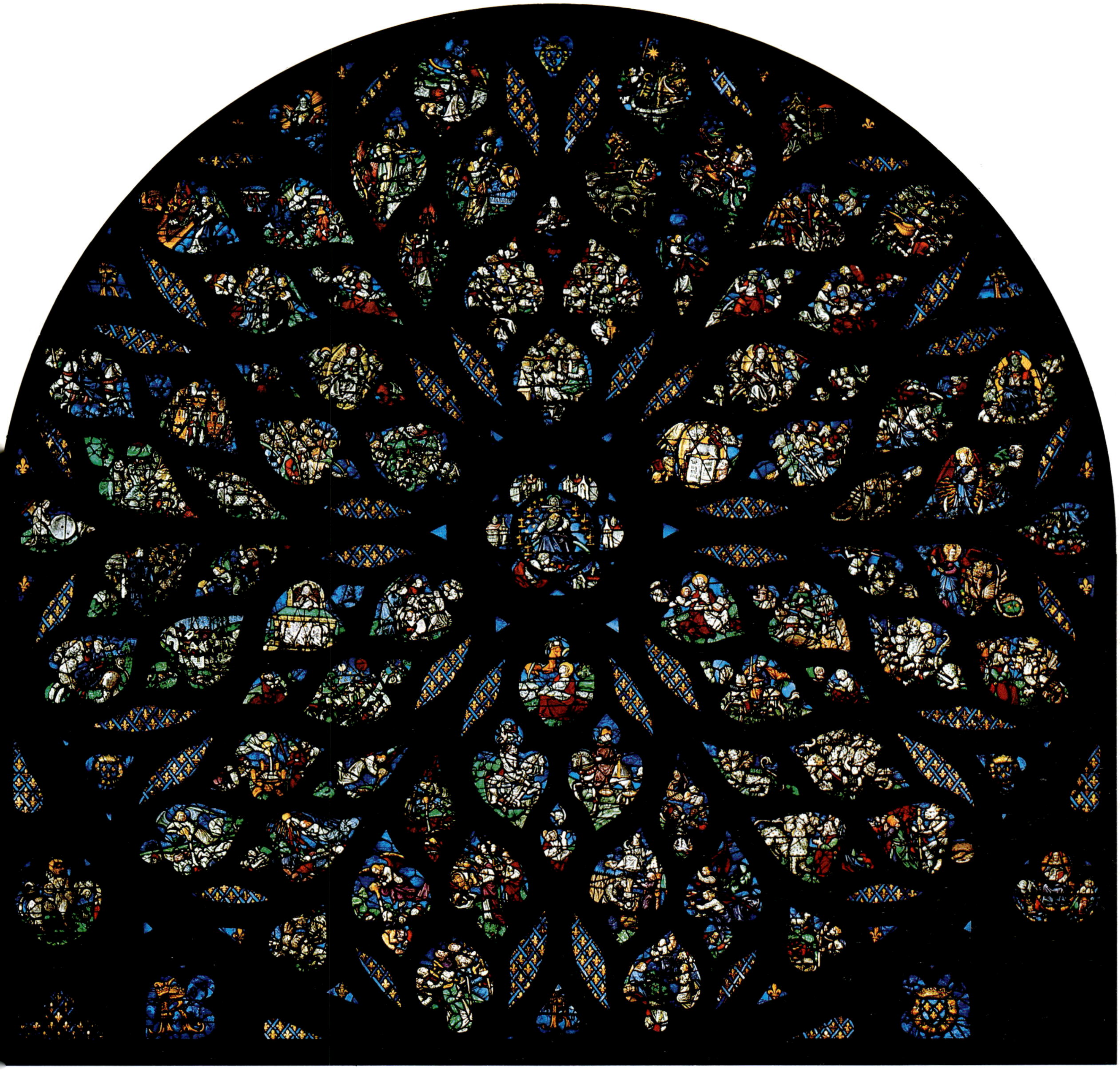

32. The west rose window of the Sainte-Chapelle.

33 to 35. The Conciergerie.

Formerly the prison of the Capetian royal palace, the Conciergerie owes its name to the concierge or lodge keeper of the royal residence. Amongst other duties, he disposed of wide powers of justice in the palace and its annexes.

The four towers overlooking the Quai de l'Horloge are the remains of the Palace wall rebuilt by Philippe le Bel. The Tour Bonbec, the most western of the towers, dates back to the time of Saint Louis. Before the restorations of the last century, it was lower than the two others. The two twin towers in the center, the Tour d'Argent and the Tour de César served as entrance to the Grand'Chambre or Great Chamber when they were built under Philippe Le Bel. Both towers still have one room with ribbed vaulting supported by finely sculpted brackets. The Tour de l'Horloge (the Clock Tower), overrestored in the last century, is more recent; it was not built before 1350 and its clock was not mounted till 1371. Originally, it had a very high basement on which there was a recessed main building, terminating in a rectangular pavilion, also recessed.

The Salle des Gens d'armes or the Hall of the Men-at-Arms—popularly known as the hall of Saint Louis—served as basement to the Grand'Salle, destroyed in the fire of 1618. It was built in two stages, first the west and then the east part. The hall, of large dimensions, is divided into four by three lines of pillars, some of which were later reinforced. This powerful construction includes some capitals decorated with foliage which soften the overall rigour of the style.

The staircase in the first bays to the north must be later than the work carried out under Philippe le Bel. It must habe been built to provide access to the famous kitchens which do not date before the mid-fourteenth century. These kitchens had originally been a separate two-story building of which only the lower hall remains. Square in plan, it has four enormous chimneys in the corners. Its roof is supported by three rows of three columns. The building's function explains why the original arches are only rough-hewn, the capitals unpolished and the bases hardly moulded.

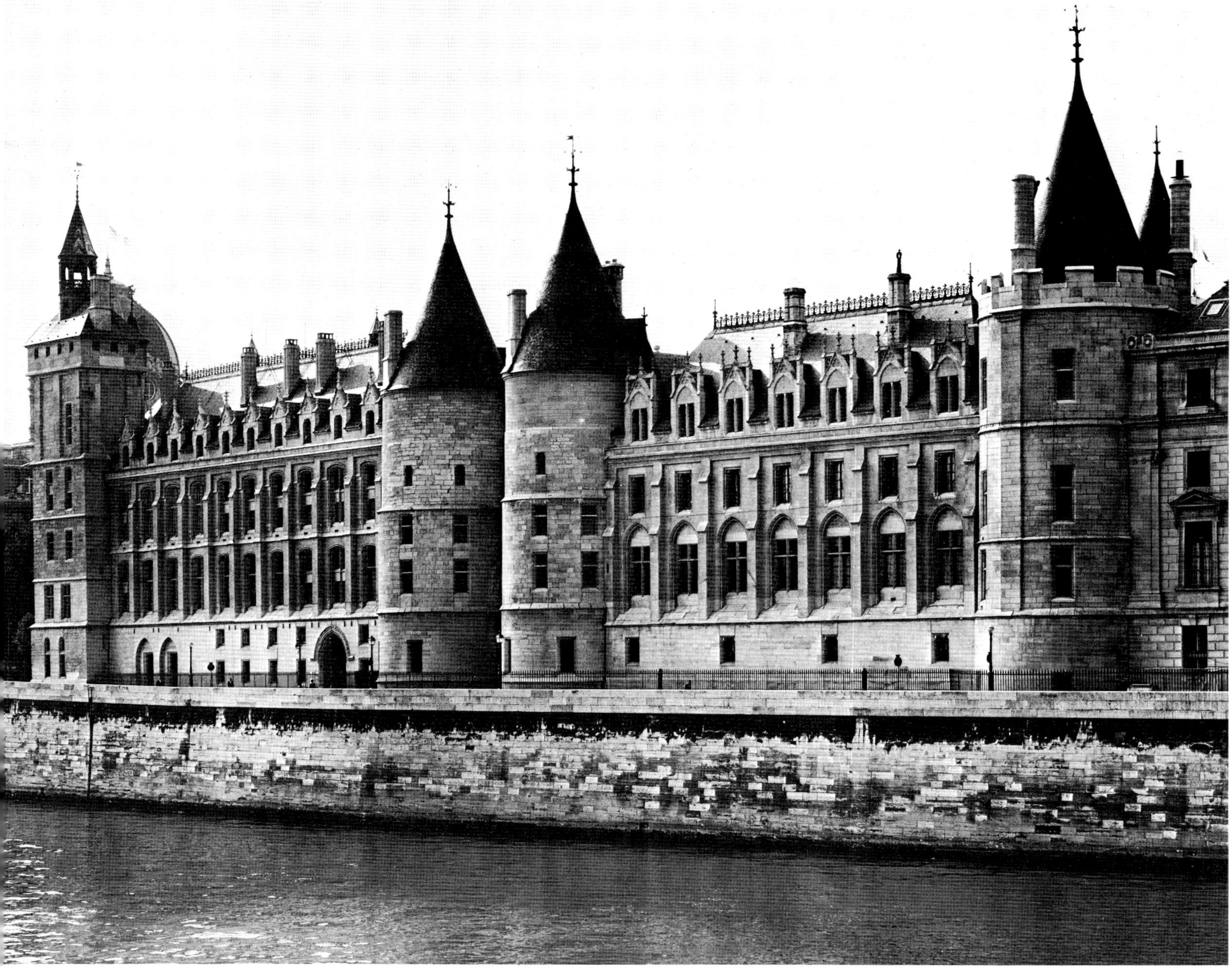

33. The Conciergerie, north wall of the Palais de la Cité, now the Palais de Justice.

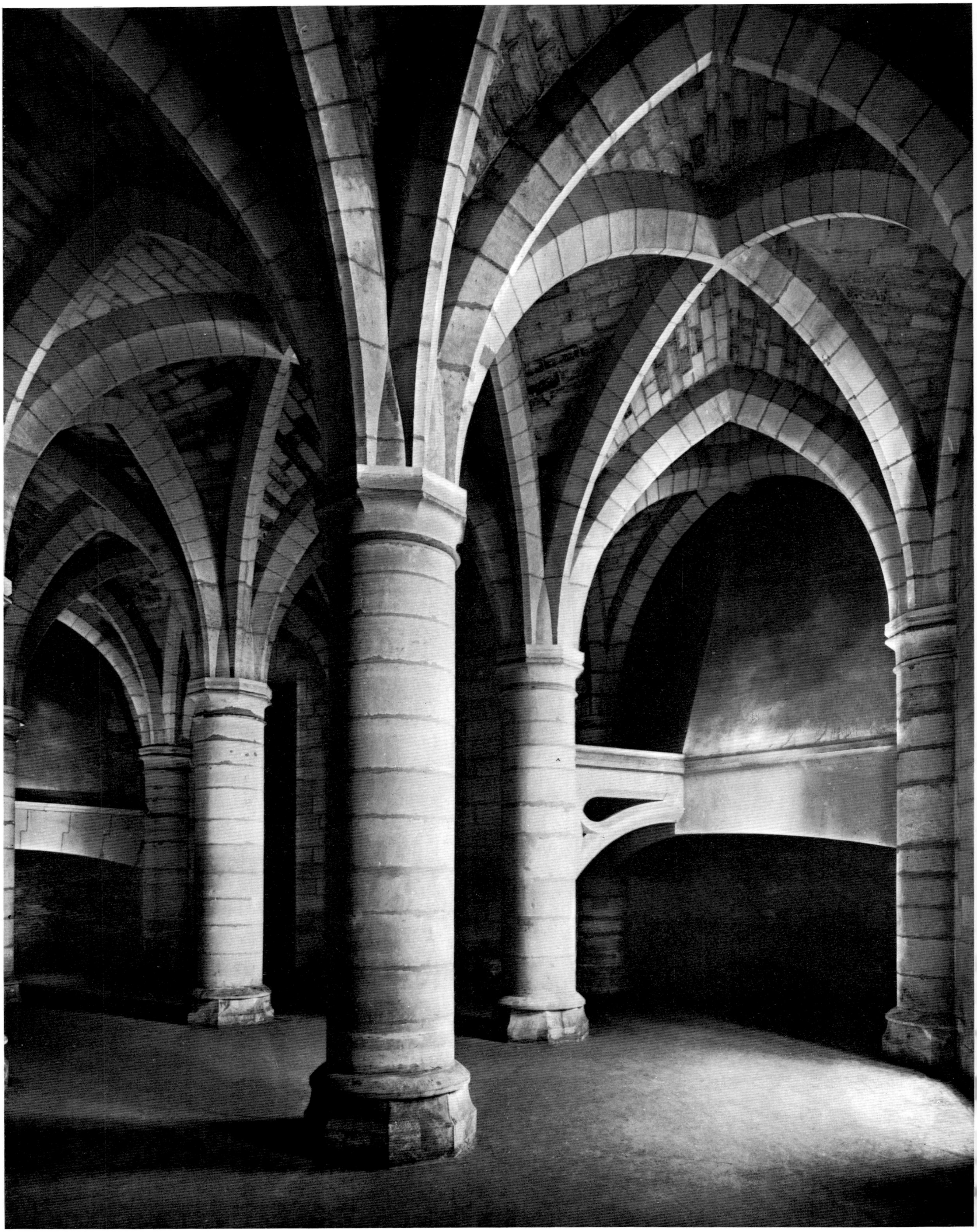

34. The kitchens of the Palais.

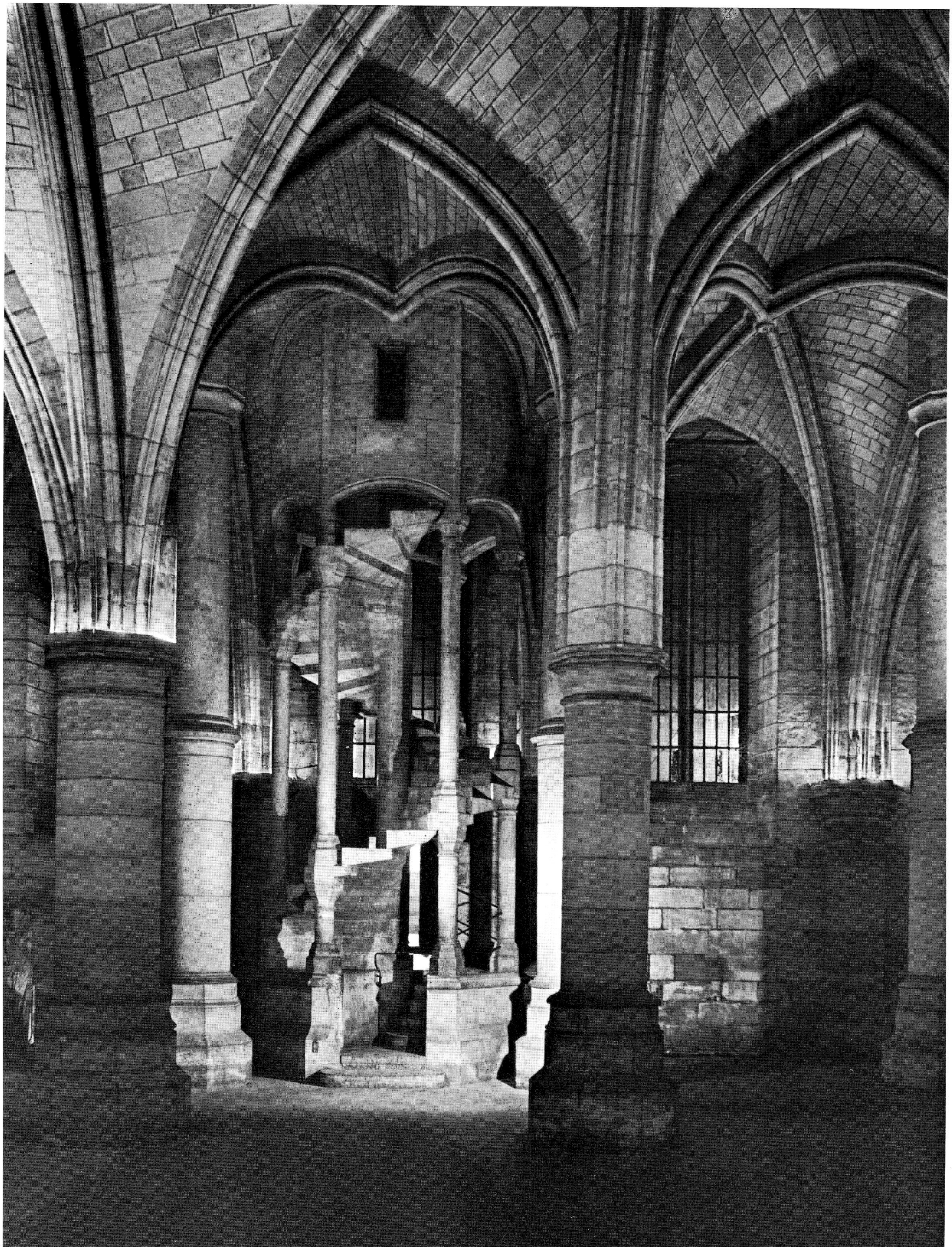

35. The staircase of the Salle des Gens d'Armes.

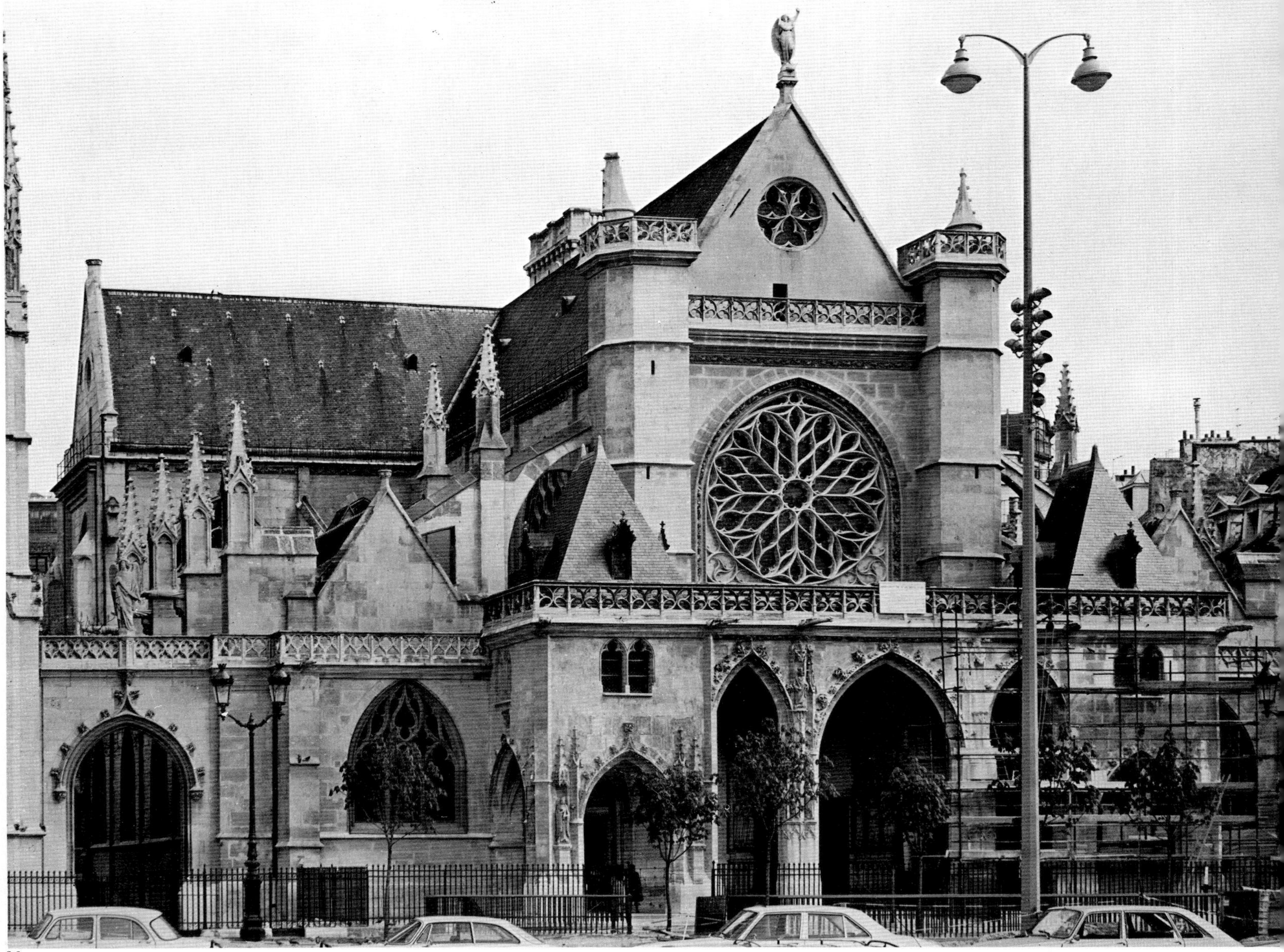
36

36 and 37. Saint-Germain-l'Auxerrois.

The church of Saint-Germain-l'Auxerrois is a composite building which, despite additions at different periods, retains a remarkable unity. The lower half of the bell-tower, set into the south aisles of the choir, dates back to the first half of the twelfth century; the portal, the choir and its first aisle were built in the first half of the thireenth century, whilst the chapel of the Virgin appears to be late thirteenth century. The building was furthermore almost entirely rebuilt in the fourteenth century. Then it was that the transept, nave and its aisles were built. The building's plan, with an interior volume of marvellous simplicity, is particularly successful. The concept of the bay has been defined anew. The window sills reach right down to the extrados of the great arcades; the wall is relieved by great openings with window tracery that dances like flames. A Burgundian-style porch, built by Jean Gaussel between 1433 and 1439, breaks the original vertical sweep of the facade with its horizontal lines.
Gothic statuary flourished till the beginning of the sixteenth century. Little has survived the ruthless destruction of the Revolution and the nineteenth century. Nevertheless Saint-Germain-l'Auxerrois still boasts an astonishing Marie L'Egyptienne, originally in the porch but now safe inside the church. This statue of Mary reflects traditional iconography: her clothes in tatters, the upper half of her body is hidden by her magnificent hair which flows to her knees. She holds the three loaves of bread which enabled her to survive sixty years in the desert. The light glides over the different surfaces of the statue to admirable effect. The delicate relief of the face with its bare, pensive brow contrasts with the lower half of her body which is heavy. The landscape at the saint's feet indicates that the work dates from around 1500.

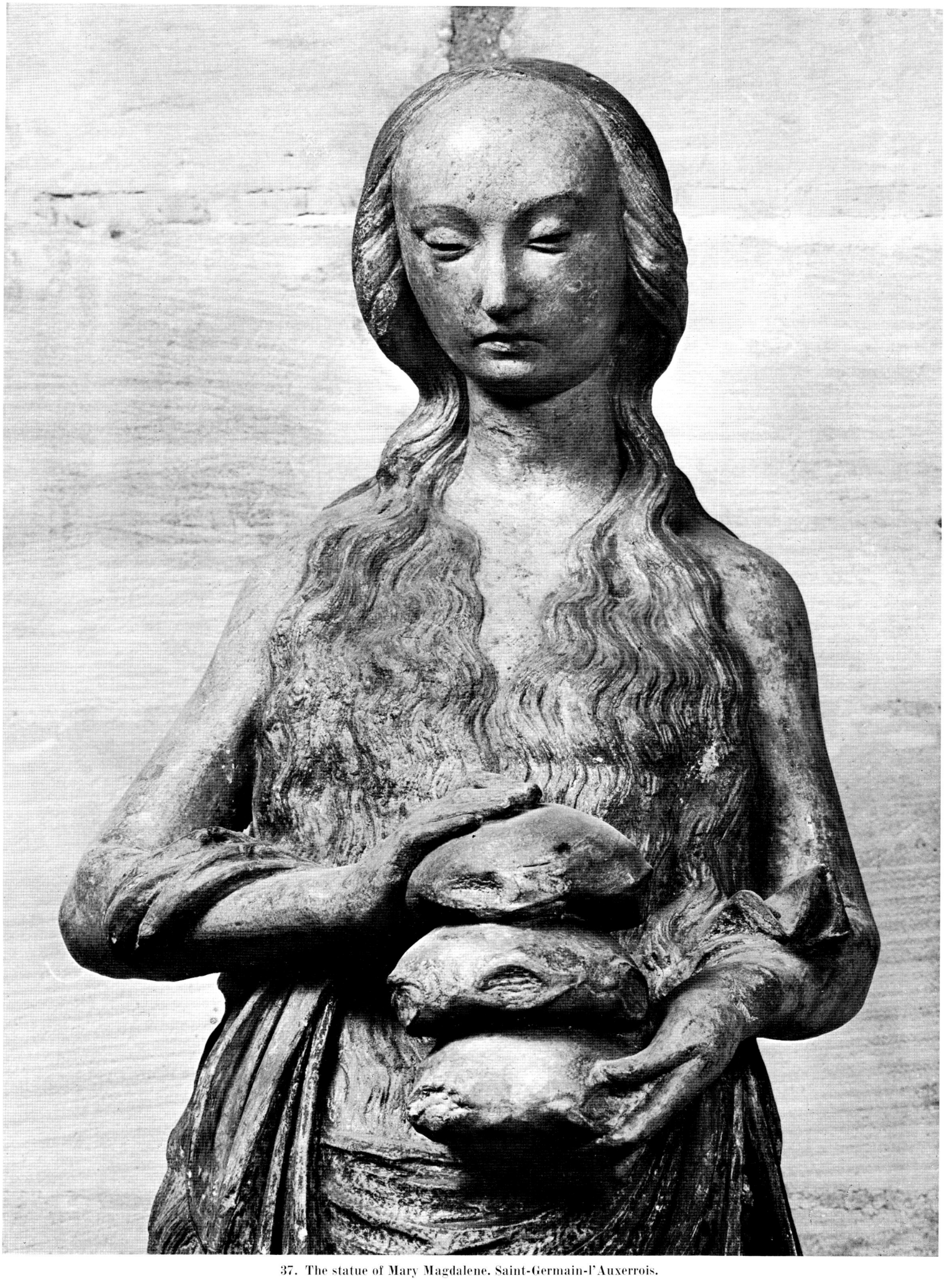

37. The statue of Mary Magdalene. Saint-Germain-l'Auxerrois.

38. Saint-Séverin.

The architecture of Saint-Séverin has suffered the consequences of population growth in its parish. It had to be constantly enlarged to accomodate the swelling tide of the faithful. The result is a picturesque building in which the different stages of building work are jumbled together in rather uncertain harmony. In the first third of the thirteenth century, the church's nave had eight bays and ended in the east with flat apse. At that time the bell-tower on the north-west corner served as entrance. In the middle of the fourteenth century, a way had to be found of enlarging the church on the open land towards the south. A second aisle was added at this point. Building work was then resumed in the middle of the following century. The five east bays of the nave were built after 1458, as were the two north aisles and the arches of the first south aisle. The bell-tower was then built between 1485 and 1487. In 1489 the choir was built on a piece of land where a former hotel had finally been demolished. It was completed in time for the ceremony in 1496. Subsequently between 1498 and 1520 a ring of chapels were merged with the aisles.

Despite the different styles of the nave, the whole achieves the unity intended by the fifteenth century architect. Indeed, when building the five east bays, he took pains to harmonise them with those of the thirteenth century, using the same plan and the same elevation, though adapting them to the style of his own period. The pillars are polygonal with sharp arrises, the triforium is pierced, the tracery of the bays is flamboyant and the Gothic arches penetrate the supports without being interrupted by the capitals. This architect's successor, who designed the apse, did not show equal respect; the discontinuance between the corners of the choir and the last bay on the right is brutal.

In the ambulatory, the Gothic arches supported by the famous central pillar seem to prolong a turning movement by virtue of the fine little columns surrounding the pillar. The effect gives an astonishing dynamism to the volume of the ambulatory circumscribed by two curves. The great opening surmounting the west door was cut and ornamented during the same period.

38. Saint-Séverin. The ambulatory and the central pillar.

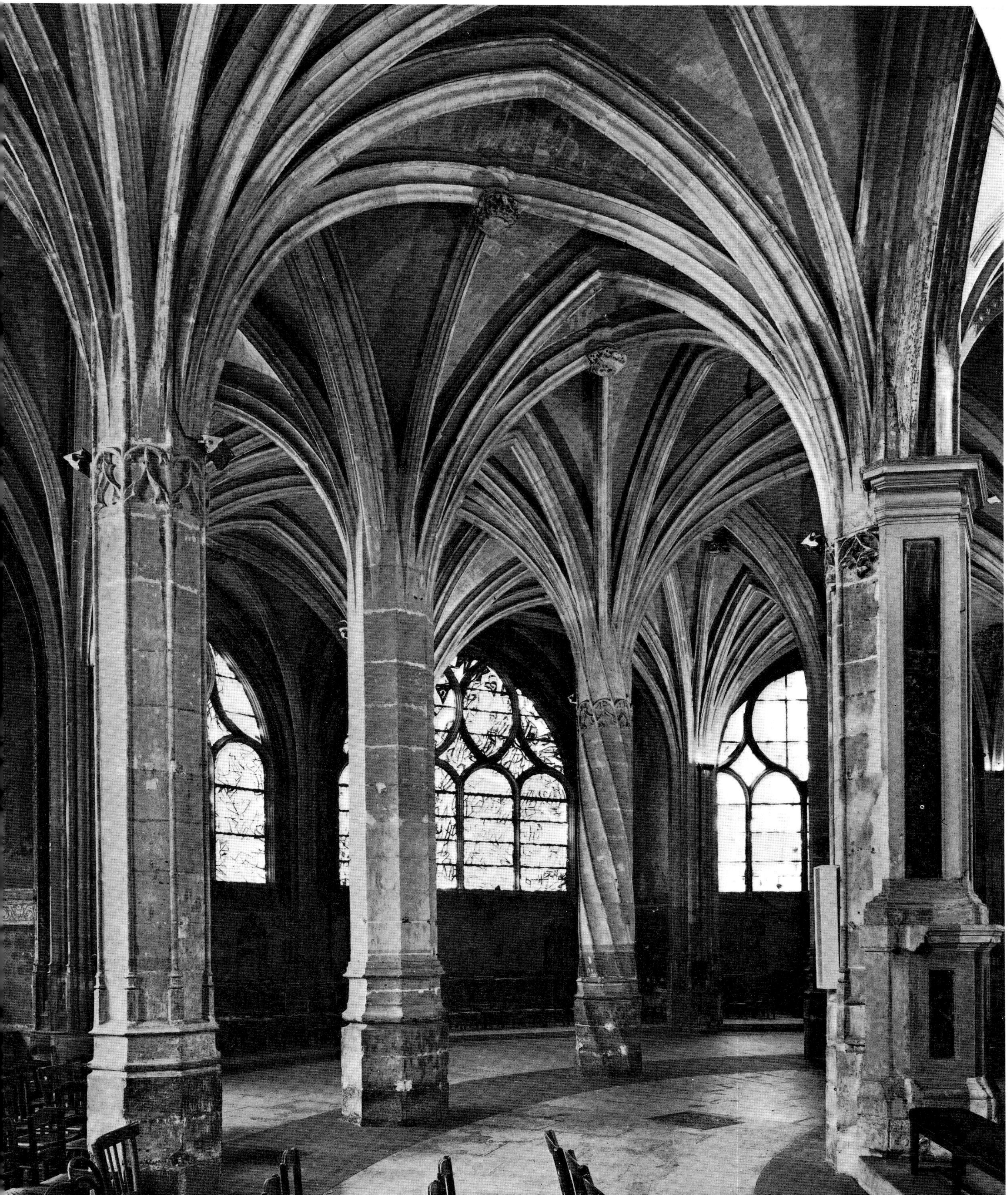

39. The portal of the Hôtel de Clisson.

The end of the forteenth century saw the blossoming of civil architecture. The impetus given by Charles V was taken up by the great lords of the period who vied with each other in building their private residences or hotels. In 1371 the future High Constable of Clisson set about building a hotel in the Marais, a quarter of Paris made fashionable by Charles V. The entrance, flanked by pepper-pot turrets, still exists today. The fortress-like style which these late fourteenth century residences still kept, is even more marked in the tower which Jean sans Peur added to the Hôtel de Bourgogne (20, Rue Etienne-Marcel) at the beginning of the fifteenth century.

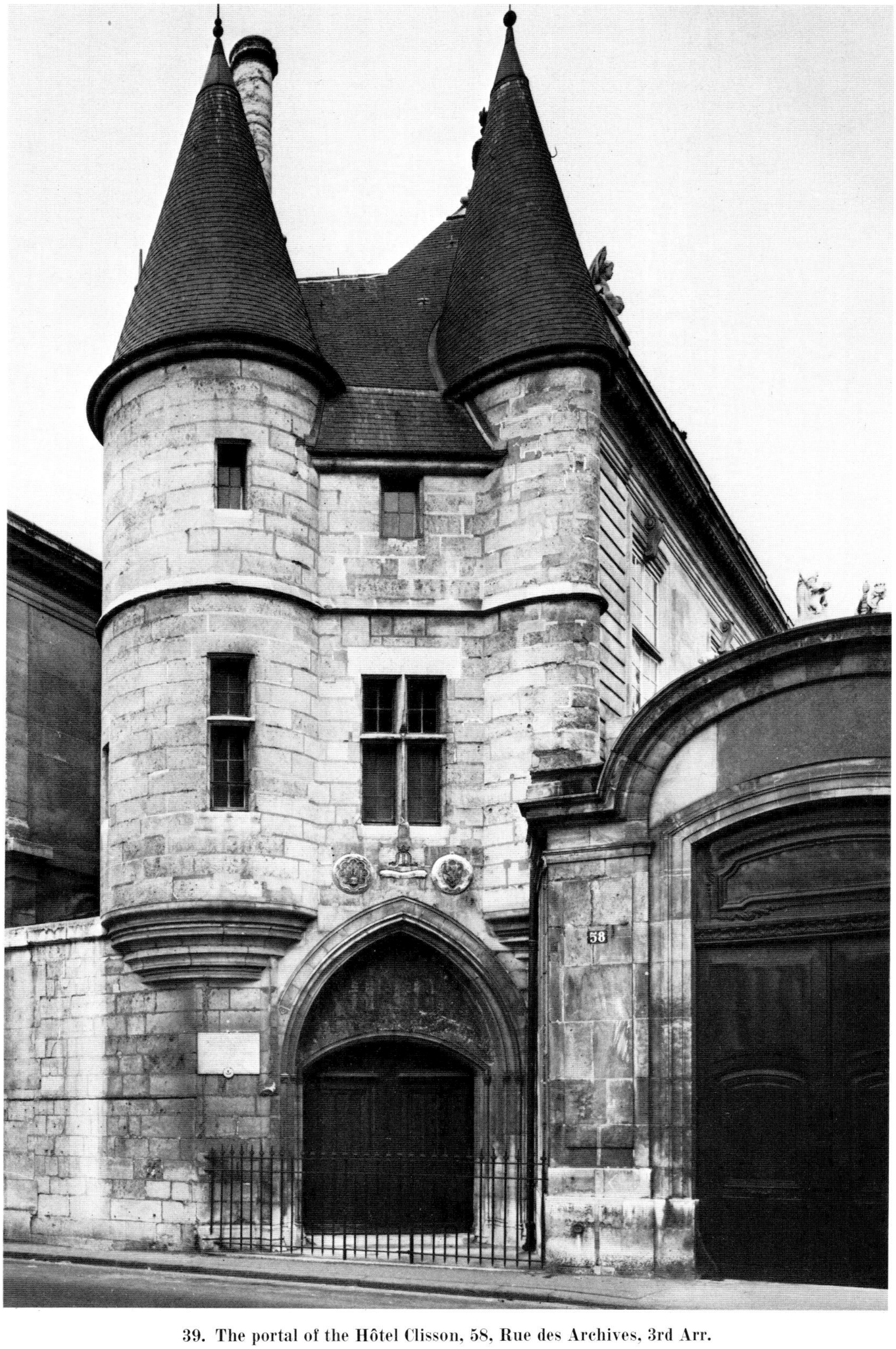

39. The portal of the Hôtel Clisson, 58, Rue des Archives, 3rd Arr.

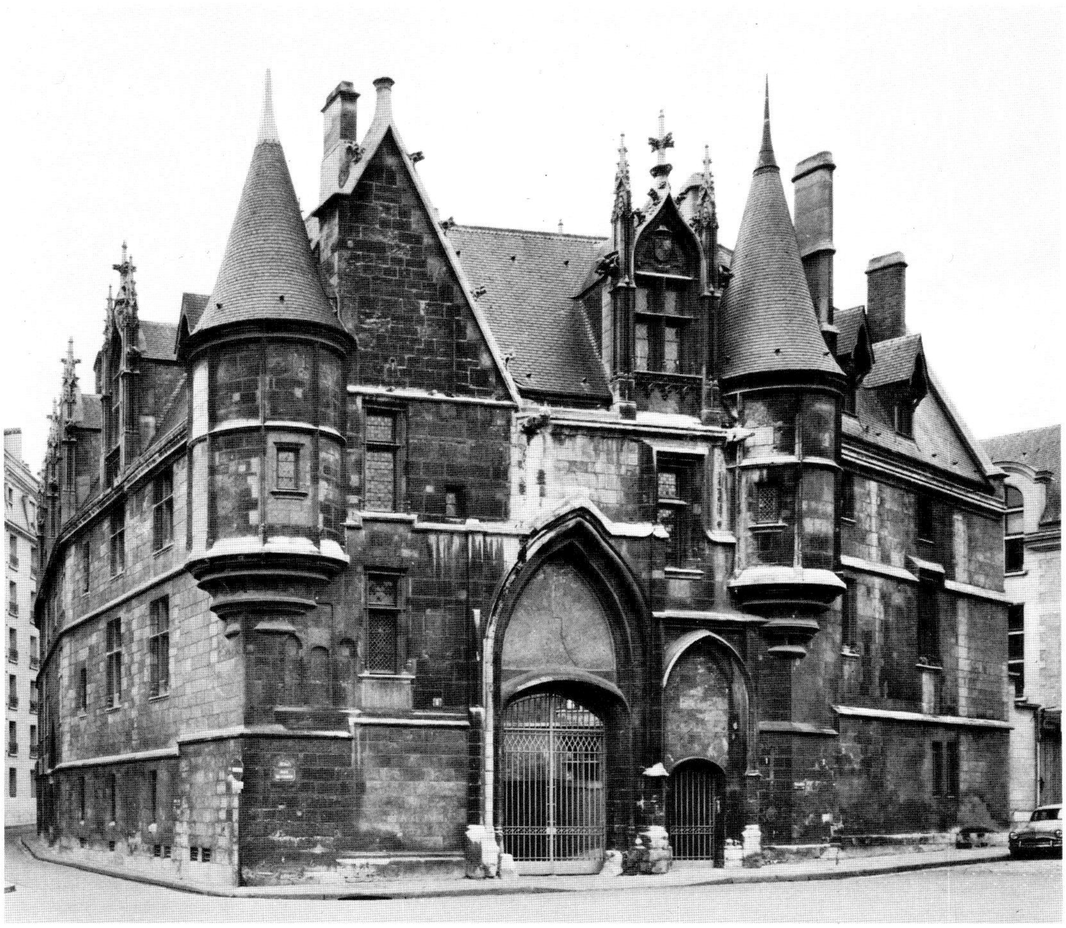

40

40. The Hôtel de Sens.

Paris still has two beautiful hotels dating from the end of the Middle Ages, one on each bank of the Seine: the hotel of the archbishops of Sens and that of the abbots of Cluny. At that time the diocese of Paris depended on the archdiocese of Sens whose archbishops, for this reason, had a residence in the capital. From 1475 on, it was entirely rebuilt. The building, polygonal on the exterior, still retains a severe military look with its three corner towers, two of them watch-towers guarding the coach gate and the entrance for pedestrians. The entrance has a flattened porch covered by a flamboyant arch. The courtyard within is surrounded by buildings, arranged with no great regularity. It is dominated by a square tower in the southwest corner. This has one rounded side and holds the spiral staircase.

41 and 42. The Hôtel de Cluny.

The abbots of the powerful Burgundian abbey of Cluny had a pied-à-terre in Paris from the thirteenth century. It was rebuilt in accordance with the style of the times by the ostentatious Jacques d'Amboise (1485-1510), brother of the cardinal. Protected from the road by a crenellated wall surrounding the courtyard, the hotel has three main buildings at right angles. The central building is cut by a projecting polygonal tower which holds the staircase. Another staircase has been fitted into a small prominence in the angle between the main building and the east wing; there is also a third one in the west wing. This wing, which backs on the Gallo-Roman baths also has a gallery with four great arcades on the ground floor. Its decorative effect is flamboyant and highly sophisticated, with its four-centered arches adorned with sculpted kale and pinnacles emphasizing the vertical divisions of the bays. The horizontal, already stressed in this facade with its double string-course broken only by the vertical lines of the uprights, dominates the north and east wings completely. Inside, the chapel with its flamboyant vaulting has kept all its original beauty. The thrust of the arches is taken by an astonishing polygonal pillar whose lightness adds to the beauty of the volume.

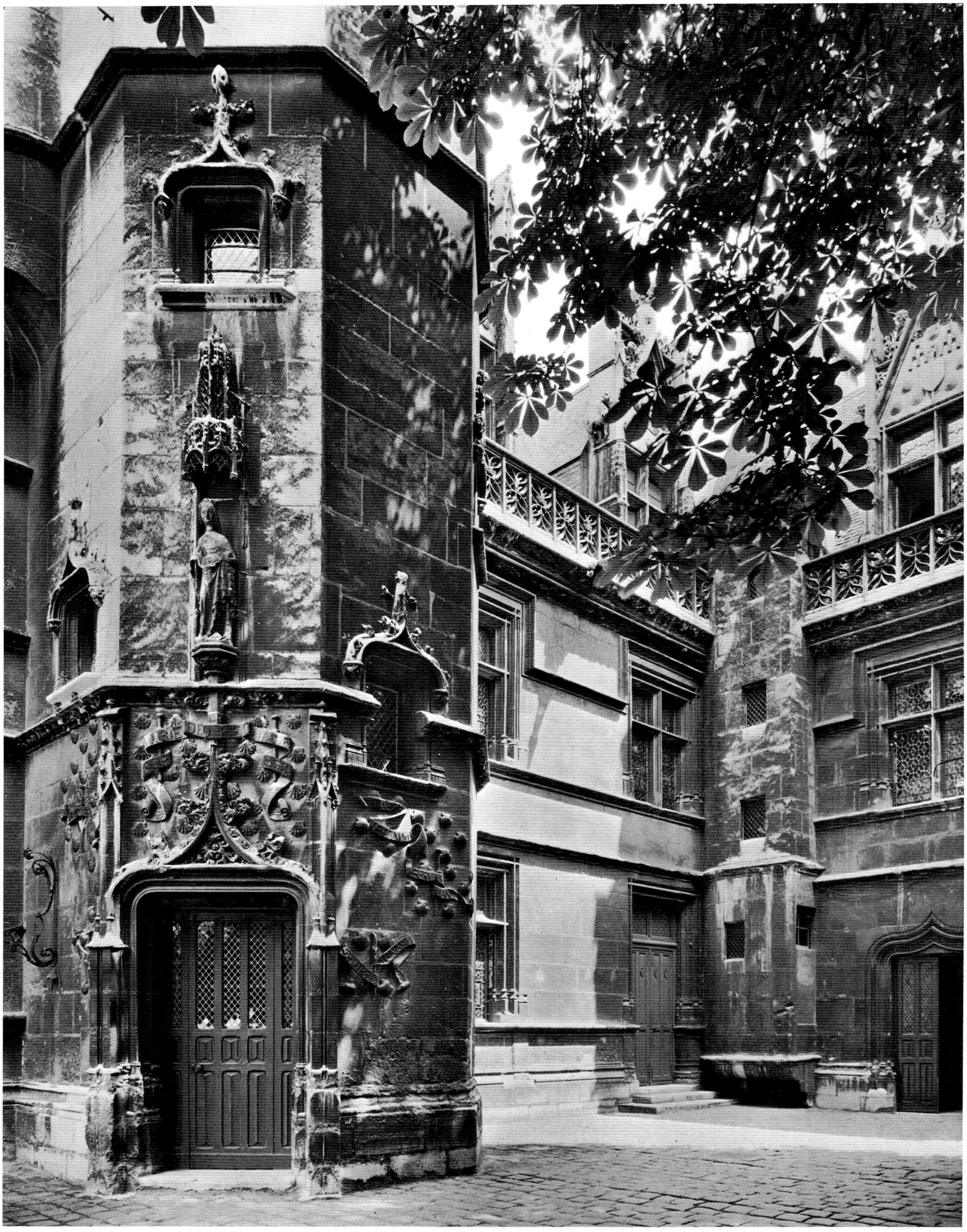

41. The Hôtel of the Abbots of Cluny. The staircase tower on the south wing.

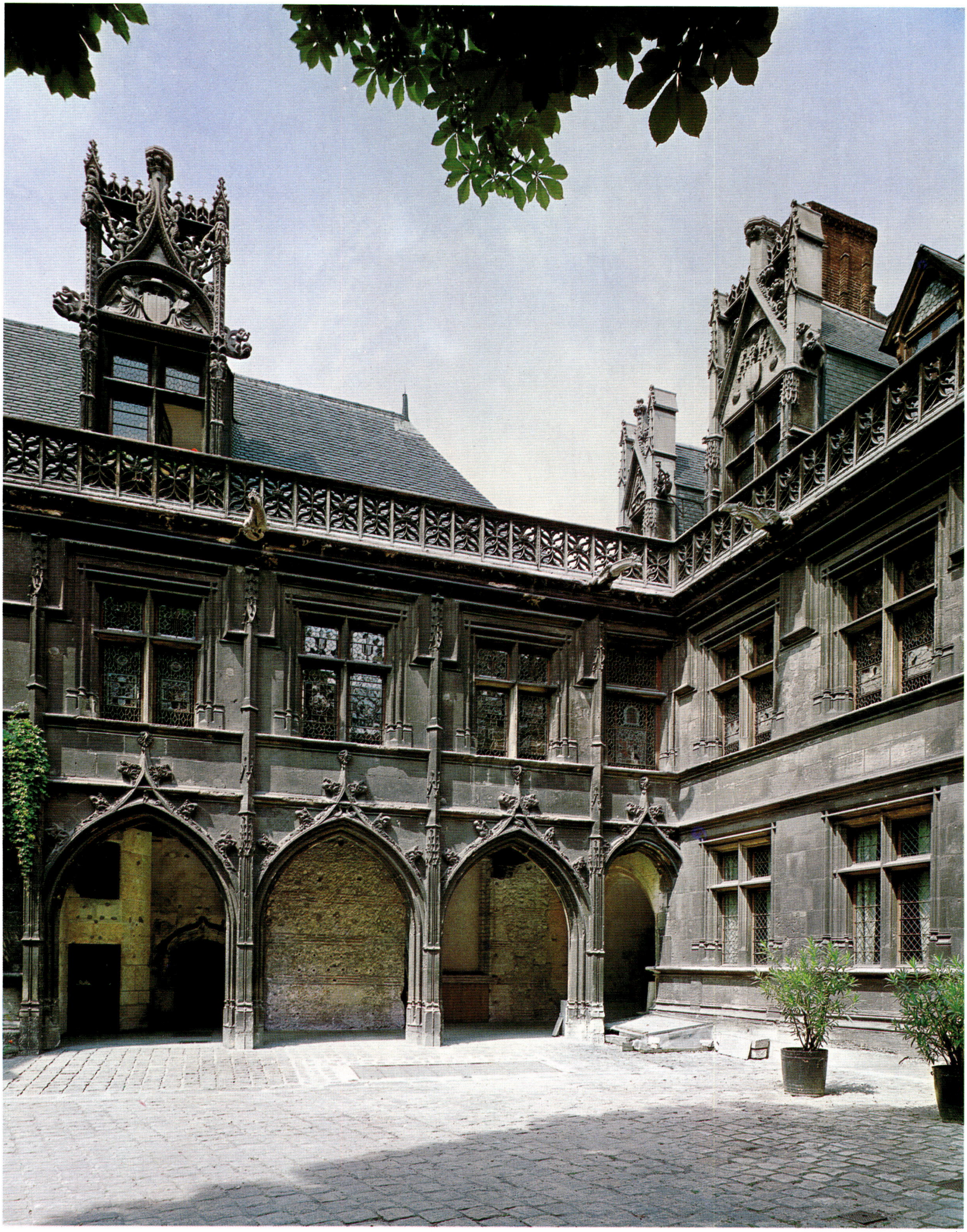

42. The Hôtel of the Abbots of Cluny. The facade on the courtyard.

43. Saint-Gervais-Saint-Protais.

At Saint-Gervais-Saint-Protais building work began in 1494, to a plan which took nearly a century to complete. During the first stage, the choir was built as well as the apse with aisles and chapels and the last three chapels to the south (1494-1578). The nave was built between 1600 and 1620. The rhythm of the bays is strongly emphasized by the ascending supports which take the thrust of the vaults. A string-course separating the window sills from the great arcades creates a horizontal line which in no way breaks the soaring lines of the bays. The wall has been reduced to its most simple expression since the splays of the high windows come right down to the extrados of the great arcades. These in turn rise to a great height, thus integrating the volume of the aisles magnificently. The very height of the bays means that no part of the building is left in shadow and the interior volume is unified by the light. By way of contrast, a certain clumsiness can be detected in the east of the building where the beams come down so low that they hide the star vault. On the exterior, the building's masses are powerfully articulated beneath an apse of admirable design. At the apse, the long, slightly corrugated buttresses alternate with the roofs of the chapels. The picturesque has been banished in favour of a monumental effect which does not square with the usual concept of flamboyant architecture.

The facade—its first stone was laid in 1616—is of regular composition and conceals the gable of the nave. Whilst following Italian models (the facade of the Gesù by Giacomo della Porta and many others), the architects of the time were still faithful to the vertical spirit and triangular composition which characterised Gothic architecture in France; they were also faithful to the classicism of Philibert de l'Orme (the avant-corps of Anet). It would seem that tradition is right in ascribing this church to Salomon de Brosse, since Clément Métezeau seems to have been involved only in the later stages. The work was prepared with the utmost care, including the making of a big wooden model (which still exists). The portal, built between 1616 and 1621 by the mason Claude Monnard, was immediately hailed as a masterpiece.

43. Saint-Gervais-Saint-Protais. The apse.

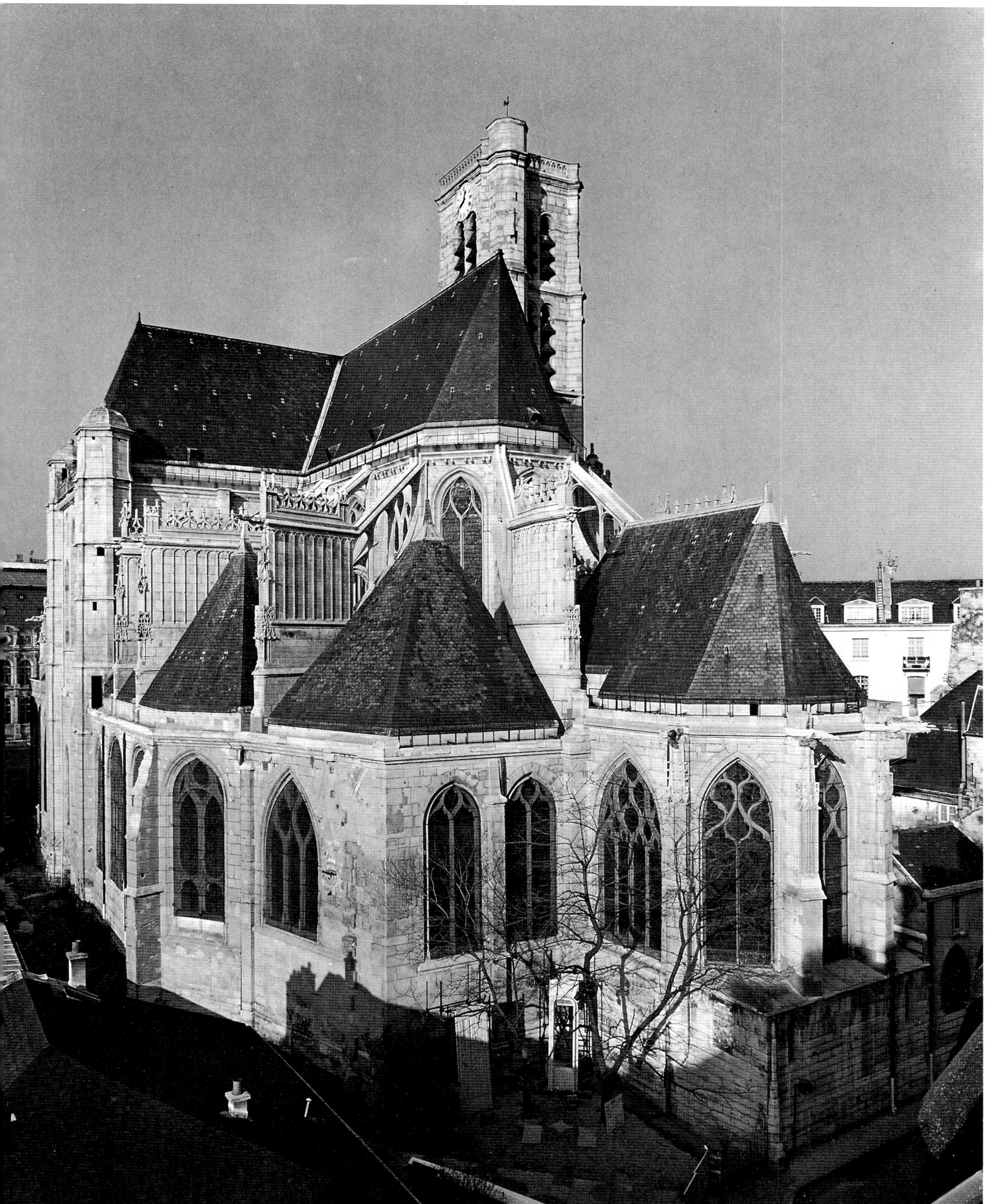

88

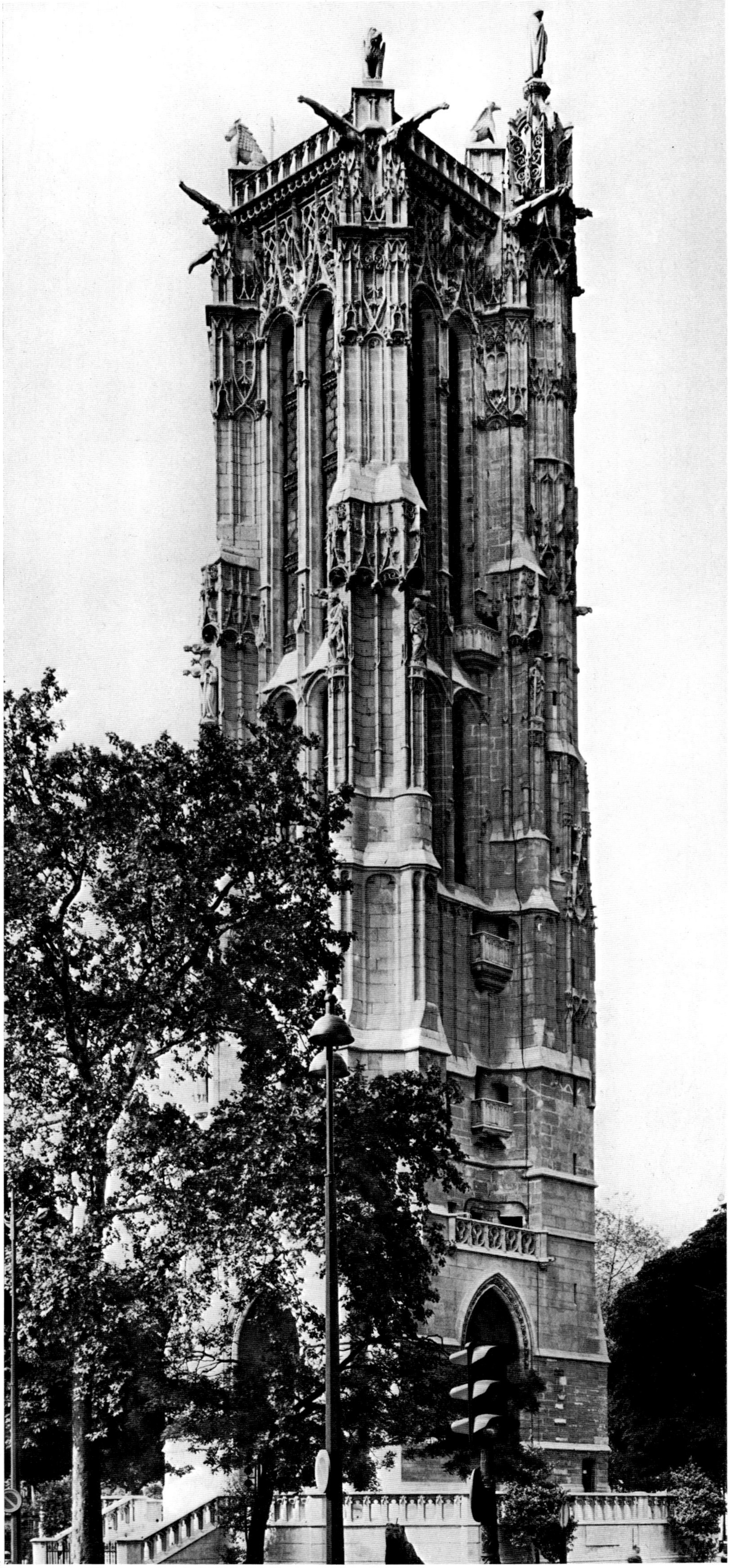

44

44. The Tour Saint-Jacques.

Buildings no earlier than the sixteenth century provide ample examples of late Gothic. Today the Tour Saint-Jacques is set apart in a square of little character. The former bell-tower of the church of Saint-Jacques-de-la-Boucherie demolished in 1797, the Tour Saint-Jacques once sheltered a rich, flamboyant portal at its base, no doubt built in the same period (1508-1512). The architect Jehan de Felin, who later worked at Saint-Aspais in Melun, for the first time took the trouble to integrate the corner buttresses into a harmonious whole. Square at the base, these buttresses become round as they rise up and disappear behind the decorative blind arcades and shallow canopies, embellished in exuberant style.

45 and 46. Saint-Eustache.

Saint-Eustache is the largest Renaissance church in France. In the Paris of those times, long attached to the Gothic style of building, it appeared in fact as a manifesto of the new art. Although in plan and structure, in the design of the bays, vaulting and portals, it remains entirely Gothic, its traditional ossature is unrecognisable by virtue of the new decorative conventions imported from Italy and with which its walls are adorned in profusion.

At first sight, the church can be disconcerting; its ample proportions suggest a cathedral, not a parish church. Saint-Eustache in fact rivals Notre-Dame (100 meters long and 43 meters wide) and its vaulting is the higher of the two (33. 40 meters). The great nave is most striking: certain elements (the great arcades, the superposed pillars and columns) are of colossal proportions. The latter are long and thin, thus not observing the cannons of antiquity, and piled up to reach the vaulting. This design, though strange, is of fascinating originality. The light flooding in through the great windows plays on the lateral planes, emphasizing each molding and creating a theatrical effect.

Saint-Eustache was completed at the beginning of the seventeenth century with a facade and two towers which were subsequently demoslished in 1688 for reasons of security. In 1754 Jean Hardouin-Mansart de Jouy, grandson of Jules Hardouin, was asked to build a new facade and a great square in front of the church to afford a clear view of it. Work on the facade was then continued by Moreaux-Desproux from 1772-1788 but the south tower was never built. At the apse the same architect put up the building which was to serve as vestry to the parish and as guard room to the market of Les Halles. On the Rue Montmartre he built the choir school and the chapel of ease.

44. The Tour Saint-Jacques.

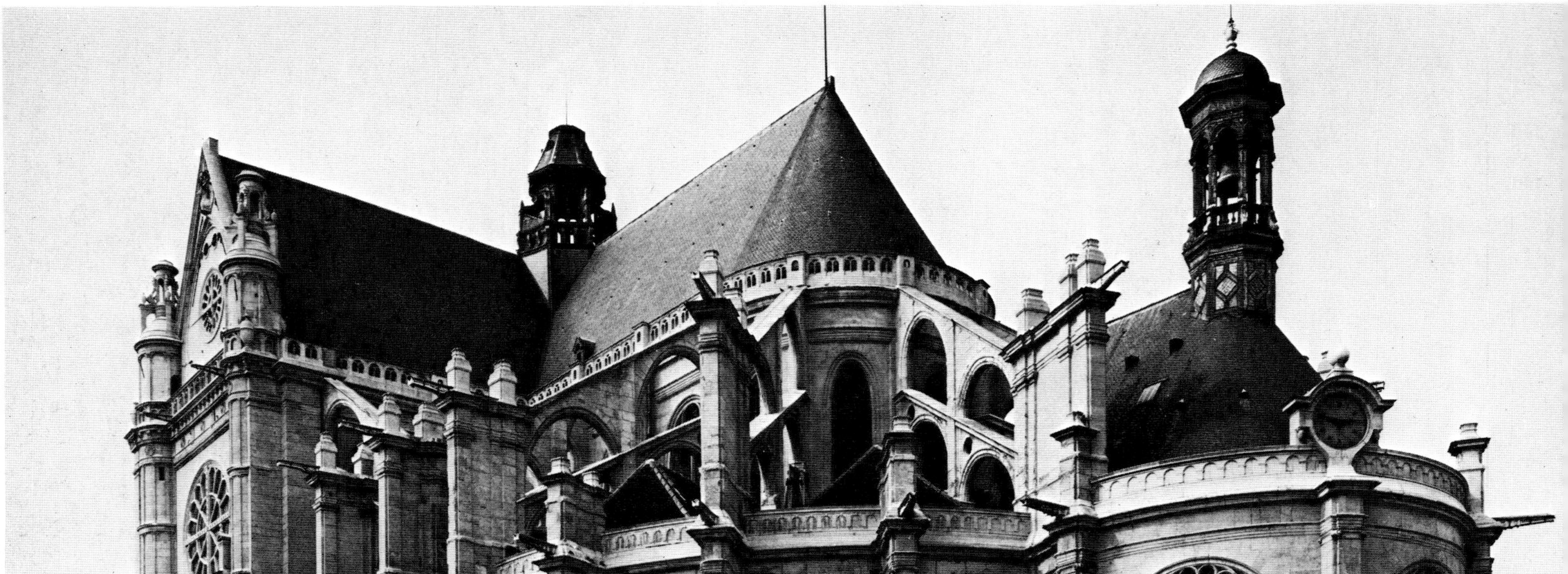

45. The apse of Saint-Eustache. At the end, the building used as a guard room, added under Louis XVI.

46. Saint-Eustache. The nave and the choir.

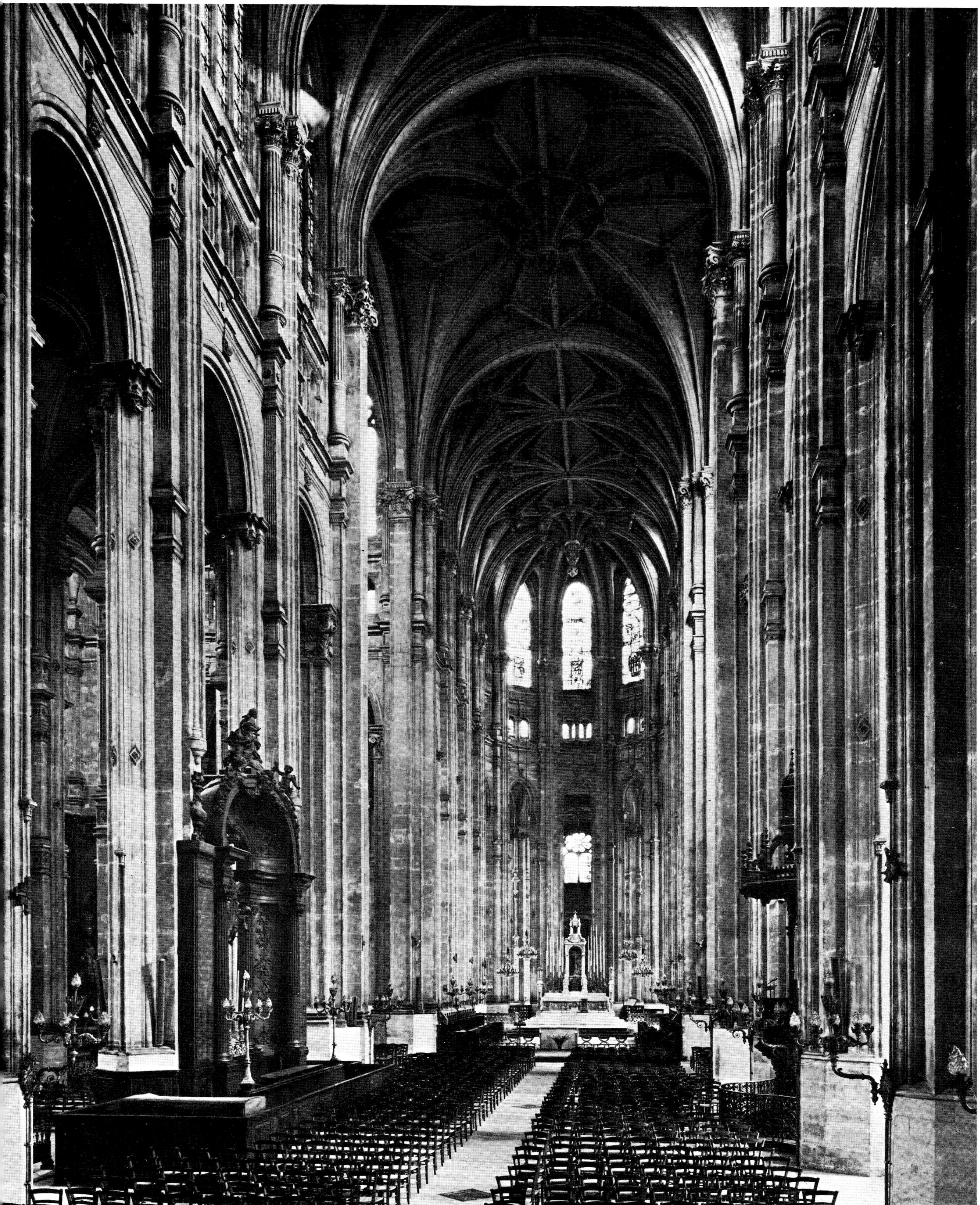

47 and 48. The Pont-Neuf and the Ile de la Cité.

Henri IV opened up the banks of the Seine for Paris. Previously, the embankments and the bridges had been covered with houses and one crossed the river without even realising it. Yet the Parisian Kings had always liked the Seine and the fact that the "Palais" was being built on the island by the river's edge bore testimony to the fact. It took the fourteenth and fifteenth century spells of residence in the Marais, far from the river and surrounded by increasingly polluted air, for the Valois to discover once again that vast panorama where the two arms of the river meet, embracing the greenery of the Jardin du Roi. The great stretches of sky and water, the massed silhouette of the city, standing out against the hills and the green of the nearby countryside, could hardly fail to impress the new residents of the Louvre. Indeed the king chose a pavilion by the river's edge as his quarters and the queens decided to have their apartments in the south wing; Catherine built the Petite Galerie to be nearer the Seine, and Henri IV built the Waterside Gallery for the same reason.

Meanwhile over on the left bank, the market town of Saint-Germain was spreading and its inhabitants were demanding a new bridge over to the other bank—one that would be nearer than the Pont Saint-Michel. Henri III chose the site: the tip of the Ile de la Cité, where the bridges over the river's two arms would meet (1577-1578). However building work was abandoned in 1584. Then in 1598, Henri IV ordered work to begin again, though he could not decide on a plan: should there be a terrace on the water, adorned perhaps with triumphal arches and pyramids as had been suggested to Henri III, or two rows of houses on the parapets? The former design was finally adopted and the Pont-Neuf was completed in 1606. To connect it with the streets on the left bank, the King had a long road built—the Rue Dauphine—and two smaller ones, the Rue Christine and the Rue d'Anjou (de Nesle), named after his children. Using plans drawn up for Henri III, he also built at the tip of the island a triangular square and two embankments lined by buildings of uniform design. In some ways the charming houses overlooking the bridge are the Propylaea of Henri IV's Paris. The houses in the Place Dauphine, meanwhile, and those on the Quai de l'Horloge and the Quai des Orfèvres have suffered at the hands of succeeding generations. There has recently been an attempt to restore those parts of the facades still remaining from the 1607 design. To recreate the closed triangle, however, now only to be seen in old drawings, one must resort to imagination. The east side of this was destroyed for the most absurd reasons—sacrificed to the new solitary facade of the Palais. The equestrian statue of Henri IV on the bridge is not the original, promised by Marie de Medici in 1605, erected in 1614 and taken down in 1792. The one we see today is a good reconstruction by Lemot (1818).

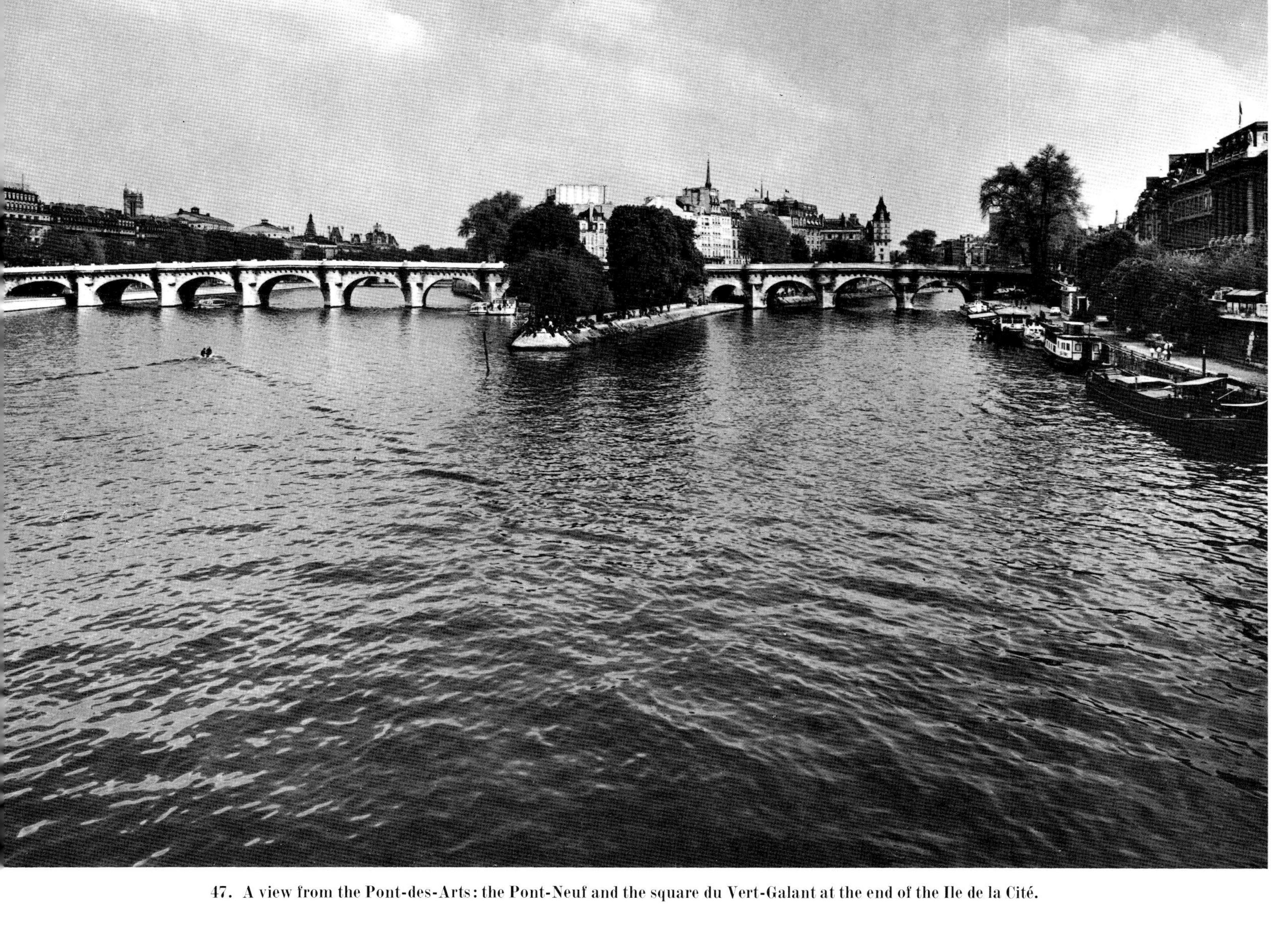

47. A view from the Pont-des-Arts: the Pont-Neuf and the square du Vert-Galant at the end of the Ile de la Cité.

48. The Pont-Neuf and its terrace;
the statue of Henri IV, opposite the houses of the Place Dauphine.

94

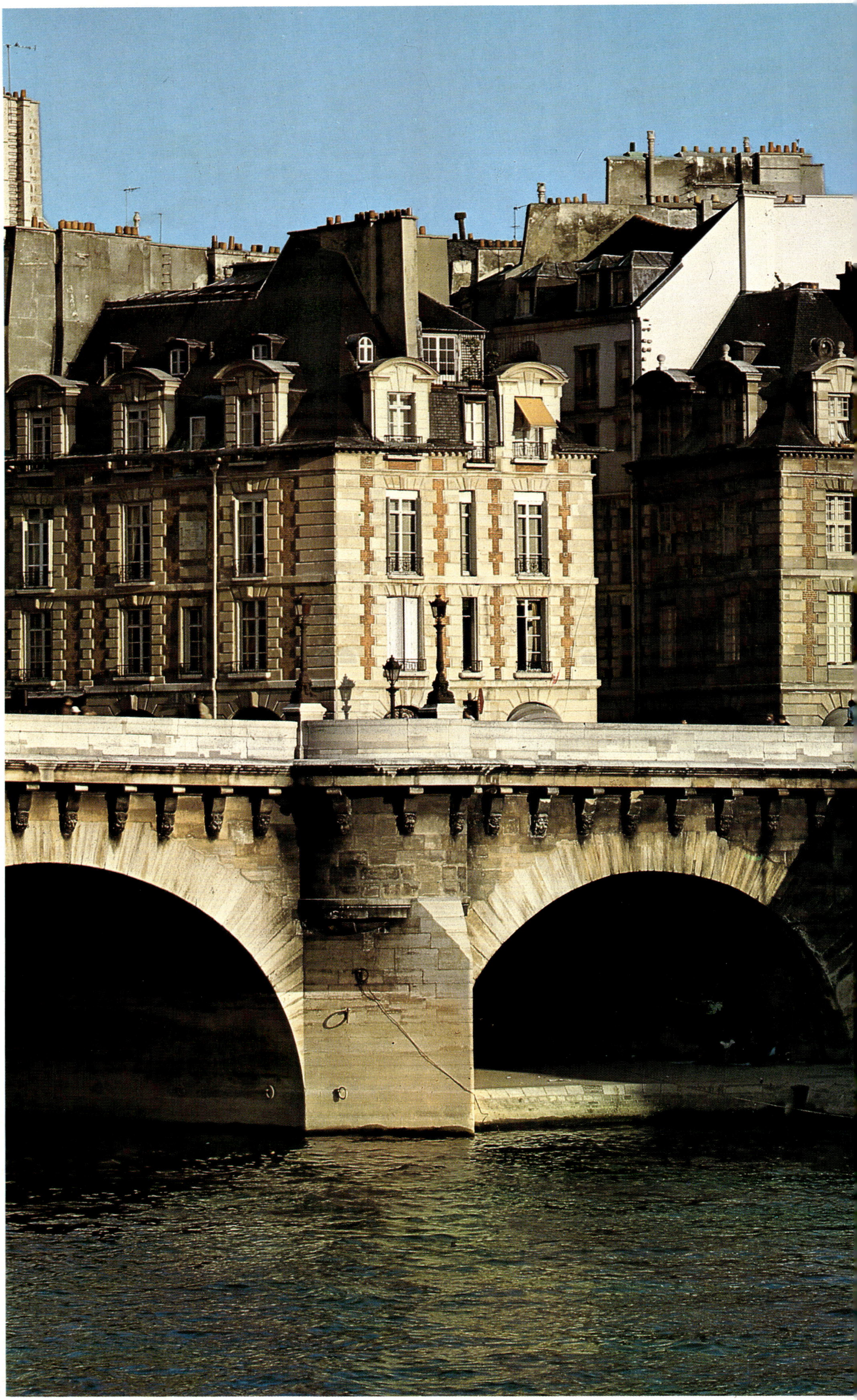

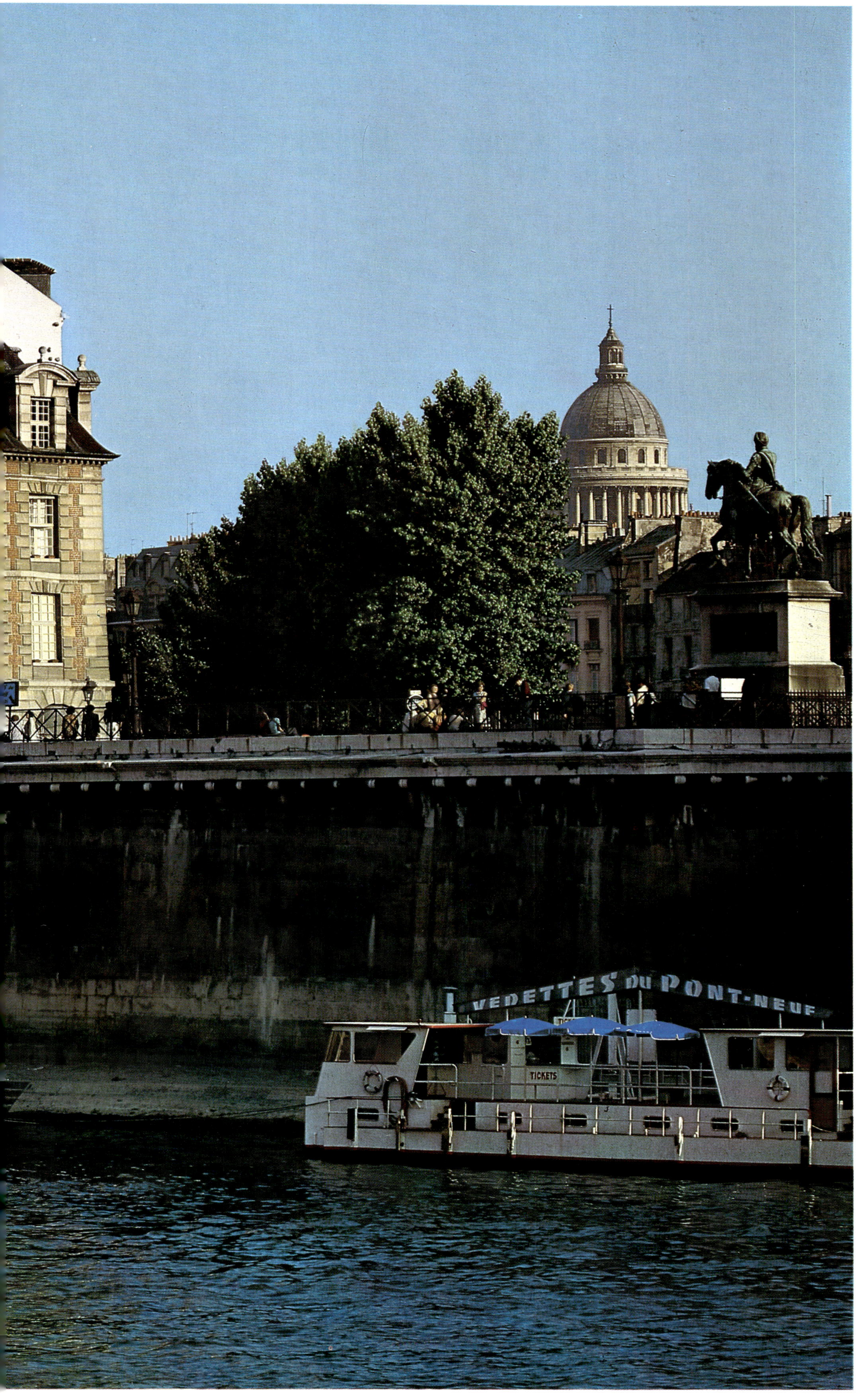
VEDETTES DU PONT-NEUF
TICKETS

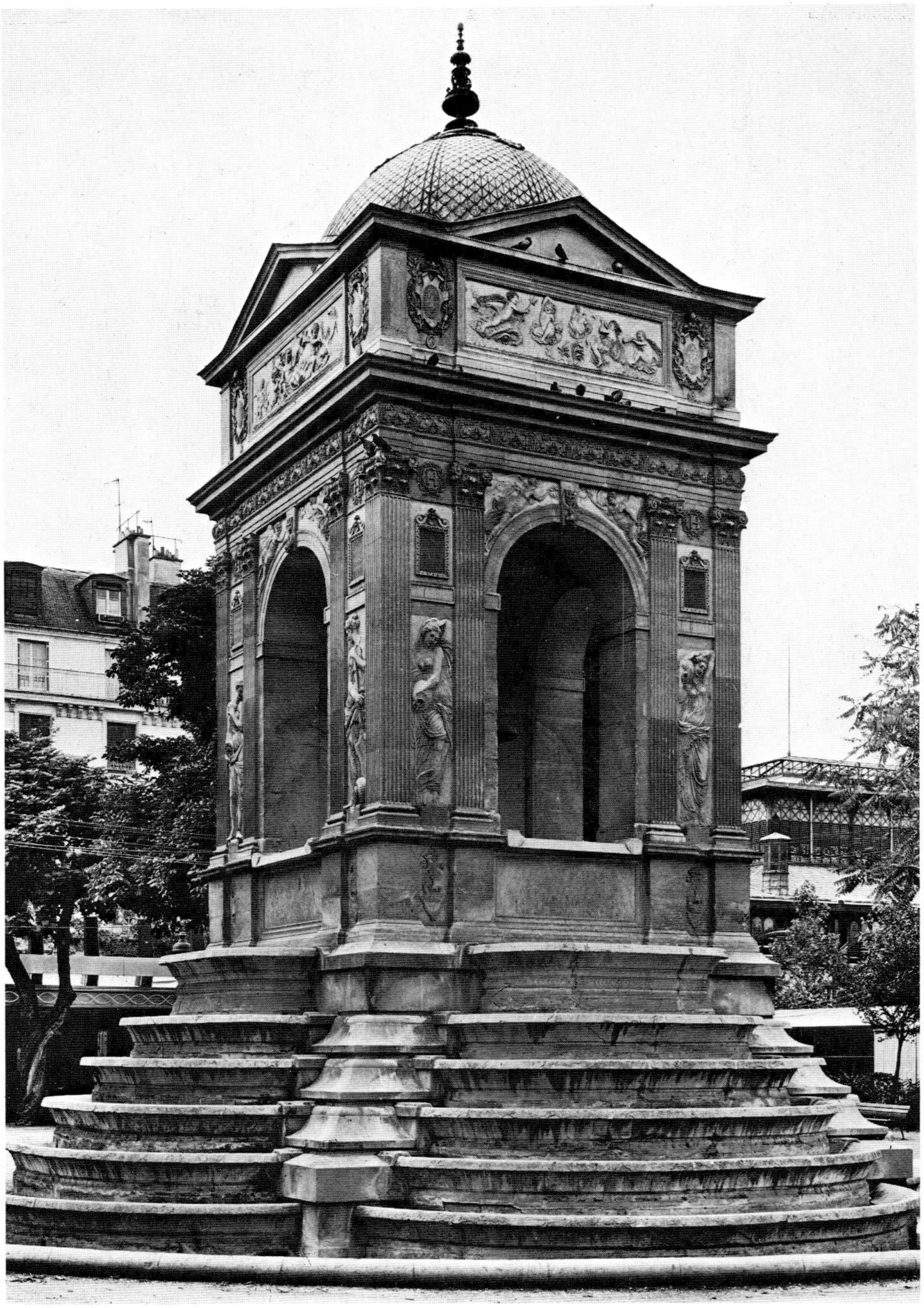

49

49 to 51. The Fountain of the Innocents.

On viewing the edifice which now adorns the Square des Innocents, it is difficult to imagine the fountain which once stood at the corner of the Rue Saint-Denis and the Rue aux Fers (the present Rue Berger). Built between 1547 and 1549 to replace a fountain dating from the time of Philippe Auguste, it supplied the inhabitants of the old Halles quarter with water. Situated on the triumphal route taken by the sovereign when he entered his city, it had three arcades of galleries used by the privileged spectators of the royal "entrances". Fountains and triumphal arches built for these occasions were always of perishable material. But the Fontaine des Innocents was an exception in that it was built to last. A temple dedicated to the water divinities, first used when Henri II entered the city in 1549. The decorations by Jean Goujon, were completed in 1550. Between the pilasters, the water nymphs pour the water gracefully from their urns. The bas reliefs of the crown and the base (the latter in the Louvre) portray sea gods lying on shells or astride sea monsters. When the decision was taken to deconsecrate the Cimetière des Innocents (cemetery) and to demolish the old church of the same name, the archeologist Quatremère de Quincy was the only one to request that the fountain be saved. It was rebuilt in quadrangular form in the center of the Marché des Innocents. Pajou completed the monument with sculptures in imitation sixteenth century style.

50 and 51. Two of the five nymphs of the Fountain of the Innocents sculpted by Jean Goujon.

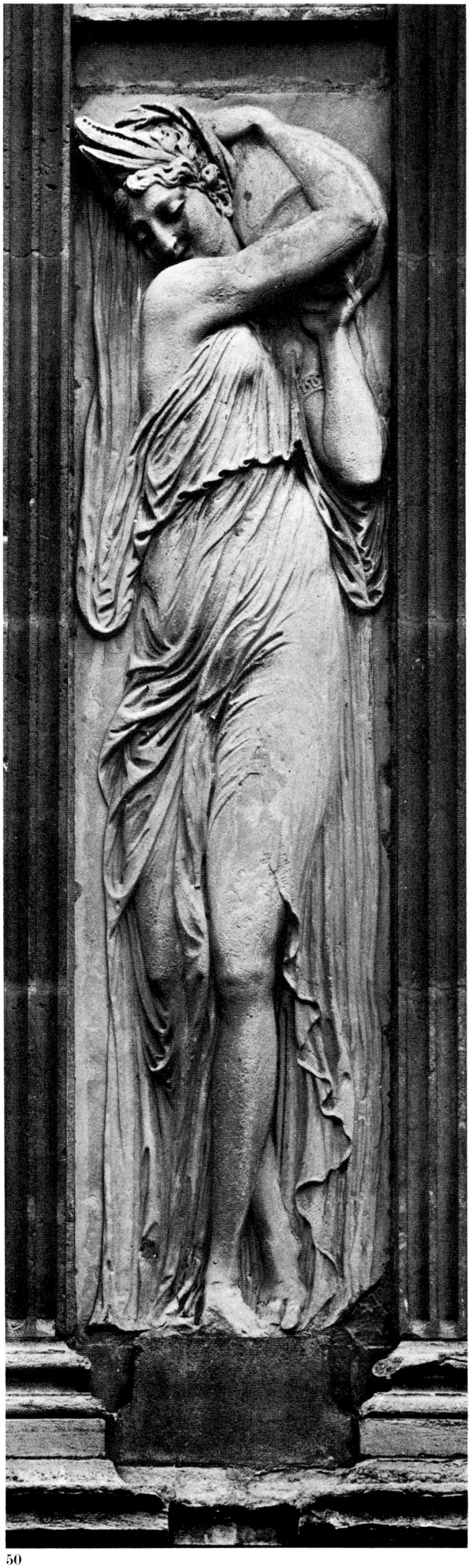
50

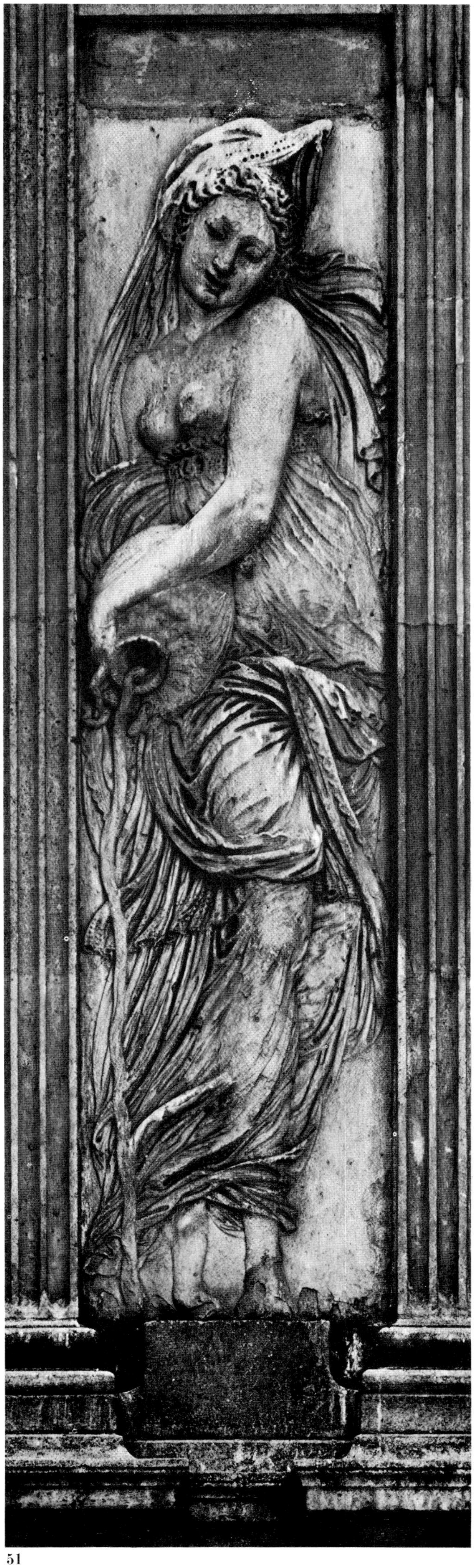
51

52. The Place des Vosges.

The Place Royale, Henri IV's famous creation, renamed the Place des Vosges in 1800, remains to this day the same enclosed area of calm. It is still a place to live and stroll in. Its colored facades betray no haughtiness in the simplicity of their irregular proportions, the little differences in ornamentation, the varying reds of the rough rendering of false brick. The pavilions stand side by side in friendly fashion on their sturdy feet, turning their faces to the sun's rays, which play on the archstones and the longitudinal lines, lengthening the shadows of the dormer windows on the great roofs.

In 1559, when Henri II died of the wound he received in the tournament of the Rue Saint-Antoine, it spelt the end for the Palais des Tournelles, old-fashioned, evil-smelling and cursed by destiny. The monarchy then finally took to the Louvre but kept the old site where a manufacture of silk, gold and silver cloth was then set up (1603) like the one in Milan. Next to the works a square was built (1605) of formal, regular design. This was a great novelty for Paris, accustomed as it was to narrow, noisy street junctions. The square was no doubt inspired by the plans for ideal towns drawn up in Italy, which also influenced the new towns of the Rhineland and Lorraine. When the unsuccessful cloth manufacture was closed down, the square then became a residential area because of the detached houses nearby, as well as a place for walks in the shelter of the arcades, and an arena for equestrian jousting. The central space, surrounded by wooden lists, was sanded and then inaugurated with the famous tournament of 1612. The houses were already built at the time.

The name of the architect remains unknown. One can only assume that the whole was designed under the guidance of a commission directed by Sully. This would have included the King's two architects, Louis Métezeau and Jacques II Androuet du Cerceau, and engineers like Claude Chastillon (who included an engraving of the square in his "Topographie françoise") as well as representatives of the City.

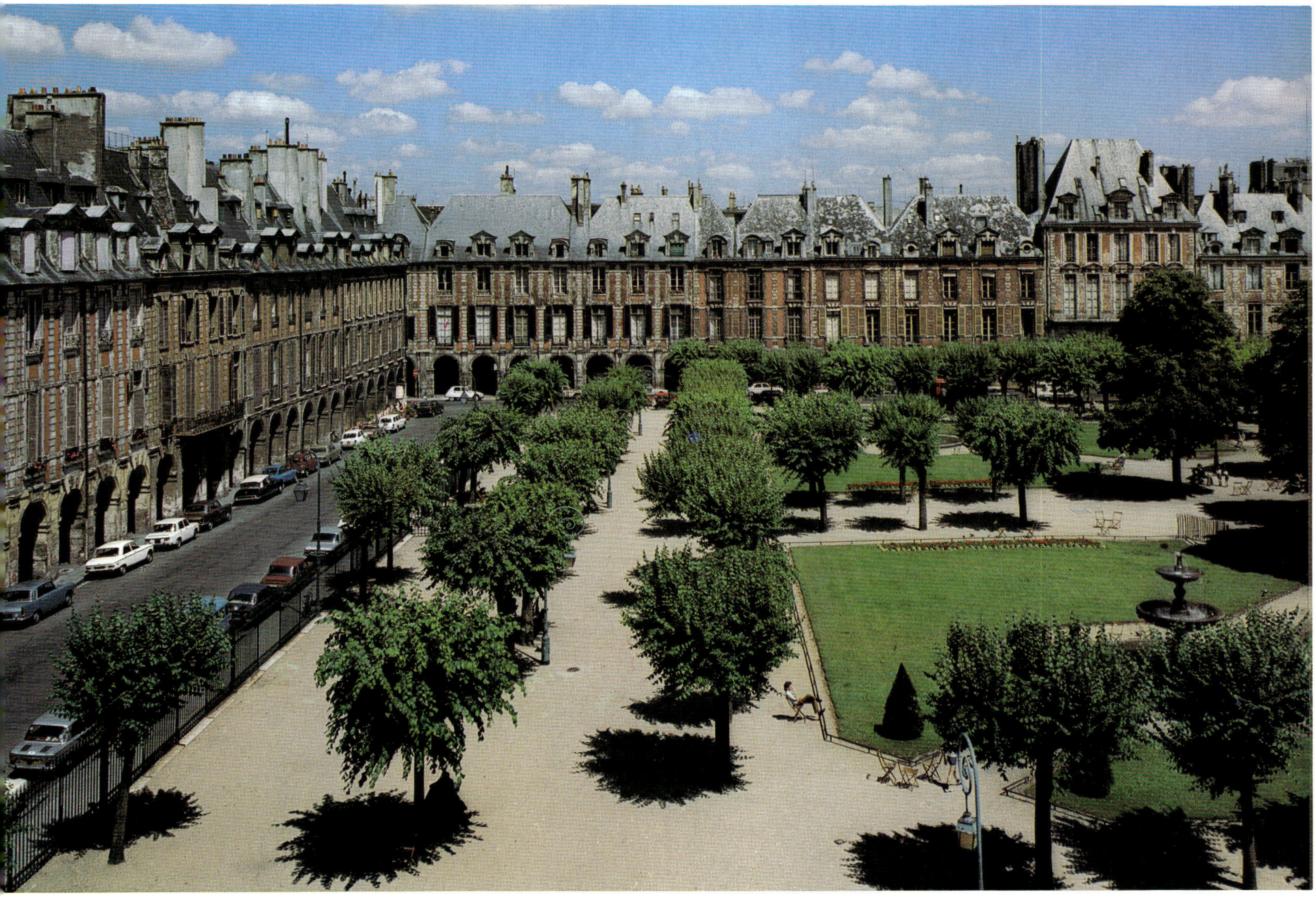

52. The Place des Vosges. In the background, to the right, the Pavillon de la Reine.

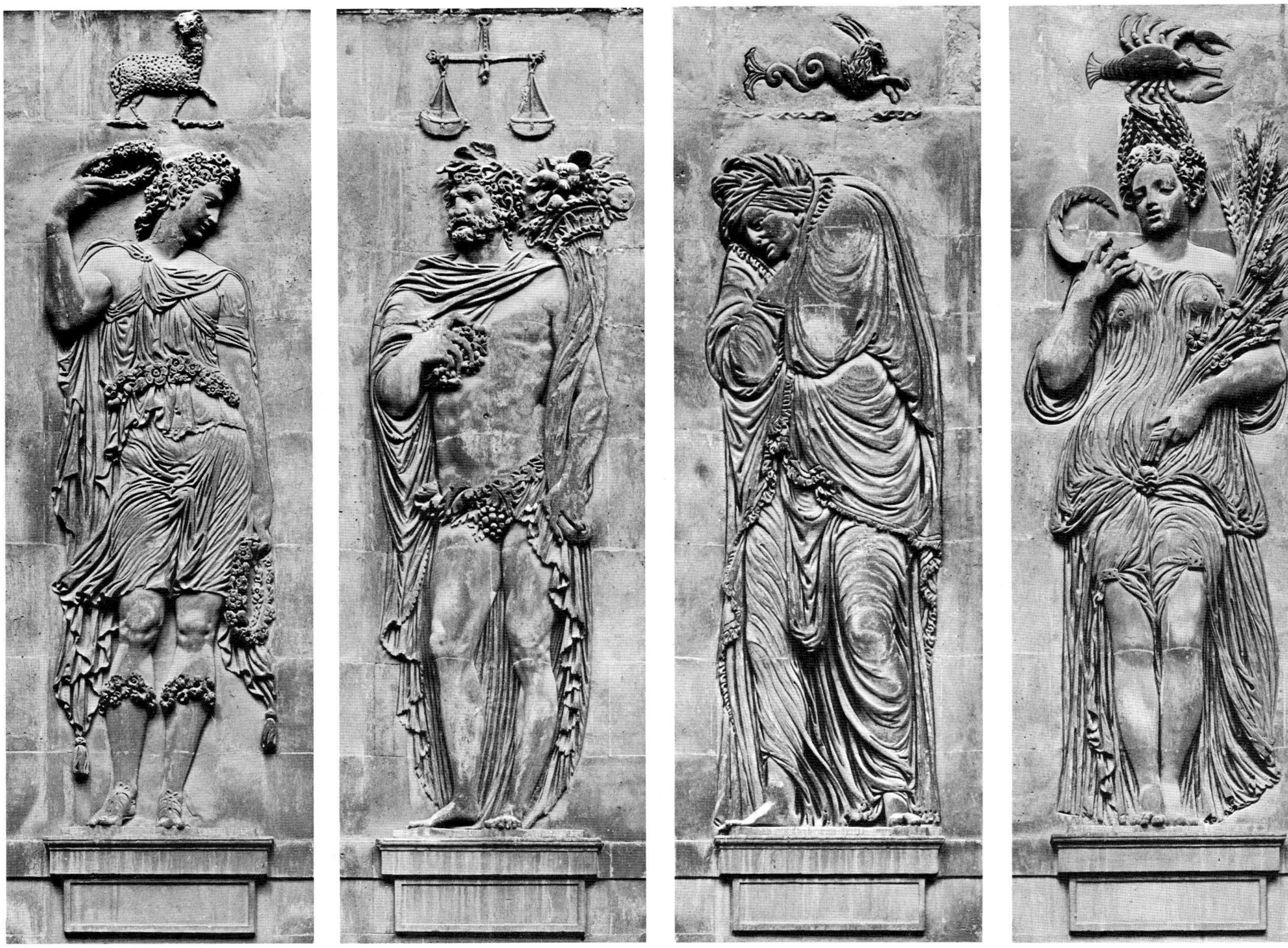

53

53. The Hôtel Carnavalet.

A magnificent private house of the sixteenth century still stands—the Hôtel Carnavalet. It was built by Jacques de Ligneris, High Court President in the Parliament of Paris, who represented the King at the first meeting of the Council of Trent. In 1545 he bought five plots of land when the domain belonging to the monks of Sainte-Catherine was divided up for sale. Three years later he commissioned the mason Nicolas Dupuis to construct a main building, flanked by two pavilions, one with a spiral staircase. The other main parts were built later, as were a low building between two pavilions, giving onto the street, and two other wings. The masterly design of the gate was attributed to Pierre Lescot by the historian Sauval in the eighteenth century. Despite the regularity of plan and openings, both new features in private town houses, and also despite the antique-style decoration, the design as a whole remains that of the traditional French residence.
It is not yet known who did the sculptures. Sauval only has one name to suggest, that of "maître Ponce" who sculpted the satyr masks in the crown of the arches. They were long thought to have been the work of Jean Goujon, though there is no evidence to this effect. However some of the pieces are of such high quality, for instance the figures on the back of the door, the spirits crowning the side doors and the lions and the figure of Abundance, overlooking the road, that Goujon's name inevitably springs to mind. The hotel belonged to Madame de Kernevenoy (Carnavalet is a distortion of the name) and was then altered several times before it became the home of the Marquise de Sévigné. Between 1660 and 1661 it was altered by François Mansart, who, whilst scrupulously respecting the work of his predecessor, added a building above the gate and transformed the wings and pavilions.

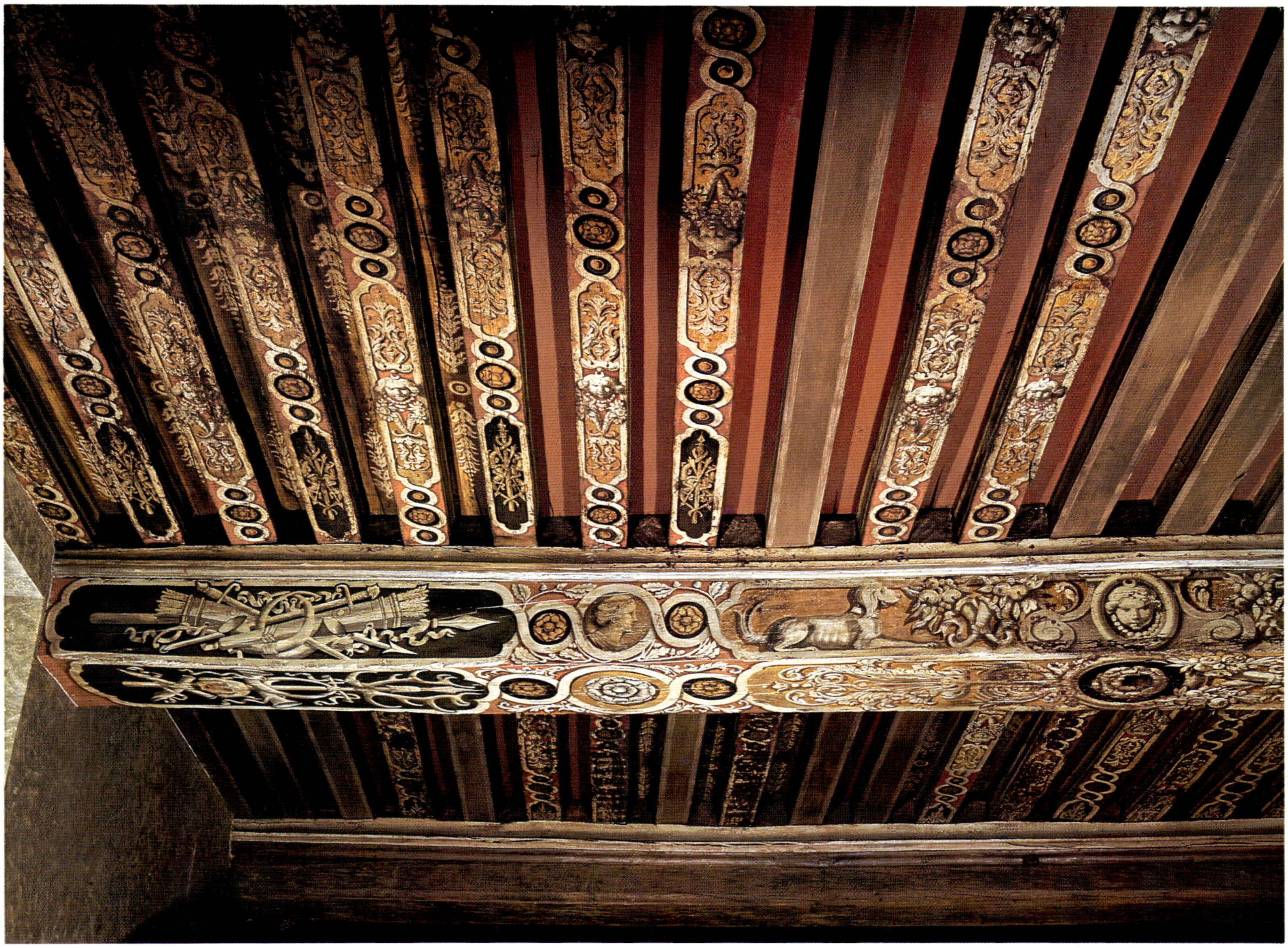

54

54. The Hôtel d'Angoulême.

Hôtels were still being built in the quarter of the domain of Sainte-Catherine in the second half of the sixteenth century. Several of them still remain, and recent restoration work has meant that we can now appreciate the style of the reigns of Charles IX and Henri III in Paris. One of the most monumental hotels was built in the Rue Pavée for Diane de France, the illegitimate daughter of Henri II, and widow of the field-marshal François de Montmorency. This hotel has been attributed to Baptiste Androuet du Cerceau, one of the du Cerceau family which became famous for its work in the Mannerist style of the end of the century (the Château de Verneuil and the Château de Charleval). In 1584 Baptiste Androuet du Cerceau, who left the country in 1585 and died around 1590, presented his plans for the transformation and extension of the existing residence bought by Diane. The inital plan does not seem to have been completed till 1611.
Since 1969 the hotel has housed the historical library of the City of Paris. The ceiling of the reading room has painted beams and joists, decorated with the weapons of Diana the huntress.

53. The Hôtel Carnavalet. The four Seasons, beneath the signs of the zodiac. Bas-reliefs decorating the piers of the main building.

54. The ceiling of the great hall of the Hôtel d'Angoulême, with the emblems of Diane de France, daughter of Henri II.

55. The Hôtel de Chalon-Luxembourg.

The main living quarters of the Hôtel de Chalon-Luxembourg are curiously composed of two identical buildings with their backs to one another between the courtyard and the garden. This lay-out suggests that under Henri IV an older building was in fact put to use again. Both buildings have their own slate roofs embellished with finials shaped like lead vases—some of the last ones still preserved in Paris. The building overlooking the garden has two little side pavilions, customary in the sixteenth century. The frames, molded tablets, dormer windows (shaped like a gendarme's hat) and the circular windows are all in stone, set off by the brick-work. The initials carved on the dormer windows indicate that the building dates back to 1608, and was commissioned by Antoine Le Fèvre de La Boderie and his wife Jeanne Le Prévost.

La Boderie was France's ambassador to London as well as being a poet. Among his relatives were two brothers who, towards the end of the sixteenth century, had written on the architectural correspondence between the terrestrial and celestial worlds. La Boderie welcomed his daughter Catherine and her husband Robert Arnauld d'Andilly to the Hôtel de Chalon-Luxembourg, and it was here that four of their thirteen famous children were born, amongst them Simon Arnauld de Pomponne. The splendid portal, adorned with the lion's muzzle, foreshadows those of the Visitation and the Invalides. The building into which the portal is let, was altered in 1667, but the portal itself most probably dates back to 1608, as does the original building.

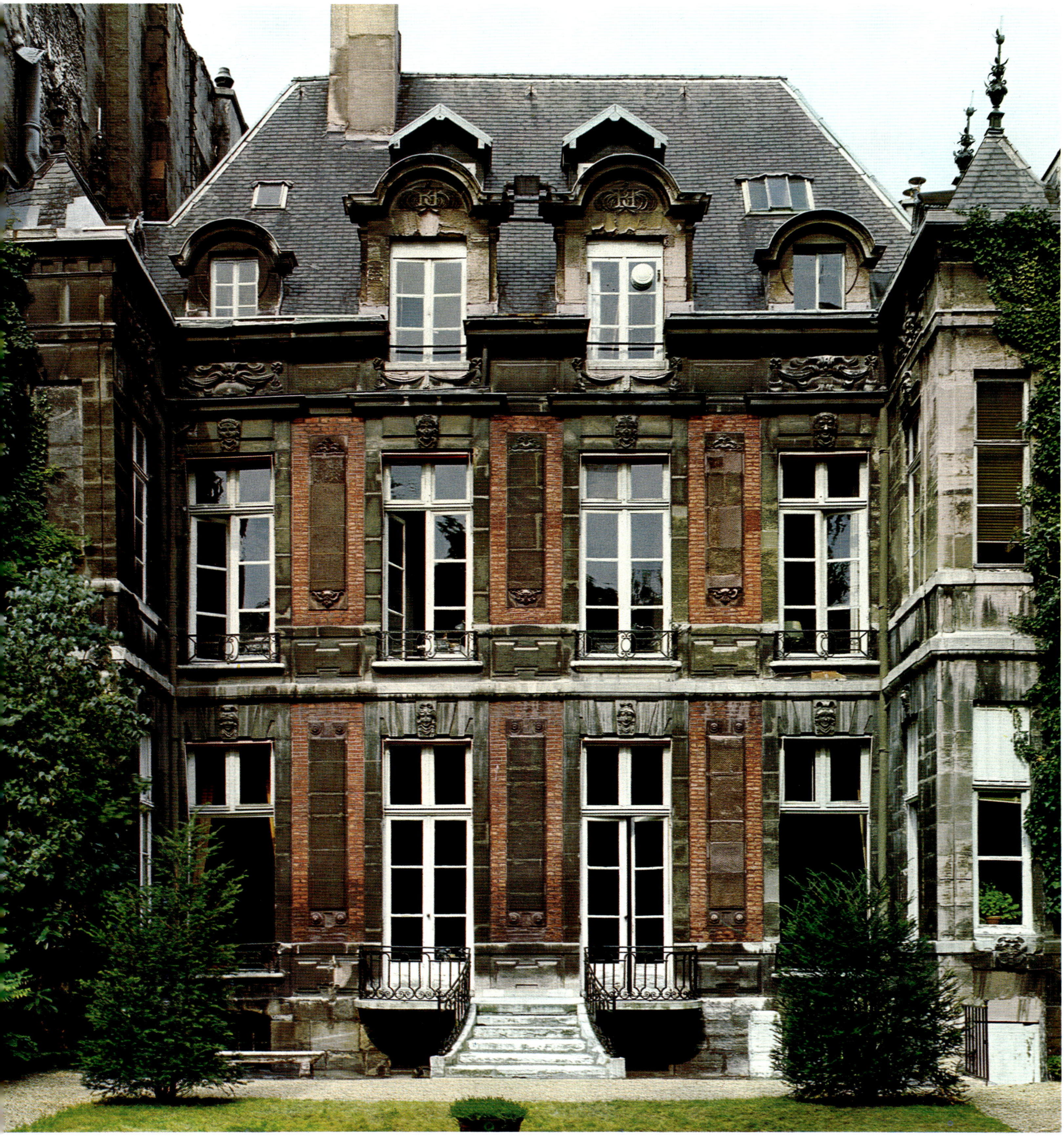

55. The Hôtel de Chalon-Luxembourg, the facade on the garden.

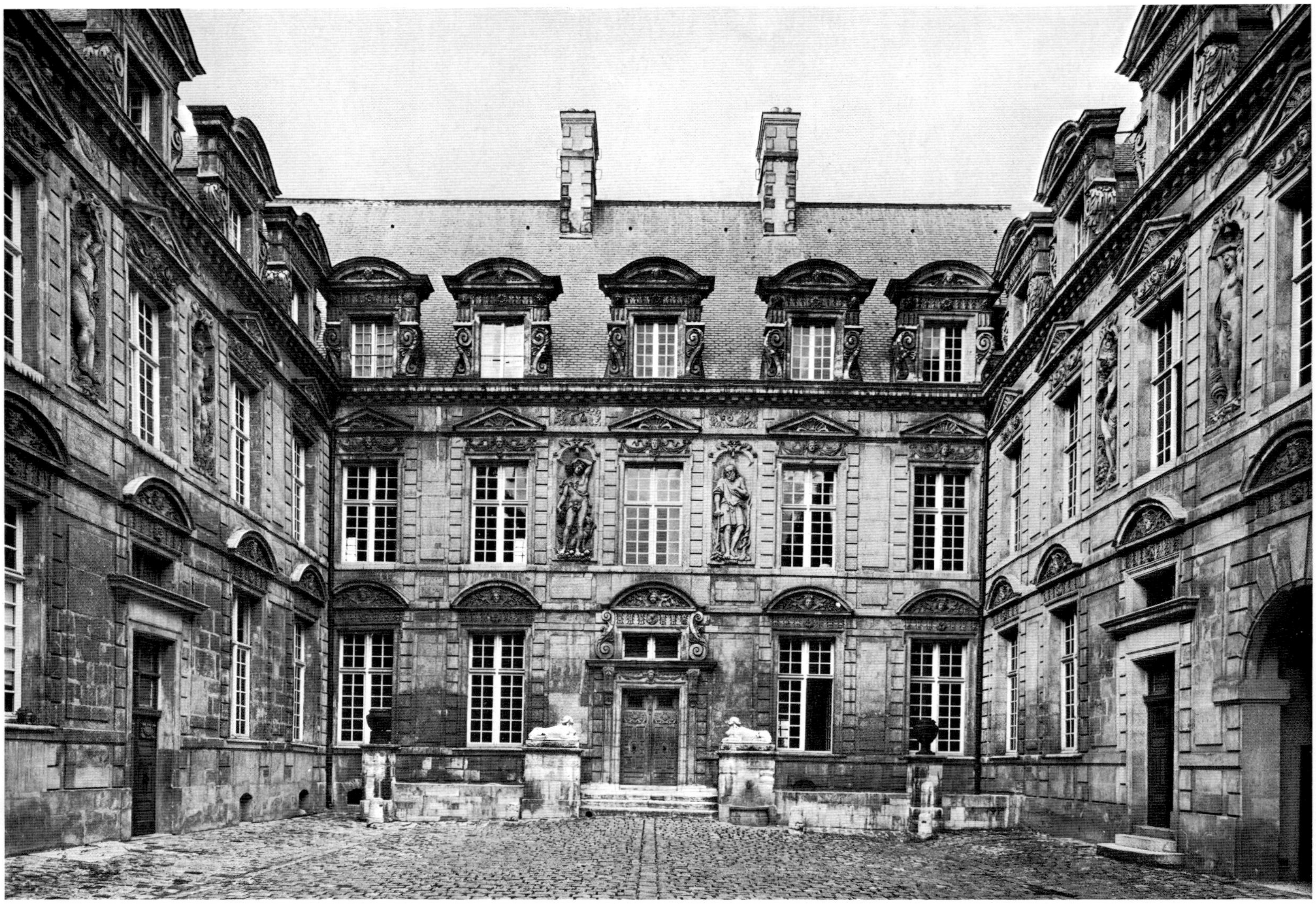

56. The Hôtel de Sully, 62, Rue Saint-Antoine, 4th Arr., the courtyard.

56. The Hôtel de Sully.

The Hôtel de Sully offers a final example of the flowery style of the Renaissance, the influence of the Hôtel Carnavalet is obvious.
In 1625-1626 Jean Androuet du Cerceau, the king's architect since 1617, constructed the main building and the two wings for a comptroller of Finance, Mesme Gallet of Petit Thouars. Soon ruined, he was then succeeded by Roland de Neufbourg who then had the houses overlooking the Rue Saint-Antoine demolished to finish the coutyard and build the pavilions overlooking the street (1628-1630). Four years later, Sully, former minister now in disgrace, bought the hotel. His grandson and great-grandson then had the apartments decorated and a wing built overlooking the garden, all with a regard for the unity of style.

57. The Hôtel Lambert.

With the sale of the two little islands of greenery where the canons of Notre-Dame used to let cows graze, a new district soon sprang up—one which escaped the constraints of the City, overlooking the river in all directions as it did.
In the city itself, living quarters and gardens were habitually built on sites deep amidst the blocks of houses. By way of contrast, the purchasers of plots of land on the embankments wanted to benefit from the vast riverscape to the full. At this point the houses were turned round, as it were. The buildings rose up high with nothing opposite them, the living quarters overlooked the decorated facades which fronted on the Seine.

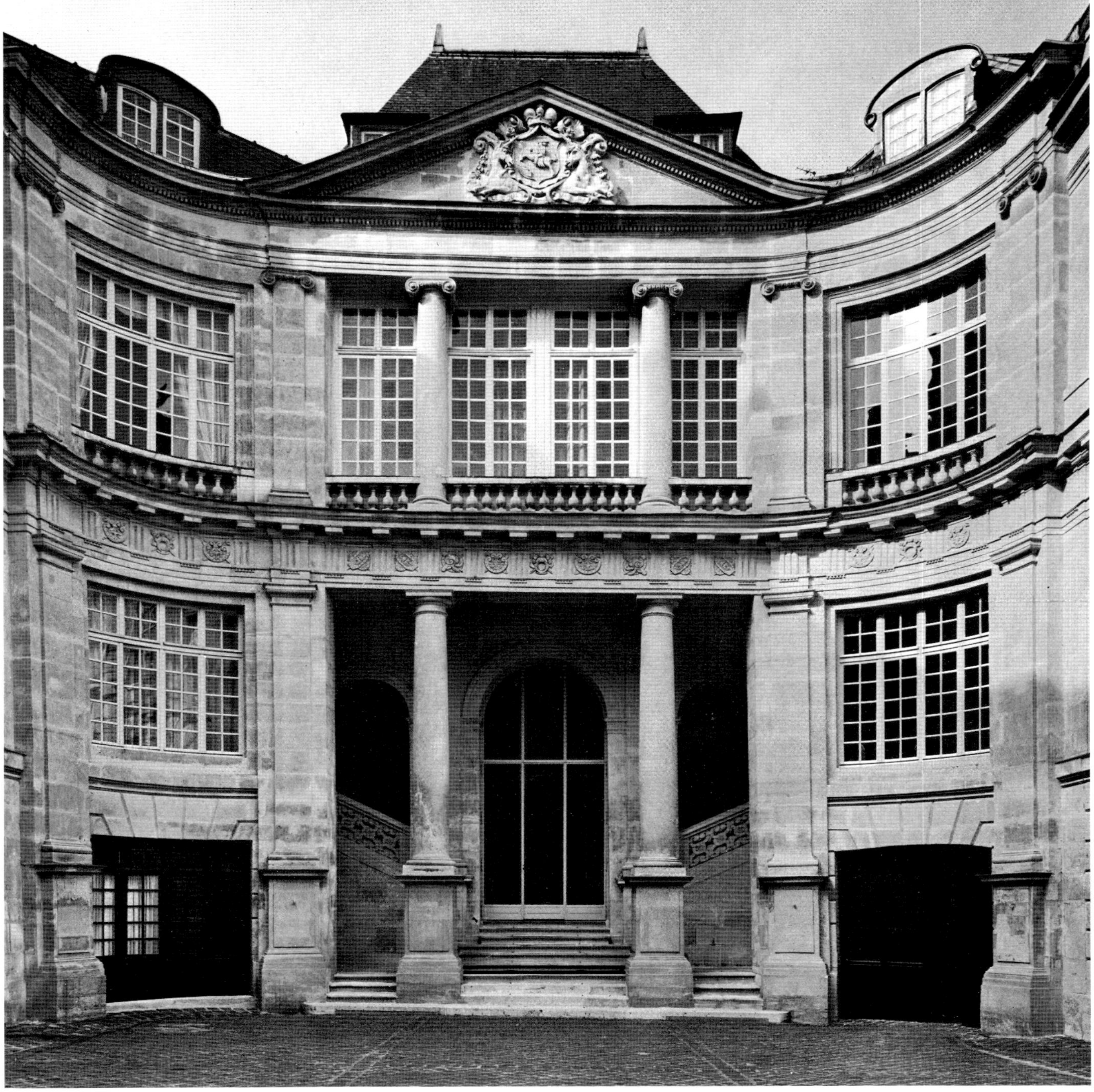

57. The Hôtel Lambert, 2, Rue Saint-Louis-en-l'Ile, 4th Arr., the facade on the courtyard.

Some of the important hotels on the island were built between 1638 and 1643. Jean-Baptiste Lambert de Thorigny, the king's adviser and secretary, bought some land in 1639. On it he built eleven houses and then, in the triangle with the best view, he built his hotel. The young Louis Le Vau, with all the support of his father's experience, drew up the plans. The residence was completed in a year (1641-1642) but its owner then died two years later. It was his brother Nicholas, maître des Comptes and later president, who had the sumptuous interior decor done. On the exterior, the house is arranged around two spaces on different levels. To the left is a courtyard with a triumphal portal giving onto the Rue Saint-Louis-en-l'Ile; at the far end, the curved facade, relieved by a portico and pediment, draws the visitor spontaneously to the staircase. On the right, the garden is on a higher level than the courtyard and the Quai d'Anjou which it borders on one side. The garden is bordered by two similar buildings, at right angles, which are embellished with a colossal Ionic Order. At the end of the garden is the gallery, to the left the main building ornamented by Eustache Le Sueur with a series of decoratively designed rooms. This interior decor was done somewhere between 1646 and 1655. The decoration of the gallery, inspired by the legend of the labours of Hercules, was done by Charles Le Brun.

58 and 59. Saint-Etienne-du-Mont.

The inhabitants of the abbey of Sainte-Geneviève had a parish church (Saint-Etienne-du-Mont) built at the beginning of the thirteenth century; this subsequently had to be rebuilt around 1492. The choir was completed around 1540, followed by the nave and the transept (1580-1586), then the facade. This building, in very simple flamboyant style with high round columns without capitals, is the home of the last rood screen in Paris. Its cross-galleries, common in the Middle Ages, were used for reading the sacred texts to the faithful who crowded the nave. They were joined to the choir which was reserved for the clerics. Many rood-screens were demolished in the eighteenth century. At Saint-Etienne-du-Mont the screen for the main arch was built from 1530-1535, followed in 1545 by the one for the spiral staircases which wind up round the columns to the light gallery surrounding the choir. This bold masterpiece has been attributed to Philibert de l'Orme. To any one acquainted with his skill, the suggestion seems likely enough, particularly if one compares the delicate choir screens with those of the Château d'Anet. The two side portals were built by Pierre Biard in 1601 and crowned with statues in his style.

The facade, built between 1610 and 1622, as the finishing touch to the new church, is one of the most free and lively works of the period when Marie de Medici reigned as queen, and then regent. It was built by the mastermason, Christophe Bardou, from drawings by Claude Guérin, sworn mason to the king. Before work started, there were various difficulties to iron out with the monks of the adjoining abbey of Sainte-Geneviève, who were determined not to give up an inch of land. For better or worse, a classic design was imposed on the great church's Gothic form, which is markedly pointed and irregular since its whole left side curves sharply to join the curve of the Rue de la Montagne-Sainte-Geneviève. The church's frontispiece is a work of true nobility, with its two levels heavily emphasized by two great pediments, one triangular and closed, the other arched and open, and both united by the abundance of decorative sculpture. Unfortunately, its major elements only date back to Baltard's restoration work of the nineteenth century. To the sides of the frontispiece and above it, the traditional structures are still clearly visible—the twin windows, the oculi, the plain walls decorated simply with scrolls, emphasizing the triangular design of the whole. This is completed by a gable so pointed that a real pediment could not in fact be designed for it. On the left, the turret of the little north portal adds an amusing touch of fantasy. The general asymmetry is moreover further accentuated by the vertical thrust of the fifteenth century bell-tower completed in 1624. Jean-François de Gondi, first archbishop of Paris, presided over the consecration of the church in 1626. The building of the Rue Clovis in 1807 entailed the demolition of the twin church on the right, the old abbey church of Sainte-Geneviève, whose proximity must have had a certain influence on the design of Saint-Etienne's facade.

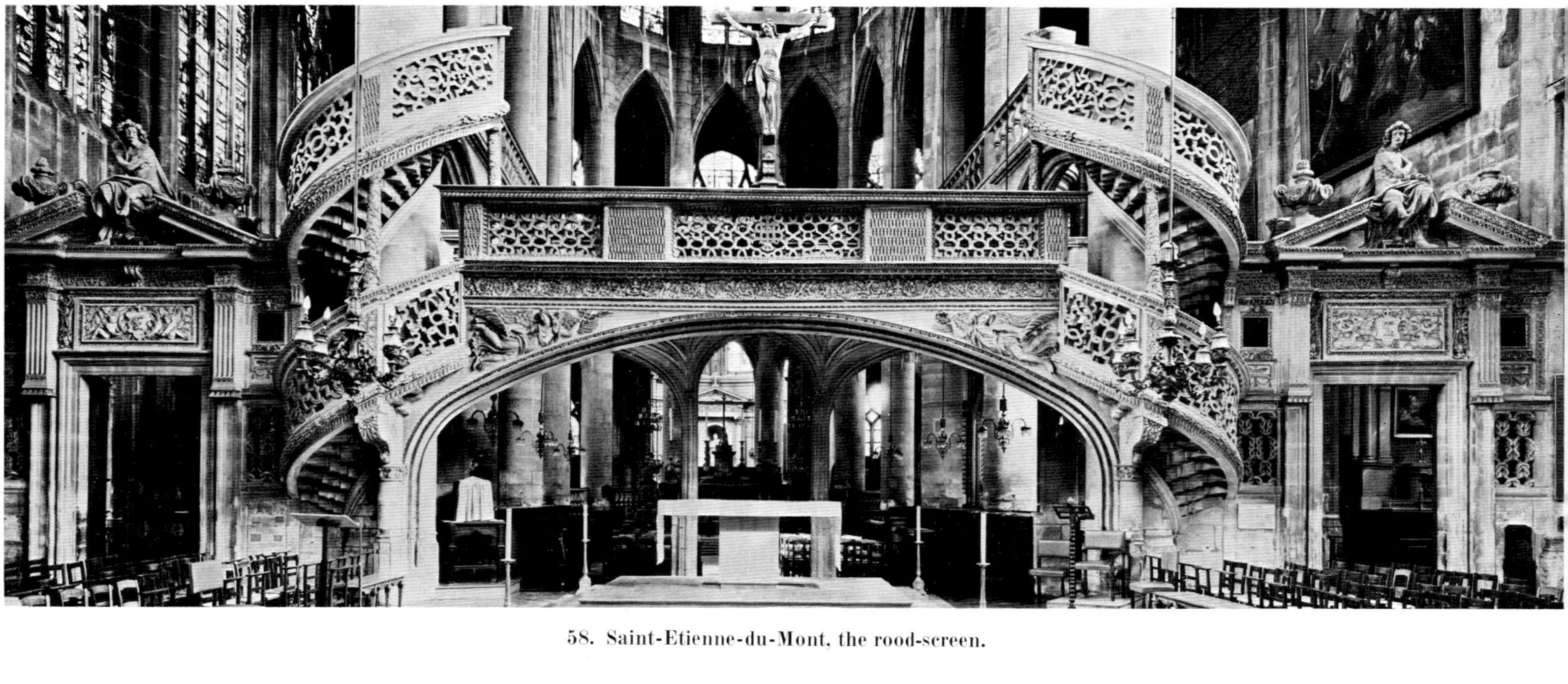

58. Saint-Etienne-du-Mont, the rood-screen.

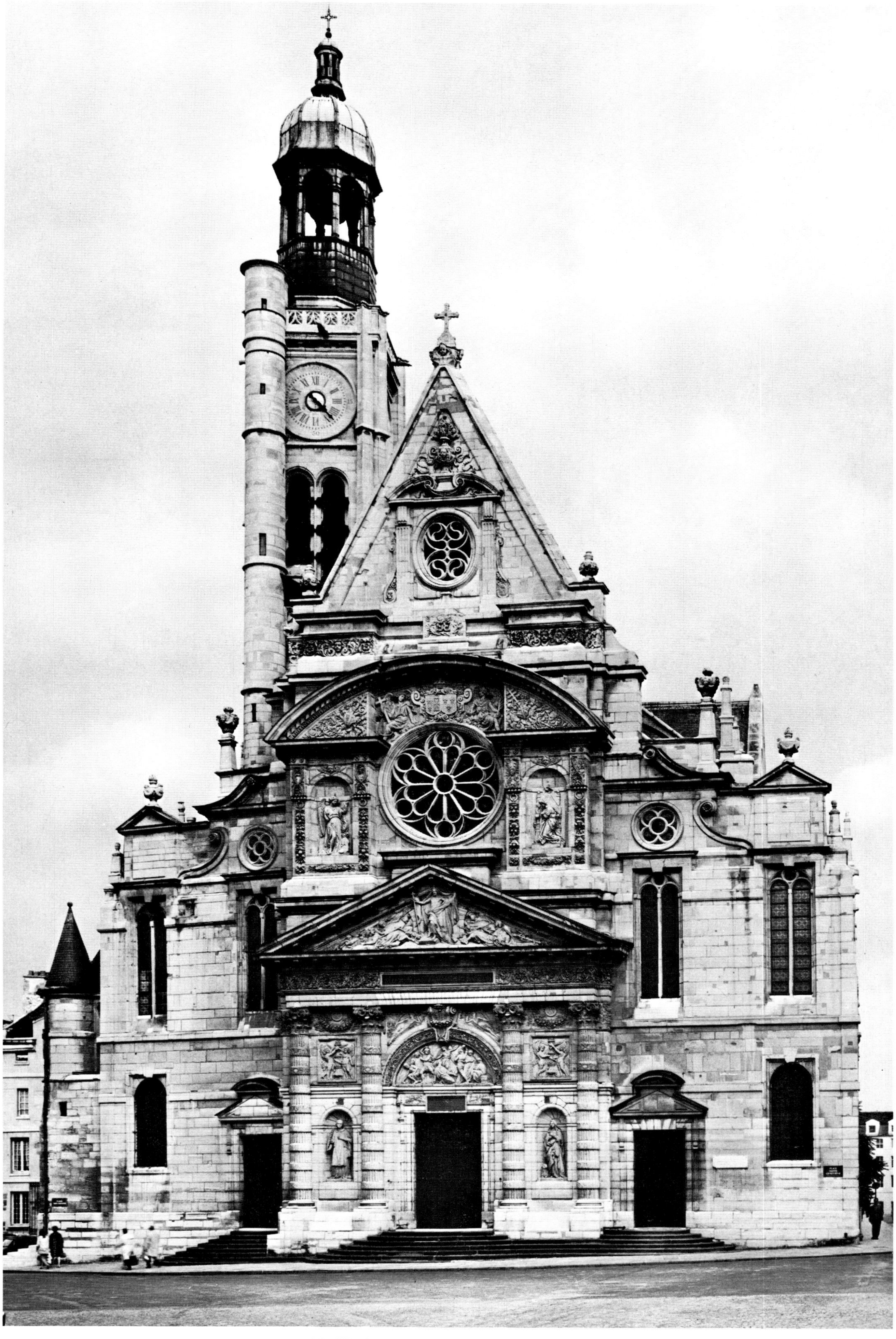

59. The facade of Saint-Etienne-du-Mont.

60. The Luxembourg Palace and the Medici Fountain.

When she was widowed, Marie de Medici wanted her own personal residence, as had her aunt, Catherine de Medici. Marie, a native of Florence, had been brought up in the Pitti Palace, Brunelleschi's masterpiece, which had subsequently been enlarged by Ammanati around the time of her birth. Marie wanted a palace which was close to the city yet also somewhat apart so that it might have a great park around it like the lovely Boboli Gardens which surround the Pitti Palace. Catherine and the kings had opted for the right bank. Marie, by way of contrast, following the example of her rival, Queen Margot, Henri IV's first wife, chose the left bank, that sacred site of monasteries. In 1611 she began buying land for her residence between the Chemin de Vaugirard and the great Carthusian monastery.
In the same year, she hastily sent one of the Métezeau architects (Louis probably) to Florence to get the plans of the Pitti Palace. The first stone of her palace was laid in 1615. It was named the Luxembourg because François de Luxembourg gave his hotel to the Queen (the Petit Luxembourg). The architect chosen was Salomon de Brosse, who was also the contractor—a fact for which he was later to be criticised. Marin de La Vallée took over from him, followed by Jean Thiriot. But the times were troubled ones and work progressed slowly. The Queen Mother took up residence for the first time in 1625. But the palace was not finished till 1631, the year she went into exile to die.
On Marie's death in 1642, the palace went to her youngest son, Gaston d'Orléans and then to his daughters. Thereafter it went to the duchess of Berry, the count of Provence, the Directoire and finally to the conservative Senate. After the work carried out in the eighteenth and nineteenth centuries, nothing was left of Marie de Medici's apartments; the ornamental woodwork which survived is now in the "Salle du livre d'or" (Room of the Golden Book). The famous Medici gallery by Rubens, finished in 1625, has been in the Louvre since 1780. The park, designed by Boyceau and laid out in 1612, has retained something of its originally ample design, despite the mutilations it suffered in 1782 and 1866. The general plan has also kept a considerable number of its original features. On the left, one can still admire the Medici Fountain or nymphaeum, a decorative vision which catches the eye, at the end of an avenue. It was doubtless inspired by the Queen's memories of the ornamental grotto in the Boboli gardens. The figures of the Rhone and the Seine are copies of the originals by Pierre Biard (1630), whilst the group of figures depicting Polyphemus coming unexpectedly upon Acis and Galatea is a nineteenth century composition by Ottin.

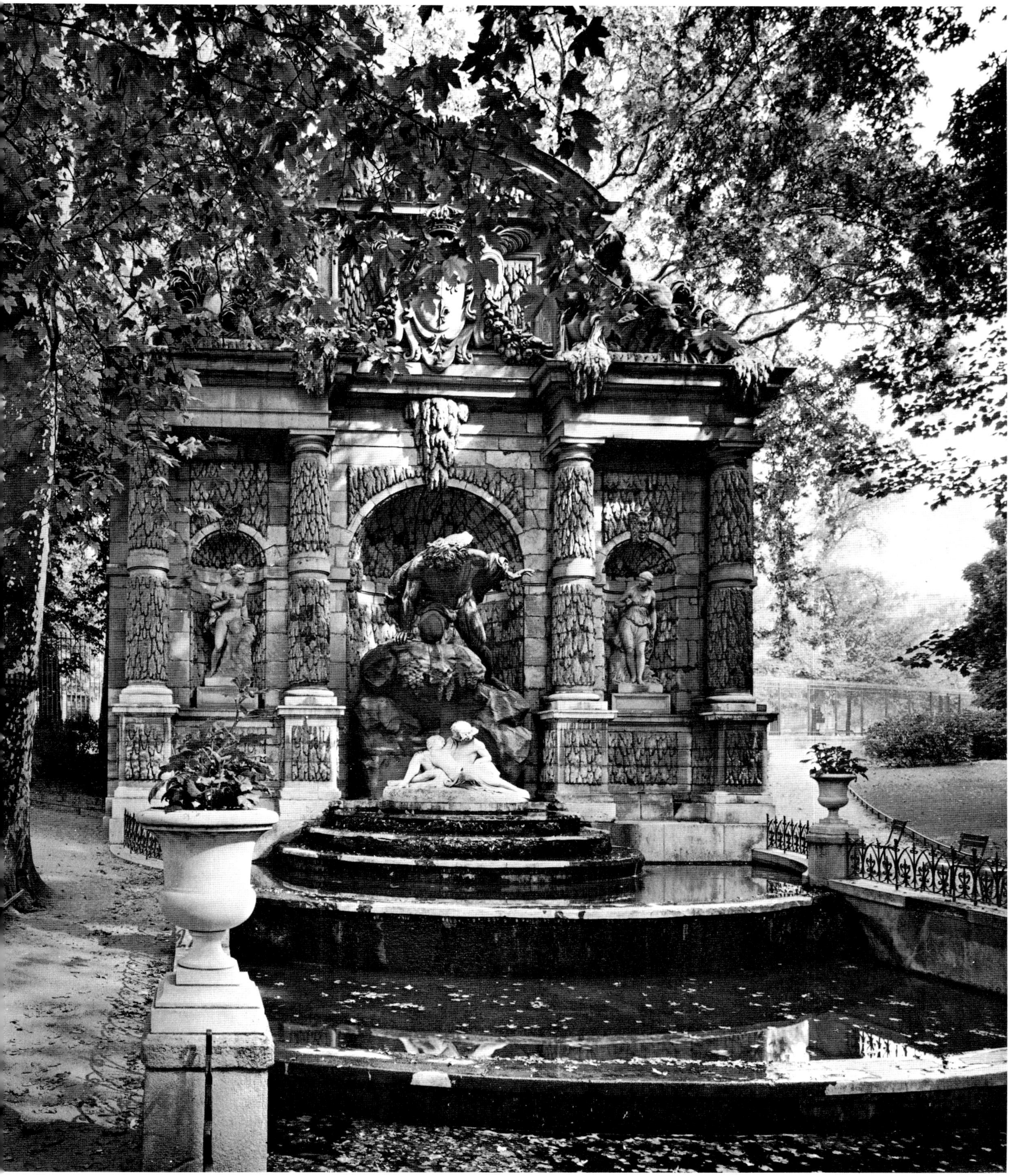

60. The Medici Fountain in the Luxembourg Garden.

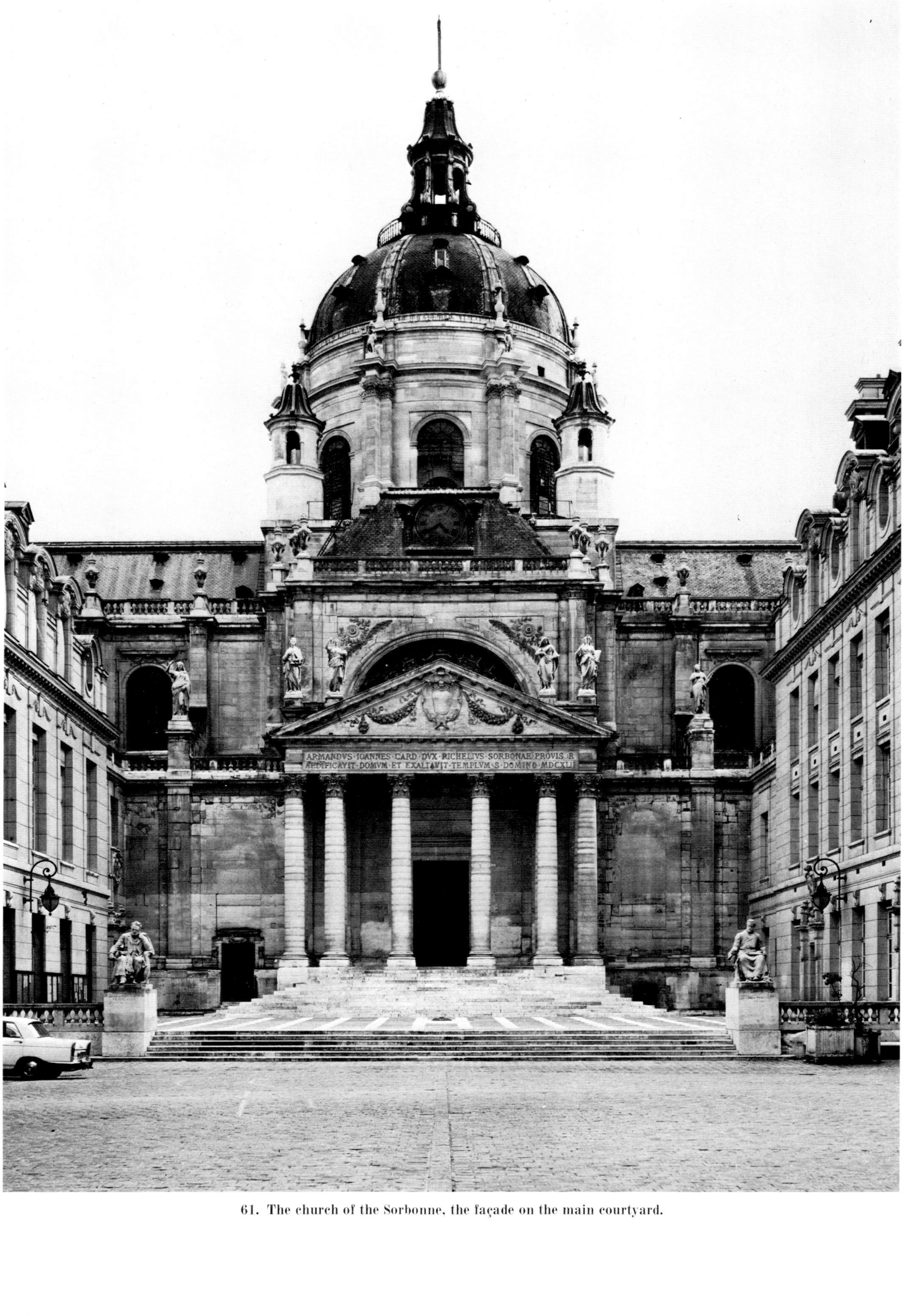

61. The church of the Sorbonne, the façade on the main courtyard.

61. The Church of the Sorbonne.

In 1622 Richelieu was elected head of the College of the Sorbonne, seat of the Theological Faculty. Four years later he decided to rebuild the old college and took on Jacques Le Mercier to do the job. In 1635 the first stone of the chapel was laid. When finished, it was as big as a church, opening onto the newly-built square to the west and onto the inside courtyard. Le Mercier finished the main work in 1642. The dome, high as the church is long, is very Romanesque in design. In its perfection, it heralds those of the Val-de-Grâce and the Invalides. Its position is such as to dominate the facade on the square, a classic design with two levels, as well as the facade on the courtyard. The latter is more original in the way it combines elements on three levels. These include a Corinthian peristyle inspired by the Pantheon in Rome, the far end of the transept, and the dome, clearly visible, framed by the pinnacles of the staircase turrets. In the church there is the admirable tomb built by Girardon in 1694. This portrays Richelieu supported by Piety and wept over by Christian Doctrine. (It was restored to its original place in 1973.)

62 and 63. The Val-de-Grâce.

The Escorial, a palace-monastery in the shadow of a church, twice inspired the architects of Paris—at the Val-de-Grâce and the Invalides. The former we owe to the piety of a Spanish queen, grand-daughter of Philippe II, who sought refuge in religious retreat. Anne of Austria took an interest in a house of Benedictines near Paris, called the Val-de-Grâce. In 1621 she installed them in the Gothic building of the "Petit-Bourbon" in the faubourg Saint-Jacques. Then in 1624 she had a few modest buildings constructed, perhaps by Le Muet. These included a small apartment which she later used during the dark times of her semi-disgrace. The birth of the long-desired son, Louis Le Déséré, Louis XIV, on September 5 1638, transformed the Queen's position. When she became regent in 1643, she decided to keep her vow and ordered that a church be built, dedicated to the Virgin Mother and her new-born son. The first stone was laid on April 1, 1645. The architect was François Mansart; his plan was on a scale unheard of at the time: it included a church, a monastery, a palace, a square of semicircular shape in front of the church. The church walls had already reached first floor level when he was thanked for his work and replaced by Le Mercier. When the latter died in 1654, the work was taken over by Le Muet, helped by Le Duc and Boutel. Together they completed the church in 1667, a few months after Anne of Austria's death.
The church rises up at the far end of a square courtyard; pavilions joined by low buildings, decorated with pediments, lend the whole a marked rhythm of design. Behind the great "Jesuit" facade, the dome rises up from a quadrangular block, its outline massive and very Roman-looking. The interior volumes are strongly influenced by the Gesù and Saint Peter's of Rome; the walls and the vaulting are decorated with the work of the sculptor, Michel Anguier. Under the dome, painted by Mignard, is the canopy, inspired by Bernini's, which rises above the beautiful Nativity by Michel Anguier (the original is in Saint-Roch).
The monastic buildings were constructed by Le Muet between 1655 and 1667. They encompassed the old buildings in a vast quadrilateral, which enclosed the cloister and was flanked by pavilions. The Queen's pavilion is amongst them, flanked by a strange little portico which must date back to the building work of 1624.

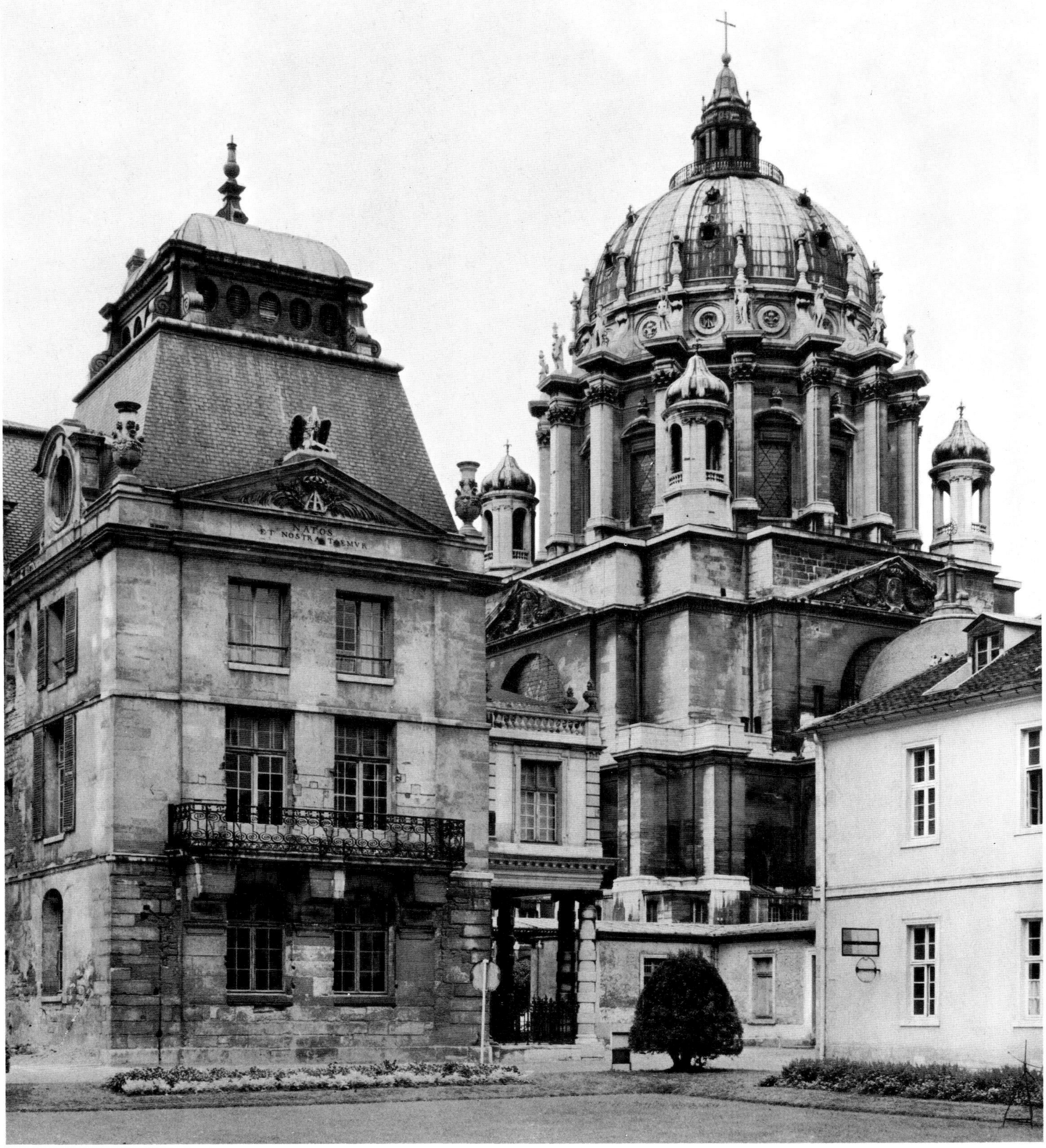

62. The apse of the Val-de-Grâce church and the pavilion of Anne of Austria.

63. The Val-de-Grâce, the interior of the church and the canopy.

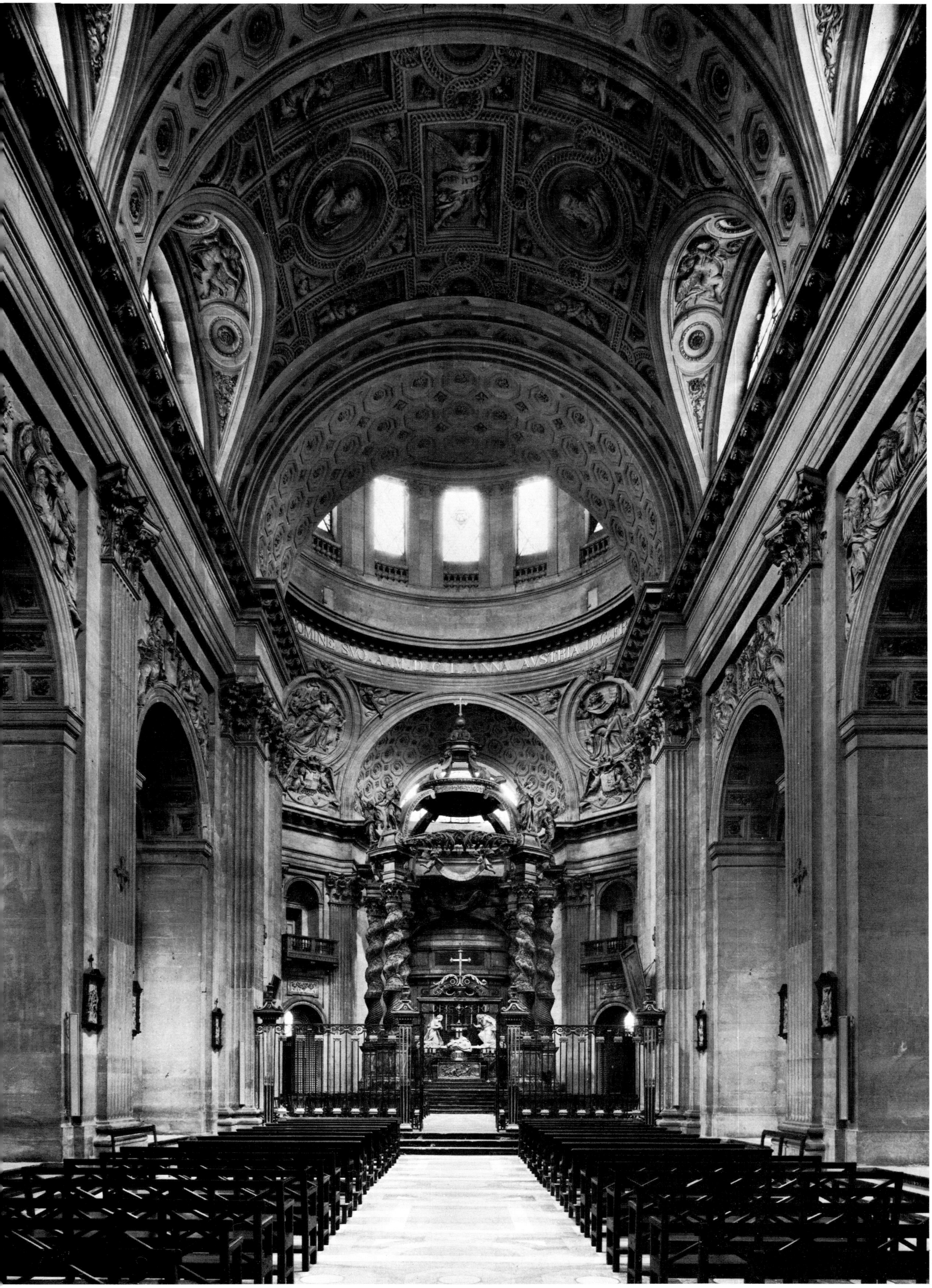
OMINE SVO A. M. D. C. L. ANNA AVSTRIA. D. G. FR

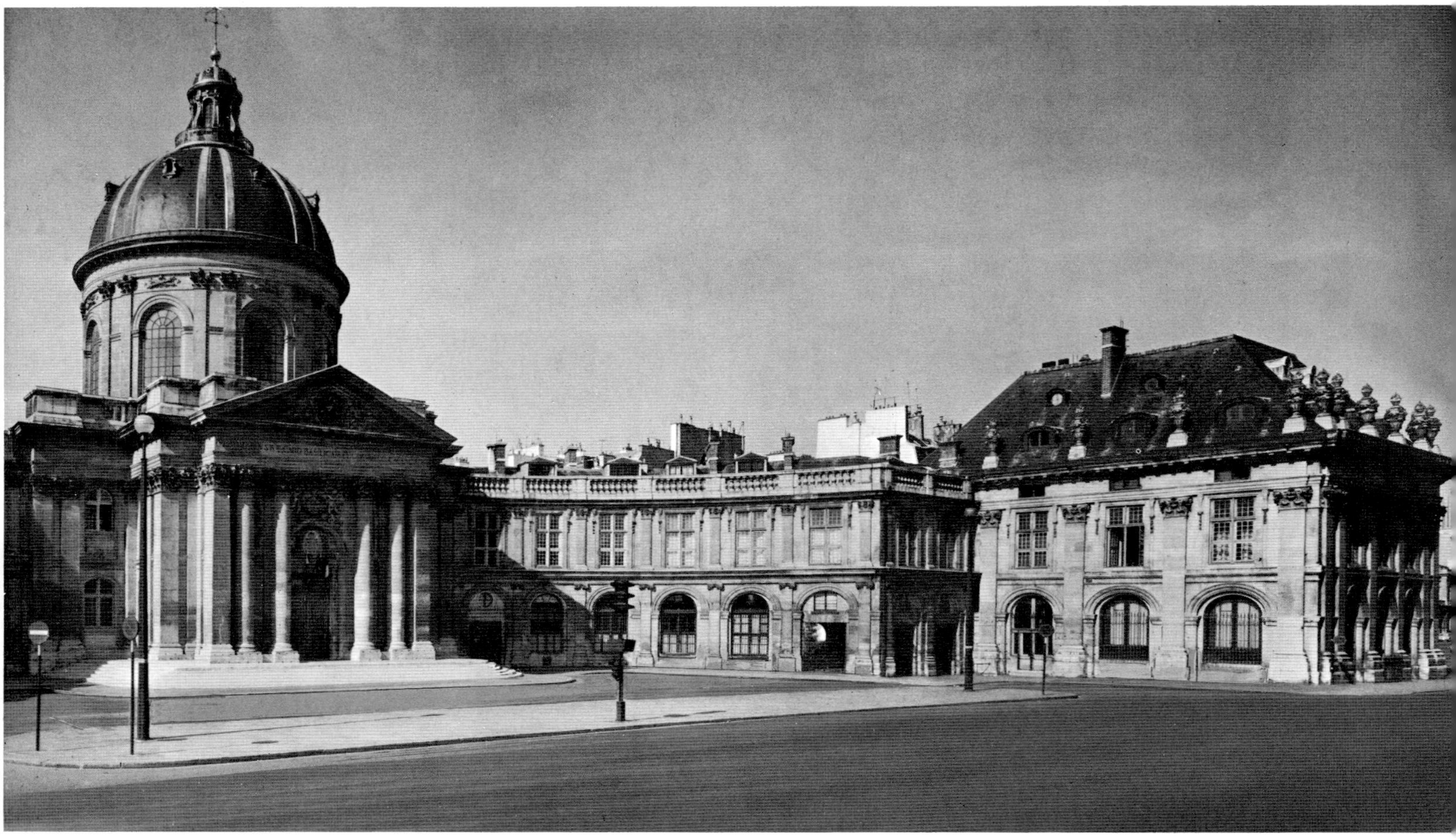

64. The Palais de l'Institut, the former Collège des Quatre-Nations; the dome and the hemicycle of the facades on the Quai Conti.

64. The Palais de l'Institut, the former Collège des Quatre-Nations.

Having failed to persuade the young king to inherit his immense fortune, Mazarin arranged a few days before his death that a large part of his wealth would go to the foundation of a college. It was to be devoted to the education of young gentlemen from Pignerol and the Piedmontese valleys, Alsace, Flanders and the Roussillon; the four provinces which Mazarin had reunited with France under the treaties of Westphalia and the Pyrenees. After hesitating somewhat, the trustees of the estate, who had chosen Le Vau as architect, finally came round to the latter's plan to build the "Collège des Quatre-Nations" opposite the Louvre, on the site of Philippe Auguste's old wall and the Nesle tower. Le Vau built the embankment with all haste and in 1662 obtained approval for a plan which resembled certain Roman designs (the church of Sainte-Agnès on the Place Navone, and the Colonnade of Bernini) but which also bore a similarity to some of François Mansart's work (the Châteaux of Berny and Blois and the church of the Minimes. The design included a chapel of central plan, covered with a dome, and built at the far end of a square of semi-circular plan and joined to two pavilions by concave wings. The three strong elements in the design, the church and the pavilions, are emphasized by roofs and by pilasters of a colossal order, dear to Le Vau. Meanwhile the wings with their narrow roofs are decorated with superposed orders. Building work was completed in 1667. The chapel has a central space of oval plan, lit by the dome and opening on all four sides onto a narthex, two chapels and a choir. Since 1806 the Institut de France has held its solemn meetings beneath the famous "dome".

65 to 67. The Louvre.

The year 1546 was to be a most important date for the capital, both from the historical point of view and for the topography of the right bank and the spread of the classic style. It was the year that François I decided to have the old Louvre rebuilt by Pierre Lescot. The Louvre had started life as a fortress, built by Philippe Auguste between 1190 and 1200. With its towers, connecting facades and dungeon, it was built to strengthen, to the west along the Seine, the King's new surrounding wall. The castle was altered by Saint Louis and by Charles V, who made it one of his occasional residences, installing his library there. Meanwhile his brother-in-law, the Duc de Bourbon, built the Hôtel du Petit-Bourbon nearby. Then the Louvre was abandoned in favour of the mansions in the east of Paris—Saint-Pol, les Tournelles, Barbette—with their galleries, great gardens, aviaries and menageries, they had more amenities to offer than the grim fortress. When François I announced in 1528 that he intended to reside in Paris as often as possible, the royal residence was still officially the Hôtel de Tournelles. But things had changed since the times of Charles V and Charles VI. Les Tournelles had aged badly and its apartments no longer suited the taste of the day; the air was humid and evil-smelling on account of a nearby sewer. The King thus dreamt of a new palace, one with the harmonious design and amenities he had admired in Italy—features he subsequently included in his new buildings at Blois, Chambord, Madrid, Villers-Cotterêts and Fontainebleau. He also dreamt of being in the fresh air, enjoying the riverscape of the Seine. As it was, his mother, Louise de Savoie set the example by building a house outside the west ramparts, in the spot called the Tuileries. Thus François I took an interest in the Louvre, which also had the advantage of being on the way to the Bois de Boulogne and his Château de Madrid there. He gave orders for the demolition of the Louvre dungeon—a symbol of the French sovereign's feudal authority over his vassals (1528). He then ordered the building of the first stone embankments alongside the château. Then he proceeded to have the royal apartements transformed—an initiative partly inspired by the visit of his brother-in-law, Charles Quint, whom he wished to impress. It was not until August 1546, a year before his death, that François I decided to have the palace rebuilt. This task he assigned not to a mason but to an intellectual, an erudite cannon of Notre-Dame and the friend of Ronsard. Thus it was that Pierre Lescot, Lord of Clagny, received an order to draw up plans for a large residential building to replace the west apartments on the Cour Carrée of the old Louvre. Having approved the plan and seen building work begin, the King the died.

His successor, Henri II, asked Lescot to carry on, though he altered the plans somewhat in 1549, moving the staircase planned for the centre to the north. Lescot completed the new building in 1555. The residential quarters are flanked by a great square pavilion known as the King's Pavilion, which replaced the south-west corner tower on the Seine side. Lescot then began work on a similar building which was to replace the Gothic main building to the south. Only the fore-part of this building was in fact completed (1556) during his lifetime. Catherine de Medici then had this wing finished in the reign of her sons. In 1574 it was joined to the south-east tower, known as the tower of the great chapel.

Though the outward facades were of sober design, those giving onto the courtyard were decorated with a new ostentation. The facade designed by Lescot was in fact immediately hailed as an exemplary work, one which proved to be an influential example. It was, in fact, the first masterly demonstration of French classicism. The modulated rhythm of its different parts, subordinated to the rigorous symmetry of the whole, and the regard for the proportions of the classic orders, are all harmoniously moderated by the original treatment of the top story. The attic story adds a note of brilliant fantasy to a work drawn up with great skill, though perhaps verging on the pedantic. One cannot look to the treaties of Vitruvius, Alberti or Serlio for the inspiration which created this noticeably straight roof, the lively frieze, the attic's great open pediments and, more especially, the figures sculpted by Jean Goujon. These are on such a large scale and endowed with such brutal power that they almost seem to rend asunder the fragile network of pillars and pediments. The top story of the south wing was unfortunately replaced under Napoléon by a second floor.

65. The new Louvre of the Valois. To the right, the Henri II facade, to the left, the Charles IX-Henri III facade, designed by Pierre Lescot. The last story of the left facade is an alteration dating from the First Empire.

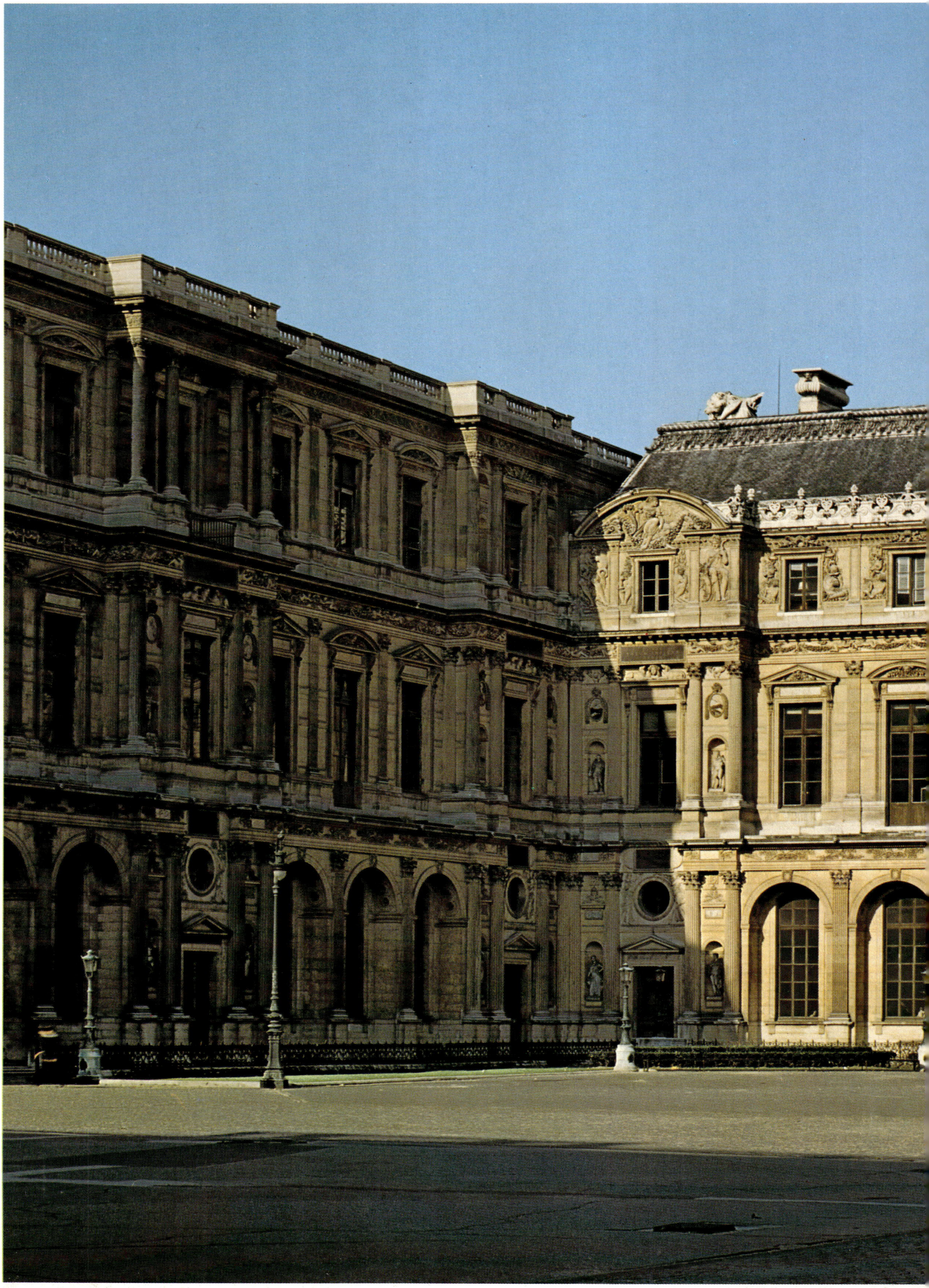

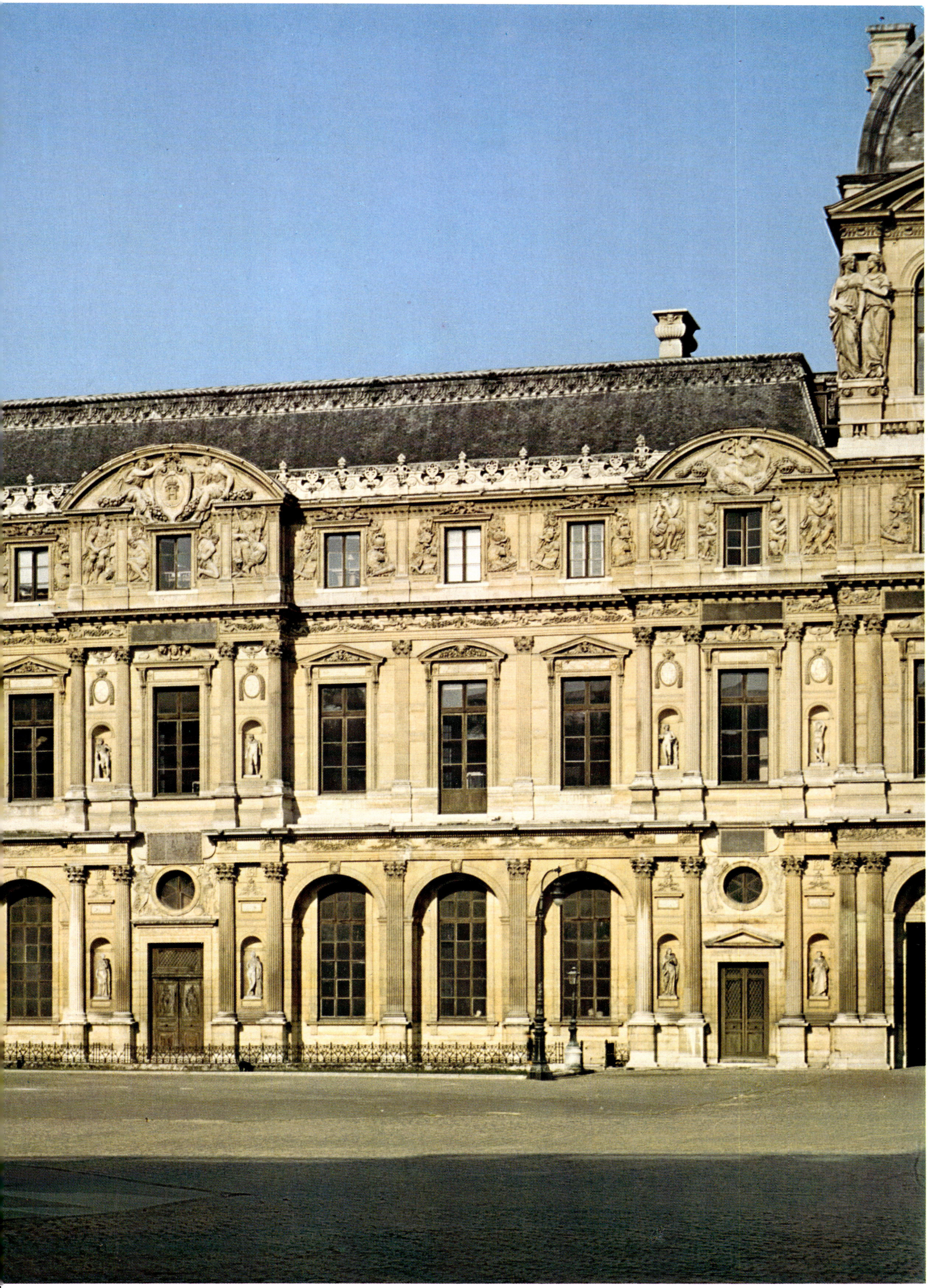

Work on the interior began shortly after the building was completed. In 1549 the great staircase was built as was the "great ballroom" on the ground floor, originally roofed with beams and not vaulted till the reign of Louis XIII. Jean Goujon added a musicians' gallery supported by four cariatids, used when balls were held. The cariatids resemble those of the Erectheion and the drawings by Goujon illustrating the translation of Vitruvius by Jean Martin, published in 1547. At the other end of the room, columns and a triumphal arch mark the seat of privilege, the "platform" with five steps leading up to it, where the royal throne was placed. The Henri II staircase, situated behind the right fore-part of the building, is made up of high rectilinear flights, roofed with an ascending cradle-vault, decorated with caissons sculpted by the team of Jean Goujon. This is a development of the design at Chenonceaux.

Henri IV ordered a new start on building work to join the Louvre with the Tuileries. Thus 1595 saw the completion of the little arcade joined to the Pavillon du Roi by a little building which spanned the moat of the Louvre on three arches. The first floor housed the Galerie des Rois, renamed the Galerie d'Apollon after the fire of 1661. The king then had the great Waterside Gallery built (1595-1608) at right angles. The eastern half, which has three storys, laden with sculptures, is most probably the work of Clément Métezeau. Most of it still remains. The western half, beyond the present day entrance, is the work of Jacques II Androuet Du Cerceau. The facades were decorated with a colossal Classic order with large alternating pediments, planned to relieve the long continuity of design and to harmonise with the Pavillon de Flore and the little gallery of the Tuileries by the same architect. This wing was unfortunately rebuilt in the Second Empire to a uniform plan.

The old Louvre was soon deemed rather mean in size and the idea of enlarging the courtyard fourfold may well have been mooted around 1555. The task was eventually undertaken by the young Louis XIII. In 1624 he had the old north wing demolished, the former site of the famous spiral staircase by Raymond du Temple. In the same year he laid the first stone of the pavilion around which the new plan subsequently took shape. The facade by Pierre Lescot, designed as a self-sufficient entity, was thus integrated into a larger design.

118 The Pavillon de l'Horloge (Clock Pavilion) is the work of Jacques Le Mercier, Richelieu's favourite architect. Its three lower storeys match Lescot's elevation. However they are surmounted by a vast story crowned by a square-plan dome. This lofty crown called for decoration on a grand scale: two pediments enclosed by a third and borne by cariatids which recall those by Jean Goujon. They were sculpted by Philippe de Buyster and Gilles Guérin after the models of their master, Jacques Sarrazin.

During his last years, Mazarin was eager to finish the Louvre. After Le Mercier's death in 1654, Le Vau, leading architect to the King, was charged with the task. In 1660 work started on the north wing of the Cour Carrée, originally undertaken by Le Mercier, and which stood at an angle to the north-west pavilion, known as the Pavillon de Beauvais. To the south wing, where building work had been done under the last Valois monarchs, Le Vau added a monumental pavilion, resembling in outline the Pavillon de l'Horloge. It had Corinthian columns of a colossal order and was crowned by a dome, subsequently to be matched by the dome of the Collège Mazarin, on the other side of the Seine. A bridge, the Pont de la Paix, was planned for the present site of the Pont des Arts. The south wing extended beyond this pavilion with a raised main building, like the others, built to Pierre Lescot's design. The wing then ended in a pavilion similar to the Pavillon du Roi, and which was apparently called the Pavillon de la Reine (Queen's Pavilion). It was finished in 1663. During those years, Le Vau also carried out work on the Petite Galerie which had been damaged by fire in 1661. He restored the ground floor, rebuilt the first floor (Galerie d'Apollon) and enlarged the building towards the west to include a theater. Its facade overlooks the Cour du Sphynx.

The east wing of the palace, looking towards Saint-Germain-l'Auxerrois, presented problems of a different nature. The monumental entrance to the palace was to be situated here, there was also a plan to move the royal apartments to this wing. Le Vau had his plan for a central pavilion approved in 1661 and building work started the following year. When the moat was excavated in 1964, the massive foundations of the facade were uncovered, in front of the present Colonnade.

66. The Pavillon de l'Horloge, in the Cour Carrée of the Louvre.

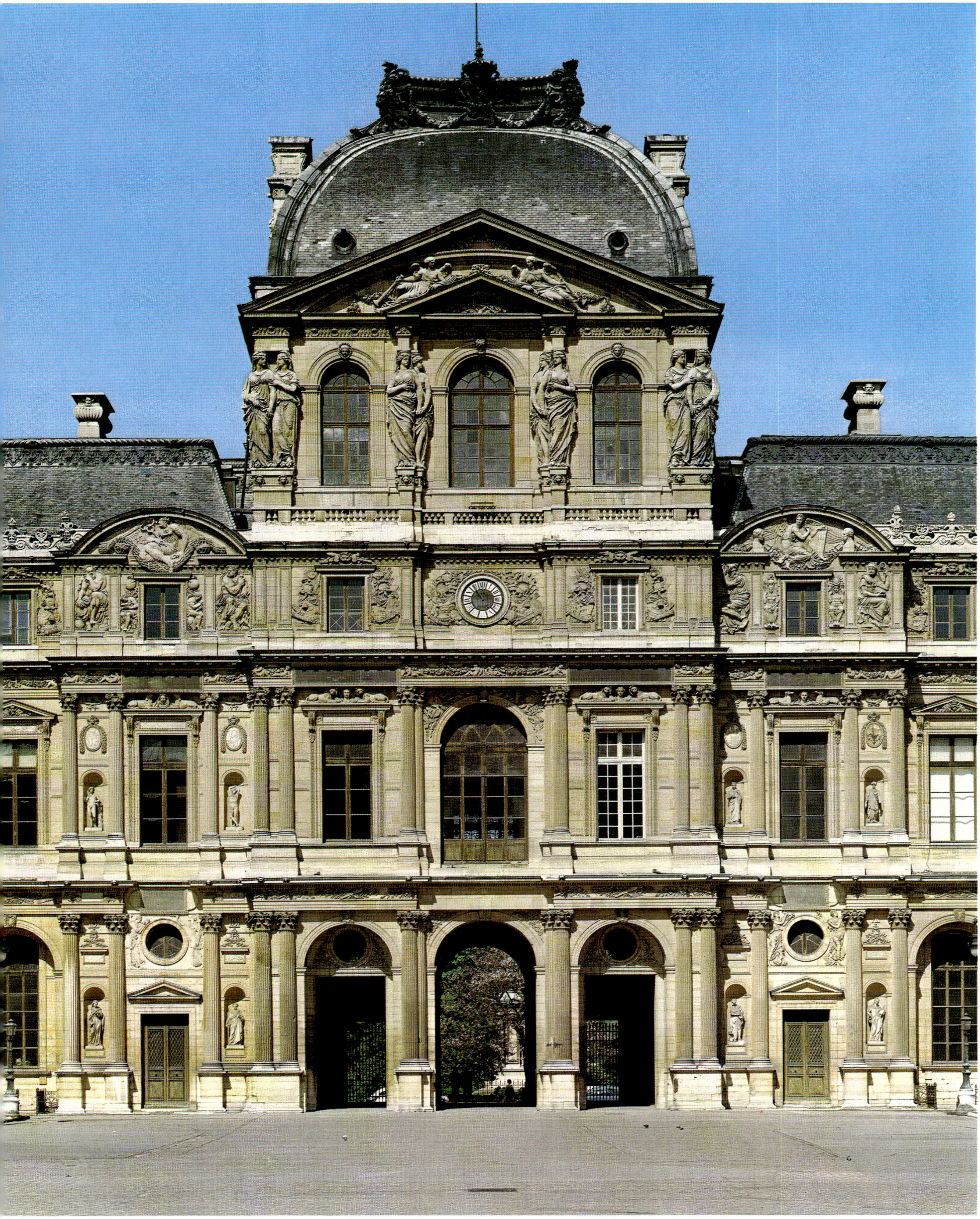

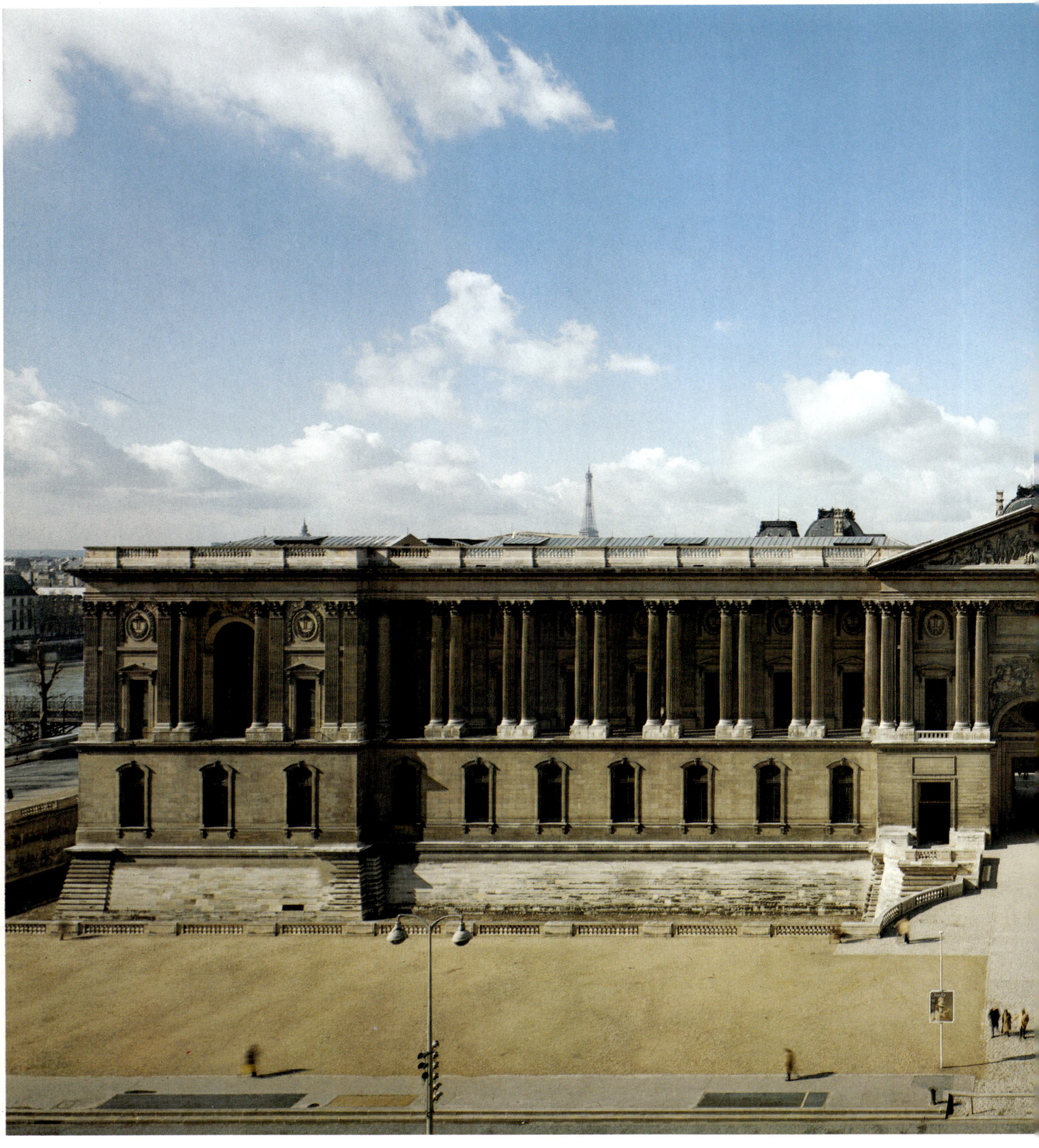

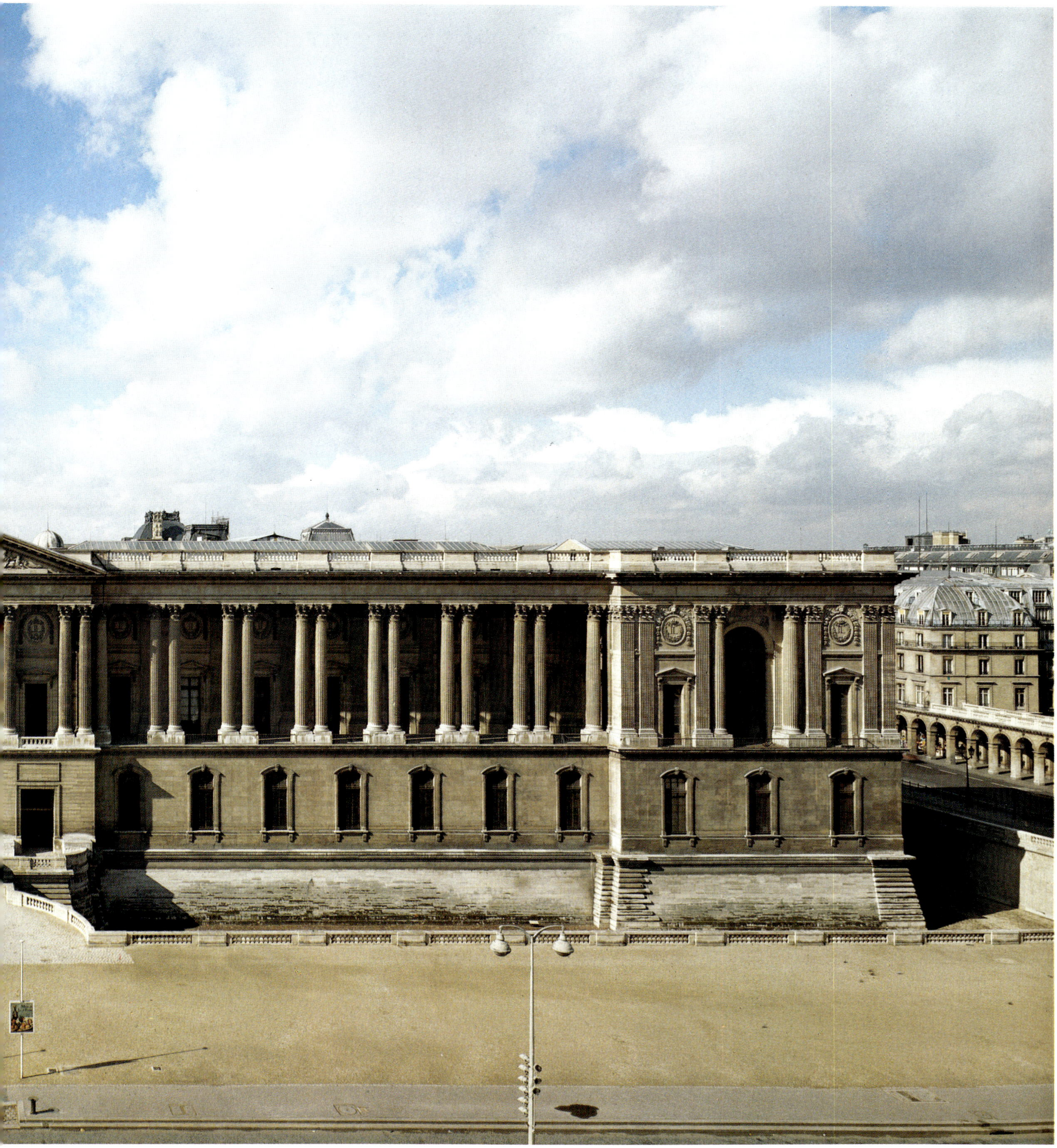

67. The Louvre Colonnade and its basement, uncovered when the moats were dug out in 1964.

Le Vau was not the only architect to have presented a plan; Marot, François Mansart had also been asked to do so... Some architects, Léonor Houdin and François le Vau in 1661 and 1662 put forward the idea of a high peristyle. Not content with these suggestions, the King then turned to the architects of Italy: first of all to Rainaldi who designed an immense building crowned with an onion-shaped dome, and then to Bernini, the glory of Rome, who had built the famous colonnade of Saint Peter's. Bernini submitted a plan in 1664 and was invited to the court by Louis XIV who received him with great pomp and ceremony (June-October 1665), appearing to take an interest in his plan. In October work began on new foundations, disturbing those laid by Le Vau. Yet when Bernini left, it had already been decided that work on his facade would not be continued since it was too Roman in design and did not harmonise with the rest of the palace. At that point Colbert summoned a commission which included Louis Le Vau, Charles Le Brun and the doctor Claude Perrault. The question as to who designed the "Colonnade" has been frequently debated. The most authoritative research suggests that a plan was adopted in 1667, probably the work of Le Vau. Whether this included the two colossal peristyles or not, the plan apparently had three high pavilions which harmonised with the animated outline of a French-style palace. When building work started the following year, this plan was modified by Perrault: the pavilions were replaced by foreparts and the facade was extended beyond the ends of the north and south wings. Because of this a new facade had to be built in front of the south wing to harmonise with the Colonnade. Building work was completed in 1674 under the watchful eye of François d'Orbay. The Colonnade was built on a high basement which was meant to be seen. In reality the moat was not dug till 1964, at André Malraux's behest; he wanted the building to be seen in the full harmony of its design, with the three-story elevation originally planned by Louis XIV's architects.

68. The Tuileries.

Philibert de l'Orme only built the main part of the immense palace which be had planned to build in 1564 on the open land named the Tuileries, after the tile-works which had once been there. Around 1570 Bullant added a pavilion to the south, then Jacques Androuet Du Cerceau built the Petite Galerie des Tuileries and the Pavillon de Flore for Henri IV. To the north, Le Vau added the theater known as the "Salle des Machines" (1659-1666), ending in the pavilion by Marsan. He then altered the center of the palace and built the great square dome (1664-1666). The palace was hardly used under the Ancien Régime; Louis XIV's forced stay there from 1789-1792 came to an end with the attack of August 10th. By way of contrast, the sovereigns of the nineteenth century made it their habitual residence: Napoléon I, Louis XVIII, Charles X, Louis-Philippe and finally Napoléon III. The palace was burnt in 1871, and then demolished in 1882.
An Italian-style garden was laid out for Catherine de Medici by Bastien Tarquin after a drawing by Carruessequi: it had squares of greenery, beds of flowers and coloured sands, a labyrinth, and a grotto decorated by Bernard Palissy with terracotta figures. In the reigns of Henri IV and Louis XIII, Jacques and Claude Mollet introduced the new art of "embroidering" with dwarf box trees. Then finally Le Nôtre was given the task of remodelling the garden (1664). He managed to conjure up a marvellous perspective from the flat, monotonous site. The view opens up along an avenue which climbs the hill of Chaillot (the Champs-Elysées). Making use of an existing embankment to the north, Le Nôtre laid out the Terrasse des Feuillants, and then built a similar one overlooking the Seine. The statues are of somewhat later date: the terminals of the octogon were put up in 1680, followed by the sculptures taken from the Parc de Marly, which included the statues of Mercury, Fame, the Rivers, Aenius and Anchises, Arria and Poetus, Hippomenus and Atlanta.

68. Fame. One of the statues by Coysevox, transferred from Marly and placed on the pilasters and west wrought iron gate of the Jardin des Tuileries in 1719.

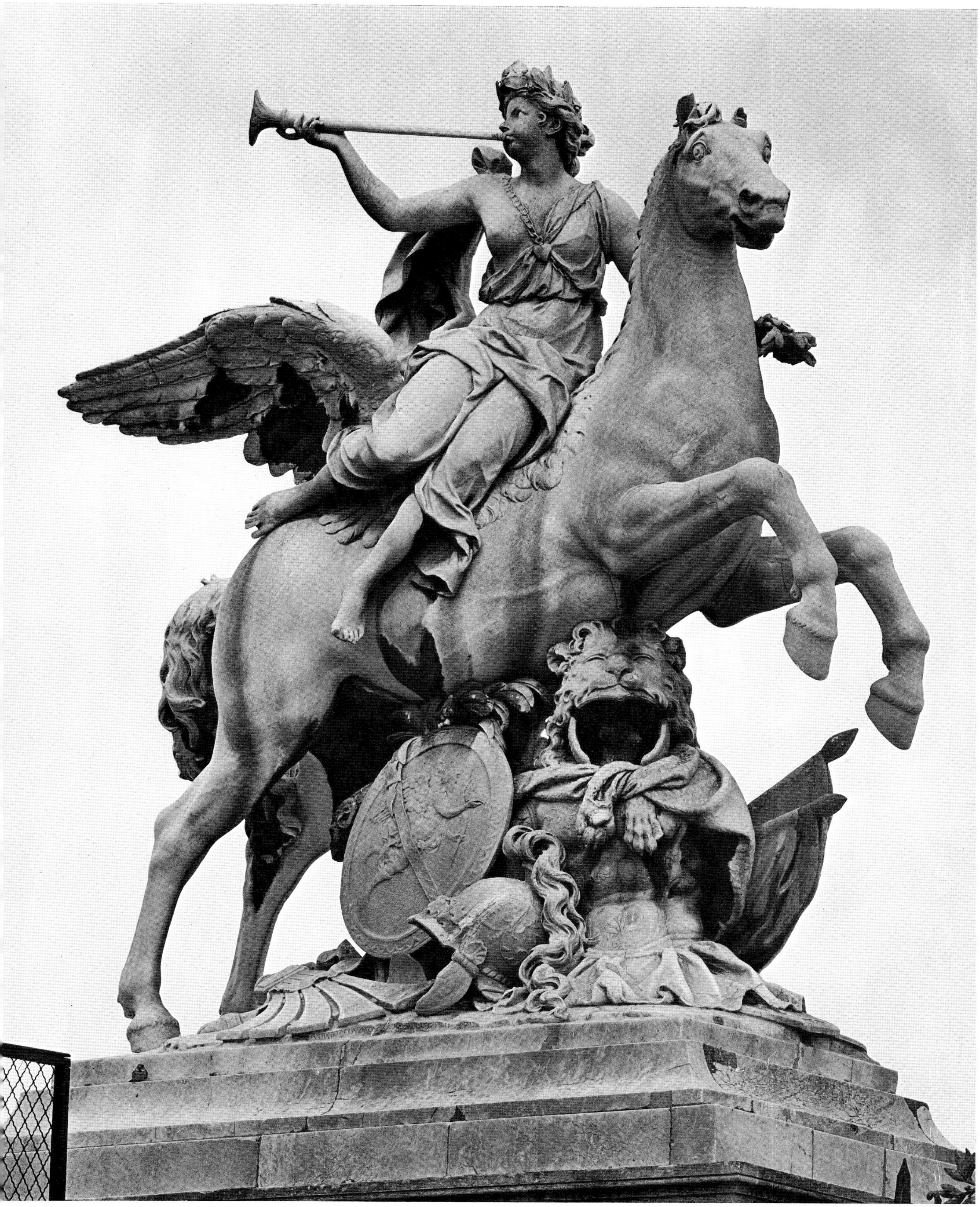

69 and 70. The Hôtel Royal des Invalides.

In 1670 Louis XIV decided, on Louvois' advice, to found a "royal hostel" where those who had served his military glory could be looked after. It was the Spanish palace-convent of the Escorial which inspired the plan for a vast monastery-like barracks, to be built on the open ground of the Plaine de Grenelle. In these surroundings "old, maimed and worn-out" soldiers could lead a simple life devoted to manual labour, regulated by the peals of the bell for Divine Service. Libéral Bruant was chosen as architect in 1670, the year of Le Vau's death. He also built the chapel of the La Salpêtrière hospital in the same year.

Bruant built the hostel with great speed: by 1674 the first pensioners were already taking up residence: This immense building, its long facade overlooking the esplanade, is designed round a vast courtyard with arcades, planned like a monastic cloister with two storeys, and flanked by four secondary courtyards. The architecture is massive in style, embellished only with dormer windows in the form of breast-plates and groups of sculptures by way of pediments. The whole is endowed with a truly military austerity which sets off the central frontispiece—a veritable triumphal arch to the glory of the King.

The royal foundation evidently required a chapel; Louvois gave the task of designing one to a young thirty-year old architect, Jules Hardouin-Mansart, whose good fortune it was to be the nephew and spiritual successor of François Mansart. The task was a difficult one as the church had to be harmoniously fitted into the general plan of the buildings. Moreover, as in the monasteries of closed orders, the areas used by the pensioners had to be completely separate from the areas open to the outside world.

Thus the church designed for the soldiers, the church of Saint-Louis, had a long traditional nave, with sober decorations, which opened onto the main courtyard. Behind it, and joined by a great bay shut off by sheets of glass, was built the glorious exterior church. It faced in the other direction overlooking, not the Seine, but the Plaine de Grenelle. This church, with its central plan crowned by a dome, is one of the most beautiful in the world.

Unlike the architects of Saint Peter's in Rome, Jules Hardouin was able to build his dome directly above the perpendicular sweep of the south front which thus acted as a base, setting it off perfectly. The first church was completed in 1679; the dome, built by Robert de Cotte and Lassurance, was finished in 1690. Its interior decor of painting and sculptures was finished by 1706. Some authors have suggested quite plausibly that Louis XIV at one point thought of building his tomb here. And here it was that Louis-Philippe had the ashes of Napoleon I enterred.

69. The Hôtel Royal des Invalides. The Church of the Dome.

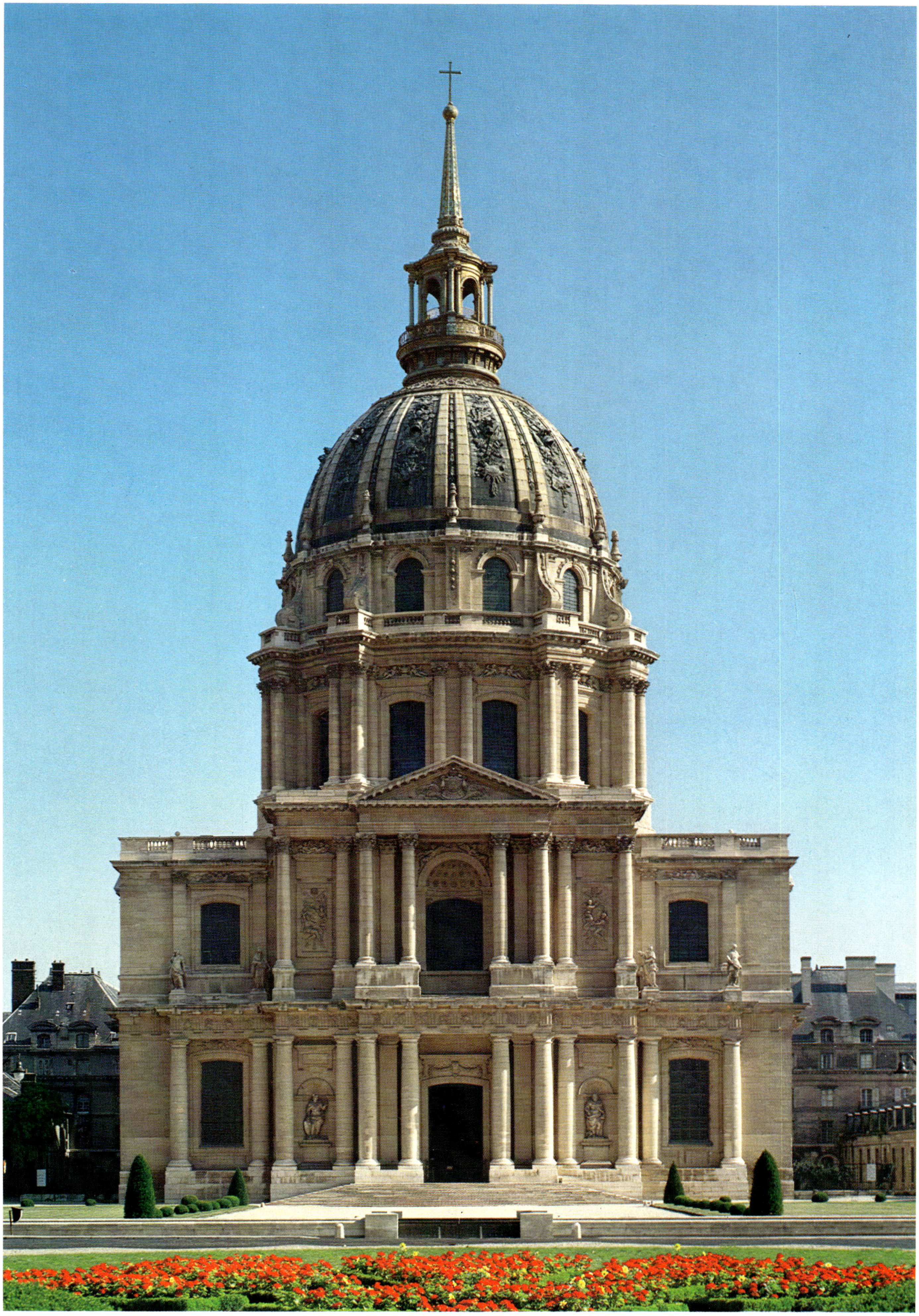

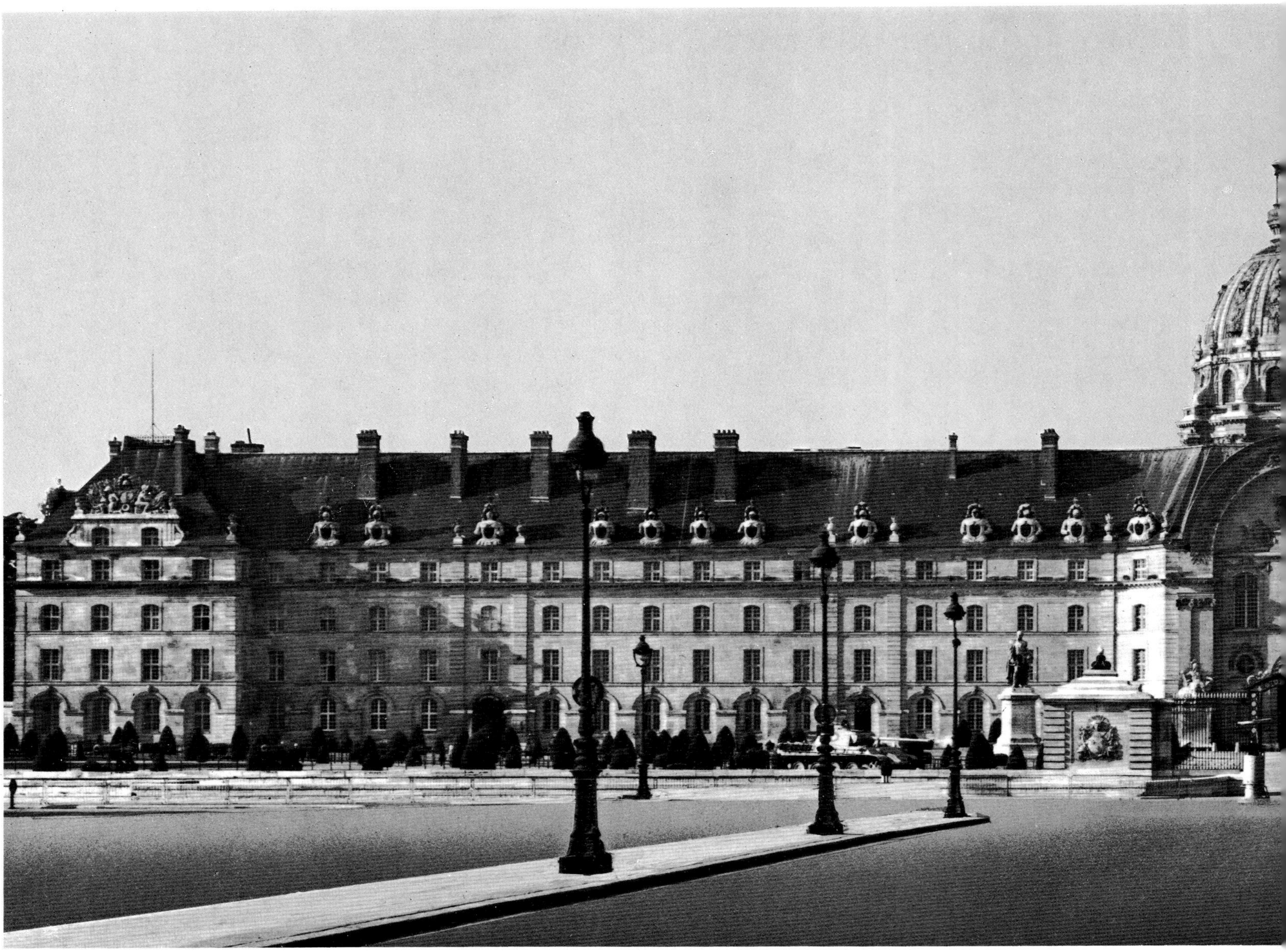

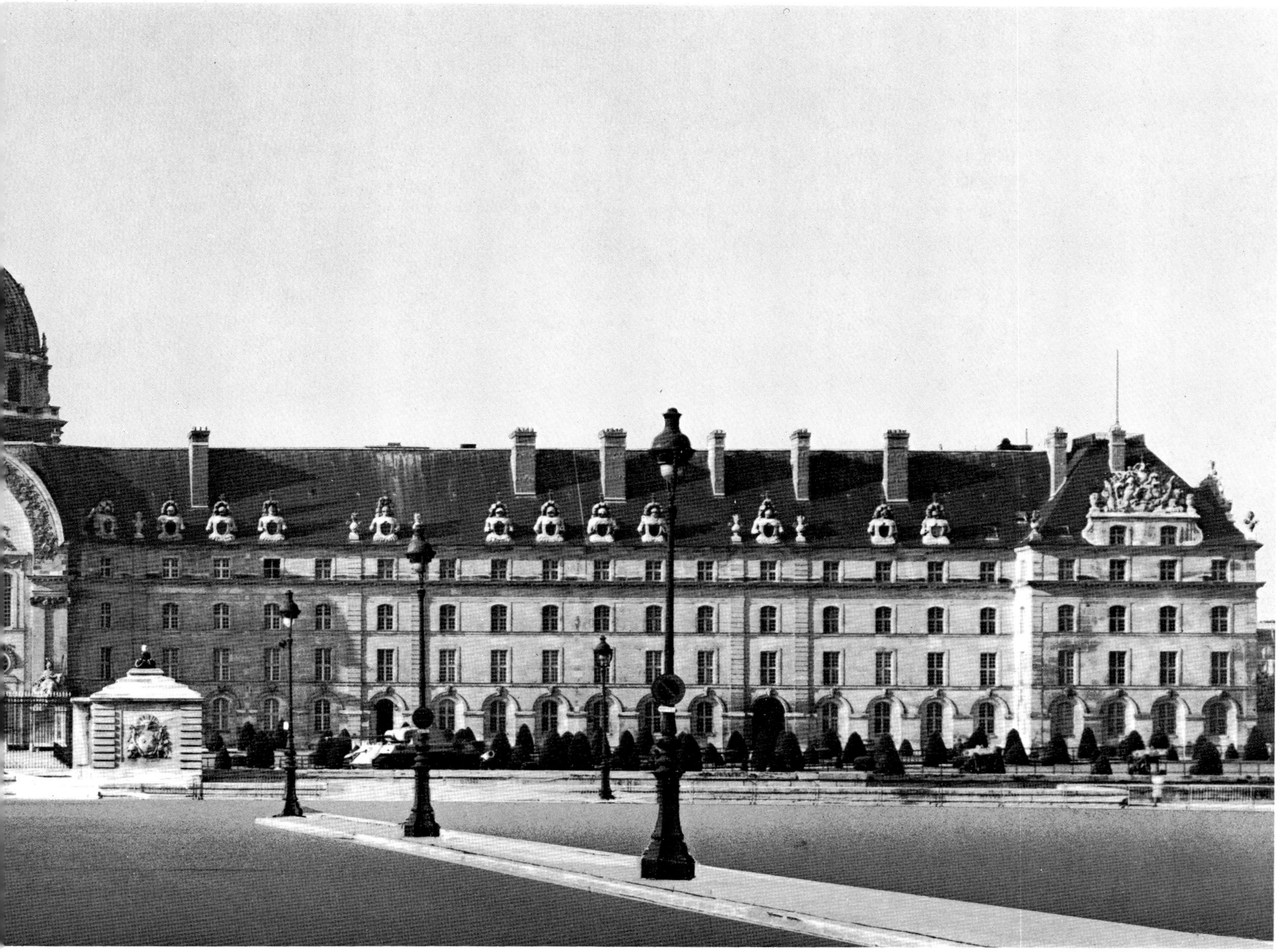

70. The Hôtel Royal des Invalides. A general view from the Esplanade.

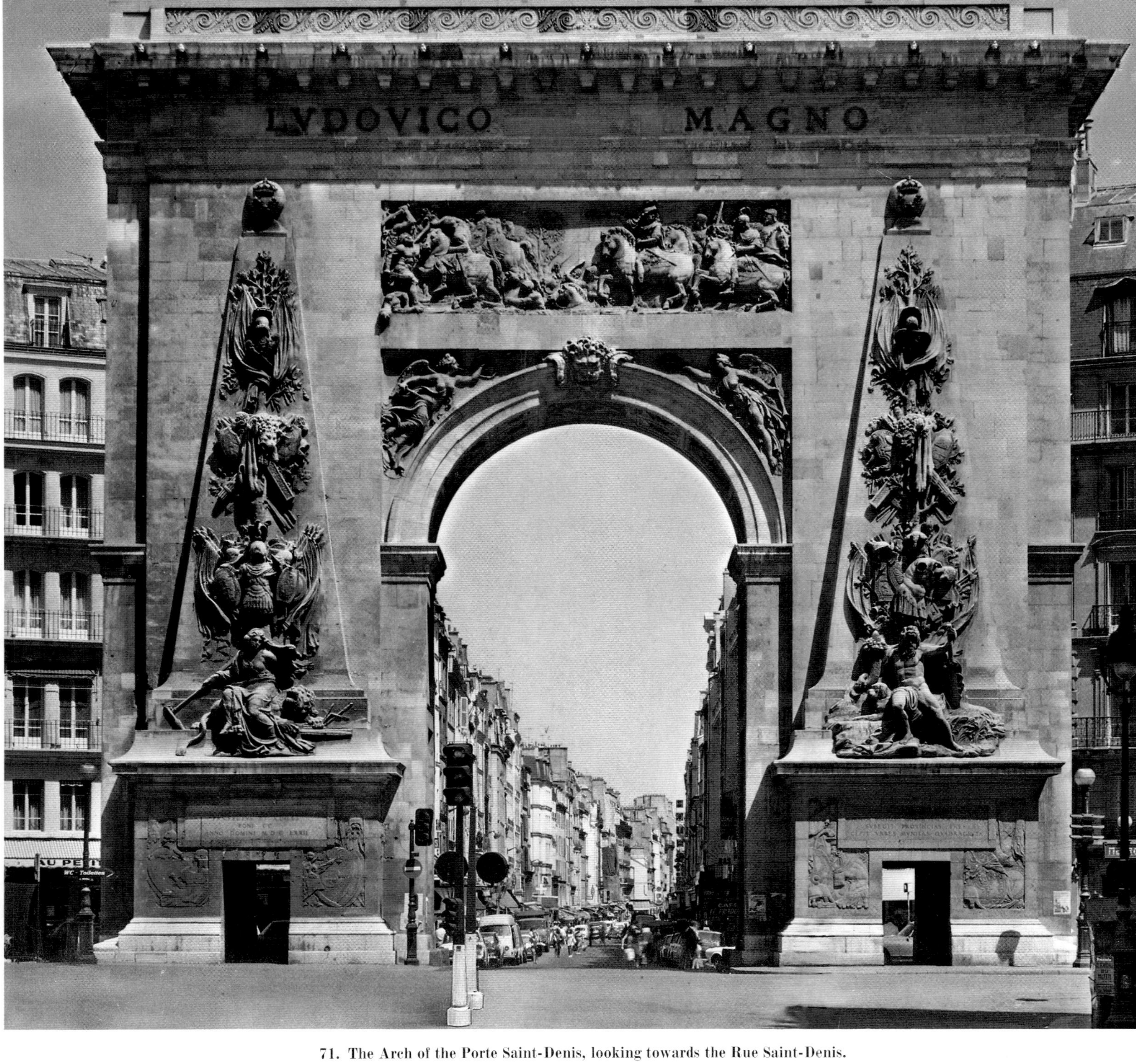

71. The Arch of the Porte Saint-Denis, looking towards the Rue Saint-Denis.

71. The Porte Saint-Denis.

Paris dwelt within the walls built to protect it against the barbarians, the Normans, the Plantaganets, and later, the Spanish of the Netherlands and the Imperials. After the campaigns of Flanders and the Franche-Comté, Louis XIV considered that the city no longer needed defences and that Vauban's fortifications on the frontiers would provide security enough. In 1670 the wall built by Charles V was demolished and replaced by a walk with trees, bordered by an ordinary wall with a toll gate. Thus the "grands boulevards" were born. To replace the fortified gates, the City decided to put up Roman-style arches. Those which stood at the Portes Saint-Bernard and Saint-Antoine no longer exist, but we still have the Porte Saint-Martin, built by Pierre Bullet (1674) and the Porte Saint-Denis. François Blondel began work on the latter in 1672. It was dedicated to the King's personal victories during the Dutch war in 1672 and 1673: the Crossing of the Rhine and the Taking of Maëstricht (bas-reliefs by Michel Anguier). The inscription LUDOVICO MAGNO recalls the medallion of 1671 when, for the first time, the City bestowed the title "the Great" on Louis XIV.

72. The Place Vendôme.

The Place Vendôme was built at the same time as the Place des Victoires. In 1677 Jules Hardouin-Mansart got together with five financiers to sell the Hôtel de Vendôme by lots. In order to attract buyers, a square was planned, to include such official institutions as the Bibliothèque Royale, the Académies, the Hôtels de Monnaies and the Hôtel des Ambassadeurs.
Hardouin-Mansart began work on this first Place Louis-le-Grand in 1685, on the orders of Louvois and at the King's expense. It was rectangular in shape, opening into the Rue Saint-Honoré, a plan repeated later in the royal Place de Bordeaux and Place de Lisbonne. Only the facades were built however, and it was amidst this hollow scenery that the equestrian statue, cast by Girardon, was erected in 1699.
When no buyers turned up, the King made over the site to the City, which then asked Hardouin-Mansart to draw up a new plan. This was adopted in 1699; it included the demolition of the 1685 facades and the building of a chamfered square, with two streets letting off it, one towards the church of the Capucines (Rue de la Paix), and the other leading towards the Rue Saint-Honoré and the Portail des Feuillants (Rue de Castiglione). The facades resemble those of the Place des Victoires but here the order is Corinthian, not Ionic. The dormer windows are an important feature and the building's fore-parts with their columns and pediments, give the whole an overall rhythm.
All this building was essentially the work of the great financiers of the Regency—Law, Pennautier, Crozat and of the architects Boffrand, Pierre Bullet and Bullet de Chamblain. The statue of Louis XIV, destroyed during the Revolution, was replaced in 1810 by the Colonne de la Grande Armée.
Ever since the Revolution, Trajan's column had haunted people's imaginations. In 1798, Poyet wanted to erect a column in honour of the French people on the terrace of the Pont-Neuf. Then in 1800 it was decided that columns should be erected in the country's various departments as well as a national column. Paris apparently had two such columns, one in the Place Vendôme, the other in the Place de la Concorde. After the battle of Austerlitz, Vivant Denon suggested that a Colonne de la Grande Armée, cast from the bronze of the Austrian canons, should be erected in the Place Vendôme. Napoléon agreed to this in 1806 and assigned the task to Gondoin and Lepère.
The spiralling bas-reliefs, which tell the story of the 1805 campaign, were designed by Bergeret, a pupil of David. In 1810, a statue of Napoléon as "Imperator" by Chaudet was added to the top of the column. The statue saw troubled times (which included the destruction of the column during the Paris Commune) and the one we see today is a copy of the original by Dumont.

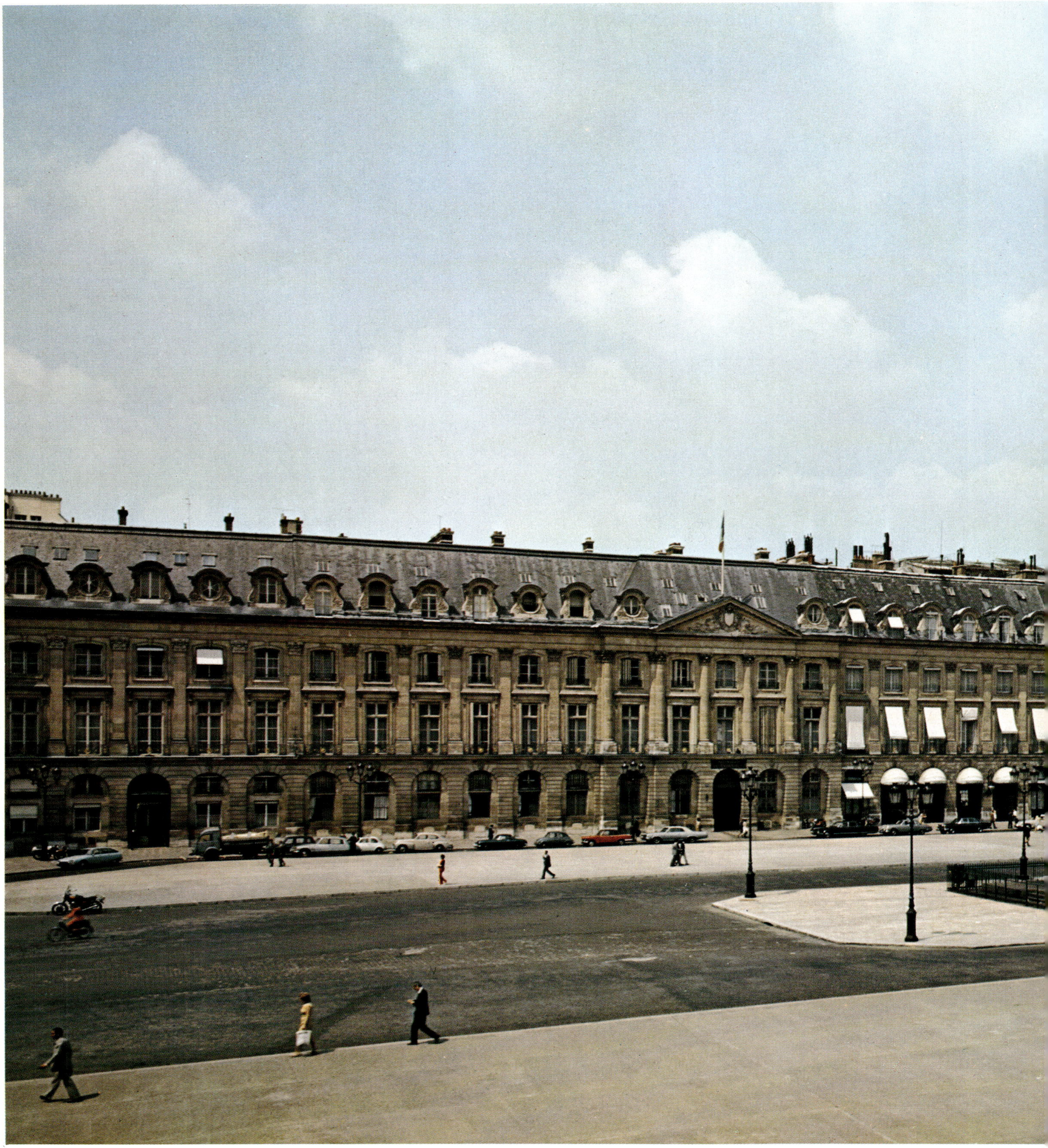

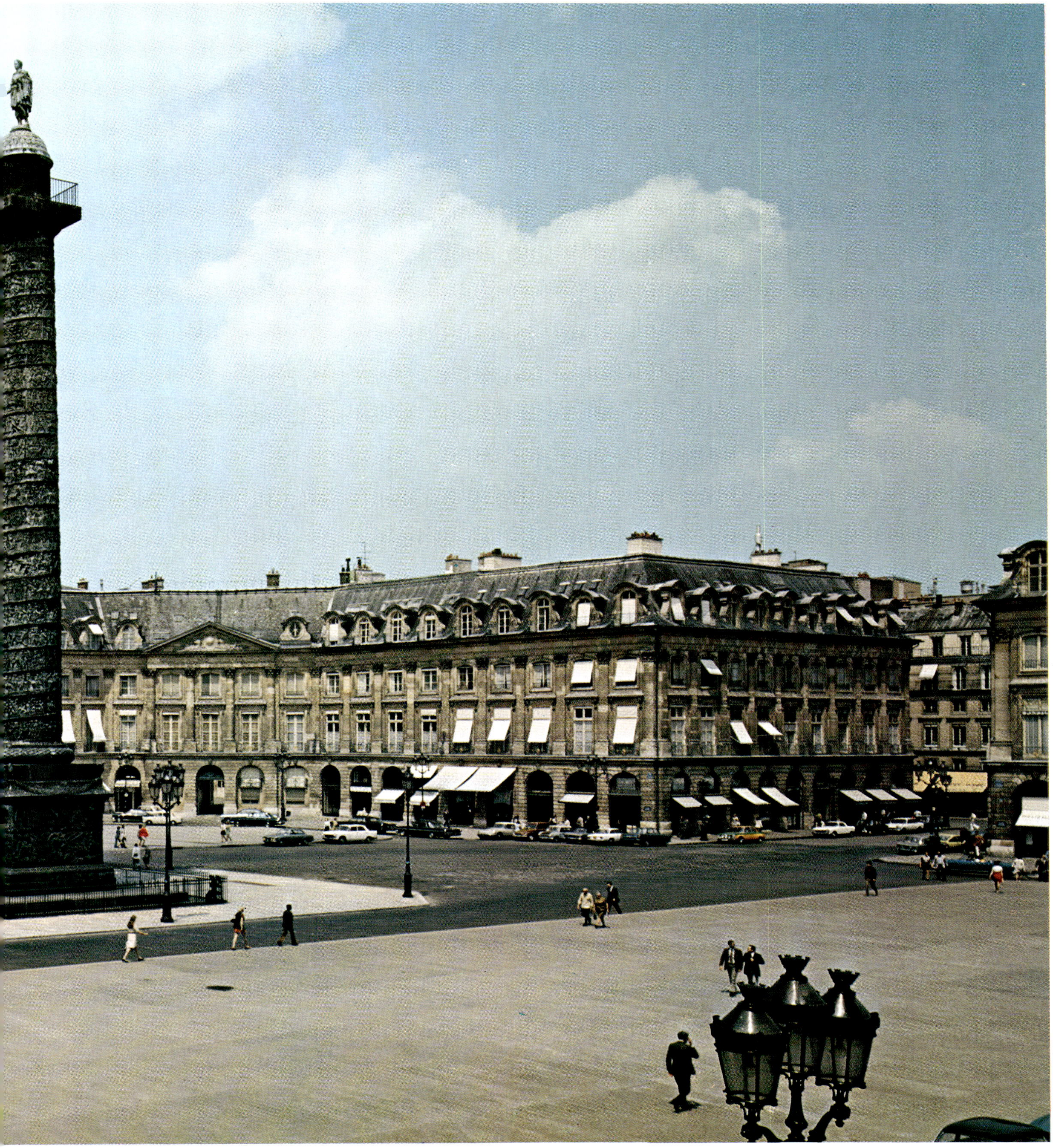

72. The Place Vendôme, formerly Place Louis-le-Grand.

73 to 75. The Hôtel de Rohan-Strasbourg.

Armand Gaston de Rohan, bishop-prince of Strasbourg, member of the Académie Française in 1704, cardinal in 1712 and High Chaplain of France, played a leading role in the first half of the eighteenth century and was also a great builder. It is to him we owe the first Château de Saverne and the Palais Rohan in Strasbourg. In Paris he had a palace built opposite that of his parents (1705-1708) and designed by the same architect, Delamair. Built on open ground, the Hôtel de Rohan-Strasbourg is quite different from the Hôtel de Soubise: its building is much higher, more wide-spreading and the decoration is more sober in style, as befits the residence of a prince of the Church.

Later on, the Cardinal de Rohan had Delamair add a vast stable yard (1725-1750). Above the gate which led, through the drinking troughs, to the fifty-two stalls, he had Robert de Lorrain sculpt a bas relief portraying the Horses of the Sun watered by servants. It is one of the most beautiful sculptures of the century.

In 1749-1750, the Cabinet des Singes (the so-called Monkey Study) was painted. Polychromy had vanished from apartments during the reign of Louis XIV to be replaced by white and gold panelling. Under Louis XV, color was gradually rediscovered, and some rooms were painted in plain light colors with contrasting white borders. The more secluded rooms and studies still occasionally kept to the tradition of "narative" decor. A painter of carriages and sedan chairs, Christophe Huet, made a speciality of it, following the tradition of the "grotesques" of Berain, Audran, Watteau and Lancret. In his work at Chantilly and Champs, his love of the exotic is reflected in the lavish use of chinoiserie and decorative monkeys, as it is at the Hôtel de Rohan-Strasbourg where he painted the Cabinet des Singes.

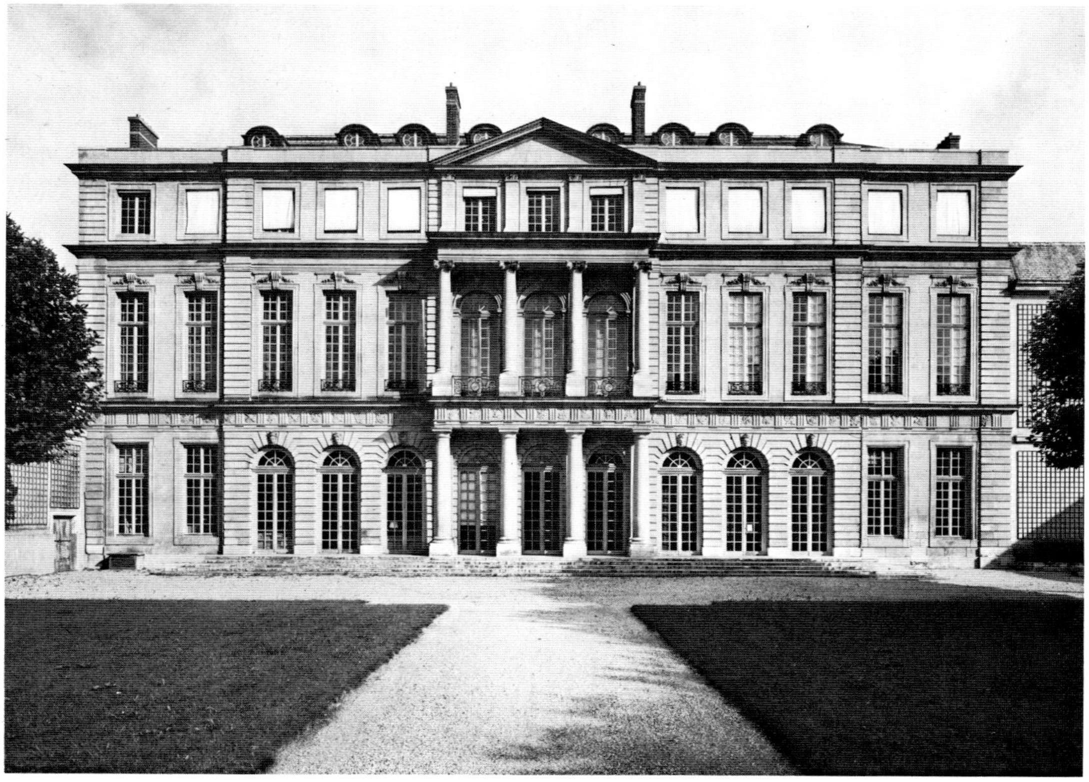

73. The Hôtel de Rohan-Strasbourg, 87, Rue Vieille-du-Temple, 3rd Arr., the facade on the garden.

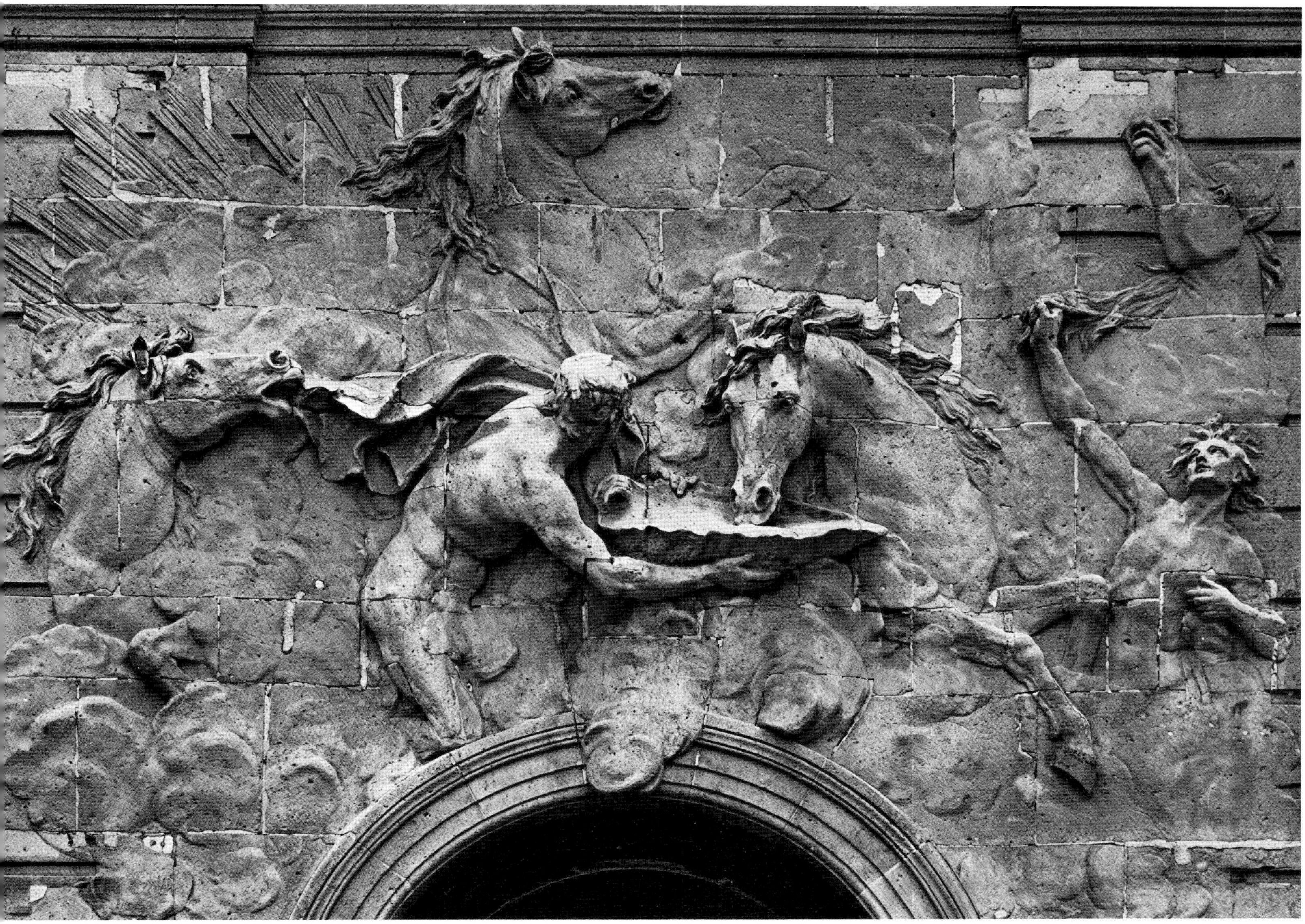

74. The horses of the Sun, by Robert Le Lorrain, bas-relief over the gateway of the Cardinal de Rohan's stables.

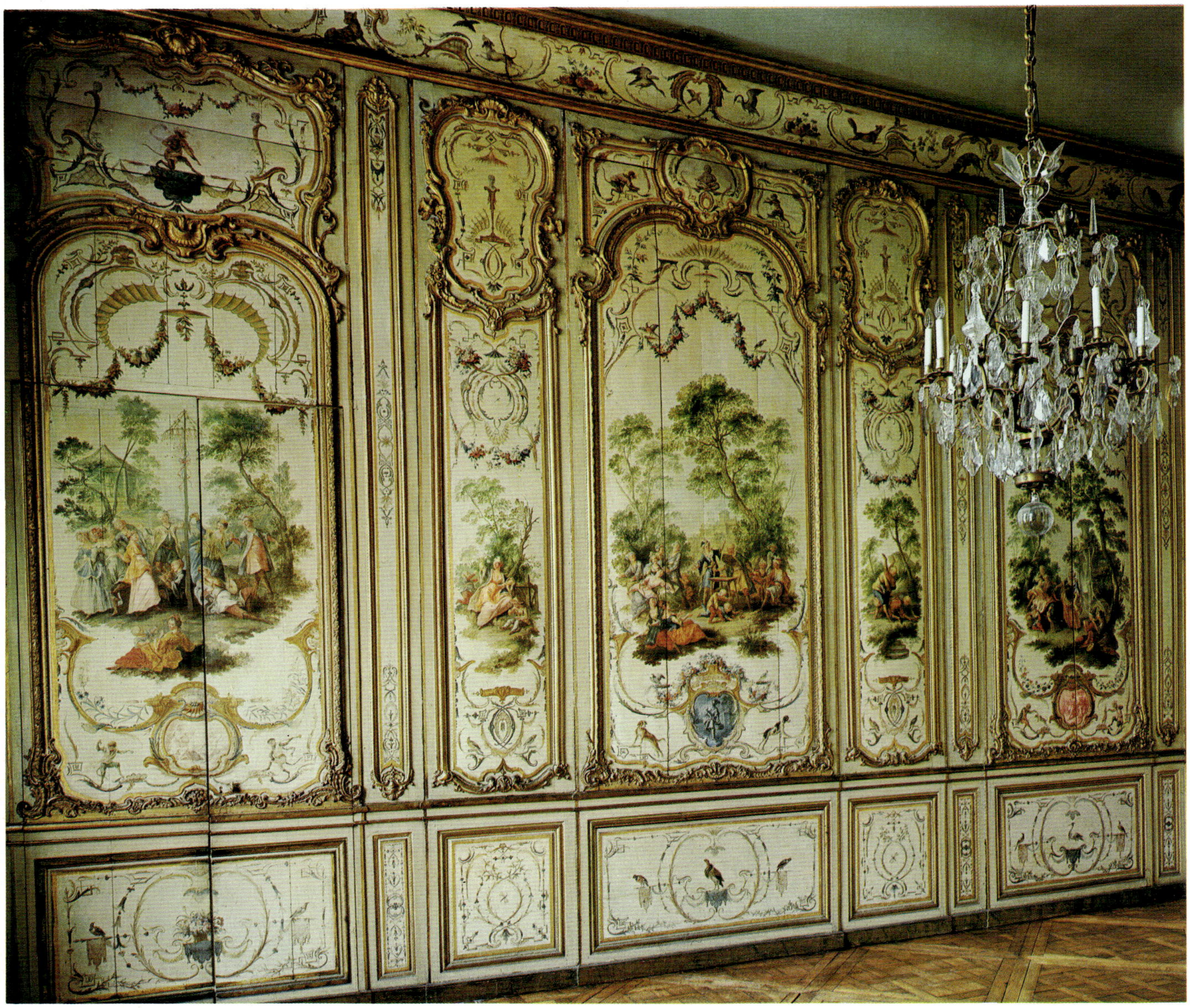

75. The Cabinet des Singes in the Hôtel de Rohan-Strasbourg.

76 and 77. The Hôtel de Rohan-Soubise.

The prince of Rohan-Soubise had his palace fitted out with a princely generosity beyond the scale of hôtels of the time. He was the husband of the beautiful Ann Chabot de Rohan who had enjoyed the favors of Louis XIV and wished to place the name of Rohan in the front rank after the princes of the blood. In 1700 they bought the old Hôtel de Guise, an immense property in the heart of the Marais, and decided to transform it. A young architect Pierre Alexis Delamair, was recommended to them by their son, the future cardinal de Rohan, and he managed to assert himself in spite of the endeavours of Hardouin-Mansart. With remarkable ingenuity Delamair used a vacant area of land which had been a riding-school to lay out a vast courtyard edged with peristyles, the size of a public square, and at the far end he covered what had been a side face of the Hôtel de Guise with classical decoration on a grand scale. He even preserved at one end the medieval turrets of the portal of Olivier de Clisson (ill. 39) probably as a reminder that the Rohans were descended from officials of the Royal household. The palace was erected from 1705-1708 but the interiors of the apartments which we see today date from thiry years later and are the most splendid eighteenth century ensemble that remains intact.

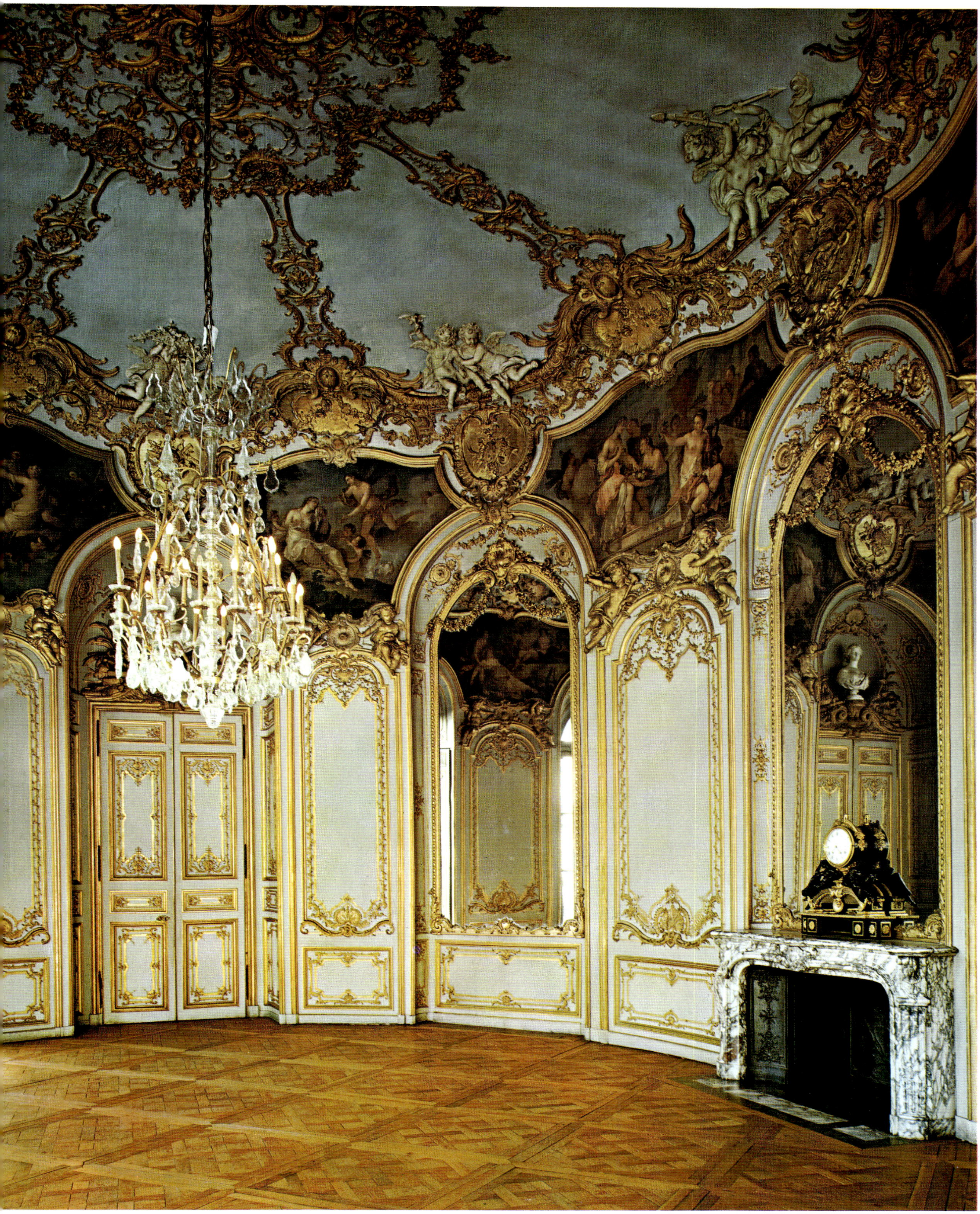

76. The oval drawing room of the Princess of Soubise.

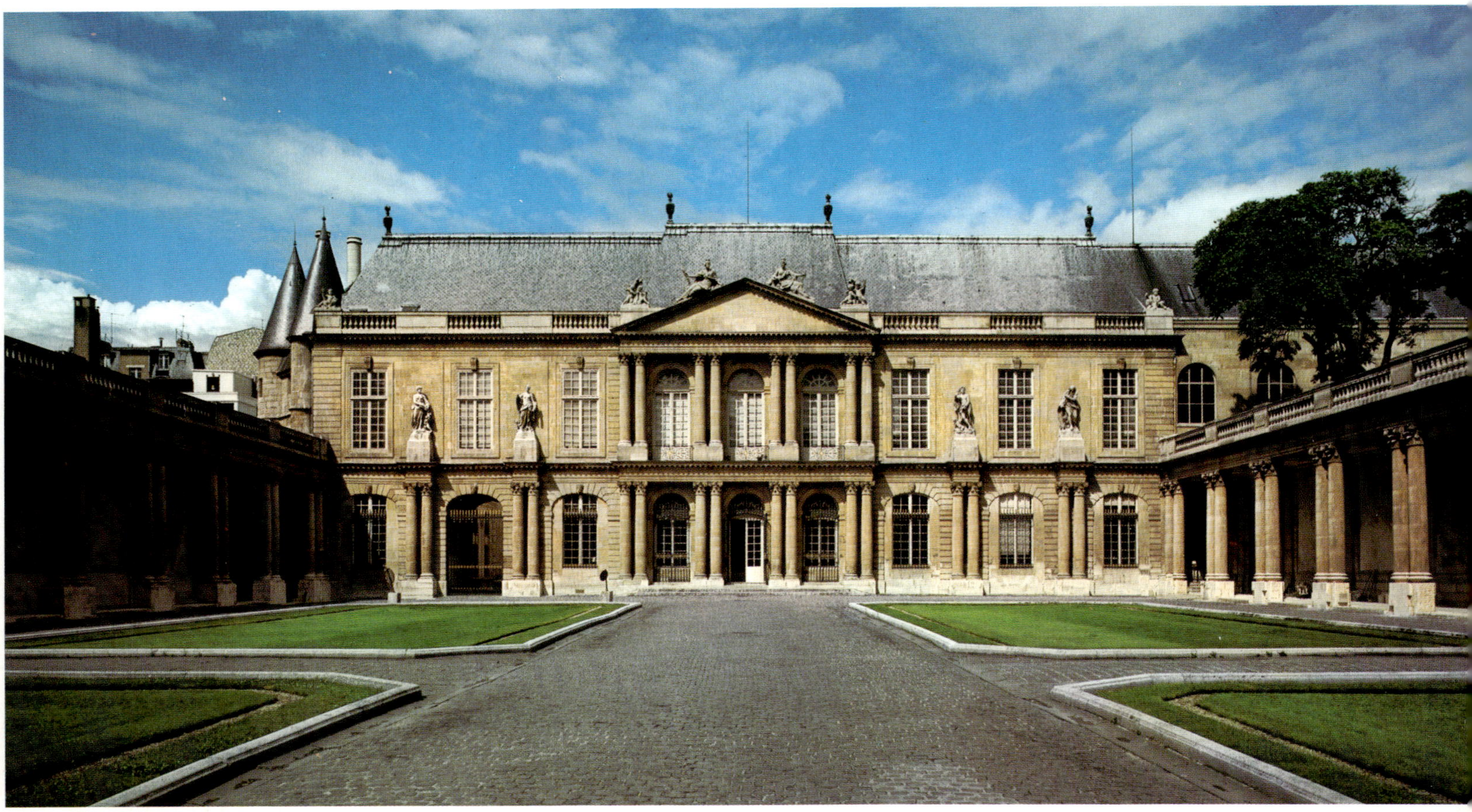

77. The Hôtel de Rohan-Soubise, 60, Rue des Francs-Bourgeois, 3rd. Arr. The National Archives.

After his re-marriage the prince Hercule-Mériadec de Rohan made sweeping changes in his whole lifestyle (1735-1739). After the old apartments Germain Boffrand built a pavilion to accommodate on both floors an oval-shaped salon.
Then he designed the panelling and stucco, calling in the finest painters: Boucher, Van Loo, Trémolières, Restout and Natoire, and the sculptors Adam the elder and the younger and Jean-Baptiste II Lemoine. An inconographic programme was decided for each room, expressed in the carvings on wood, the panelling, the cornices, the white stucco work, the gilding, yellow or green, matt or brilliant, married with the vivid colors of the lintels and the crimson damask of the tapestries in the alcoves, the drapes on the beds and the furniture. The prince's bedroom on the ground floor, recently restored, is dedicated to famous mythological couples, painted on the lintels, and masculine virtues, sculptured in the wainscoting. The oval drawing room into which it leads is painted in blue-green and decorated with bas-reliefs representing the sciences and the arts, and is one of the most harmonious masterpieces of the eighteenth century.
On the upper floor, the princess's state room is devoted to the theme of the education of a young beauty, painted over the lintels, and the loves of Jupiter, carved in the wainscoting and the cornice. The oval drawing room, so luxuriantly decorated that it was copied for Ludwig II of Bavaria at Herrenchiemsee Castle, is dedicated to Psyche, whose adventures are painted by Natoire. The gilded lattice of the ceiling is reminiscent of an open-air arbour. The rhythm of the arcades, the progression of reliefs from floor to ceiling, and the proportion between oval axes and height, make this room the great masterpiece of rococo art.

78. The Hôtel de Toulouse.

When Louis Phélypeaux de La Vrillière, wealthy secretary of State to Louis XIII, had a hôtel built for himself near the Palais Cardinal, he asked François Mansart to provide for a long gallery in the garden where he could house a part of his important collection of paintings (1635-1638). Huge historical paintings were set into the panelling of the first floor beneath a barrel-vault decorated by François Perrier on the model of the Farnese gallery. In 1705 the hôtel was bought by Raulin Rouille de Jouy, a tax-farmer, whose widow in her turn sold it in 1713 to Louis-Alexandre de Bourbon, Count of Toulouse, Admiral of France and son of Louis XIV and Madame de Montespan.

The prince had the hôtel transformed by Robert de Cotte. Except for the vault paintings, the gallery was stripped and fitted with sumptuous panelling designed by the sculptor Vasse (1719). The piers were furnished with pilasters, the alcoves facing the windows fitted with mirrors, the entrance door and the monumental hearth at each end surmounted with marine deities—an allusion to his office of Admiral of France; the great paintings, augmented by more, were replaced in the piers. Assigned later to the State Press and then to the Bank of France, this magnificent dwelling was bit by bit demolished and reconstructed during the nineteenth century, including the gilded Gallery, which was reconstituted in 1870-1875 from prints. Only Vassé's sculptures (wood and stucco) were used again.

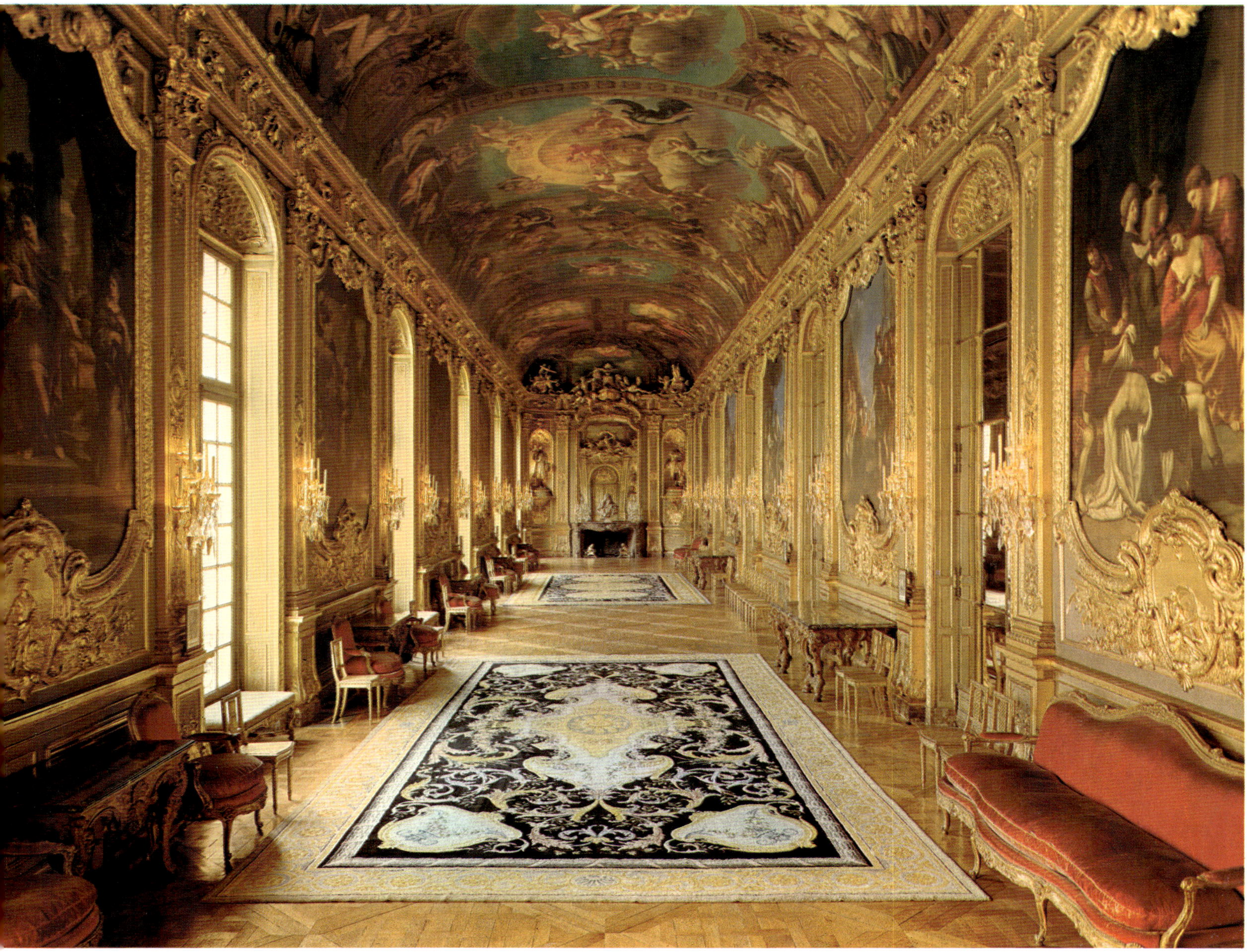

78. The Golden Gallery in the Hôtel de Toulouse, now the Bank of France, 1-3, Rue de La-Vrillière, 1st Arr.

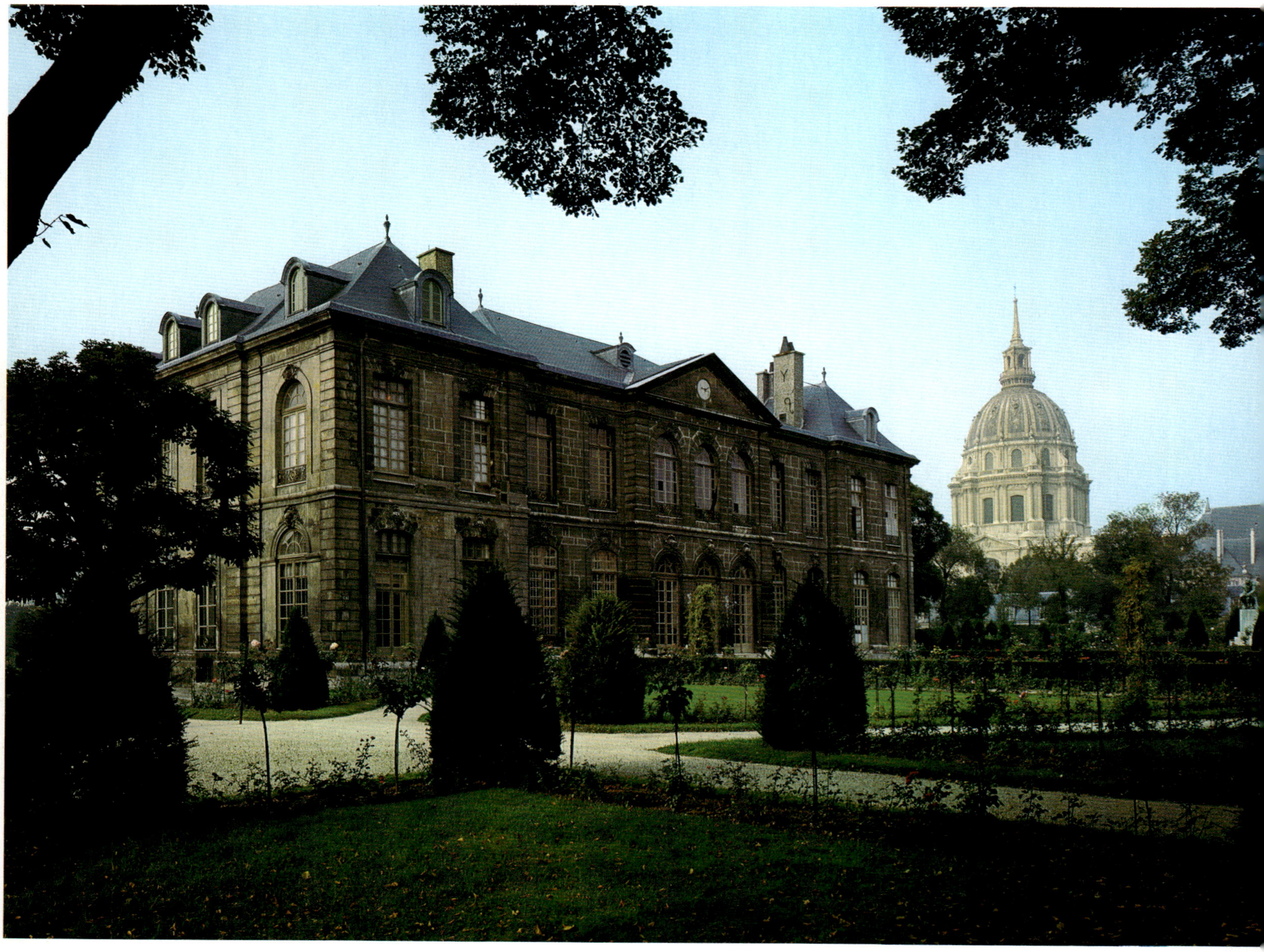

79 and 80. The Hôtel Peyrenc de Moras, subsequently the Hôtel Biron, 77, rue de Varenne, 7th Arr., today the Rodin Museum. The facade on the entrance side seen from the little garden (79). The facade on the park (80).

79 and 80. The Hôtel Biron, the Rodin Museum.

From the end of the seventeenth century, architects strove to dissociate the main building of a hôtel from its courtyard and outbuildings. The culmination of this was the hôtel Biron, isolated on all sides and surrounded by gardens, erected at the furthest end of the faubourg Saint-Germain on a green site where the English park added for the duc de Biron blended in perfectly.
The hôtel is traditionally attributed to Jacques V Gabriel, whose design was supposedly carried out by Jean Aubert. Recent research has proved that the essential role was played by Aubert himself, builder of the celebrated Chantilly Stables. The spacious site at the corner of the Rue de Varenne and the Boulevard des Invalides (laid in 1704) had been acquired by Abraham Peyrenc, a former wigmaker who had become wealthy through the system of the

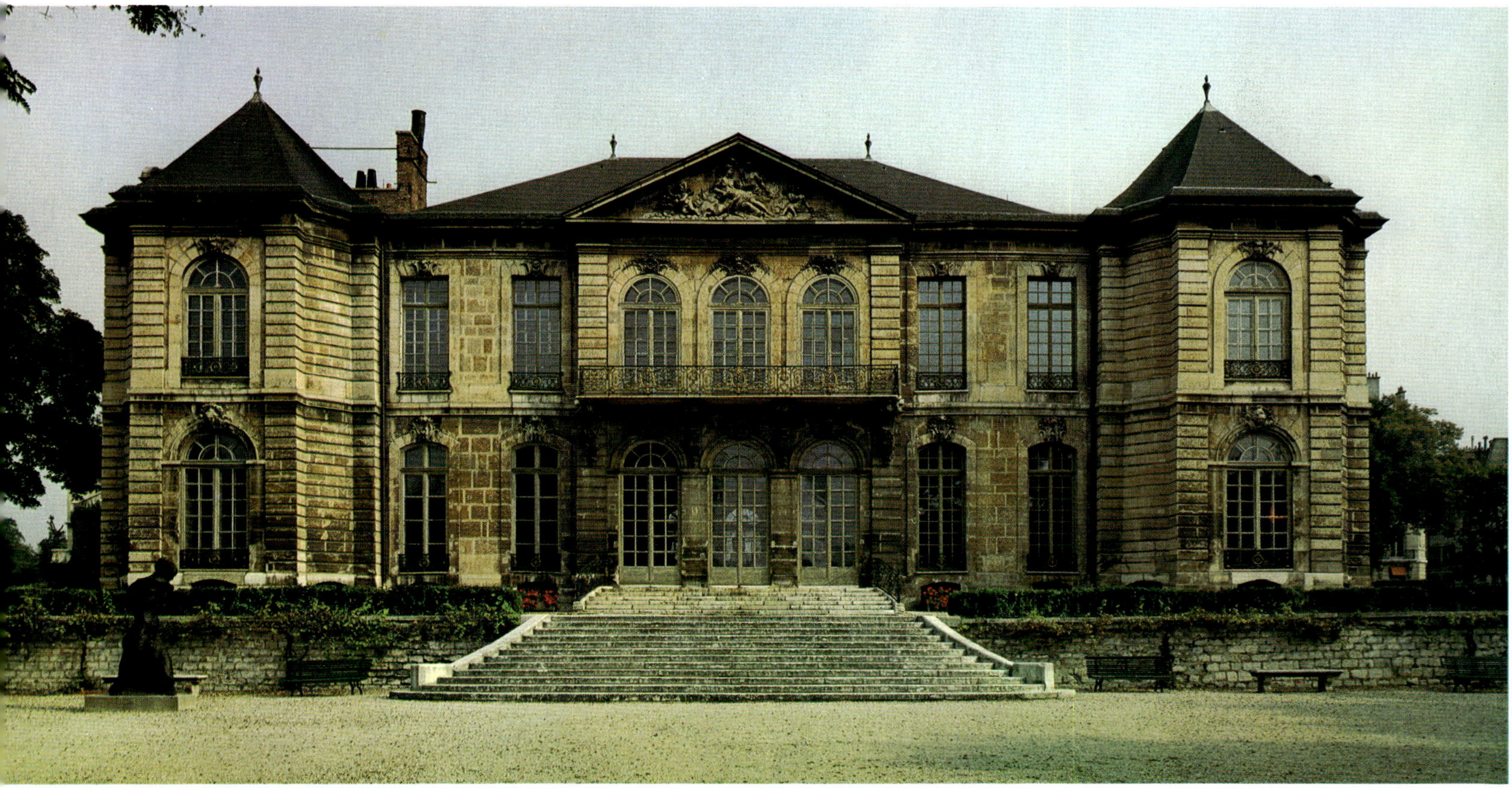

Law, latterly Mr Moras and an official of the State, bailiff of the Condé family. Construction went on from 1728 to 1730. The outbuildings and offices were grouped around the stable yard at the corner of the two streets, and the kitchens connected by an underground passage with the dining room.
Placed on a wide area of raised ground, the hôtel is livened by projecting parts on its main facades, with separate roofs. These, on the park side, enclose the extremities of two large oval rooms. The whole has a picturesque harmony which, like the persistent use of corner stones, is typical of Aubert's style. Peyrenc died here in 1732. His widow sold the hôtel to a princess of the blood, the duchesse de Maine, who spent her last years (1736-1753) there. It then became the residence of Louis-Antoine de Gontaut, duc de Biron, marshal of France, who gave ostentatious receptions there and opened the gardens to the people of Paris. Since 1910 it has been the Rodin Museum.

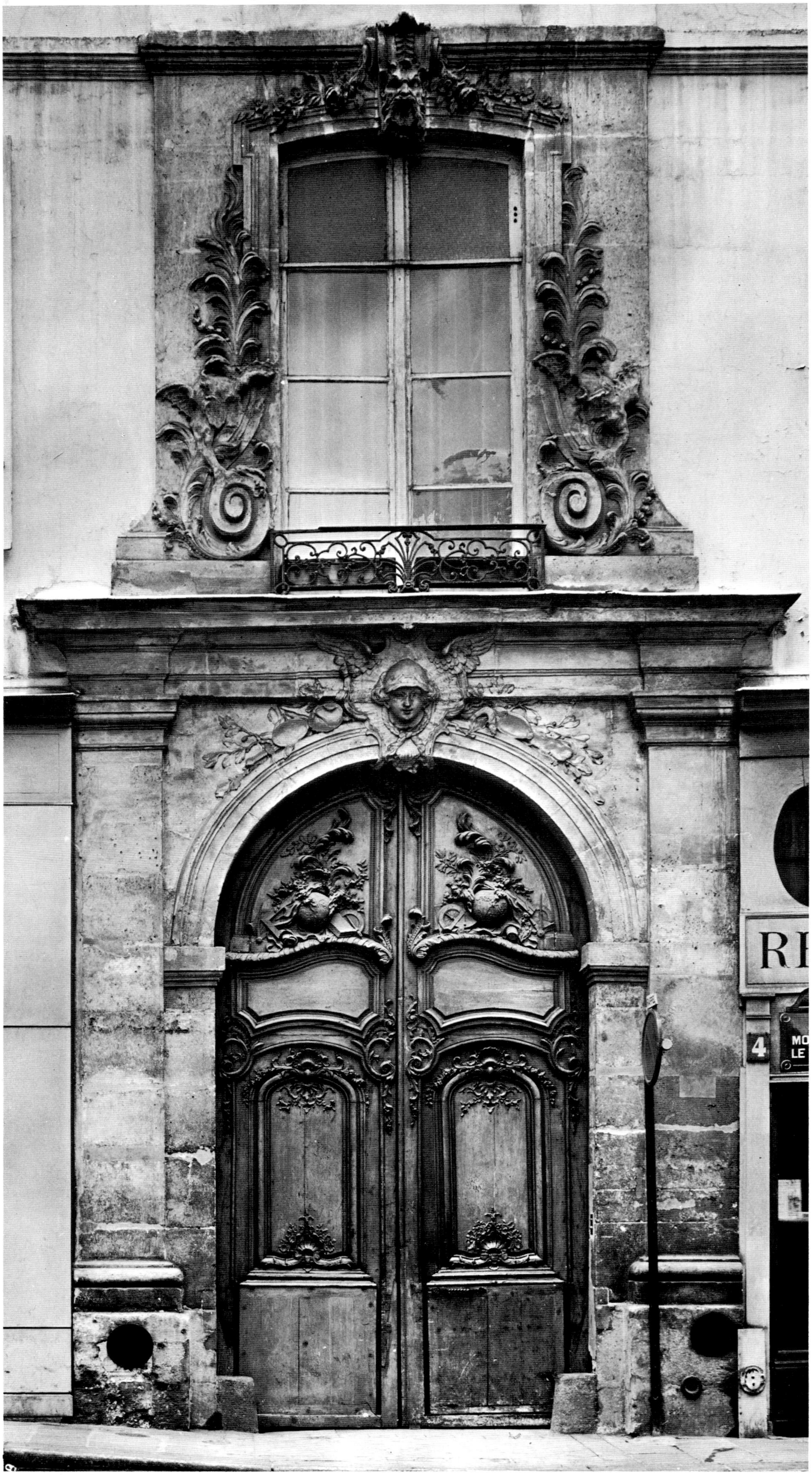

81

81. The Portal of No. 4, Rue Monsieur-le-Prince.

The rococo art, which scarcely appeared on the frontages of the great Parisian hotels (while it inspired their interiors), often figured on more humble facades such as 29 Rue de la Parcheminerie, 151 Rue Saint-Jacques, 27 Rue Lhommond, 151 Boulevard de Sébastopol, 2 Rue de la Jussienne and at the Hôtels Chenizot and d'Ecquevilly. The main door to Nº 4 Rue Monsieur-le-Prince served as entrance, beneath a house known as the "Hôtel de Bacq", to the alleyway "of the Rich Farmer", which led to No. 3 Rue de Condé and was closed in 1779. When and by whom it was conceived is unknown, but the leavers of the door, with their carvings symbolic of the sciences, the Mercury on the keystone, and the palm-scrolls at the windows are the work of a great artist who was a contemporary of Oppenord and Pineau.

81. The portal of No. 4, Rue Monsieur-le-Prince, 6th Arr.

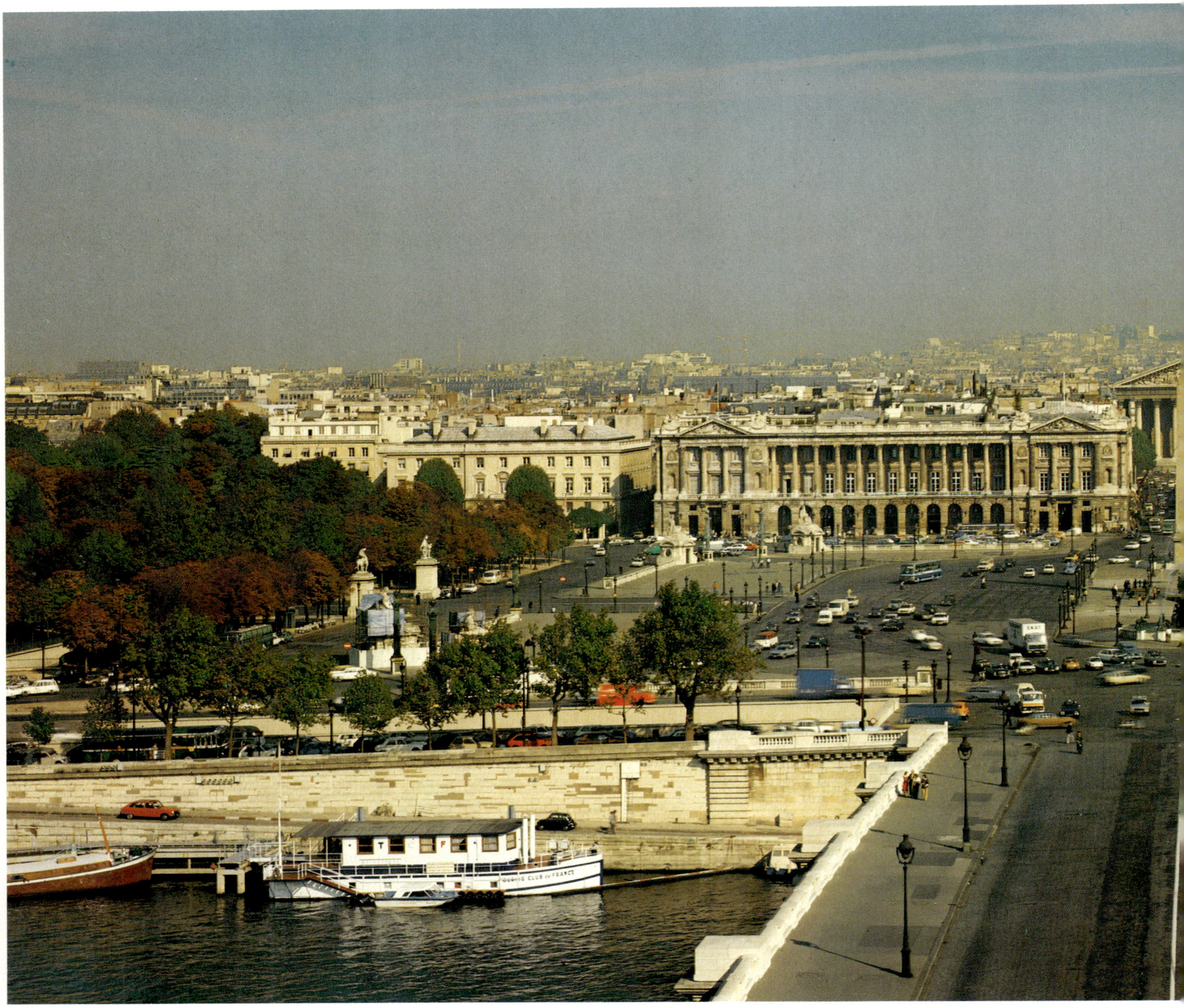

82. The Place de la Concorde.

After the treaty of Aix-la-Chapelle the city wished to honor the glorious name of Louis XV and on 27 June 1748 decided to erect an equestrian statue of him, while the Academy of architecture proposed laying out a square. The 90 projects that flowed in to the count of Argenson placed the square in various districts of Paris. Louis XV selected an unoccupied area of land which belonged to him, at the end of the Tuileries gardens (1750), from the viewpoint of the "great promenade" designed by Marie de Medici and transformed by Le Nôtre (the Champs-Elysées). In 1753 a second competition attracted 19 plans. The King instructed Gabriel to blend all their advantages into a new plan which provided for a single large building on the north side, divided eventually to allow the Rue Royale to pass through. Louis XV Square was laid out in 1757-1772. It was not crossed, as it is today, by traffic ways (the Concorde Bridge had not been envisaged) and formed a great mall for pedestrians, isolated by

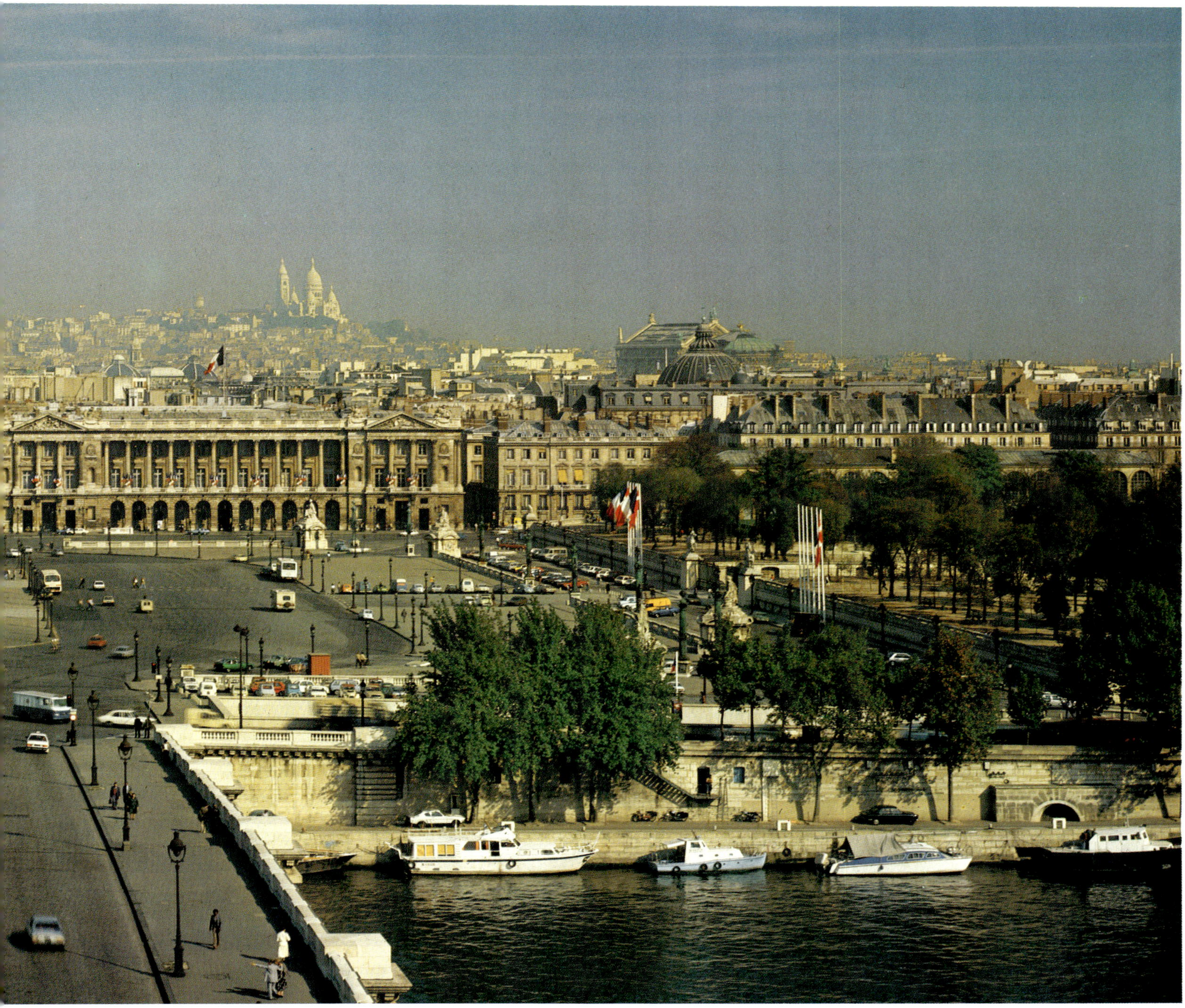

82. Place de la Concorde. Buildings by Gabriel: the Ministry of the Navy, and to the left, the Hôtel Crillon.

balustrades and masonry ditches. The equestrian statue was cast in bronze by Bouchardon in 1758 and unveiled in 1763 on a pedestal by Pigalle, only to be pulled down less than thirty years later. The plinth of the statue of Louis XV on "Revolution" square needed a new effigy. They placed Liberty there, facing the scaffold of the guillotine, and at the same time they placed Marly horses, groups by Coustou sculpted for the Marly watering-pond in 1739, at the entrance to the Champs-Elysées; then the National Convention bequeathed to the Directoire a square named Place de la Concorde. Hundreds of plans were submitted, Napoleon wanted a central fountain, Louis XVIII a new statue of Louis XV, Charles X a monument to Louis XVI. Avoiding any political symbolism, Louis-Philippe adopted in 1833 the plan by Hittorff: to erect the Luxor Obelisk, which Mehmet Ali had just given to France, between two fountains placed in imitation of those before St Peter's at Rome, with twenty lampstands in the form of rostral columns and eight statues representing cities of France on Gabriel's sentry-boxes. The square was finished in 1840.

83. Saint-Roch.

Saint-Roch was completed at the same time as Saint-Sulpice. The church had been undertaken by Le Mercier in 1653. From 1706-1710 Jules Hardouin-Mansart, followed by Pierre Bullet, built the beautiful oval-shaped chapel of the Virgin. In 1722 the vaults were built. The finishing touch was the great portal of which the first stone was laid by Robert de Cotte in 1736. The facade follows the classical plan which has since been so often copied in Paris, but the double columns, the sharply projecting pediment where the royal coat of arms once stood, and the high staircase where it is perched, all give the building special breadth in the narrow Rue Saint-Honoré.

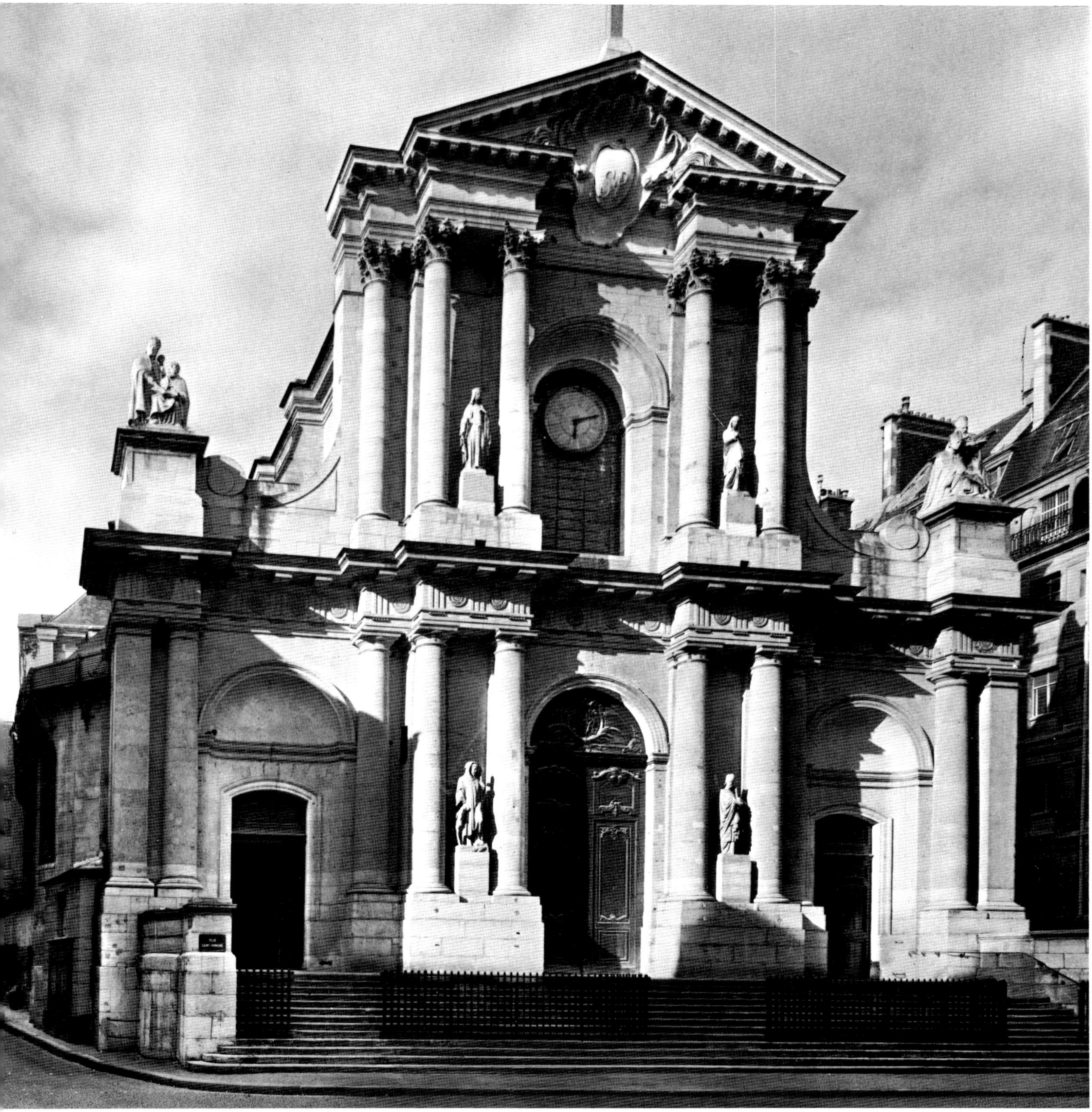

83. The facade of the church of Saint-Roch.

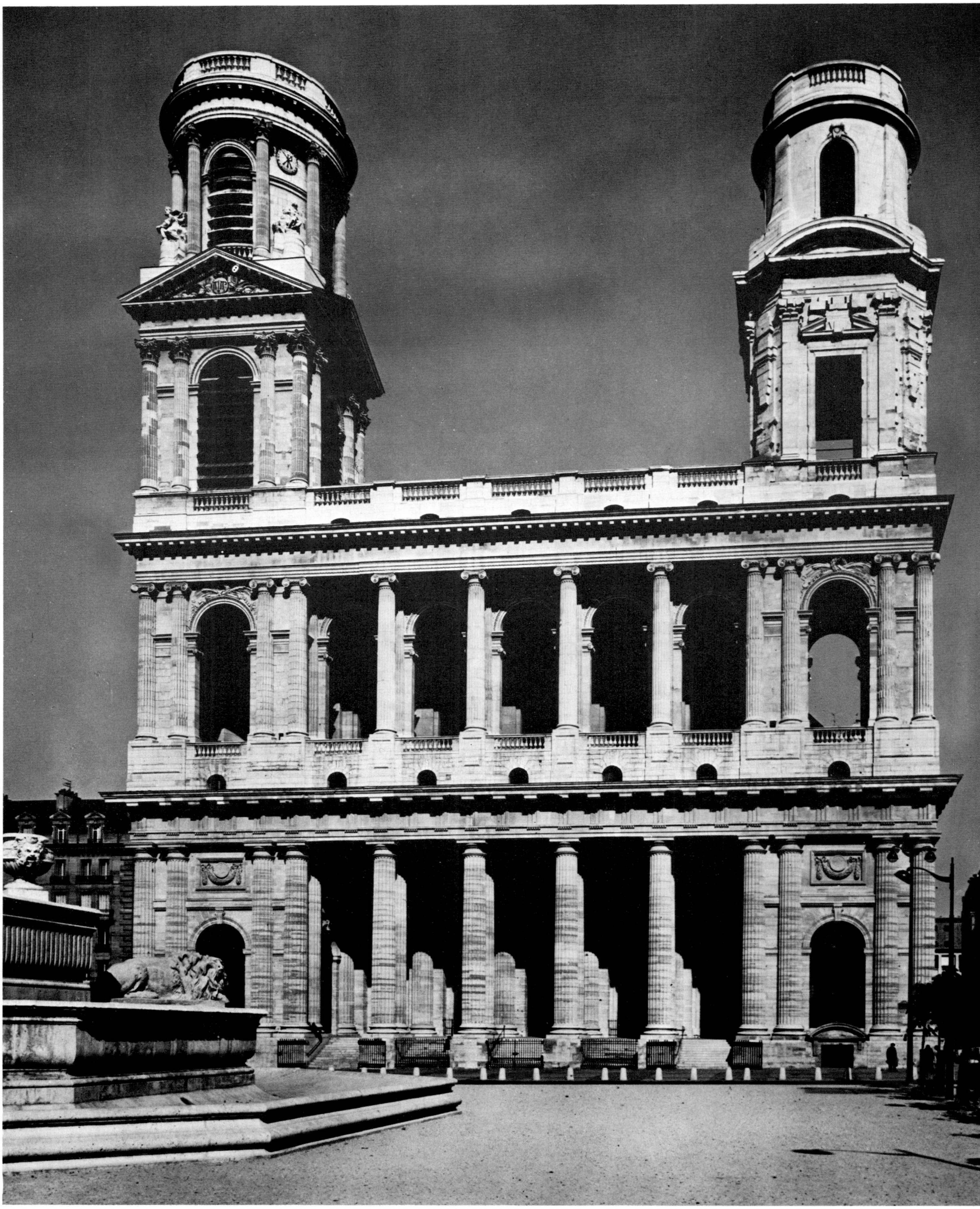

84. Saint-Sulpice, the facade.

84. Saint-Sulpice.

The importance of the market town of Saint-Germain grew as it spread out around the old abbey, and this meant a church had to be built. It was dedicated to Saint Sulpice and, from the early thirteenth century, had the rank of parish church. Rebuilt and enlarged during the Middle Ages, it was still not large enough to cater for the great numbers of the faithful in its immense parish. Thus when Jean-Jacques Ollier was appointed vicar (1642), he decided to have it rebuilt. Christophe Gamard, the architect of Saint-Germain-des-Prés was approached; he drew up plans for a building three times the size. The first stone was laid by Anne of Austria in 1646. Gamard died three years later and was replaced on the job by Louis Le Vau, who enlarged the plans even further. After Le Vau's death in 1670, his plans were then taken up by Daniel Gittard. The vast scale of the building and the splendor and majesty of its classical architecture make it the cathedral of the left bank. Work started on the choir and the left transept.
But, owing to lack of funds, building work then stopped in 1674, leaving the church reduced to a choir and the left transept. Forty years later, the vicar, Languet de Gergy, ordered that work be resumed again in 1718, thanks to a collection, supplemented by lotteries. The right transept was finished in 1723, and the nave ten years later. Since he adopted the general plan of his predecessors, Oppenord had little chance to express his powerful personality, with its bent towards the "rococo", except, that is, in the interior design of the far ends of the transept, which are rounded into alcoves with cherubs sculpted by Slodtz.
During the same period, an architect of Italian origin, Servandoni, a famous designer of festivals and operas, was asked to decorate the chapel of the Virgin: the dome was painted by Lemoine in 1731-1732. It was Wailly who painted the chapel the third time round (1774) and that is how it remains today, with the Virgin of Pigalle, standing like an apparition in an alcove lit as though by an invisible window.
After a competition had been held, Servandoni was also asked to build the great west front (1733-1749). In his plan, this was to overlook a great square surrounded by houses of uniform design (only number 6 was ever built). He built two great superposed porticos, thus forming a narthex between two towers whose upper stories were never built. He was inspired to a certain extent by the design of the Gothic cathedrals, except that the space between the towers was too great to achieve a harmonious proportion.
After his death in 1766, the Academy of Architecture discussed the thorny question of a crowning for the facade; Oudot de Maclaurin was asked to finish the two towers, whilst Patte was asked to build a great pediment, which was subsquently destroyed by lightning in 1770. At that point Chalgrin replaced the pediment with a balustrade surmounted by four colossal statues, and he also altered the north tower. The great organ-chest is also his work.

85. The Panthéon.

In 1744, after his illness at Metz, Louis XV had vowed to build a new church dedicated to Sainte Geneviève, patron saint of Paris, to replace the old abbey church. A decree of the Council in 1754 ordered its construction and the marquis of Marigny selected Jacques-Germain-Soufflot, with whom he had traveled in Italy during his famous journey of 1750 which was to hasten the advent of the new style inspired by Antiquity. Soufflot came back from Rome and his plan was approved by the King in 1757. It envisaged, at the top of the Sainte-Geneviève hill, a semicircular area setting off the acede of a vaste basilica. Excavations revealed that the site was dangerously undermined by pottery wells. The first stone was laid in 1764, but Soufflot continued to modify his plans and costs soon began to exceed the original estimate. Cracks, which a rival had warned about since 1770, appeared in 1778. Exhausted by work, Soufflot died in 1780 before starting on the dome. This was erected by his pupil Maximilien Brebion, assisted by Rondelet and Soufflot le Romain, and completed in 1790, only a year before the church became the "French Pantheon" dedicated to great men by the Constituant Assembly. It was then that the great windows were walled up so that light could only enter from above, as in the temples of antiquity. At the same time the ornamentation had been replaced by a patriotic decor; work on it went on throughout the nineteenth century. For a domed church, the Pantheon was a break with precedent. Where, previously, skilful transitions between volumes had been sought, Soufflot, on the contrary, preferred open and bold juxtaposition. While his exterior was a recreation of the forms of Roman antiquity, his interior was intended to be inspired by Gothic cathedrals in which the heavy supports of classical art were replaced by slim, elegant columns and ogival vaulting. "By using the Greek orders", he declared to the Academy in 1762, "one can approach the lightness of Gothic monuments—and make a great saving in materials". Moreover, to satisfy Soufflot's requirements, Rondelet invented the reinforced concrete girder to put together the great facade.

85. The Panthéon.

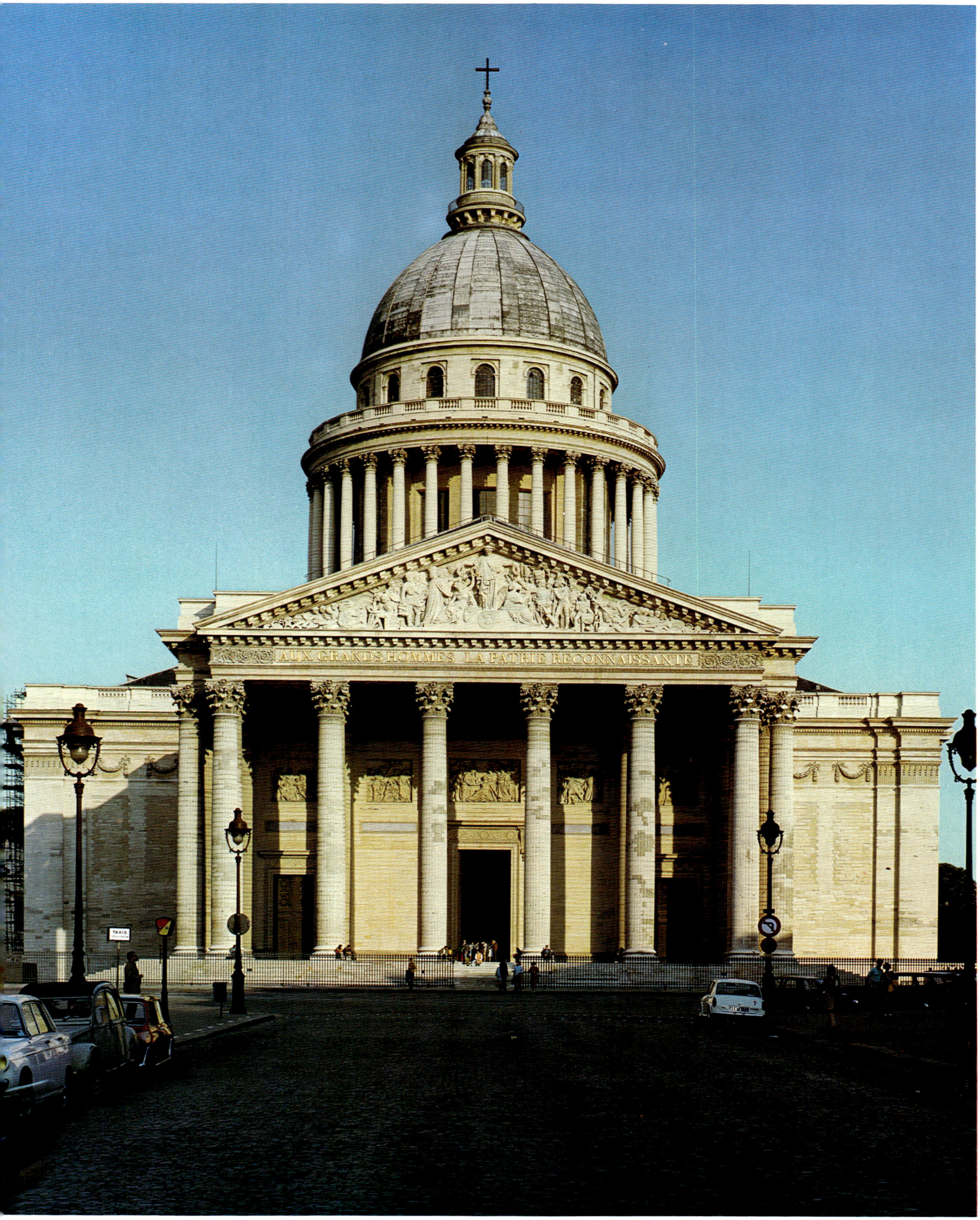
AUX GRANDS HOMMES LA PATRIE RECONNAISSANTE
TAXIS

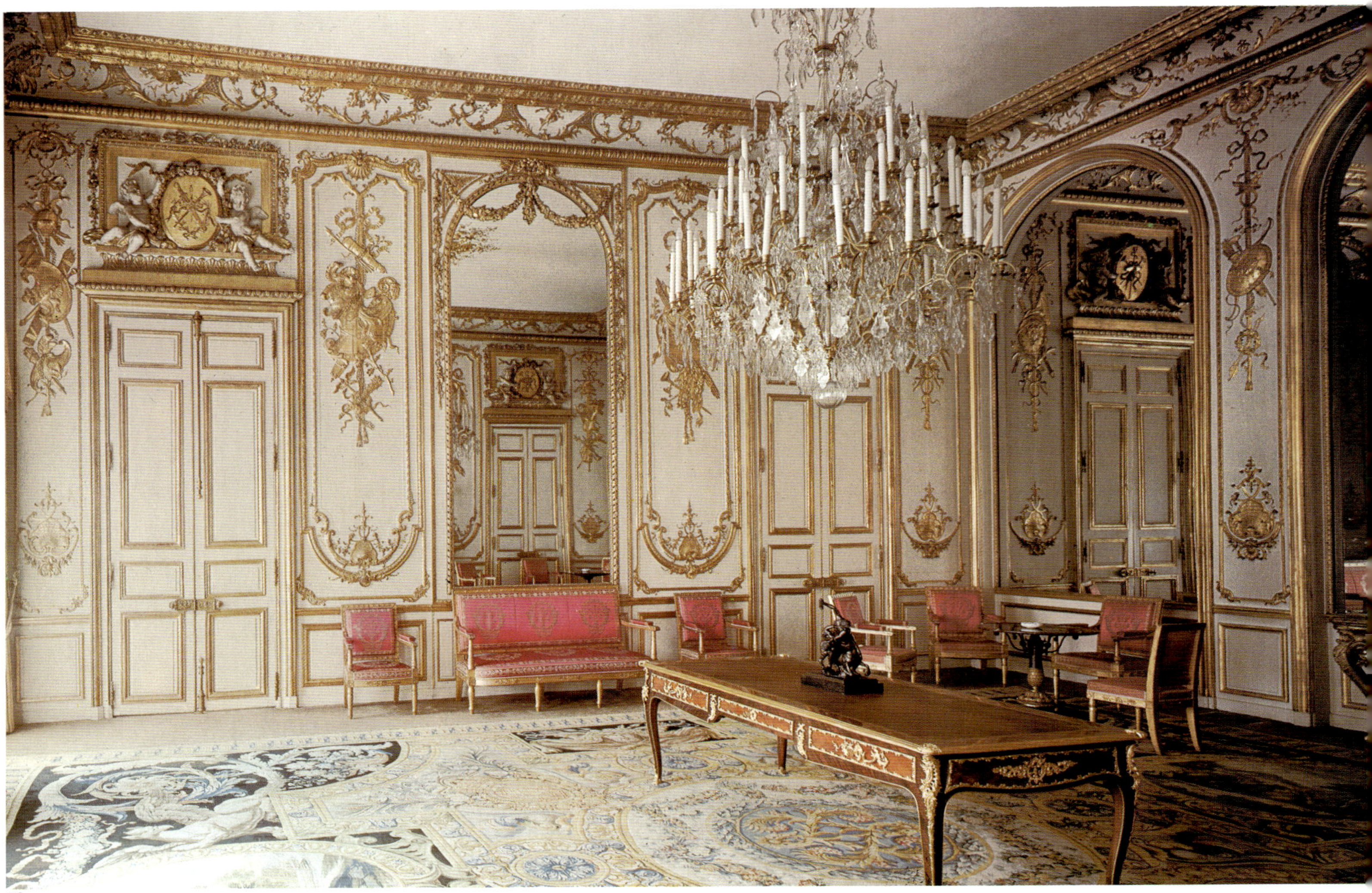
86

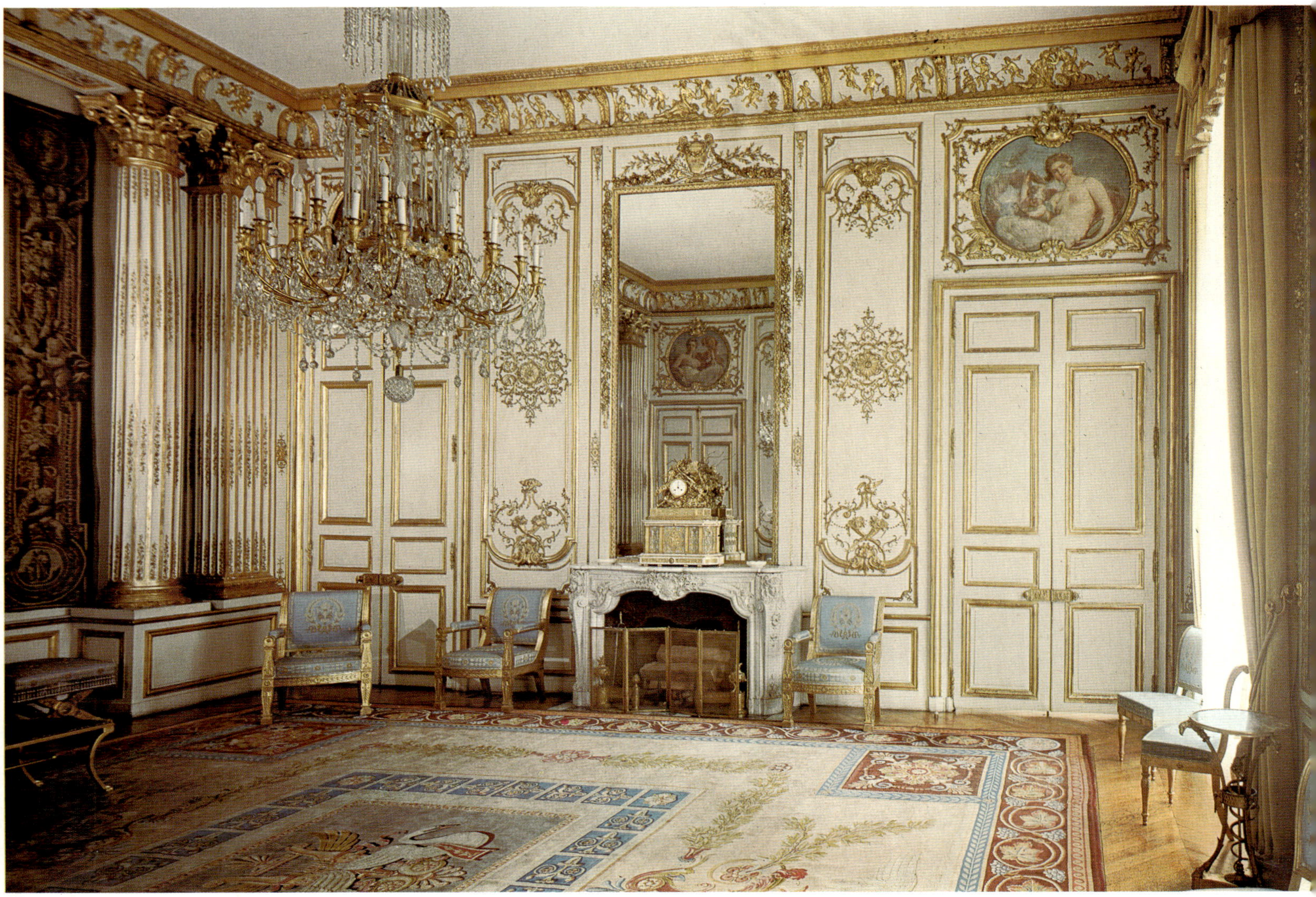
87

86 and 87. The Elysée Palace.

The Elysée has not escaped the fate of Versailles. Constantly lived in by personages of the highest rank, it has undergone a succession of transformations in accordance with taste until the present day. This is scarcely evident from the exterior. Apart from the great triumphal entrance door on the faubourg Saint-Honoré, erected under Napoléon III, the large hall added by Sadi Carnot on the garden side, and other, less obvious additions, the palace, recently restored, still looks much as it did when it was built in 1718 by the architect Claude Mollet along the Champs Elysées as the residence of the count of Evreux, a member of the illustrious Bouillon family, an intimate of the Regent and son-in-law of the banker Antoine Crozat. Situated at that time far from any other habitation, surrounded by a garden to which the Regent in his generosity added a half-moon shaped area of land which still encroaches on to the Avenue Gabriel, the Hôtel d'Evreux was completed in 1722. Surviving from that time are some ground floor rooms, the Portrait Room, whose charming wood-panelled lintels are fine enough to be attributed to Oppenord, and the Ambassadors' Room, where the trophies of battle were designed in 1723 by Jules-Michel Hardouin and carved by Lange. The count of Evreux died in 1753 and the palace was purchased by the Marquise de Pompadour who had it embellished by Lassurance, Boucher and Van Loo. The room still known as the hemicycle—although one president of the Republic has blocked in the alcove hemicycle to install a lift—was the marquises's bedchamber. The beautiful cornice dates from the time of the count of Evreux, the panelling was certainly carved for the marquise, while the lintels are late nineteenth century.

The residence then passed into the hands of the financier Beaujon; the lintels in the Ambassadors' Room are by Boullée and were among the alterations made by Beaujon. Next it became the "Elysée-Bourbon" for the duchess of Bourbon, then accommodated Murat, the Empress Joséphine and Tsar Alexander; it was there that Napoléon signed his second abdication. Thirty-three years later, his nephew the prince-president took possession of it and prepared his coup d'Etat within its walls. Finally, since 1871 it has been the residence of successive Presidents of France.

86 and 87. The Elysée Palace, 55, Rue du Faubourg Saint-Honoré, 8th Arr. The Ambassadors' drawing room, the great drawing room of Madame de Pompadour (86). The hemicycle drawing room, former bedroom of Madame de Pompadour (87).

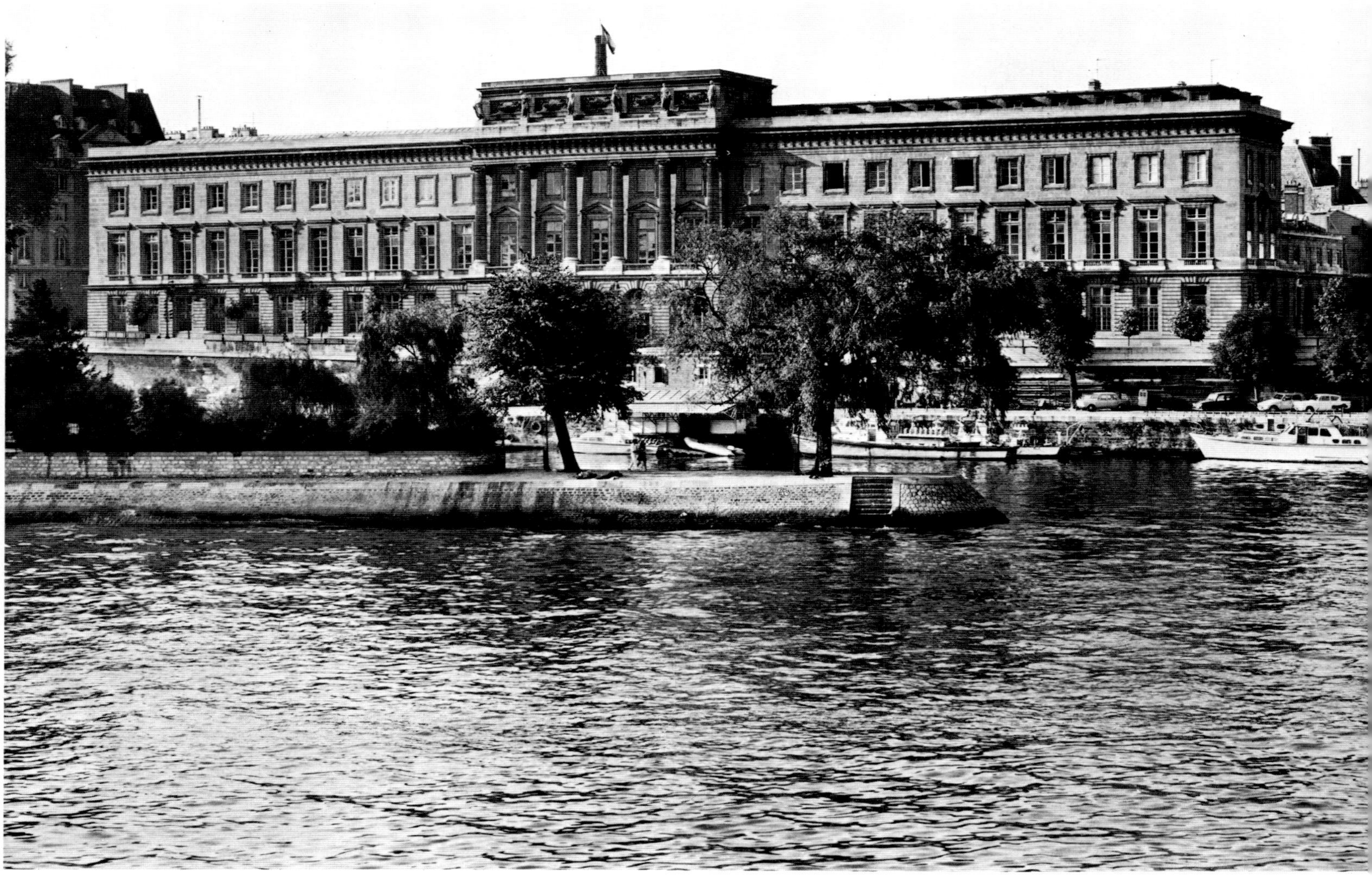

88. The Mint, 11, Quai de Conti, 6th Arr.

88. The Mint.

In 1768 Louis XV decided to build a new Mint and chose a magnificent site along the Seine opposite the Louvre. The Hôtel de Conti was pulled down, the first stone was laid in 1771 and the building completed in six years. Jacques-Denis Antoine, who was selected by competition, went for simplicity. Along the 117 meter frontage he only permitted the absolute minimum of decoration to avoid baldness and focussed interest on the central pavilion with its pillars and its attic story embellished with allegorical statues. The great staircase and the great drawing room are arranged with more emphasis while retaining beautiful monumental proportions.

89. The Church of Saint-Louis-en-l'Ile.

The parish church of the Ile Saint-Louis was begun in 1664 by Louis Le Vau. The nave was built from 1702-1723 by Gabriel Le Duc and Jacques Doucet, the transept followed and, above the crossing, a dome surmounted by a bell-tower which was struck by lightning in 1740. It was replaced by a charming openwork belfry over the entrance door in 1765. On the side overhanging the street, the clock, like a flying flag, marks the church entrance. The great facade on the Rue Poulletier was never built.

90. Rue des Colonnes.

The initial events of the Revolution did not bring construction to a halt in Paris. The great building operations that had been begun in previous years were continued along the Boulevard des Invalides, for example, and Rue Duroc (with Brongniart as architect), or on the land taken from the Luxembourg Gardens by the Count of Provence (Rue de Fleurus), or the completion of Rue de l'Odéon and the Place du Palais-Bourbon, etc. New roads were built across private estates and lined with buildings of uniform design, like Rue Mandar (1790) and Rue des Colonnes (1794). The latter prefigures the Rue de Rivoli. There was a private house on this site belonging to the Marquis Chaspou de Verneuil and which faced on to the Rue des Filles-Saint-Thomas. Since it was the property of an émigré it was confiscated and sold by lots. A private passage (made into a public thoroughfare in 1798) was built from the Rue des Filles-Saint-Thomas to the Théâtre Feydeau in the street of the same name. Those who bought plots of land had to abide by the contract of the 15 frimaire, Year III (5December 1794) which scheduled the construction of houses of uniform design. These were to have "public galleries six feet in width, at ground floor and mezzanine levels; these galleries shall be supported by columns topped with semi-circular arches, making in all thirty-six bays on each side. The houses shall be four square stories high, with slate-tiled attics." In a few cases, the interesting form of these buildings has been preserved. The columns are still there—Grecian Doric, without bases, as had been fashionable for fifteen years or so before the houses were built; they are not topped by horizontal architraves, as they would have been in Antiquity, but by archways which allow light through to the mezzanine floor; the external surface of these arcades is decorated with a very simple intaglio design, and each capital is crowned by a little palm. The architect has done his best to find an antique motif for the window sills and used little clusters of columns.

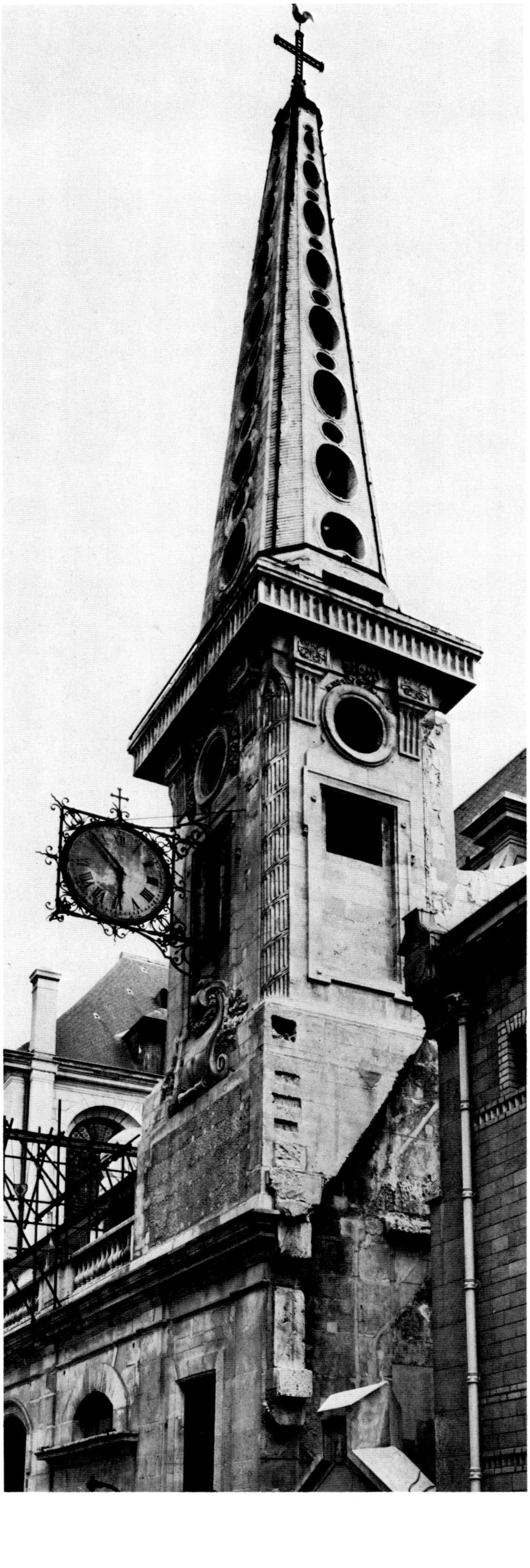

89

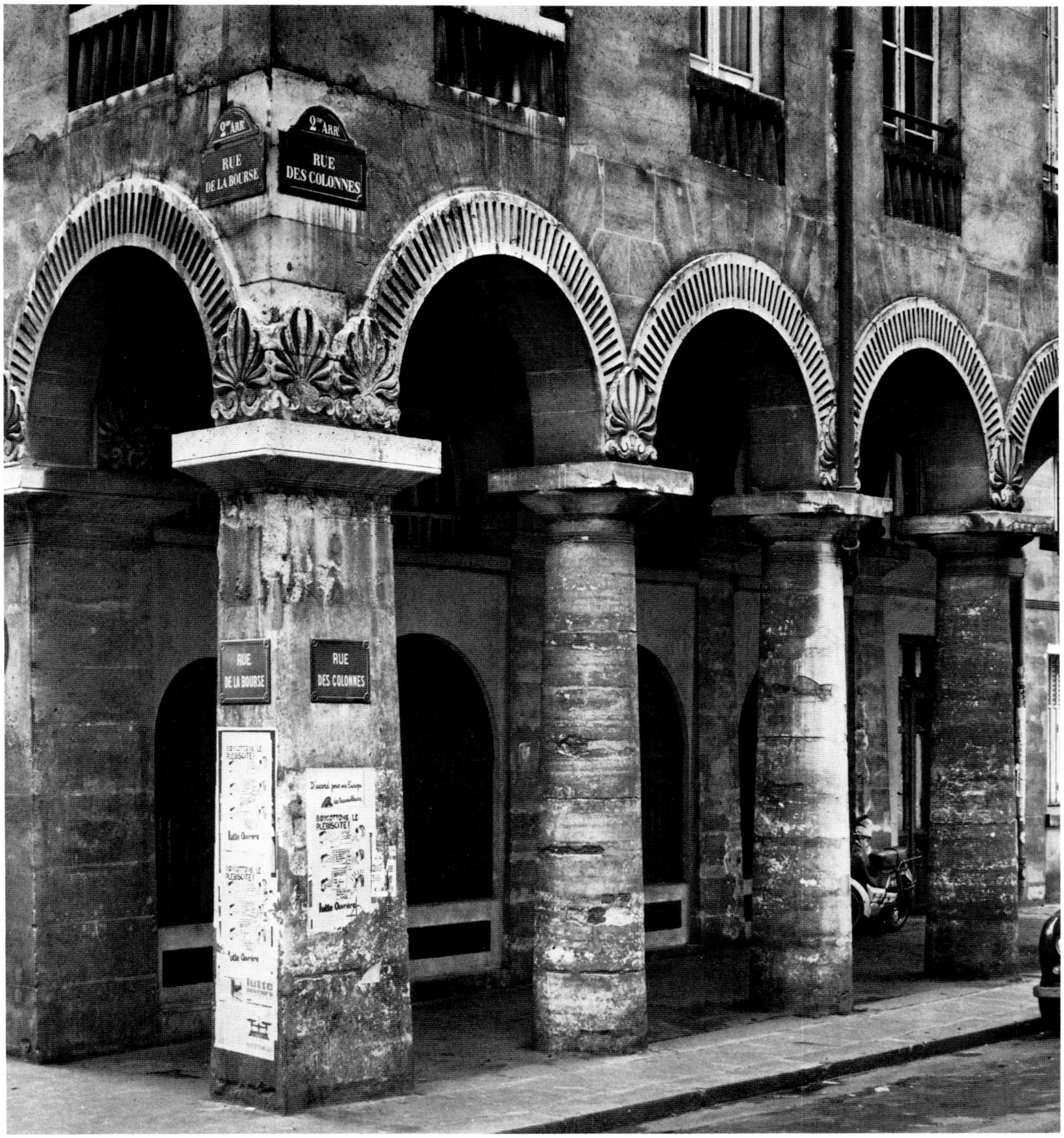

90. The Spartan style of the Revolution: the houses of the Rue des Colonnes, 2nd Arr.

89. The bell-tower of the church of Saint-Louis-en-l'Ile.

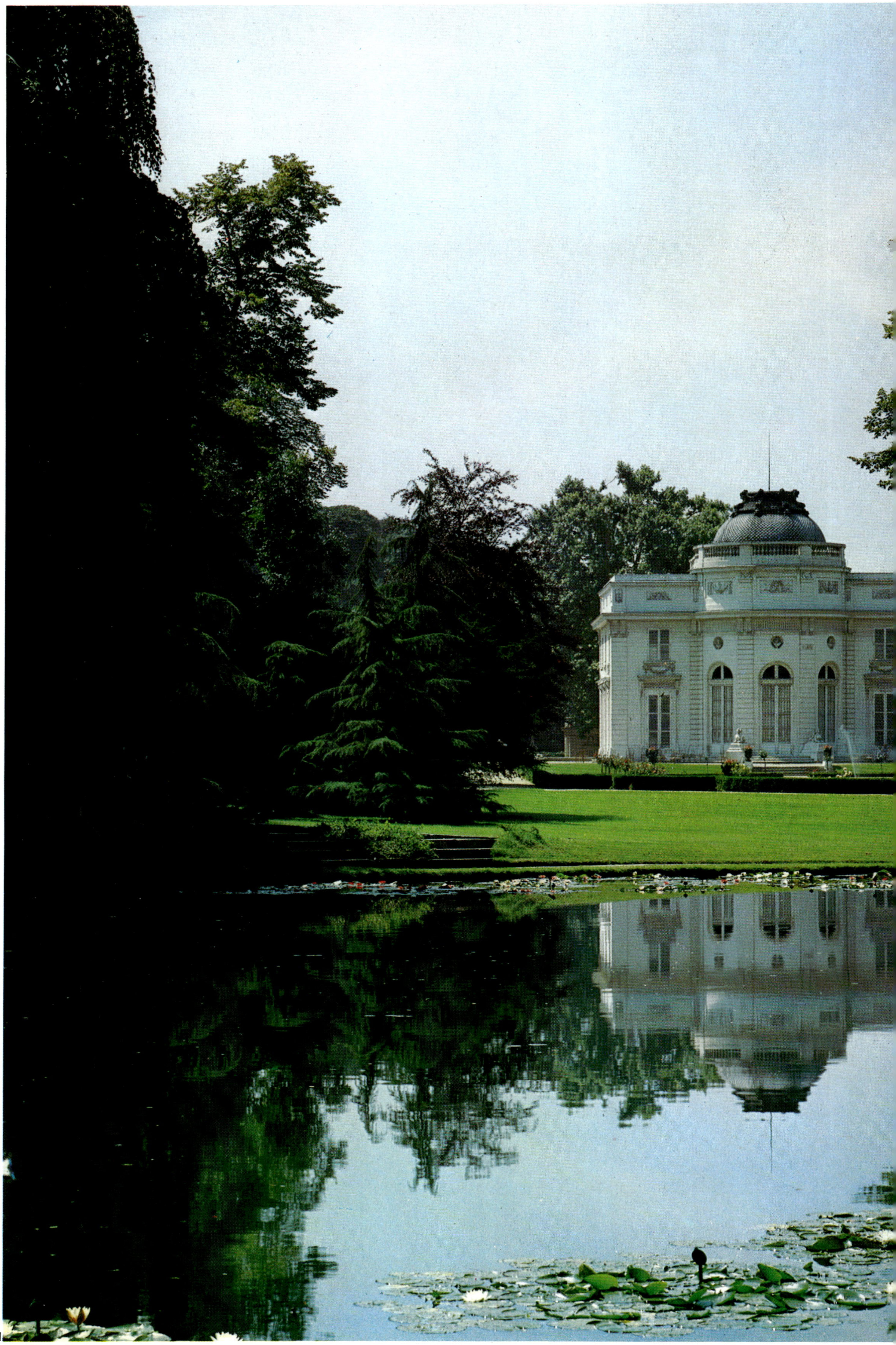

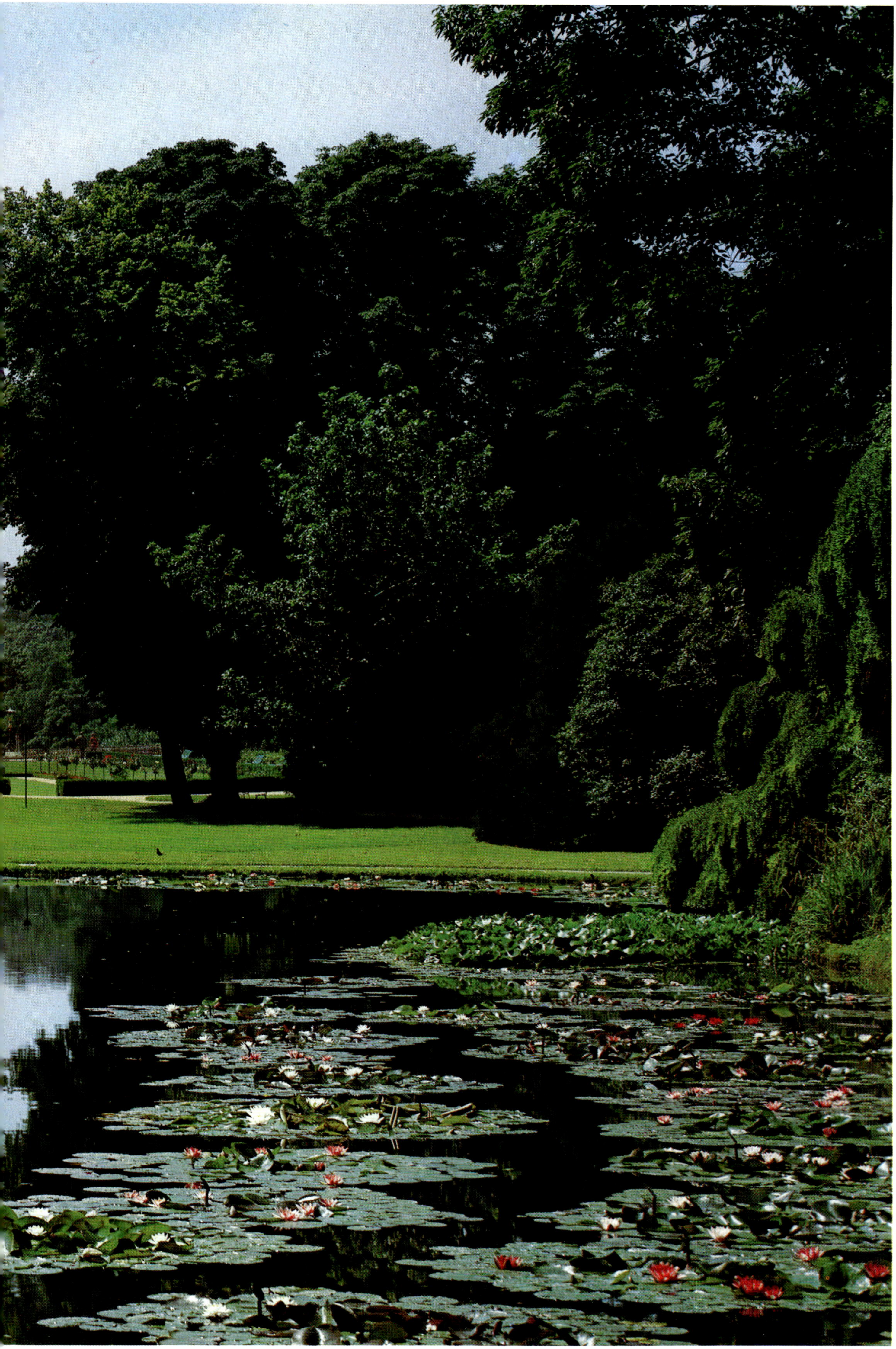

91. The Pavillon de Bagatelle in the Bois de Boulogne.

Under Louis XVI the fashion was for small houses, follies, curios, bagatelles—provided they were expensive ones. The nobility had them built for themselves or for actresses, on the boulevards and in Montparnasse, but also in the outskirts of Paris—Belleville, Pantin, Charonne and Neuilly. Bélanger, a man of the new generation, made it his speciality. In 1777 he had bought his way into the office of architect to the count of Artois. In the same year the prince, who was vying in prodigality with his sister-in-law the queen Marie-Antoinette, had a wager of 100,000 livres that he would have a little folly in the Bois de Boulogne rebuilt during the Queen's stay at Choisy. Bélanger drew up the plans in 48 hours and the pavilion was completed in 64 days at a cost of more than a million livres, with its outbuildings, gardens and grottos. The Bagatelle was raised higher by Sir Richard Wallace in the nineteenth century. A part of the attic and certain openings must therefore be disregarded in order to rediscover Bélanger's simple volumes—a cube, penetrated from the garden side by a cylindre which accommodates a circular drawing room.

92. The Palais-Royal.

The Duke of Chartres, the future Philippe-Egalité, had in 1780 received from his father, the Duke of Orléans, the entire Palais-Royal as an advancement on his inheritance. The former palace of Cardinal Richelieu, bequeathed to the Crown and then given to the Orléans family, had been modified and enlarged several times, on the last occasion by Cartaud, Constant d'Ivry and Moreau-Desproux in 1750-1769. The facades on the Place du Palais-Royal side, and a part of those overlooking the gardens, date from this time.

In this fashionable district it was very tempting for the prince to increase his revenue by making the best use of the enormous gardens on to which the houses in the Rue de Richelieu, Rue des Petits-Champs, Rue de Radziwill and Rue des Bons-Enfants backed directly. The prince had made the acquaintance of the architect Victor Louis at a masonic gathering at Bordeaux, where he was building the great theater. Now, in 1781, he asked him to design a series of identical houses for rent along the fringes of the garden, reducing its area proportionately. Building was completed in 1784. The scheme was the following: the blocks had a continuous peristyle, open on to the garden through arcades as in the Place des Vosges. Small shops surmounted by mezzanine flors opened on to the peristyle; above them, the apartments were arranged on three levels, first floor, mezzanine and, in the roofing, an attic story. Three new streets separated these buildings from the older architecture; they were named after the prince's son, Valois, Montpensier and Beaujolais.

Louis' first plan had been very simple, but preference was given to a more elaborate decor like that proposed by the same architect for the Place Ludovise in Bordeaux. The rhythm of the whole is imparted by colossal pilasters of composite order supporting a frieze decorated with garlands, a cornice and a balustrade laden with vases; a delicately carved decor embellishes the extrados of the arcades and the pictures above the windows. We know that the shops quickly found purchasers and that the Palais-Royal rapidly became a centre of trade, leisure and debauchery without equal in all Paris.

91. The Pavillon de Bagatelle in the Bois de Boulogne.

92. The arcades and the garden of the Palais-Royal seen through the Orleans Arcade, a closed shopping arcade, built by Fontaine in 1829, opened out into a peristyle in 1935.

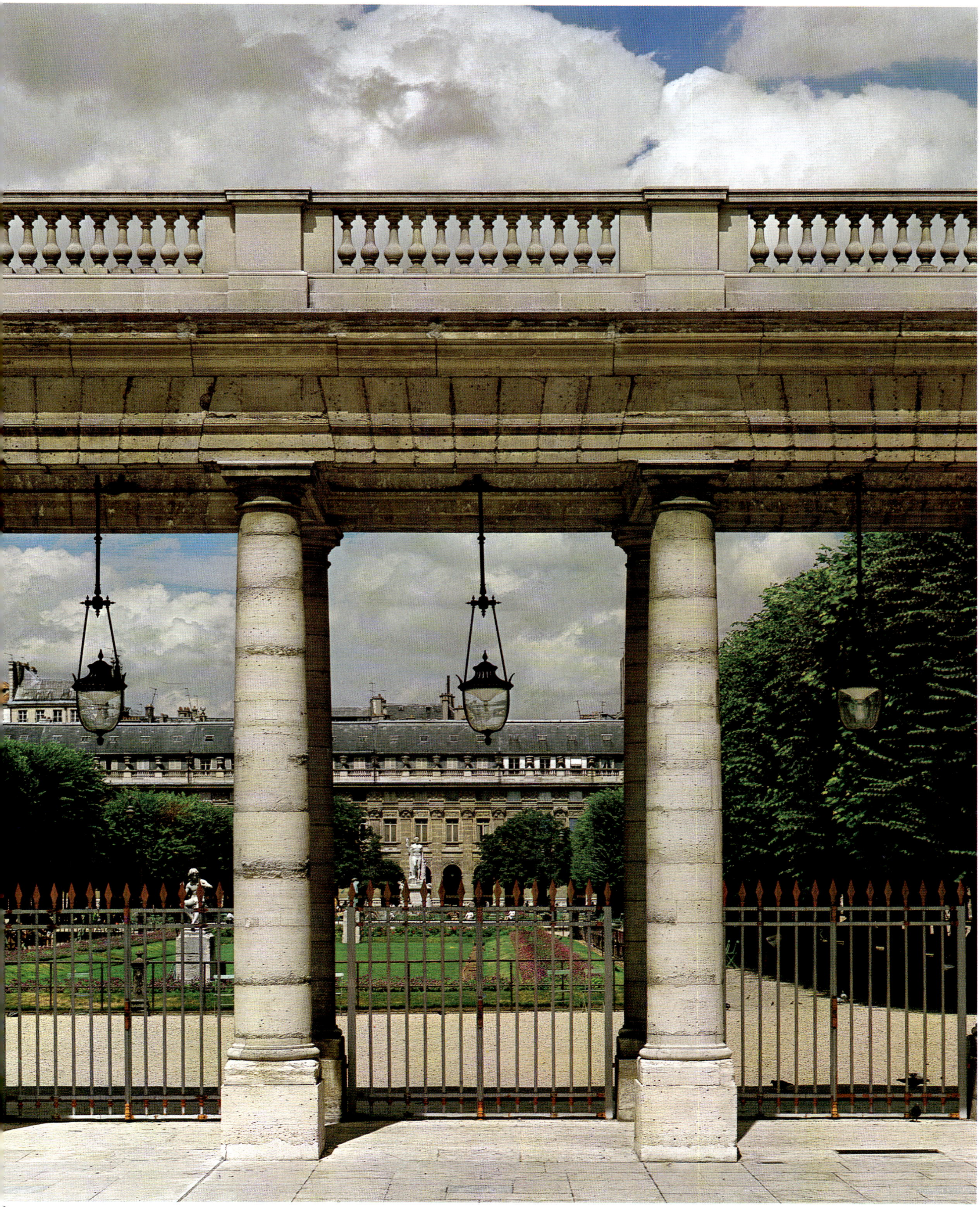

93. The Hôtel de Beauharnais.

In 1803 Eugène de Beauharnais purchased the former de Torcy residence and decided to transform it. Two years later, he was apointed vice-roy of Italy and handed supervision of the project over to his mother, the Empress Josephine. Like her son, she too allowed the architect Bataille to run up excessive costs. Napoléon was not pleased when he was presented with the bill: "I have just had a bill for 1,500,000 francs for your house. That is an exorbitant sum... you should never do anything without an estimate and an understanding that the figure quoted will not be exceeded. The architect has asked for as much as he felt like—you are just pouring money down the drain." He confiscated the building and used it to house his brother Jérôme; then in 1811 he handed it back to Eugène and his sister Hortense. The house has been restored by the German Embassy which has occupied the premises since 1871.

Prince Eugène began his renovations by adding to the first courtyard a great Egyptian stucco portico with two columns topped by lotus-flower capitals, which has been attributed to Jean-Augustin Renard. No expense was spared in decorating the apartments. The dominant theme was Greco-Roman rather than Egyptian. There is an echo of the Alexandrian elegance of the frescoes of Pompei in the flurries of arabesques and grotesques, the painted scenes and the slim little columns which decorate Queen Hortense's bed and are repeated in her bathroom. Leading off the bathroom was a Turkish boudoir where the Queen of Holland could rest after the heat of the bath. It is reminiscent of those eighteenth century Turkish fantasies which had been revived by tales of the Egyptian and Palestinian campaigns. The painted frieze which runs around the top of the room seems to draw on the same sources used by Ingres for his "Turkish Bath". His first "Woman bathing" does in fact date from 1807.

The Salon des Saisons has all the icy splendour of the Empire style. The unyielding white and gold decor is relieved by Pompeian scenes on the doors and by the huge canvasses in the style of Prud'hon or Girodet (and attributed to Charles de Boisfremont) which depict allegories of the four seasons.

93. The drawing room of the Seasons at the Hôtel de Beauharnais, the former Hôtel de Torcy, now the German Embassy, 78, Rue de Lille, 7th Arr.

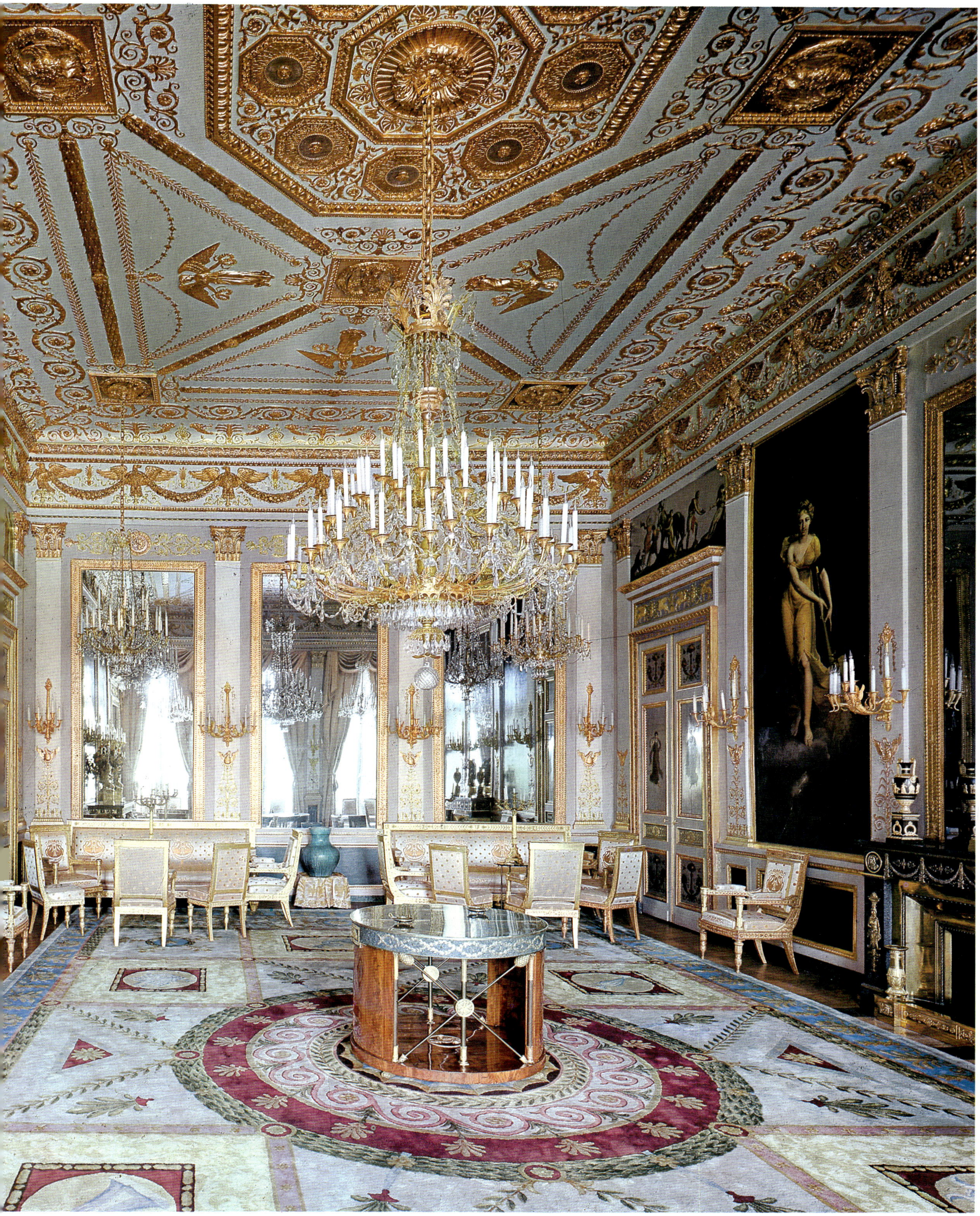

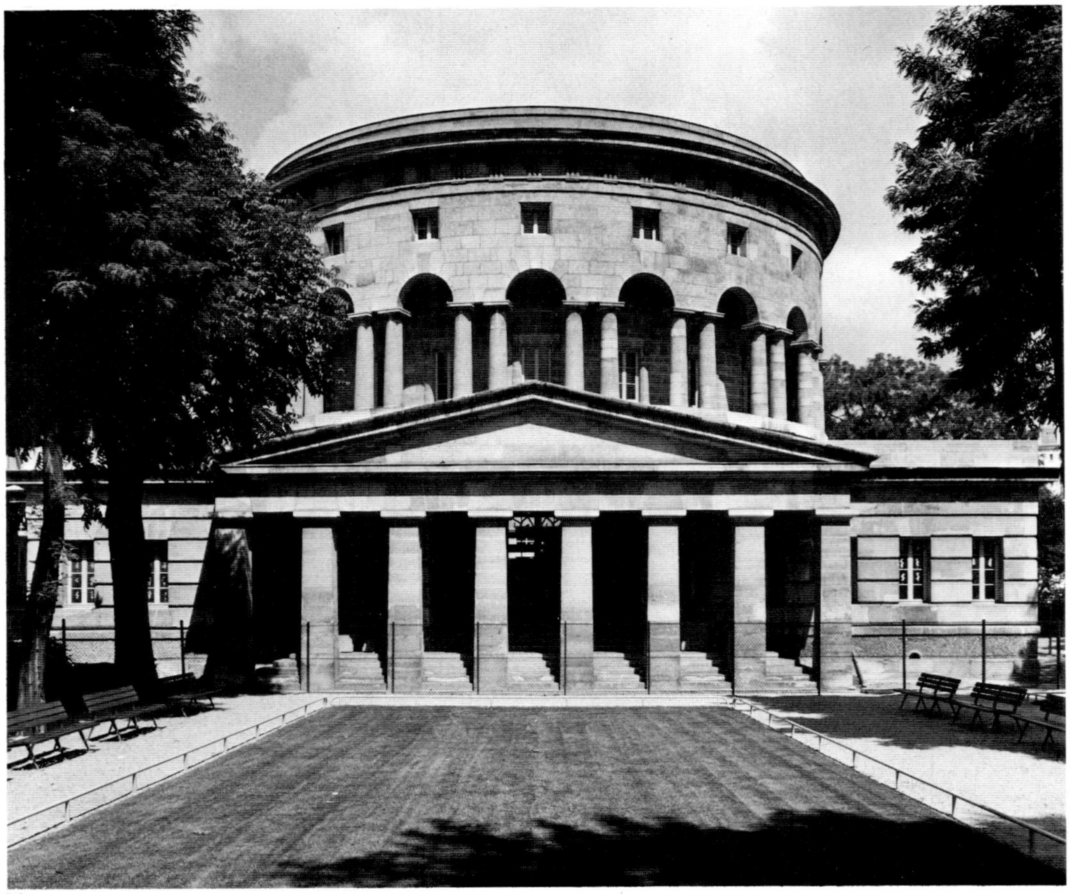

94

94. The Rotunda of la Villette.

The Farmers General were instructed to levy an import duty on certain basic commodities coming into Paris—wine, livestock, wood, coal... A third of the revenue went to the City and two thirds to the State. Smuggling and the new districts that were being built made it necessary to put up a wall around the city with toll collection points. Despite public protest the decision was taken in 1785 and Ledoux was placed in charge of the task. Far from restricting himself to the utilitarian structures that were required of him, the architect conceived each entrance gate as a monumental portal proclaiming the capital's grandeur. Work was completed in 1790. Of the 54 works built only four remain today: the gates of the Throne and of Hell, consisting of square pavilions, and the rotundas of Chartres and La Villette. The Rotunda of La Villette, situated between two gates, the Saint-Martin Gate (Rue de Flandre, in the direction of the Netherlands) and the Pantin Gate (Avenue de Pantin then Jean-Jaurès, in the direction of Germany), accommodated the offices of a collector and several inspectors, a guard corps and some warehouses. The design, inspired by Palladio's Villa Rotunda, is a combination of square, cross and circle, but predominance is given, above the vast base decorated with porticos, to a cylinder indented with an austere colonnade. The rotunda has just been restored and now houses the Paris Regional Archaeological Excavations Directorate.

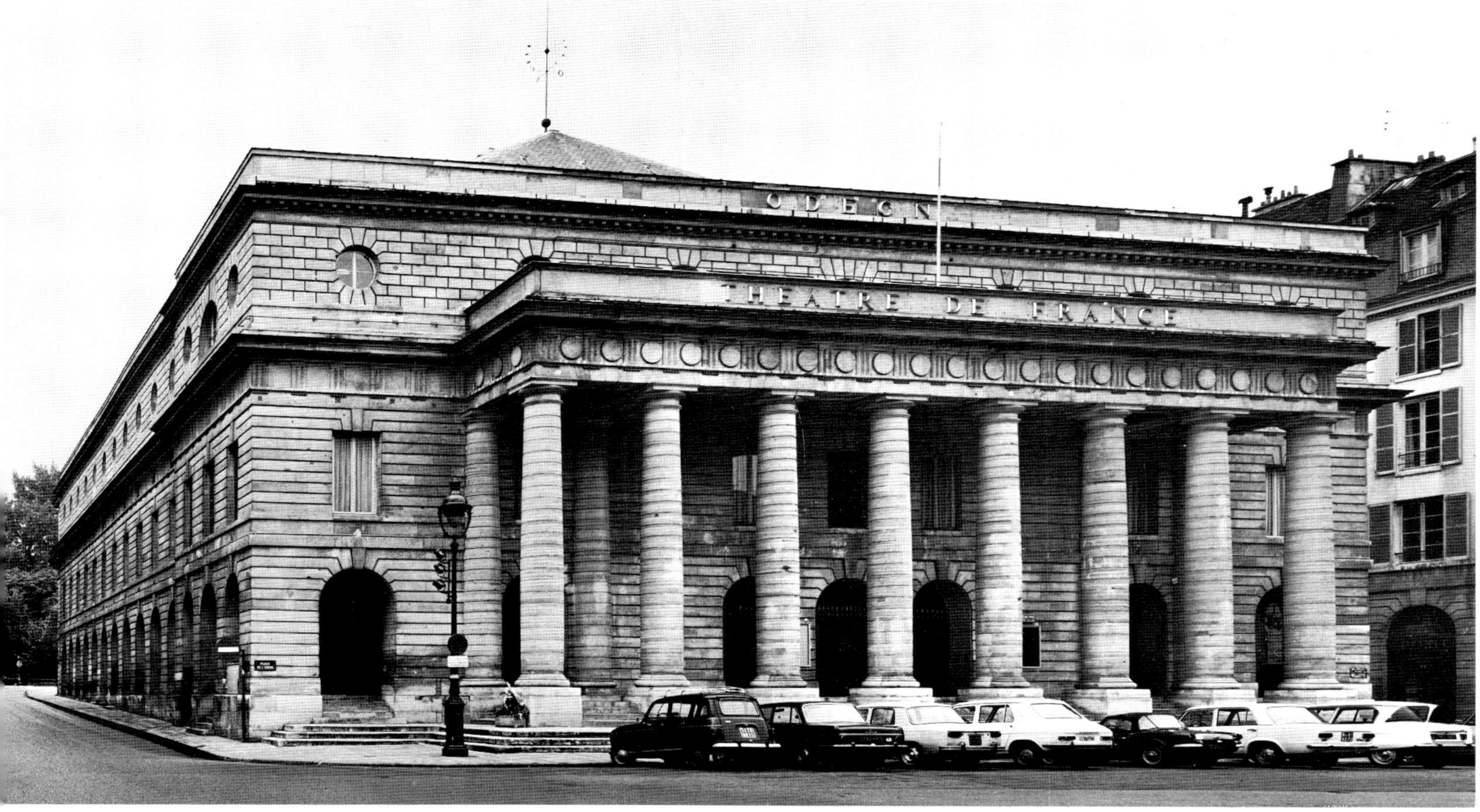

95. The Théâtre de l'Odéon.

The construction of a theater for the Comédie Française had been projected ever since the Company had left Rue de l'Ancienne Comédie in 1770. The prince of Condé offered to put the vast hotel he had inherited near the Luxembourg at their disposal. Numerous plans were submitted, but, as far back as 1767, the young Charles de Wailly, who had studied the monuments of antiquity and of baroque Rome, had embarked on the preliminary design work with Marie-Joseph Peyre, at Marigny's request. In 1778 they were given the order and the theater was built in three years. The exterior is very simple, the only embellishments being an enormous portico and two arcades which spanned the two side streets (demolished in 1818). The interior, the two great staircases, the foyer and the auditorium were extremely sumptuous. The theater was opened by the Queen in 1782 with a performance of Racine's Iphigénie, was burned down in 1799 and 1818 but rebuilt in every detail.
On the triangular site of the Hôtel de Condé, Peyre and Wailly marked out a semicircular area in front of the theater with radiating streets. The buildings round the square were designed by them, those in the streets by lesser known architects, and the whole was characterised by a sober, neo-classical style with borrowings from the Greek architecture of Paestum. For the first time a public building had been constructed with a group of residential buildings and a network of new roadways, carefully designed to show off the theater itself.

96. The Madeleine.

Facing each other across the Place de la Concorde are two imperial colonnades—to the South a temple to Law (the Palais Bourbon) and to the north a temple to Glory. When Napoléon came to power the church of Saint Madeleine was still in the process of construction on the northern extension of the Rue Royale. It was a huge edifice in the style of the Panthéon, and had been started by Contant d'Ivry in 1764 and modified by Couture. During the Revolution and the Empire the intention had been to put it to secular use and turn it into a library, an Opéra House, the Stock Exchange, or a museum. Remembering advice given him by Vivant Denon, Napoléon sent orders from Poland in 1806 that the building should be completed as a "monument to the Grande Armée". Some one hundred architects submitted plans. The one chosen by the Emperor was a Roman temple designed by Pierre Vignon. Work began, but as the years went by it seemed superfluous to devote funds to this monument to pure glory, and so Napoléon decided to hand the temple over to the Catholic Church. The "Madeleine" was not completed until 1842, under Louis-Philippe. Its pagan architecture was preserved: its sculptures are the only external indication of its Christian affinities.

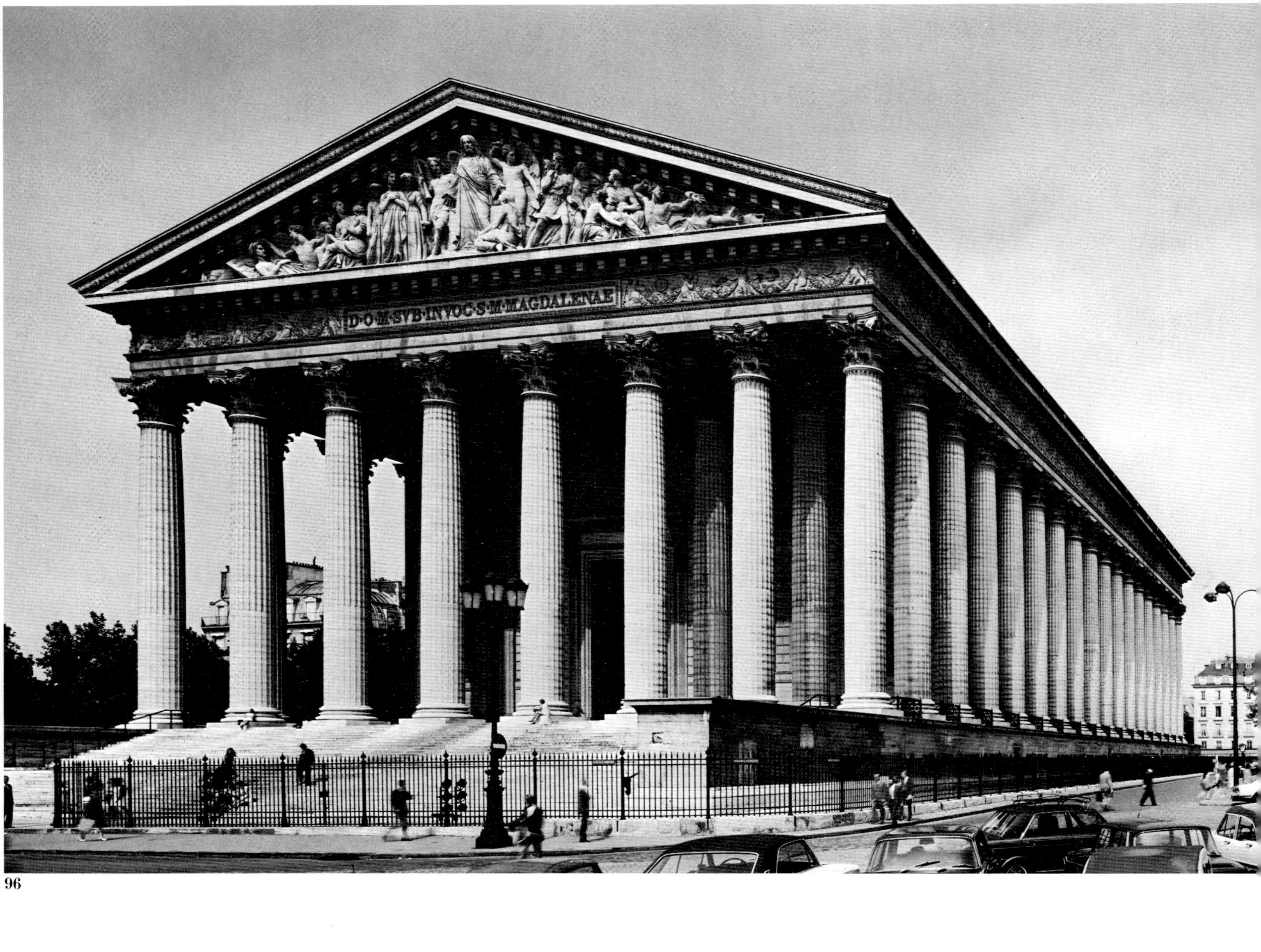

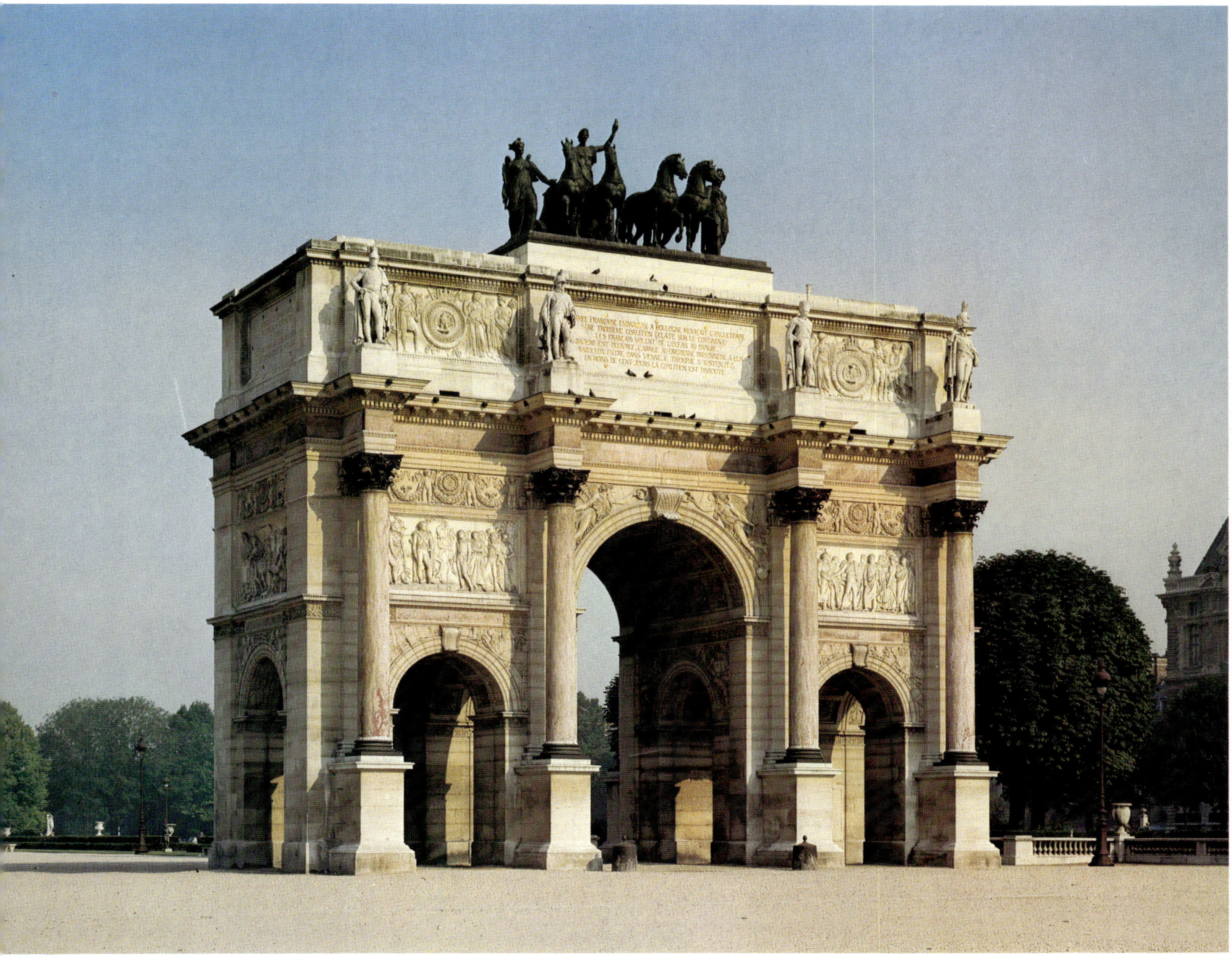

97. The Carrousel Arch.

A monumental gateway was put up in front of the Tuileries imperial residence in 1806. Percier and Fontaine drew inspiration from the arch of Septimus Severus in Rome to commemorate the victory at Marengo, but added their own innovations in the form of polychrome materials and prolific sculpture which depicts the crack corps of the Grande Armée in their uniforms. Now that the Tuileries Palace has gone, the Carrousel Arch is seen to its best advantage, standing there in isolation, the most perfect monument to be erected under the Empire.

98. The Arc de Triomphe de l'Etoile.

Great prestige monuments like the Invalides or Place Louis XV could be completed in a monarch's lifetime only during the long reigns of Louis XIV and Louis XV. Napoléon's star did not remain long enough in the ascendant for him to see the completion of the most costly monuments to his glory, the Madeleine and the triumphal arch at l'Etoile. These two edifices received very different dedications.

The Carrousel Arch had been built in 1806 to commemorate Marengo and to mark the entrance to the Tuileries. But the Emperor was not satisfied. He wanted a great city gate to catch the eye of foreign visitors; the Carrousel was merely the gateway to a castle. Napoléon was envious of the Saint-Denis gate, that monument to Louis XIV. By February 1806 a new plan was being considered. Initially, the site was to have been at the Place de la Bastille but that idea was soon abandoned in favour of the Etoile roundabout on Chaillot hill at the top of the Champs-Elysées. "The monument will be visible from a great distance and would not obscure any view", claimed Champagny. "It would be visible from the Neuilly heights and from Place de la Concorde. The visitor arriving in Paris will be filled with admiration... when he leaves, he will remember it as a striking symbol of the outstanding beauty of our capital city."

Work began in August 1806 from designs by Chalgrin. His model was the arch of Titus with a single span but built on a gigantic scale (it was to be 50 meters high). The Emperor was given some idea of how it was to look from scaffolding covered with painted canvas in 1810. By 1814 the walls were only a few meters high. The Bourbons resumed work on it in 1832 in honour of the Spanish Campaign that was so dear to Chateaubriand. While architects argued over Chalgrin's plans (he had died in 1811), the masonry slowly rose to the attic storey.

It fell to Louis-Philippe, that admirer of the splendours of the Empire, to finish the triumphal arch and restore it to its original fuction as a celebration of the Grande Armée. Huyot, then Blouet, were the last architects to work on it and the monument was unveiled on July 29th 1836. It is a sober and powerful edifice, and does credit to Chalgrin's genius. The great flat surfaces of the pillars (fortunately, columns were ruled out) magnificently display the immense bas-reliefs which were commissioned in 1833 from Etex, Cortot and Rude. The splendid, spirited "Departure of the Volunteers in 1792" by Rude far outshines the cold allegories of his rivals.

98. The Arc de Triomphe de l'Etoile. On the right, the "Departure of the Volunteers in 1792", bas-relief by Rude.

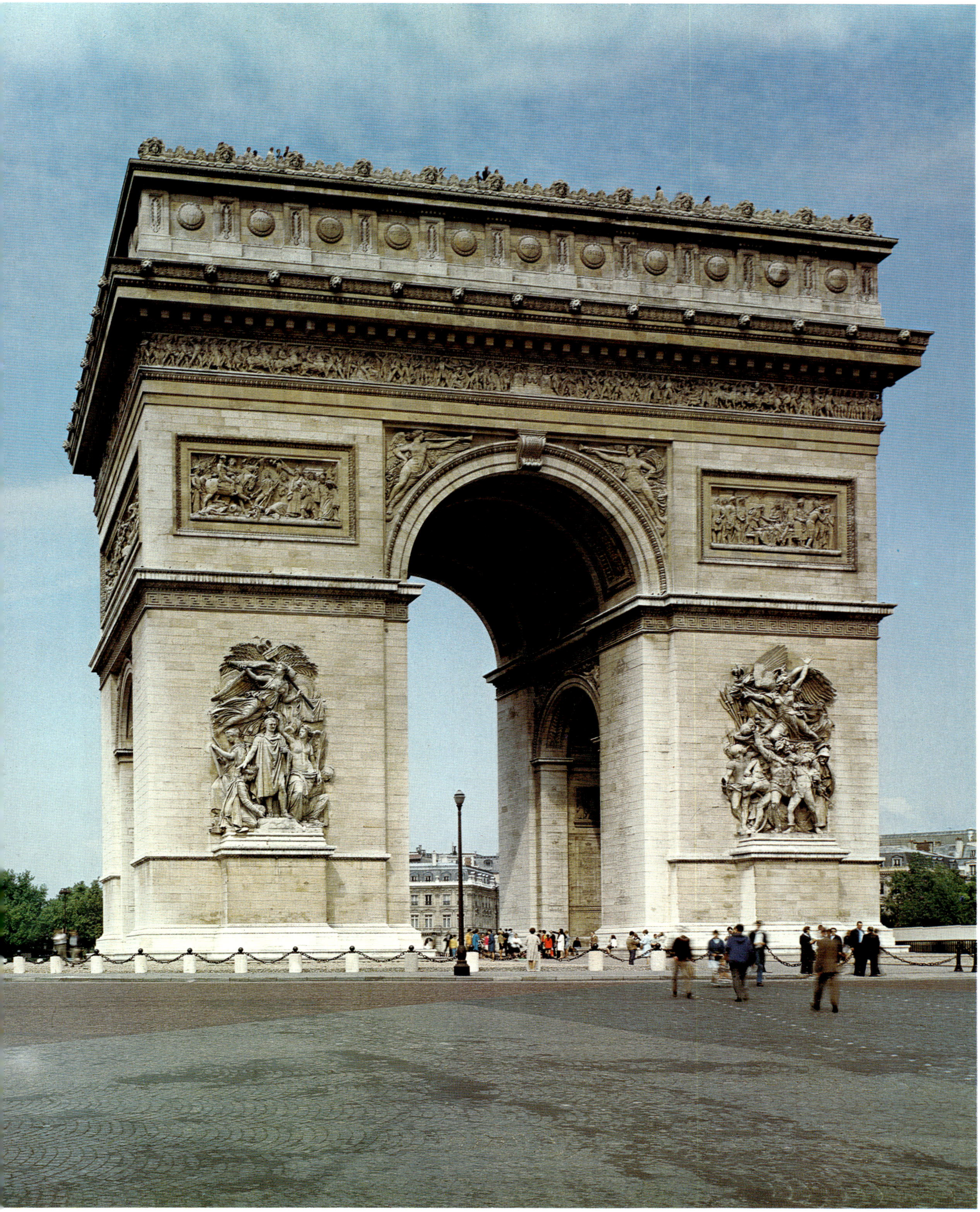

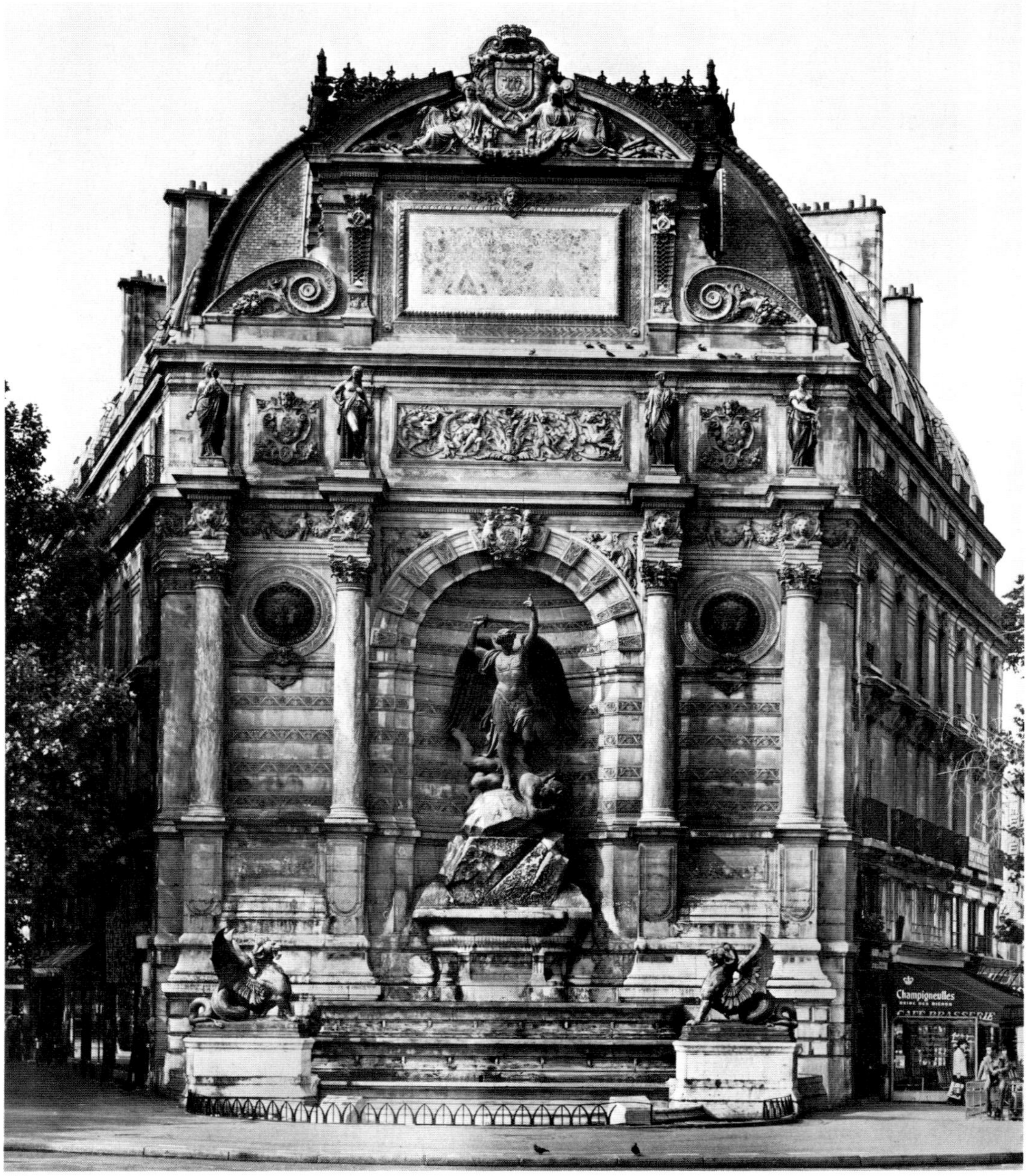

99

99. The Saint-Michel Fountain.

The roads that Haussmann cut through the city were planned so that they would lead up to some "feature". It was a constant preoccupation at the time. The Boulevard de Sébastopol leads one's eye up to the dome of the Tribunal de commerce; Boulevard Henri IV leads to the Panthéon. Since the Boulevard Saint-Michel was not a straight extension of the Boulevard du Palais, Davioud built a monumental fountain at the focal point; it is dedicated to Saint Michael and was inspired by the Trevi fountain and the Medici fountain in the Luxembourg Gardens. The central group is by Duret.

100. The Gare du Nord.

The only material that could be used to construct the wide spanned canopies over the great railway departure halls was, of course, metal. The first departure hall, by Belgique, was built in 1846 and replaced by Hittorff's Gare du Nord (1856-1864). The facade preserves the classical order with its great arcades, pilastres and statues, and it does have a certain elegance. Although it quite clearly prepares us for the great central hall, it provoked a scathing attack from Viollet-le-Duc: "The new Gare du Nord is perhaps the grossest error that the Academy's exclusive doctrines have yet been responsible for." At the same period, however, Viel and Barrault were making a similar compromise in their design for the Palace of Industry for the 1855 Exhibition. Public opinion approved of the Gare du Nord: "It is a veritable temple to steam", declared « Le Magasin pittoresque » in an article which went on to admire the great hall, 70 meters wide, with its glass roof, its rows of cast-iron columns, and its brightly colored polychrome decor.

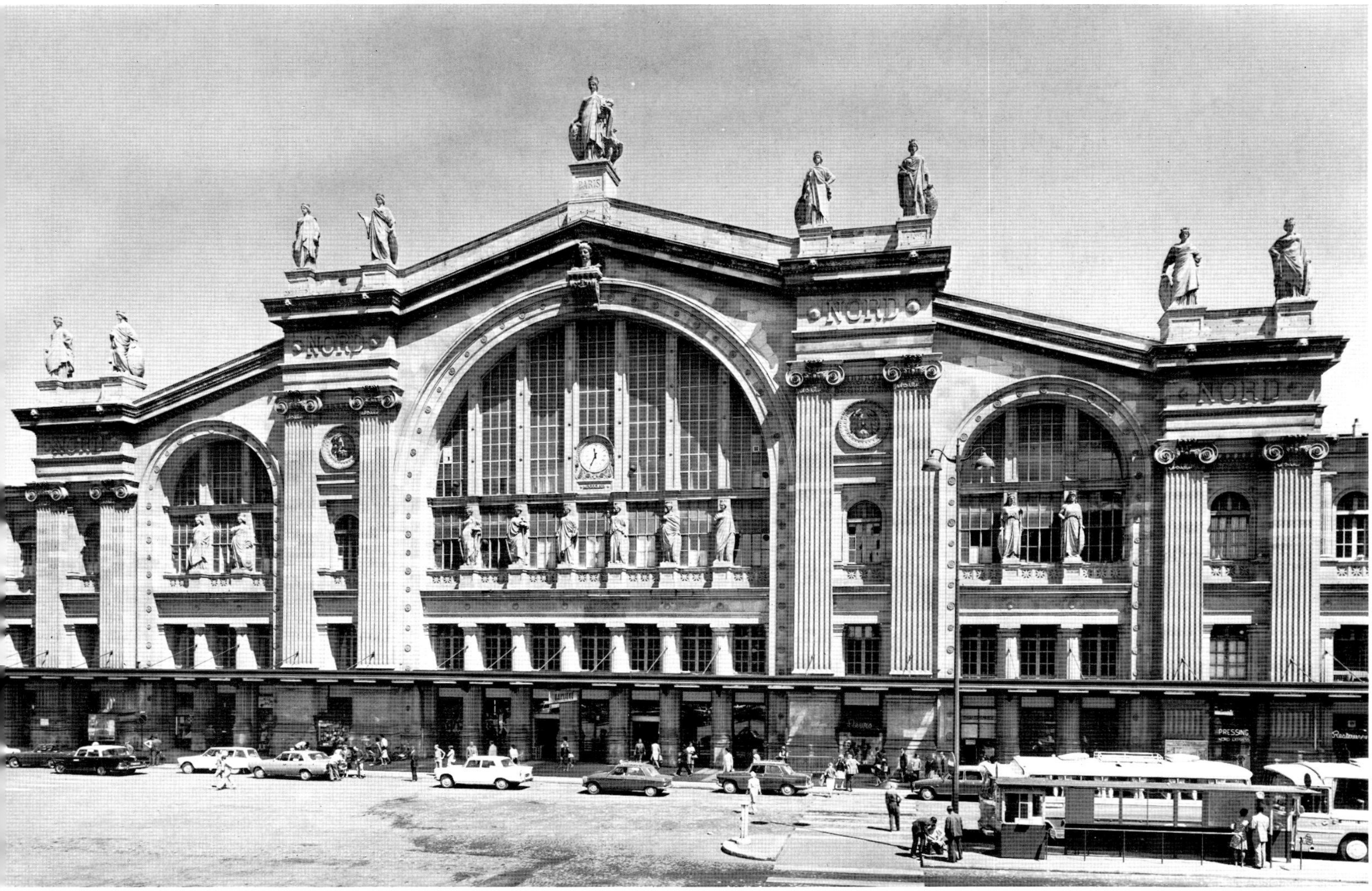

101. The Buttes-Chaumont Park.

The desire for areas of greenery was a novel in Parisian town-planning, and was largely due to Napoléon III's personal intervention: he had seen how important they were considered to be in England. As the city spread and the countryside receded, nature had to be brought back into the town by artificial means, if Parisians were not to be asphyxiated. In addition to the royal Tuileries and Luxembourg gardens, the Emperor had five large parks created at the four points of the compass—Boulogne in the west, Monceau and the Buttes-Chaumont to the north, Vincennes to the east, and Montsouris to the south. A large number of squares were also laid out. Two names are associated with this scheme: Adolphe Alphand, an engineer, and the horticulturalist Barillet-Deschamps. Alphand's most extraordinary creation was the Buttes-Chaumont park. The former village of Belleville had become part of the capital by a decree of 1860, but it was a sinister spot—Montfaucon had been hanged there on the bare hills scarred with lime-pits. In only three years (1864-1867) Alphand completely transformed the site. The natural escarpments were used to their best advantage: he had Davioud build a little imitation-Tivoli temple on the summit, he spanned the ravine with a brick bridge, and laid out the gardens with a waterfall, a lake, grottos, and greenery planted in rich loam which was carted to the barren hillside at great expense.

101. The Buttes-Chaumont Park.

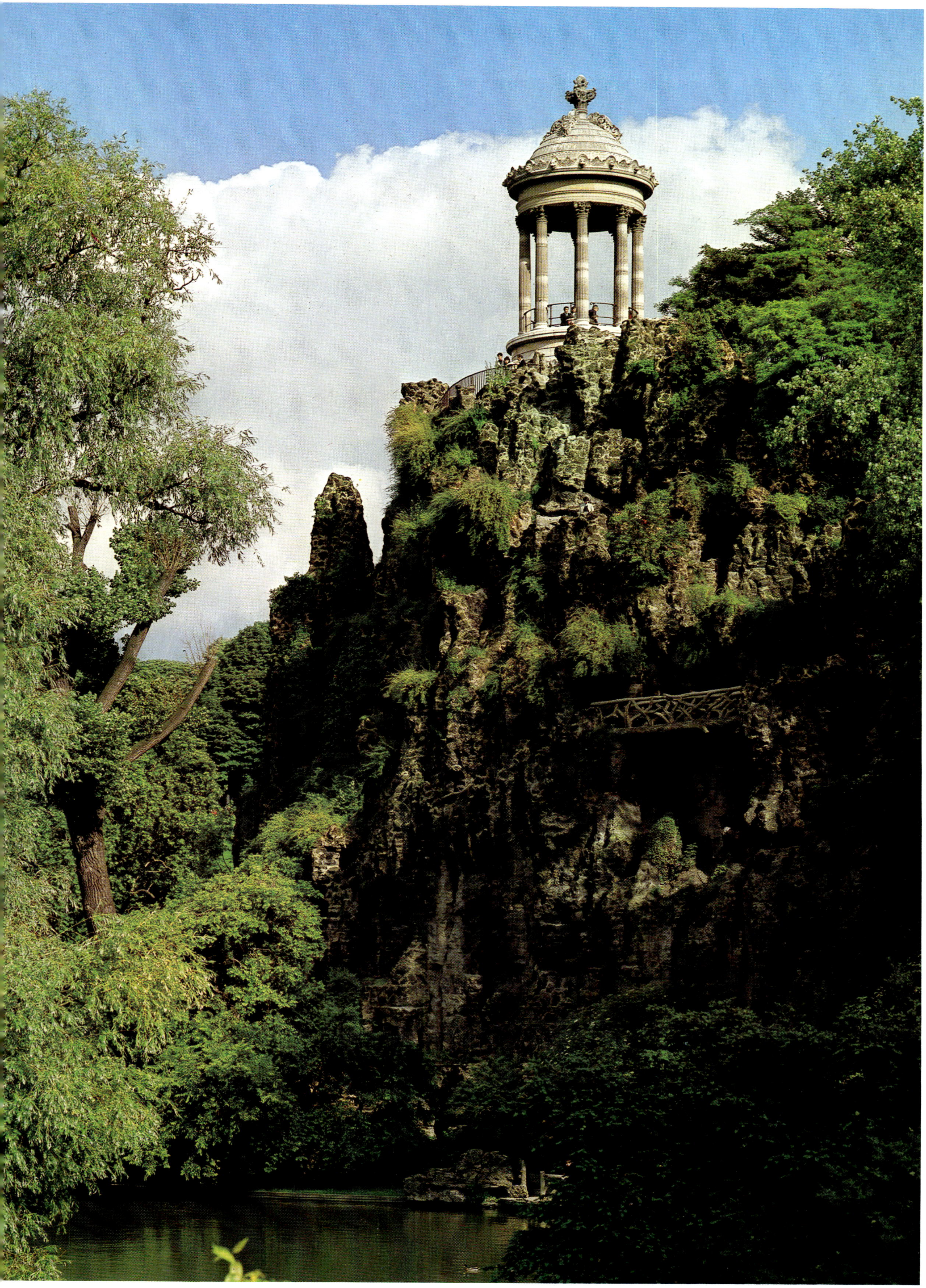

102. The Opéra.

One building that has come to symbolise the Second Empire even more than the Louvre is the Opéra. The war of 1870-1871 prevented Napoléon III from inaugurating the building. It was not completed until the Third Republic was underway, and the honor of opening it on January 5th, 1875 fell to Marshall Mac-Mahon. The Royal Academy of Music had been based in no fewer than twelve concert halls since it was founded in 1669. Romantic opera spent its heyday in a temporary hall which had been put up in twelve months (1820) in Rue Le-Peletier. Paris had become the international center of the music world, and an opera house worthy of Parisian music lovers had long been felt necessary. 171 designs (including one by the Empress) were submitted to a competition in 1860. The jury chose Charles Garnier's. He had been influenced by Italy, Greece and the Near East, and had a taste for rich materials, polychrome marble and mosaics. He handled them with casual eclecticism to produce what he himself called "Napoléon III style". The foundation stone was laid in 1862; the estimate of 34 million francs was not exceeded.

Even Viollet-le-Duc was disconcerted by the size of the undertaking. Everything is on an immense scale—the facade and its peristyle, the huge foyer, the staircase, the Emperor's wing, the subscribers' wing, and the stage which rises to a height of 60 meters to allow clearance room for the most complicated machinery. Even the administrative buildings are huge. The central area—what one might call the transept crossing—houses the auditorium which can seat 2156 in its five galleries. Garnier has managed to combine these elements in a subtle interplay of carefully graded spaces and volumes. The rectangular mass of the foyer comes first, then the dome of the auditorium etched against the immense gable of the stage. Groups of sculpture emphasize its strong points, and Apollo brandishes his lyre on the temple's pinnacle. The group representing "Dance" which Carpeaux sculpted for the facade is so full of movement and vitality, and contrasts so strongly with his rivals' stiff, formal groups that it scandalised respectable bourgeois gentlemen of the period.

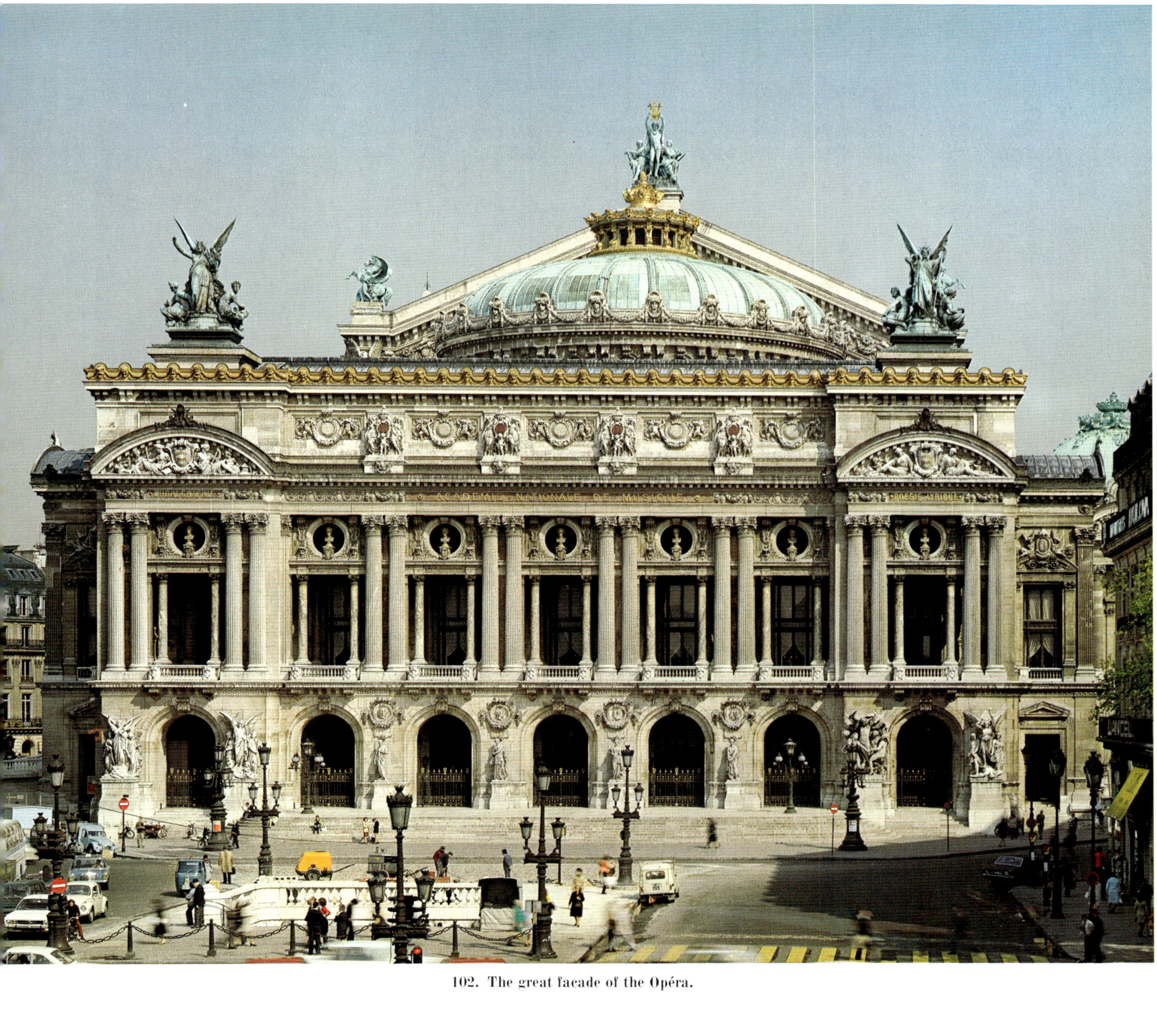

102. The great facade of the Opéra.

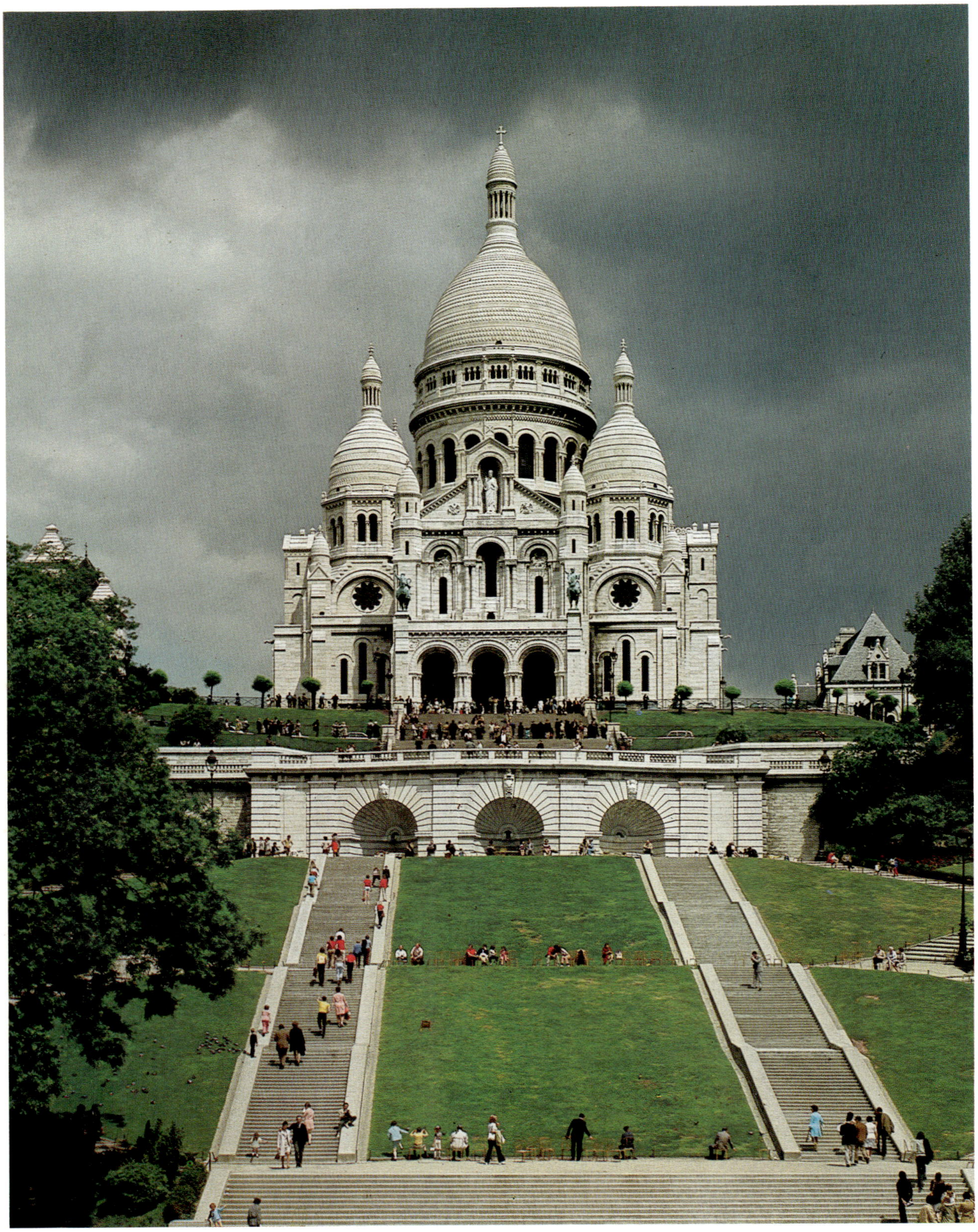

103. The Sacré-Cœur Basilica.

103. The Sacré-Cœur Basilica.

After building so many neo-Gothic, neo-Renaissance and neo-Roman churches, architects continued their search for forgotten styles from the past. Paul Abadie developed a "Romano-byzantine" style, inspired by the domed churches of south-west France and particularly by the church of Saint-Front de Périgueux which he had vigorously restored. During the Franco-Prussian war of 1870 Alexandre Legentil and Hubert Rohault de Fleury had suggested that a basilica dedicated to the Sacred Heart be built as a plea for the salvation of France and the "liberation" of Pope Pius IX. The proposal was approved by the National Assembly on July 24, 1873, and Cardinal Guibert chose Montmartre hill for the site. Abadie won the competition held to select an architect, and was commissioned to build an immense basilica, a place of pilgrimage which would be visible from a great distance and would look out over the vast panorama of Paris. When his plans were carried out, it was as if the city had been topped by a gigantic crown. Work on the basilica began in 1875 and was completed in the very year which saw France plunged into a new war—1914.

Only when seen from a distance does this massive, white, multi-domed edifice acquire a certain majesty—its distinctive shape has become a familiar part of the Paris skyline, silhouetted on the summit of the ancient mound that was once consecrated to Mercury. But when one draws closer and crosses the square in front of it and goes inside, one is confronted with meaningless arrangements of space, over-confident and ill-proportioned domes, hopelessly ugly sculpture and mosaics, and above all with the cold pallor of the building material. Far from mellowing with age, this Château-Landon stone becomes whiter as the years go by.

104. The Eiffel Tower.

The Eiffel Tower marks the sudden beginning of a daring new era of metal and engineers. Bourgeois houses complete with columns, pediments, and all the worn-out showiness of Academicism were still being built along the Boulevard Haussmann, but classical architecture had breathed its last. The universal exhibitions had already set an example for ambitious research to provide larger and larger premises for exhibitions and visitors. Four years after London's Crystal Palace, the exhibition of 1855 left behind it a Palace of Industry built of stone, iron and glass; the 1867 exhibition could only offer a 482 meter long hangar; the one held in 1878 had not only the Trocadéro but also a 725 meter palace built entirely of metal to a design by Léopold Hardy. By that date metal roof-trusses with a span of 35.60 meters were available. The exhibition of 1889 went even further and produced three memorable metal constructions: the palace of Arts, by Jean Formigé; the Machine Gallery, by Ch. L. Dutert, and lastly, the Eiffel Tower, the only one of the three that is still standing. For the first time an iron structure was not trying to imitate the little columns, arches, and latticework of stone architecture, or the patterns of Antiquity; it was a naked construction displaying its raw state, with all its rivets and molding lines visible. Metal construction specialists had been thinking for some time about building a tower. In 1884, Koechlin and Nouguier, the engineers working with Gustave Eiffel's firm, proposed a plan for a "pylon 300 meters high" to their director. It was to have the same system of metal piers, on a vertical axis this time, as they had used to form the curving arches of the Garabit viaduct. Eiffel, the engineer and Sauvestre, the architect, submitted their plan to the exhibition jury, and it was accepted. Work began on January 28th,1887 and the tower was completed on March 31st,1889. "The hideous column of rivetted metal" met with an extremely hostile reception. Techniques of metal construction were quite far advanced by the time the tower came to be built, but the clean curve sweeping the four pylons together still seems daring and elegant with the changing skies of Paris shining through the fine network of girders.

104. The Eiffel Tower, seen from the terrace of the Chaillot Palace.

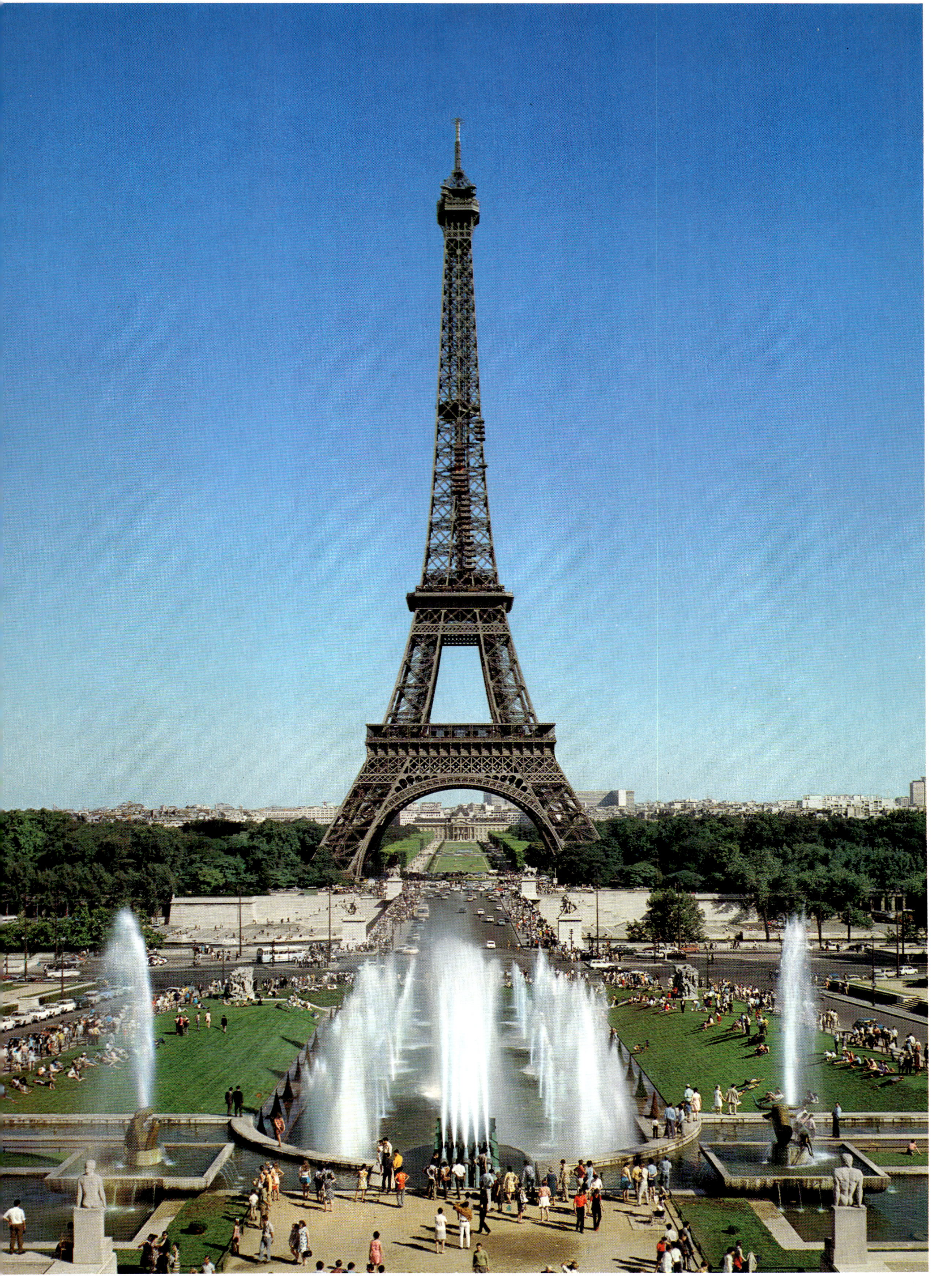

105. The Alexander III Bridge.

The most beautiful survival from the exhibition of 1900 is the Pont Alexandre III. The Franco-Russian alliance was being celebrated at the time and the French were doing all they could to please their new friends: the avenue was named after Nicolas II, and the bridge after his father Alexander III. The Tsar came in person to lay the foundation stone on October 7th, 1896. Resal and Alby, the engineers who had built the Pont Mirabeau, designed the bridge's great single span, which consists of fifteen iron trusses covering 107.50 meters. The bronze decoration in high Pompadour style seems most appropriate: Georges Récipon designed the candelabras, garlands and children, as well as the nymphs of the Seine and the Neva who recline at the top of the arch. Cassien-Bernard and Cousin's great pylons support gilded pegasuses at each end. Their silhouette is the only remnant of the lively scenes that once filled the Invalides esplanade for a whole year.

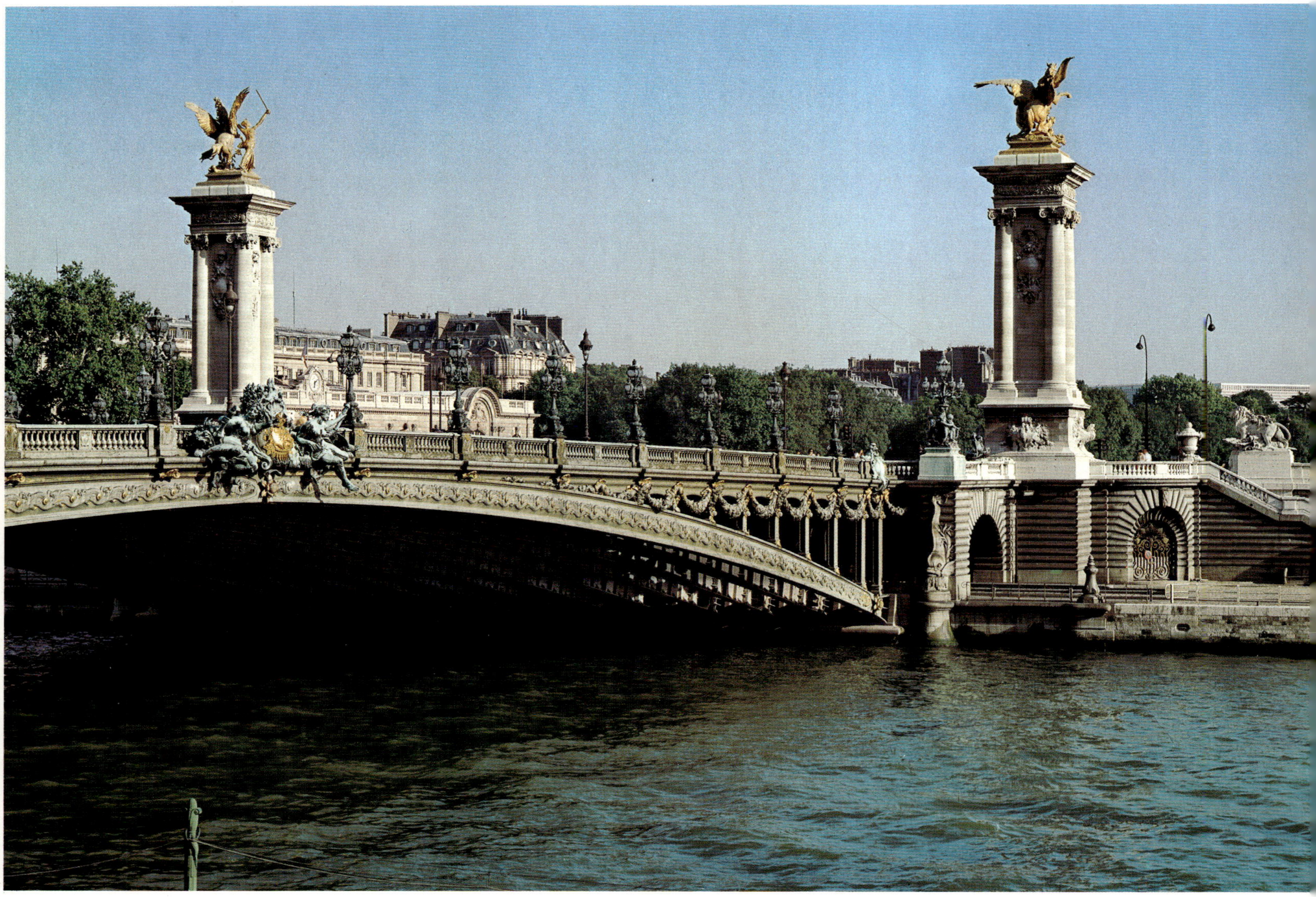

105. The Alexander III Bridge.

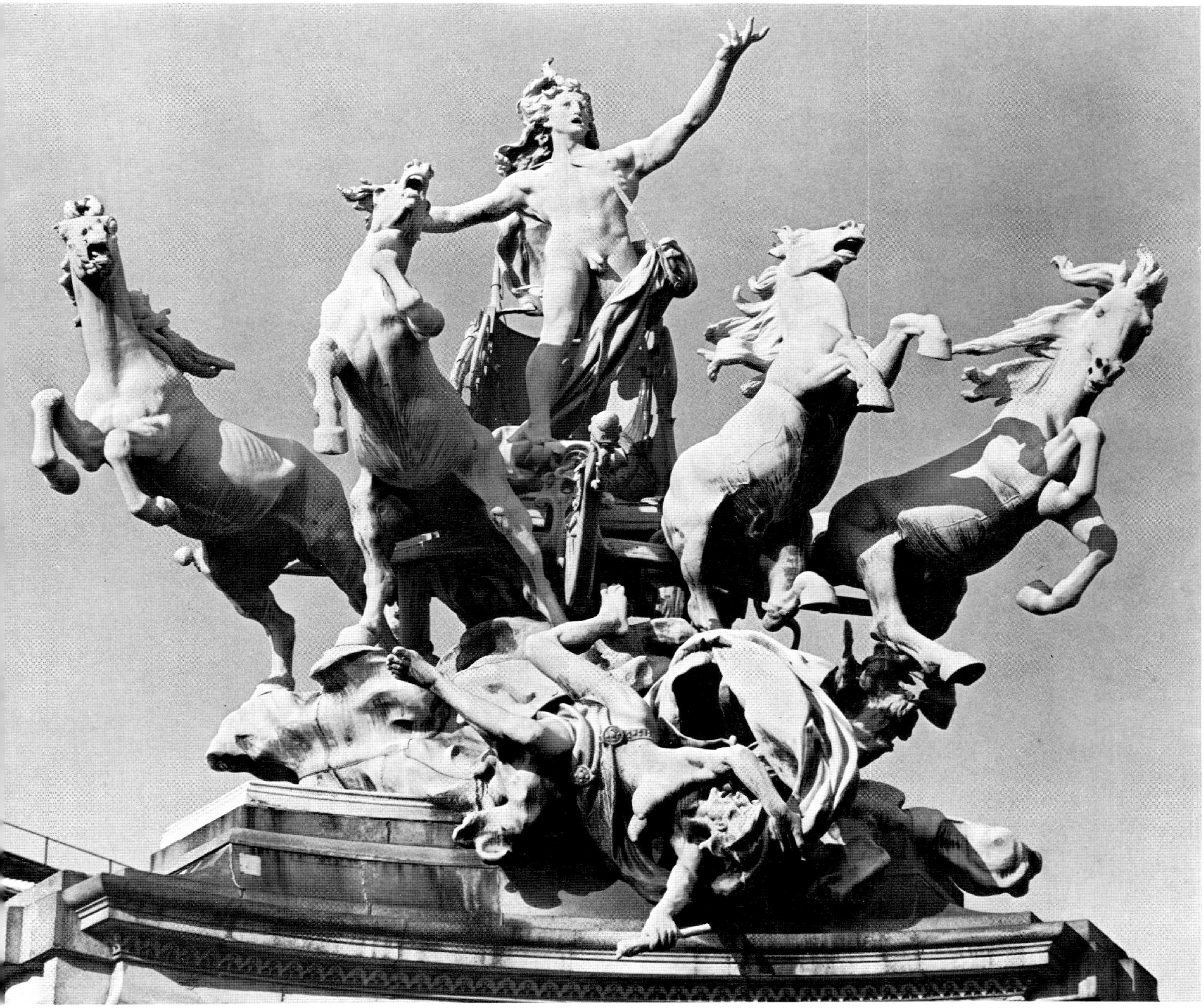

106. One of the quadrigas by Récipon, over the portals of the Grand Palais.

106. The Grand Palais.

The century drew to a close amidst feverish preparations for the Great Exhibition of 1900. Lots of little confections covered with minarets, domes, distorted pyramids, flagpoles and lanterns spread down the Invalides esplanade and along the Champ-de-Mars. Palaces from all corners of the world went up along the banks of the Seine and cast reflections in the Grand Canal. A new style was about to dawn, and this was eclecticism's last great saturnalia. Two palaces on the Avenue Nicolas II (now the Avenue Winston-Churchill) still remain from the centenary exhibition. Charles Girault's Petit Palais to the east is a refined but pompous pastiche of 17th and 18th century styles. The Grand Palais to the west is an immense hall suitable for all kinds of spectacles, from industrial or art exhibitions to show-jumping events. It covers a huge area (40 000 square meters) and was built to an asymmetrical plan, with several facades. This complex piece of work was carried out by several architects under Girault's direction. Thomas and Louvet were both involved, but it was Deglane who was responsible for the main part of the project—the glass hall surrounded by colonnades heavily decorated. Two striking bronze quadrigas by Georges Récipon surge out above the doorways.

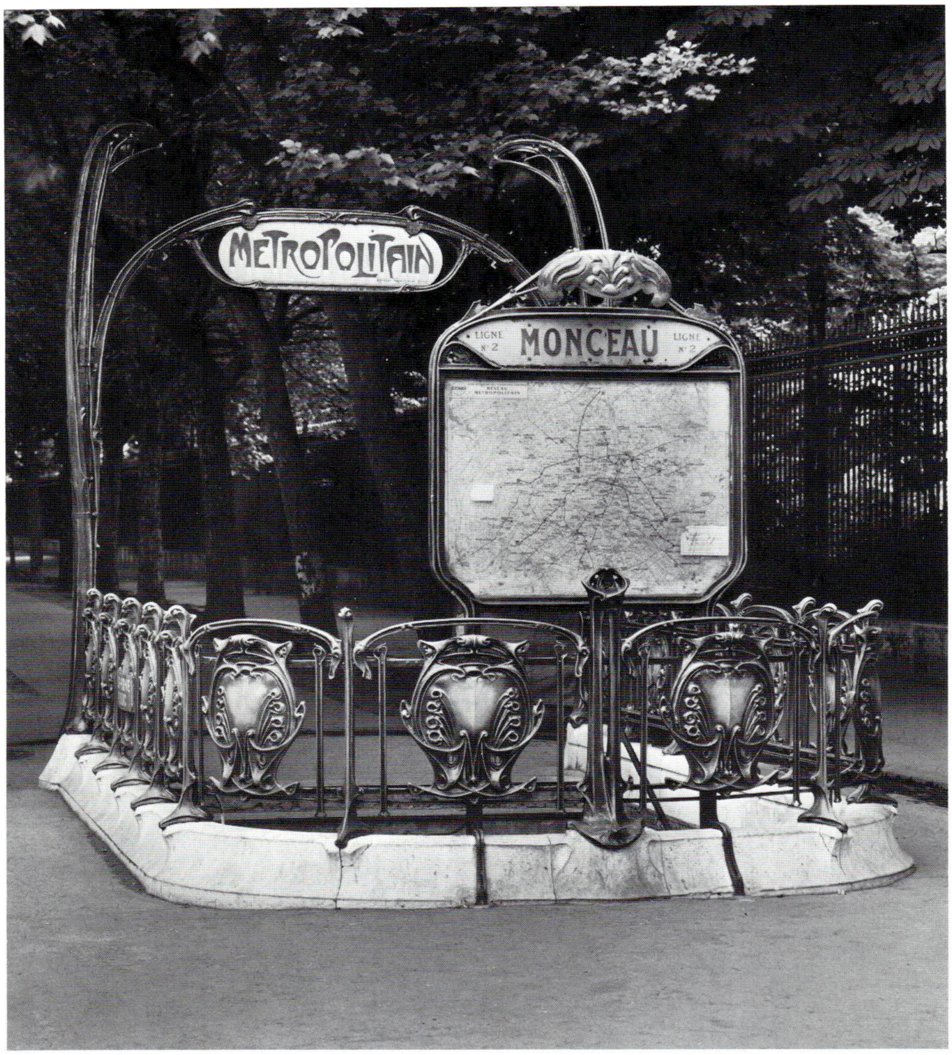

107. The entrance to the Monceau underground station.

107. Métro entrance railings, designed by Guimard.

Parisians associate the name of Guimard with the entrance railing of their first métro: it is no mean claim to fame. Guimard was an innovator who benefited from the general enthusiasm for the 1900 exhibition, for he received the official commission as soon as the State had given the city the go-ahead to build a "metropolitan underground tramway" (1889). The first line (Vincennes-Maillot) was opened on July 19th 1900. Guimard's metalwork is both functional and decorative, and the same undulating movement is repeated on the railings, the lights, the sign and the panel for the map, and sometimes even on the glass roof. His creepers and strange medallions, painted in a shade of green which emphasizes their plant-like qualities, no longer raise a smile; they are admired like open-air sculpture, as if a bouquet of Parisian flowers had pushed its way up through a crack in the pavement to delight passers-by.

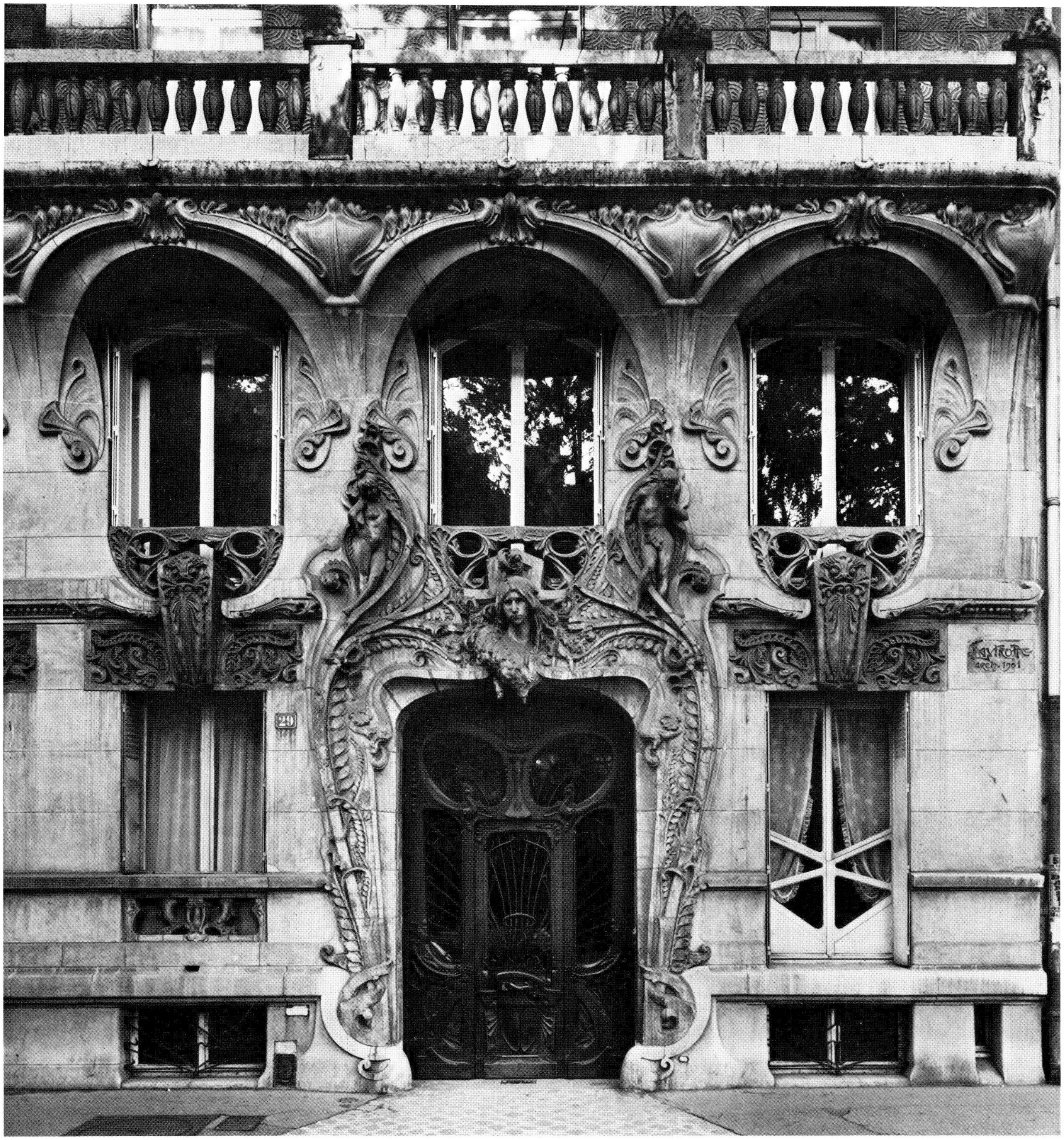

108. The entrance to No. 29, Avenue Rapp, 7th Arr.

108. Entrance to No. 29, Avenue Rapp.

Guimard was able to strike a balance between functional necessity and decoration. Moreover, the themes of his designs are basically antinaturalistic, and he remained true to the spirit of Horta with his preference for stems rather than leaves. But this asceticism soon gave way to the flowery extravagances of the "nouille" style, under pressure from the Belle Epoque's taste for girl-flowers, women with streaming locks, ingenuous children, irises and butterflies. The finest example of this is Jules Lavirotte's block of flats on the Avenue Rapp (1901), which also heralds a return to a kind of eclecticism. Its sinister doorway is reminiscent both of Rodin's Porte de l'Enfer and of the doorway to the Cabaret des Truands on the Boulevard de Clichy.

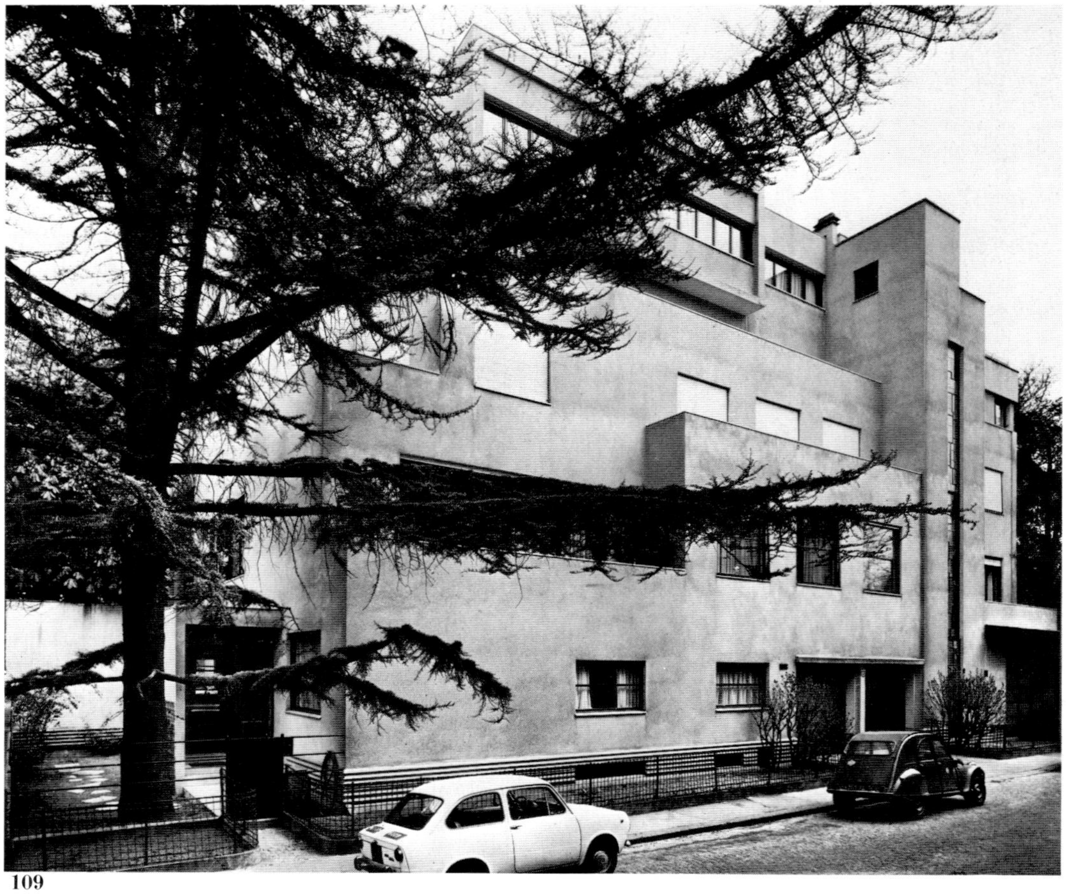
109

109. Private residence, Rue Mallet-Stevens.

After 1919, building seemed stuck in a new academic rut, exemplified by so many of the massive and unimaginative ministries and blocks of flats put up in the inter-war period. The French either misunderstood or were quite unaware of modern international architecture. A few isolated examples prove that even though there were few public or private clients, there was no shortage of creative talent: Robert Mallet-Stevens, Pierre Chareau, Henri Sauvage, Francis Jourdain... and, of course, Le Corbusier. Mallet-Stevens' work has not received the acclaim it deserves, but it in fact shows cubist architecture at its most harmonious. "The cube is the basis of architecture", he wrote in 1924. The complex of private houses he built at Auteuil along the road that was made in 1927 and named after him, is a kind of city of the arts, since every house has had personal features added to suit the activities of its occupant—architect, musician, film-maker or painter. They create a cheerful effect with their sharp outlines and pale roughcast walls with the trees close by, and all the surfaces respond to the slightest ray of light. The idea of the facade has been abandoned in favour of volumes which fit into one another and correspond to the internal structure where Mallet-Stevens wanted to have furniture with very clean lines.

110. Saint-Christophe-de-Javel.

Saint-Christophe-de-Javel is traditional in design and has medieval overtones, but it nevertheless inaugurated a new building technique: the use of prefabricated sections. Concrete is poured into molds beforehand, instead of being put up in shuttering. This accounts for the slightly industrial look of the molding, although it has still managed to keep a few art nouveau twists and turns. It was built between 1926 and 1934 by Charles-Henri Besnard, and once again shows how difficult it is for new techniques to break free from traditional forms. The frescoes which cover the walls cannot soften the overall harshness of the building while the latticework of the windows is very typical of the 1930s.

110. The church of Saint-Christophe-de-Javel.

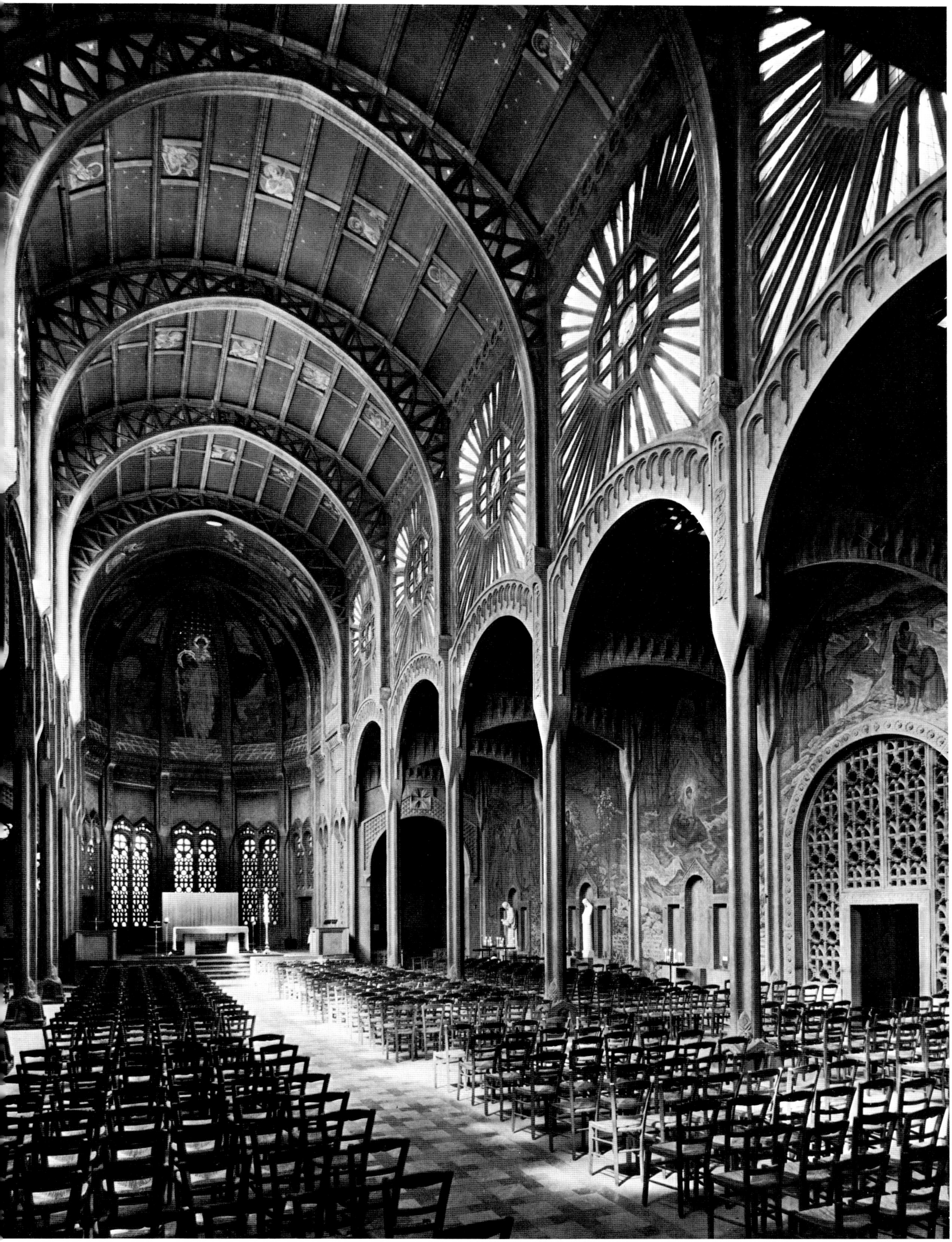

111. The Chaillot Palace.

The style of the 1937 exhibition is like a caricature of Perret's academicism. At a time when functionalism was very much in vogue, buildings devoted to the arts were still palaces. The two Modern Art Museums, by Dondel, Aubert, Viard and Dastugue are like a great theatrical backdrop—temporary architecture without weight or reality where all the requirements of a museum have deliberately been sacrificed. The new Palais de Chaillot by Carlu, Boileau and Azéma uses the renovated wings of the old Tracadéro in an immense structure in the form of an amphitheater. The old central building was demolished and replaced by an underground auditorium covered by a terrace. From a distance, the Place du Tracadéro can be seen through this wide opening.

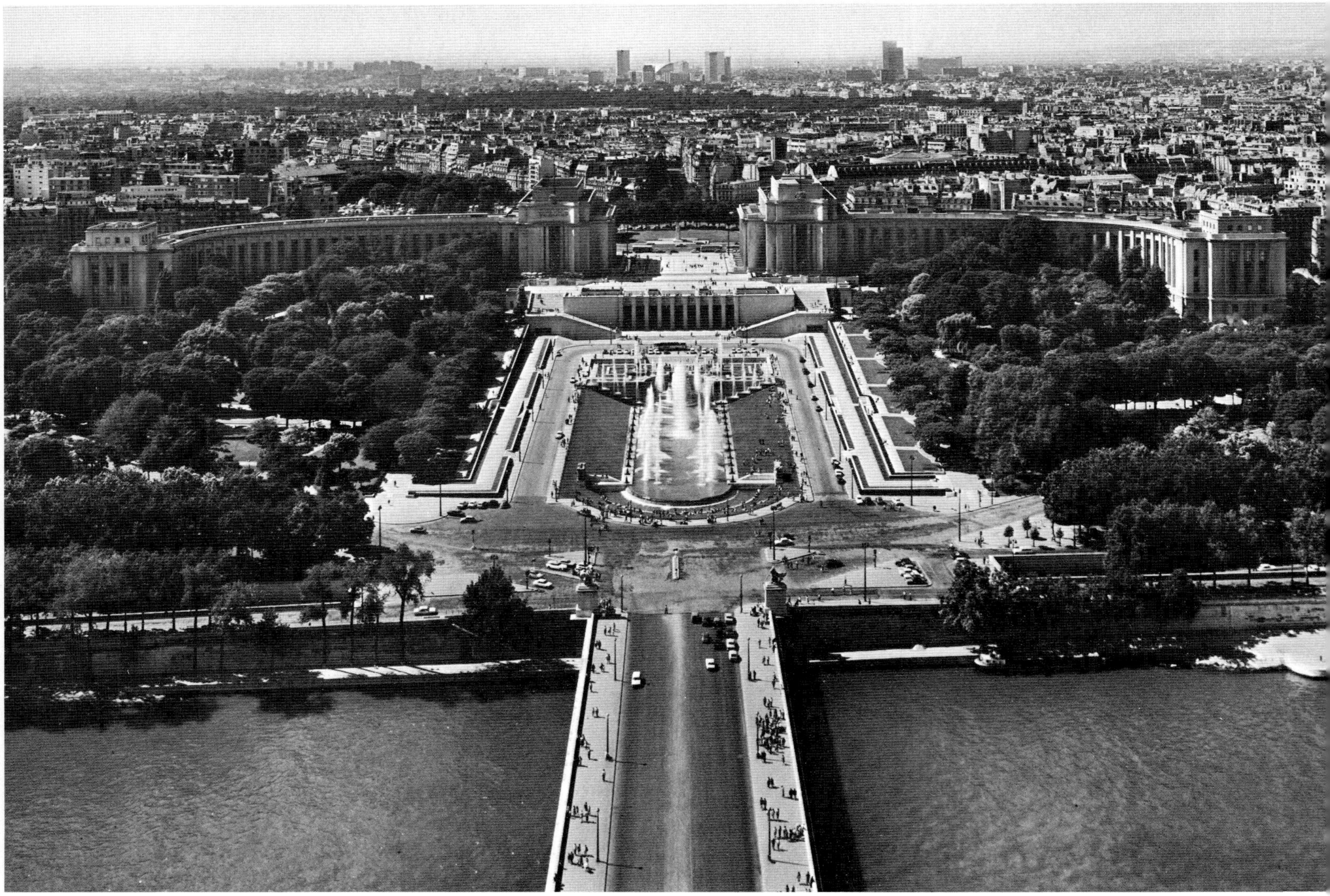

111. The Chaillot Palace. In the background the sky-scrapers of the Défense.

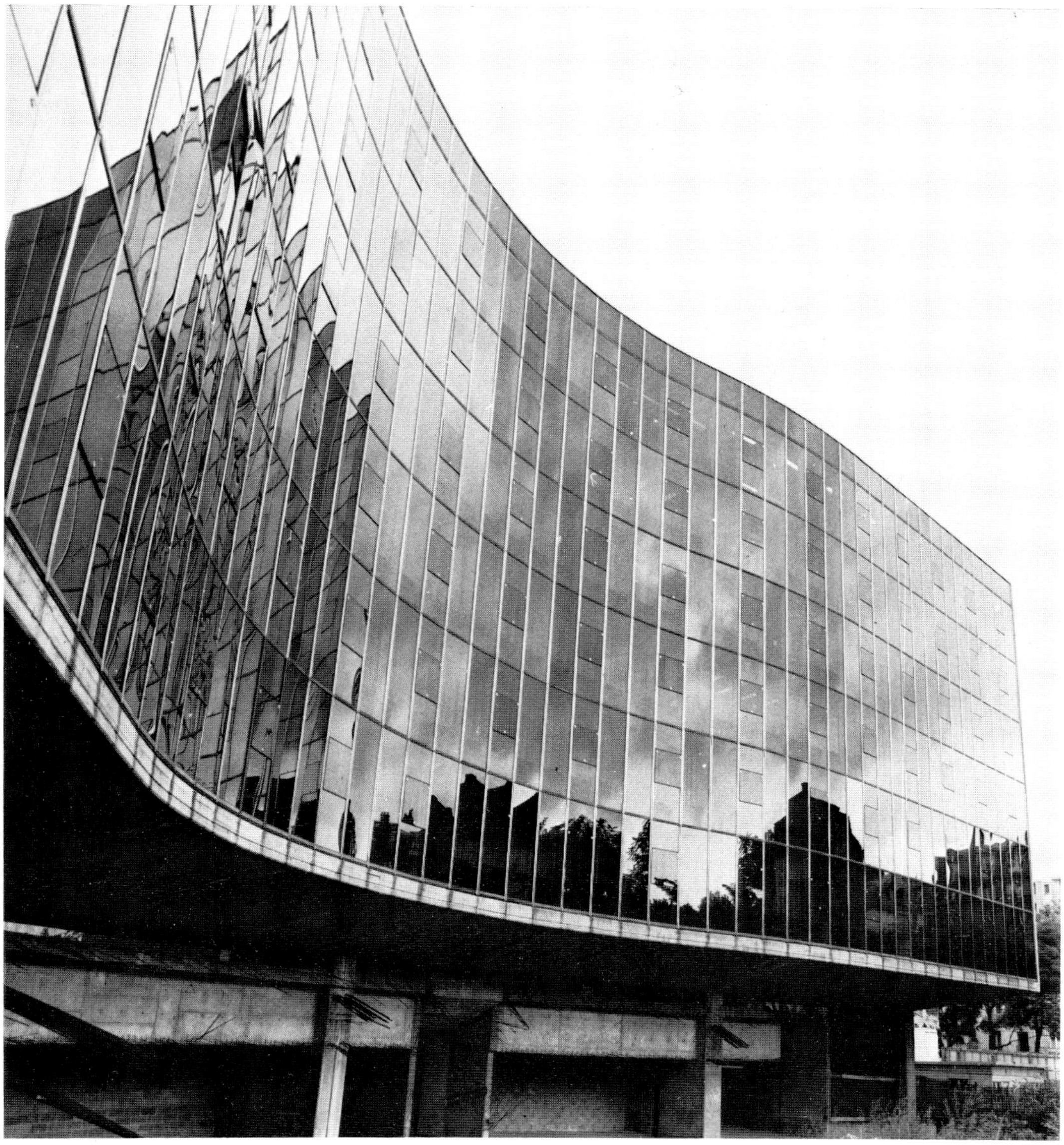

112. The headquarters of the French Communist Party, 2, Place du Colonel-Fabien, 19th Arr.

112. The French Communist Party Headquarters.

When the time came to build its new headquarters, the Communist Party turned to a Brasilian architect of international repute, Oscar Niemeyer, a pupil of Le Corbusier and the man who designed Brasilia. With the help of Jean Deroche and Paul Chémétov, he constructed the building (1970-1971) along lines reminiscent of the Unesco structure with its fluid volume raised on piles. The complete transparency of the building produces the effect of an enormous concave mirror in which the surroundings are reflected.

113. The Georges Pompidou National Center of Art and Culture.

In December 1969, Georges Pompidou, President of the Republic, conceived a plan to build a cultural center on the Beaubourg plain in the heart of Paris. It was to be devoted to contemporary art, and house an enormous library covering all spheres of knowledge. A competition was held in 1971, and the winning design by architects Renzo Piano and Richard Rogers for a "living information center" was carried out between 1972 and 1977.
The Center houses the National Museum of Modern Art (CNAM), the public reading library, the Industrial Production Centre (CCI), and the Institute for Research and Coordination in Accoustics and Music (IRCAM).

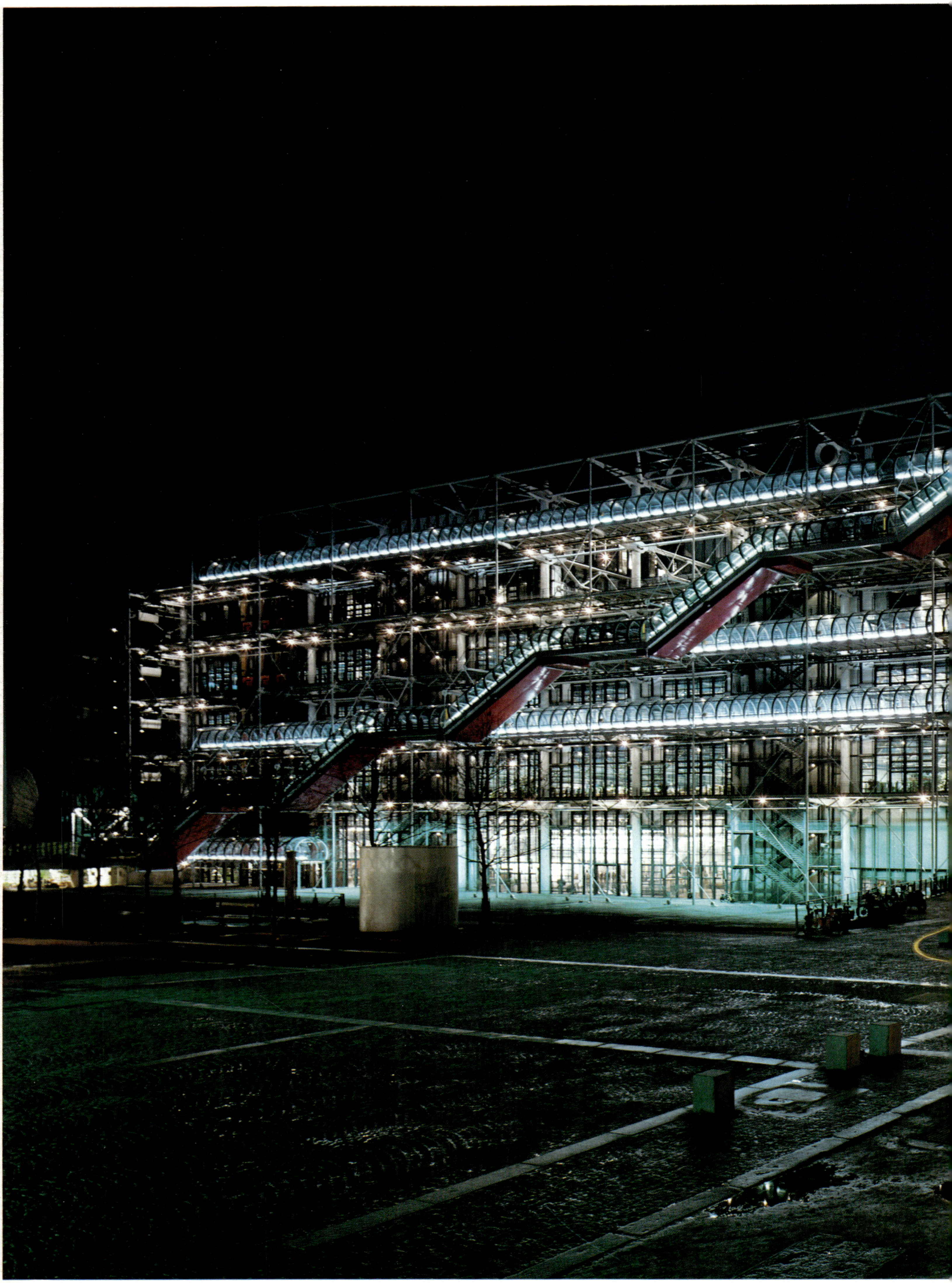

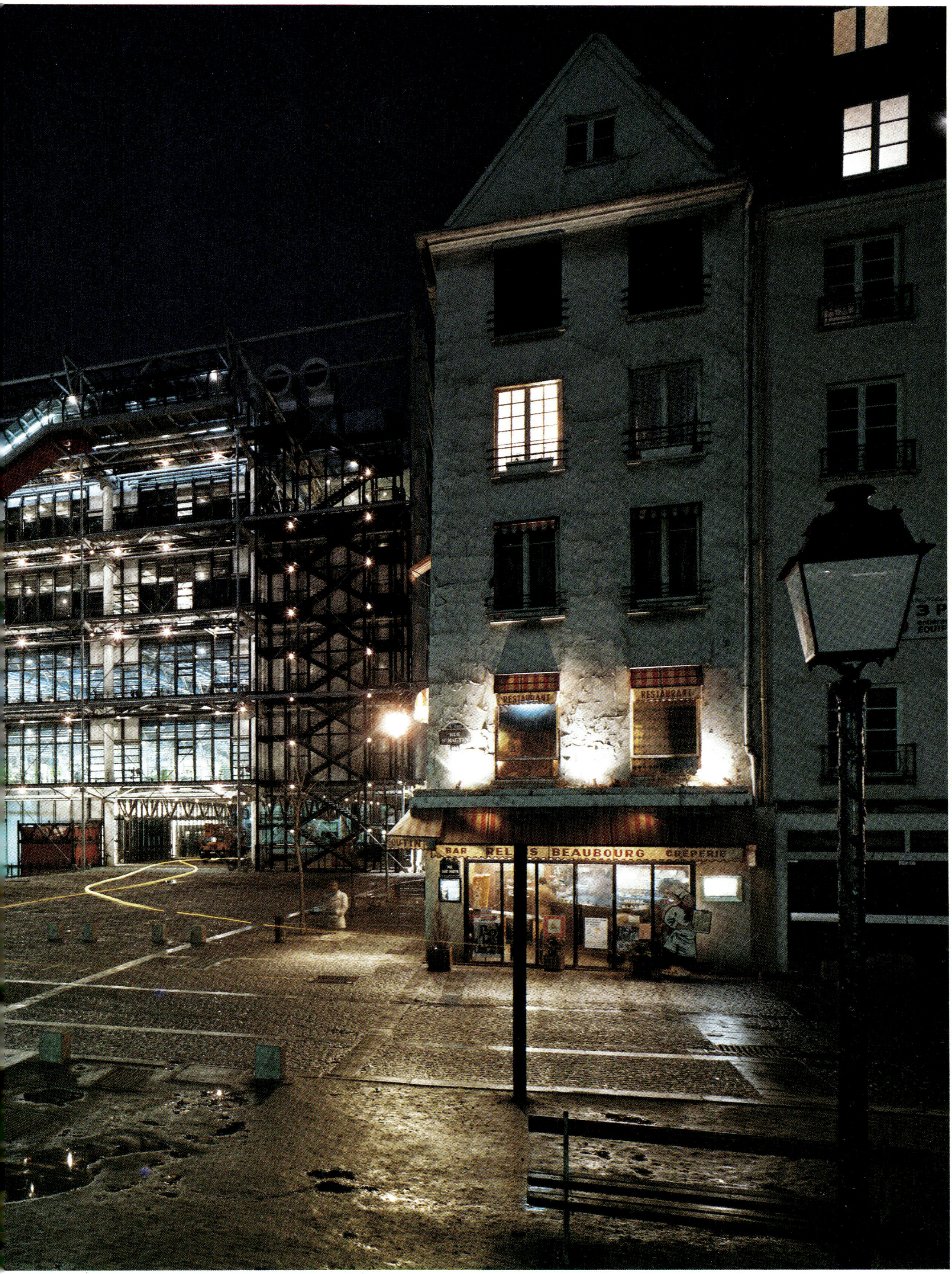
RESTAURANT
RESTAURANT
BAR
BEAUBOURG
CRÊPERIE

ALPHABETICAL LIST OF ILLUSTRATIONS WITH ARRONDISSEMENT NUMBERS

LIST OF ILLUSTRATIONS BY ARRONDISSEMENTS WITH ADDRESSES

1st Arrondissement

2nd Arrondissement

3rd Arrondissement

4th Arrondissement

5th Arrondissement

6th Arrondissement

7th Arrondissement

8th Arrondissement

9th Arrondissement

10th Arrondissement

15th Arrondissement

16th Arrondissement

18th Arrondissement

19th Arrondissement

"Paris", set in Didot, published by Arts et Métiers Graphiques, Paris, on behalf of Flammarion. Printing by Les Imprimeries Réunies S.A., Lausanne, completed 17 December, 1979.

A BOOK BY YVES RIVIÈRE AND DANIÈLE ALPERS

Publisher's number 10461 ISBN 2-08-200179-2

The photographs in this book (photo-engraving Bussière, Paris) are by Max and Albert Hirmer, with the exception of the following: 24, National Museums; 76, Jean-Claude Varga; 78, Bank of France; 9, 22, 23, 67, 82, 113, François Walch and Jacques L'Hoir, Paris (photo-engraving Imprimeries Réunies S.A., Lausanne, for the last six illustrations).

Printed in Switzerland